A Fine-Tuned Universe

A Fine-Tuned Universe

The Quest for God in Science and Theology

The 2009 Gifford Lectures

Alister E. McGrath

WESTMINSTER
JOHN KNOX PRESS
LOUISVILLE · KENTUCKY

© 2009 Alister E. McGrath

First edition
Westminster John Knox Press
Louisville, Kentucky 40202

Scripture quotations from the New Revised Standard Version of the Bible are copyright © 1989 by the Division of Christian Education of the National Council of the Churches of Christ in the U.S.A. and are used by permission.

Book design by Sharon Adams
Cover design by Night & Day Design

PRINTED IN THE UNITED STATES OF AMERICA

09 10 11 12 13 14 15 16 17 18—10 9 8 7 6 5 4 3 2 1

Library of Congress Cataloging-in-Publication Data

McGrath, Alister E., 1953–
    A fine-tuned universe : the quest for God in science and theology / Alister E. McGrath.—1st ed.
        p. cm.
    Includes bibliographical references and index.
    ISBN 978-0-664-23310-5 (alk. paper)
    1. Natural theology.   2. Religion and science.   3. God.   4. Religion.   5. Theology.
6. Science.   I. Title.
    BL183.M34 2009
    261.5'5—dc22

                                                                                    2008028006

∞ The paper used in this publication meets the minimum requirements of the American National Standard for Information Sciences—Permanence of Paper for Printed Library Materials, ANSI Z39.48-1992.

Westminster John Knox Press advocates the responsible use of our natural resources. The text paper of this book is made from at least 30% post-consumer waste.

In memory of

John Macquarrie (1919–2007)
and
Thomas Forsyth Torrance (1913–2007)

Contents

Introduction   ix

  1. Yearning to Make Sense of Things   1

A Trinitarian Natural Theology   9

  2. The Crisis of Confidence in Modern
Natural Theology   11

  3. Renewing the Vision for Natural Theology   21

  4. Challenges to a Renewed Natural Theology   35

  5. Natural Theology and the Explanation of Reality   51

  6. The Dynamics of a Trinitarian Natural Theology   61

  7. Surprising Facts: Counterfactuals
and Natural Theology   83

  8. Augustine of Hippo on Creation:
A Theological Lens   95

Fine-Tuning: Observations and Interpretations   109

  9. In the Beginning: The Constants of the Universe   111

10. Can These Bones Live? The Origins of Life   127

11. The Matrix of Life: The Curious Chemistry
of Water   143

12. Chemical Catalysts and the Constraints of Evolution   155

13. The Origins of Complexity: The Mechanism
of Evolution   167

14. The Outcomes of Evolution: The Directionality
of Evolution   183

15. An Emergent Creation and Natural Theology   203

Conclusion   217

Bibliography   223

Index   259

Introduction

The topic of this book is the quest for God in the natural sciences and Christian theology, traditionally known as "natural theology." Although this has been a subject of human interest since the dawn of recorded history, it has been given a new injection of intellectual energy in recent years by theologians and philosophers, but above all by natural scientists.[1] Natural theology languished in the intellectual doldrums for much of the twentieth century, especially within Protestantism.[2] It was seen as tired and stale, a relic of a less-critical age in theology and a more-credulous age in science. The relentless advance of scientific explanation, matched by a corresponding retreat by Christian theology from the public domain, meant that natural theology seemed to be beached on the sands, left stranded as the tide that had once lent it such intellectual buoyancy had slowly ebbed away.[3]

Yet there is every sign that natural theology is now emerging from its period of eclipse. There is growing sympathy for the view that natural theology can provide a deeper understanding on fundamental issues such as the fine-tuning of the universe, where science can "throw up questions that point beyond itself and

1. John Polkinghorne, "Where Is Natural Theology Today?" *Science and Christian Belief* 18 (2006): 169–79. Two landmark works which have catalyzed this development are John Barrow and Frank J. Tipler, *The Anthropic Cosmological Principle* (Oxford: Oxford University Press, 1986); and Simon Conway Morris, *Life's Solution: Inevitable Humans in a Lonely Universe* (Cambridge: Cambridge University Press, 2003).

2. See the detailed analysis in Christoph Kock, *Natürliche Theologie: Ein evangelischer Streitbegriff* (Neukirchen-Vluyn: Neukirchener Verlag, 2001). For a more philosophical perspective, see Bernd Irlenborn, "Abschied von der 'natürlichen Theologie'? Eine sprachphilosophische Standortbestimmung," *Theologie und Philosophie* 78 (2003): 545–57.

3. One of the best-known recent scientific critiques of "natural theology" is by Richard Dawkins, *The Blind Watchmaker: Why the Evidence of Evolution Reveals a Universe without Design* (New York: W. W. Norton, 1986), which is critical of William Paley's famous image of God as the "watchmaker." For comment, see Alister E. McGrath, *Dawkins' God: Genes, Memes and the Meaning of Life* (Oxford: Blackwell Publishing, 2004), 49–81.

transcend its power to answer."[4] Might natural theology once more act as a conceptual bridge between the worlds of science and religion? Or as a meeting place for theology, literature, and the arts?

There is clearly a need to recover a vision for natural theology that is both securely rooted in the long tradition of Christian theological reflection and adequately adapted to our understandings of the natural world. My own interest in establishing a theologically rigorous engagement with the natural sciences led me to appreciate the importance of natural theology as a means of engaging the world of nature. In my *Scientific Theology* (2001–3), I offered an account of how the theological legitimacy and utility of natural theology might be reaffirmed and placed upon a solid theological foundation.[5] Although these volumes focused on the important question of how the working assumptions and methods of Christian theology and the natural sciences might interact with and illuminate each other, the enterprise of natural theology emerged as a particularly important interface between the two. This clearly pointed to the need for a more-detailed study of the focus, scope, and limits of a natural theology.

An invitation to deliver the Riddell Memorial Lectures at Newcastle University in 2008 allowed me to develop this approach with greater rigor. In *The Open Secret: A New Vision for Natural Theology* (2008), I attempted to develop a distinctively Christian approach to natural theology by retrieving and reformulating older approaches that have been marginalized or regarded as outmoded in recent years, establishing them on more-secure intellectual foundations. The fundamental thesis of the book is that if nature is to disclose the transcendent, it must be "seen" or "read" in certain specific ways—ways that are not themselves necessarily mandated by nature itself. It is argued that Christian theology provides a *schema* or interpretative framework by which nature may be "seen" in a way that enables and authorizes it to connect with the transcendent. Natural theology is here understood as an intellectual enterprise authorized and resourced by the rich Trinitarian ontology of the Christian faith. The enterprise of natural theology is thus one of discernment, of seeing nature in a certain way, of viewing it through a particular and specific set of spectacles.[6] It has important resonances with the persistent human interest in the notion of access to the transcendent.[7]

The Open Secret was conceived as an explorative work (an *essai*, in the proper sense of the term), an attempt to lay the ground for the renewal and revalidation of natural theology, fundamentally as a legitimate aspect of Christian theology, but also as a contribution to a wider cultural discussion. This book was written in the conviction that there is a real and urgent case for the renewal and reorien-

4. John Polkinghorne, *Science and Creation: The Search for Understanding* (London: SPCK, 1988), 23.

5. See in particular Alister E. McGrath, *A Scientific Theology*, vol. 1, *Nature* (London: Continuum, 2001), 241–305. Some of the themes explored in this work were developed further in Alister E. McGrath, *The Order of Things: Explorations in Scientific Theology* (Oxford: Blackwell, 2006).

6. Alister E. McGrath, *The Open Secret: A New Vision for Natural Theology* (Oxford: Blackwell, 2008), 1–20.

7. Ibid., 23–79.

tation of natural theology, involving the dogmatic relocation of the discipline within the sphere of systematic theology, and the conceptual expansion of the notion beyond the idea of making rational sense of the world to embrace the traditional quest for truth, beauty, and goodness. Yet although the work traverses a substantial amount of territory, the method that it proposes needs further calibration and application—above all, by being applied to a specific case study, drawn from the observation of the natural world.

I was delighted to be asked to deliver the 2009 Gifford Lectures at the University of Aberdeen, since this offered me the welcome opportunity to expand my approach to natural theology. Adam Lord Gifford (1820–97) stipulated that these lectures were to be dedicated to "promoting, advancing, teaching, and diffusing the study of Natural Theology."[8] While Lord Gifford and I share a common enthusiasm for natural theology, we nevertheless define it in significantly different ways. These lectures made it possible for me to expand and develop the approach mapped out in *The Open Secret*, especially through exploring the degree of "empirical fit" between theory and observation which results from the application of this approach. As I had been involved for some years in discussions relating to anthropic phenomena in the natural sciences, it seemed highly appropriate to consider how these might relate to the tasks and goals of a renewed natural theology. What are the implications for a natural theology of the apparent fine-tuning of the cosmos?

It is a relatively new question for modern science. Since the seventeenth century, it had been widely assumed that no special initial conditions were required for the emergence of a life-bearing universe.[9] Yet in the last few decades, it has become clear that this is not the case. There has been a growing realization of the extraordinary degree of contingency for the initial conditions of the universe, if heavy elements, planets, and ultimately complex life were to develop. The life-bearing properties of the universe are highly sensitive to the values of the fundamental forces and constants of nature. The theoretical physicist Lee Smolin points to the importance of this point in relation to the development of stars:[10]

> The existence of stars rests on several delicate balances between the different forces in nature. These require that the parameters that govern how strongly these forces act be tuned just so. In many cases, a small turn of the dial in one direction or another results in a world not only without stars, but with much less structure than our universe.

A life-bearing universe is far more constrained than had been realized. This has led many to speak of the universe being "fine-tuned" for life. This is, of course, an inexact metaphor, in that it is resistant to quantification;[11] it perhaps is best

8. For the history of these lectures, see Larry Witham, *The Measure of God: Our Century-Long Struggle to Reconcile Science and Religion* (San Francisco: HarperSanFrancisco, 2005).

9. Ernan McMullin, "Indifference Principle and Anthropic Principle in Cosmology," *Studies in the History and Philosophy of Science* 24 (1993): 359–89.

10. Lee Smolin, *The Life of the Cosmos* (New York: Oxford University Press, 1997), 37.

11. Neil A. Manson, *God and Design: The Teleological Argument and Modern Science* (London: Routledge, 2003), 8–11.

seen as articulating an intuition, rather than formulating a precise mathematical deduction. Furthermore, the term is ambivalent, denoting both *fecundity* and *fragility*. The former tends to be the case in cosmological contexts, in which "fine-tuned" systems are robust, leading to fruitful outcomes. The latter often applies to biological situations, in which a system is vulnerable through being so adapted to its present environment that it cannot cope with significant changes. Our concern throughout this work is primarily, but not exclusively, with the first understanding of "fine-tuning." But what, if anything, does this *mean*?

The term "anthropic principle," introduced by Brandon Carter in 1974, has come to be widely used as a way of speaking of the curious properties of the universe.[12] The universe, it seems, is intriguingly friendly toward life. Did the universe encourage the emergence of humanity (*anthrōpos*), who might observe its puzzling features and reflect on their significance?[13] The term "anthropic" is not particularly helpful and has been challenged on several grounds; it has, however, established its presence in the field, and it is now difficult to find an alternative term.[14] Yet though the "anthropic principle" is perhaps better seen as a statement and contextualization of the issue, rather than anything even approaching its solution,[15] it is widely agreed that the observation of "fine-tuning" in the universe requires explanation—an explanation which is potentially of considerable theological significance.[16]

This book aims to take this discussion further, both in terms of developing a natural theology which is adapted to intellectual engagement with the natural sciences, and contributing toward the scientific, philosophical, and theological discussion of the wider meaning of anthropic phenomena. I do not argue that fine-tuning represents a proof of the Christian belief in God; I nevertheless insist that it is consonant with the Christian vision of God, *which is believed to be true*

12. Brandon Carter, "Large Number Coincidences and the Anthropic Principle," in *Confrontation of Cosmological Theories with Observational Data*, ed. M. S. Longair (Boston: D. Reidel, 1974), 291–98. For the interesting but somewhat problematic suggestion that such lines of argument predate the emergence of modern cosmology, see Milan Cirkovic, "Ancient Origins of a Modern Anthropic Cosmological Argument," *Astronomical and Astrophysical Transactions* 22 (2003): 879–86.

13. Carter himself emphasized the importance of observers for the existence of "anthropic" phenomena: see Brandon Carter, "The Anthropic Principle and Its Implications for Biological Evolution," *Philosophical Transactions of the Royal Society* A 310 (1983): 347–63.

14. In other disciplines, the term "anthropic" is used to designate human agency or activity within nature—for example, in speaking of "anthropic perturbation" of ecosystems. The term "biocentric" has been suggested as an alternative means of designating the apparent biofriendliness of the cosmos, following its use in the writings of the Harvard chemist Lawrence J. Henderson (1878–1942). For example, Michael Denton speaks of "biocentric adaptations in the design of the cosmos": see Michael Denton, *Nature's Destiny: How the Laws of Biology Reveal Purpose in the Universe* (New York: Free Press, 1998), 14. Paul Davies prefers to use the term "biophilic"; see Paul Davies, "Universes Galore: Where Will It All End?" in *Universe or Multiverse?* ed. Bernard Carr (Cambridge: Cambridge University Press, 2007), 487–505.

15. Ernan McMullin, "Fine-Tuning the Universe?" in *Science, Technology, and Religious Ideas*, ed. Mark H. Shale and George W. Shields (Lanham, MD: University Press of America, 1994), 97–125.

16. Robin Collins, "A Scientific Argument for the Existence of God: The Fine-Tuning Design Argument," in *Reason for the Hope Within*, ed. Michael J. Murray (Grand Rapids: Eerdmans, 1999), 47–75.

on other grounds, in that it offers a significant degree of intellectual resonance at points of importance.[17] While this "proves" nothing, it is nonetheless deeply suggestive. Might it be, to use the luminous phrase of C. S. Lewis, a "clue to the meaning of the universe"?

The fundamental point here is that there are many things about the natural world that appear strange to us, such as its apparent fine-tuning. The American philosopher Charles Peirce (1839–1914) argued that what he termed "surprising facts" were a fundamental stimulus to the advancement of human thought. Yet Peirce perhaps fails to make the point that certain facts are surprising only because they are seen in a certain way. We all approach the observation of nature with a set of inherited or acquired assumptions, a mental map which helps us to make sense of what we observe.[18] The central argument of this book is simple: that certain facts are observed which are indeed "surprising." Yet we can easily imagine a standpoint from which they are *not* surprising and might even be anticipated. The Christian vision of reality, which has its own distinct evidential basis and intrinsic rationality, offers us a standpoint from which we may view the natural world and see certain things that others might indeed regard as puzzling or strange—such as fine-tuning—as consonant with the greater picture that the Christian has to offer.

This book aims to extend the discussion and analysis of fine-tuning in nature and to offer what I hope will prove to be a helpful theological framework on the basis of which these may be explained. It is my hope to bring both theological rigor and enthusiasm into the increasingly interesting and productive discussion of these phenomena within the scientific community, which has generally tended to marginalize theology—not on account of any perception that theology is irrelevant to this discussion, but on account of the slightly more disturbing discernment that many professional theologians do not appear to regard it as particularly significant or potentially fruitful.[19]

There is clearly more to be said about instances of apparent fine-tuning than the concession of their existence. This book sets out a defensible and principled approach to natural theology, which seeks to identify and explain phenomena within the context of the framework provided by a Trinitarian natural theology. A natural theology, when shaped and informed by the fundamental themes of the Christian tradition—in short, a *Trinitarian* natural theology—can act as a point of convergence between the Christian faith, the arts and literature, and above all the natural sciences, opening up important possibilities for dialogue, cross-fertilization, and mutual enrichment. A Trinitarian approach to natural theology allows the Christian faith to shine its own distinct intellectual light on the

17. For a critical evaluation of this theme in the writings of John Polkinghorne, see Bernd Irlenborn, "Konsonanz von Theologie und Naturwissenschaft? Fundamentaltheologische Bemerkungen zum interdisziplinären Ansatz von John Polkinghorne," *Trierer theologische Zeitung* 113 (2004): 98–117.

18. For the importance of such a mental map or schema in natural theology, see McGrath, *Open Secret*, 80–110, esp. 86–92.

19. There are, of course, significant exceptions: see, e.g., Keith Ward, *Religion and Creation* (Oxford: Oxford University Press, 1996), 297–300.

landscape of reality, releasing humanity from introspective self-preoccupation, and illuminating and inspiring our study of the natural world. Such an approach to natural theology is fully capable of confronting the spectrum of complexities of the natural world without intellectual evasion, distortion, or misrepresentation.

This book thus sets out to establish and explore the intellectual virtues of a Trinitarian natural theology, chiefly by considering the significance of the observation of fine-tuning or anthropic phenomena in any coherent account of reality. It represents a contribution both to the contemporary dialogue between the natural sciences and Christian theology on the one hand, and to the long-standing debate within the Christian academic community concerning the theological legitimacy and significance of natural theology on the other. It also opens up the possibility of recovering a religiously traditional yet scientifically coherent creation story for our generation.[20] I trust it will be clear that I have little sympathy for Stephen Jay Gould's well-intentioned but ultimately misguided notion of "nonoverlapping magisteria" in science and religion; rather, I hold that the natural sciences and Christian theology represent distinct areas of intellectual inquiry which nevertheless offer each other possibilities of cross-fertilization on account of the interpenetration of their subjects and methods.

Having argued for the explanatory fecundity and power of a Trinitarian natural theology, I then turn to consider certain aspects of the natural world that clearly require explanation—namely, evidence of fine-tuning within nature. A substantial part of this volume is devoted to a scientific analysis of the notion of fine-tuning, partly because of its obvious relevance to natural theology, and partly on account of Lord Gifford's stipulation that I am to treat natural theology "as a strictly natural science, the greatest of all possible sciences."[21] Much work on anthropic phenomena has focused on the significance of the cosmological constants for the emergence of life. This section of the work expands this analysis substantially, showing how anthropic phenomena can be identified in the realms of chemistry, biochemistry, and evolutionary biology. It is argued that the existence of these phenomena can be accounted for on the basis of the Christian vision of reality, especially the forms of natural theology that it generates and sustains.

It remains for me to thank those who have been instrumental in the writing of this work. I am grateful to the University of Aberdeen for the welcome invitation to deliver the 2009 Gifford Lectures, of which this work is an expanded version. I wish to thank especially Professor Trevor Salmon, Professor Robert Frost, Dr. Duncan Heddle, and Sarah Berry for their efficient organization and hospitality throughout my time in Aberdeen. Harris Manchester College, Oxford, provided me with an outstanding scholarly community, within which I

20. A point made by Karl Giberson, "The Anthropic Principle: A Postmodern Creation Myth?" *Journal of Interdisciplinary Studies* 9 (1997): 63–90.

21. William James's classic *The Varieties of Religious Experience* (1902), based on the 1901 Gifford Lectures at Edinburgh University, reflects the terms of this will: see Hendrika Vande Kemp, "The Gifford Lectures on Natural Theology: Historical Background to James's '*Varieties*,'" *Streams of William James* 4 (2002): 2–8.

was able to research the fundamental themes of this book. The John Templeton Foundation provided financial assistance for this project, without which this book could never have been written. I have also benefitted considerably from scholarly collegiality and wish to acknowledge in particular the help of Denis Alexander, John Barrow, Simon Conway Morris, Rodney Holder, Ard Louis, R. J. P. Williams, and Wilson C. K. Poon. I also gladly acknowledge helpful conversations with Justin Barrett, John Hedley Brooke, Bernard Carr, Joanna Collicutt, Paul Davies, Peter Harrison, Richard Swinburne, and Keith Ward. I myself remain responsible for any errors of interpretation or fact.

This work is dedicated to the memory of two of Scotland's greatest twentieth-century theologians, John Macquarrie (1919–2007) and Thomas Forsyth Torrance (1913–2007). Each made significant contributions to our understanding of natural theology, as well as offering me personal support and encouragement in my own theological pilgrimage. They are both greatly missed.

Alister E. McGrath
Oxford 2008

Chapter 1

Yearning to Make Sense of Things

It is a truth of nature that we yearn to make sense of nature. "Religious faith," wrote William James, is basically "faith in the existence of an unseen order of some kind in which the riddles of the natural order may be found and explained."[1] Human beings long to make sense of things—to identify patterns in the rich fabric of nature, to offer explanations for what happens around them, and to reflect on the meaning of their lives.[2] It is as if our intellectual antennae are tuned to discern clues

---

1. William James, *The Will to Believe* (New York: Dover Publications, 1956), 51.
2. This is fundamental to the natural sciences, as noted by Peter R. Dear, *The Intelligibility of Nature: How Science Makes Sense of the World* (Chicago: University of Chicago Press, 2006), 173: "The hallmark of natural philosophy is its stress on *intelligibility*; it takes natural phenomena and tries to account for them in ways that not only hold together logically, but also rest on assumptions that seem right, to make sense." See the excellent multidisciplinary analysis, primarily from an anthropological perspective, in Mary E. Clark, *In Search of Human Nature* (London: Routledge, 2002), 160–91. There is also a particularly useful discussion in Eric Klinger, "The Search for Meaning in Evolutionary Perspective and Its Clinical Implications," in *The Human Quest for Meaning: A Handbook of Psychological Research and Clinical Applications*, ed. P. T. P. Wong and P. S. Fry (Mahwah, NJ: Erlbaum, 1998), 27–50. Note also the points made about the human perceptual "trip-wire" which generates meaning from fragmentary events: Scott Atran and Ara Norenzayan, "Religion's Evolutionary Landscape: Counterintuition, Commitment, Compassion, Communion," *Behavioral and Brain Sciences* 27 (2004): 713–70.

to purpose and meaning around us, clues built into the structure of the world.[3] "The pursuit of discovery," Michael Polanyi noted, is "guided by sensing the presence of a hidden reality toward which our clues are pointing."[4] Small wonder, then, that men and women have pondered what they observe around them, alert to the possibility of deeper levels of meaning lying beneath the surface of experience.

The quest for meaning transcends historical and cultural boundaries, even if cultures and individuals within them may offer very different accounts of what that meaning of life might be.[5] For example, based on extensive personal interviews, Roy Baumeister proposes that four basic needs—purpose, efficacy, value, and self-worth—appear to underlie the human quest for meaning, understood as "shared mental representations of possible relationships among things, events, and relationships."[6]

So why is this quest for meaning so important? Stefan Schulz-Hardt and Dieter Frey suggest that three main reasons may be identified as lying behind the universality of this quest.[7] First, it gives stability to existence, allowing people to orientate themselves in life. Second, it offers a defense mechanism in the face of a perceived threat of meaninglessness, which can overwhelm individuals and leave them unable to cope with life. The perception of meaninglessness can thus lead to distressing negative outcomes, such as depression, attempted suicide, alcoholism, or addiction. And third, it can be understood as the subjective response to an objective reality, in which the individual attempts to realign their internal world to conform to a deeper order of things, which is believed to exist independently of them. The subjective quest for meaning is thus grounded in a conviction that such a meaning exists objectively and can be discovered by those with the will and ability to do so.[8]

History reinforces our appreciation of the importance of this quest for meaning for human identity. Our distant ancestors studied the stars, aware that knowledge of their movements enabled them to navigate the world's oceans and predict the flooding of the Nile. Yet human interest in the night sky went far beyond

3. Adriaan T. Peperzak, *The Quest for Meaning: Friends of Wisdom from Plato to Levinas* (New York: Fordham University Press, 2003), 1–6. On attentional bias in human perception, see Michael I. Posner and Steven E. Petersen, "The Attentional System of the Human Brain," *Annual Review of Neuroscience* 13 (1990): 25–42.

4. Michael Polanyi, *The Tacit Dimension* (Garden City, NY: Doubleday, 1967), 24. Note how Polanyi specifically links this with the idea of "religious discovery."

5. See the rich seam of material from Asia offered in Tiziano Terzani, *A Fortune-Teller Told Me* (London: HarperCollins, 1997). The theme of "nothingness" features more prominently in Asian than in Western accounts of meaning: Victor Florian and Lonnie R. Snowden, "Fear of Personal Death and Positive Life Regard: A Study of Different Ethnic and Religious-Affiliated American College Students," *Journal of Cross-Cultural Psychology* 20 (1989): 64–79.

6. Roy F. Baumeister, *Meanings of Life* (New York: Guilford Press, 1991), 15.

7. Stefan Schulz-Hardt and Dieter Frey, "Das Sinnprinzip: Ein Standbein des Homo Psychologicus," in *Bericht über den 40. Kongress der Deutschen Gesellschaft für Psychologie in München 1996; Schwerpunktthema: Wissen und Handeln*, ed. H. Mandl (Göttingen: Hogrefe Verlag, 1997), 870–76.

8. This is a central theme of the wisdom literature of the ancient Near East and is frequently echoed in biblical works such as Proverbs and Job: see Katharine J. Dell, *The Book of Proverbs in Social and Theological Context* (Cambridge: Cambridge University Press, 2006), 125–54.

questions of mere utility. Might, many wondered, these silent pinpricks of light in the velvet darkness of the heavens disclose something deeper about the origins and goals of life? Might they bear witness to a deeper moral and intellectual order of things, with which humans could align themselves? Might nature be studded and emblazoned with clues to its meanings, and human minds shaped so that these might be identified, and their significance grasped?

It is a thought that has captivated the imagination of generations, from the dawn of civilization to the present day. True wisdom was about discerning the deeper structure of reality, lying beneath its surface appearance. The book of Job, one of the finest examples of the wisdom literature of the ancient Near East, speaks of wisdom as something that is hidden, that is to be found deep within Earth, its true meaning hidden from a casual and superficial glance.[9] The emergence of the discipline of semiotics has encouraged us to see natural objects and entities as signs, pointing beyond themselves, representing and communicating themselves. To find the true significance of things requires the development of habits of reading and directions of gaze that enable the reflective observer of nature to discern meaning where others see happenstance and accident. Or to use an image from Polanyi, where some hear a noise, others hear a tune.[10]

Polanyi's image is illuminating and highlights the importance of the human capacity to discern significance. Any such judgment involves at least a degree of intuition. "Our capacity for discerning meaningful aggregates, as distinct from chance aggregates, is an ultimate power of our personal judgment. It can be aided by explicit argument but never determined by it: our final decision will always remain tacit."[11] The human mind is able to discern what it regards as patterns within nature, patterns that are laden with significance and meaning. Similarly, the abiding popularity of detective fiction testifies to the human desire to make sense of clues, riddles, and mysteries, and the satisfaction that is derived from their resolution.[12] C. S. Lewis alluded to this when he suggested that "right and wrong" were "clues to the meaning of the universe."[13]

9. Paul S. Fiddes, "'Where Shall Wisdom Be Found?' Job 28 as a Riddle for Ancient and Modern Readers," in *After the Exile: Essays in Honor of Rex Mason*, ed. John Barton and David Reimer, 171–90 (Macon, GA: Mercer University Press, 1996). For a classic study of the significance of this piece of Wisdom Literature, see H. H. Rowley, "The Book of Job and Its Meaning," *Bulletin of the John Rylands Library* 41 (1958): 162–207. For theological reflections on Job's quest for wisdom, see David Ford, *Christian Wisdom: Desiring God and Learning in Love* (Cambridge: Cambridge University Press, 2007), 90–119.

10. Michael Polanyi, "Science and Reality," *British Journal for the Philosophy of Science* 18 (1967): 177–96, esp. 190–91.

11. Ibid., 191.

12. For a superb exploration of the relevance of the forms of abductive thinking developed in Charles Peirce's 1909 essay "Guessing" to crime fiction, see Thomas A. Sebeok and Jean Umiker-Sebeok, "'You Know My Method': A Juxtaposition of Charles S. Peirce and Sherlock Holmes," in *The Sign of Three: Dupin, Holmes, Peirce*, ed. Umberto Eco and Thomas A. Sebeok (Bloomington: Indiana University Press, 1983), 11–54.

13. This is the title of the fist major section of Lewis's work *Mere Christianity*, which takes the form of a restatement of the argument from morality: C. S. Lewis, *Mere Christianity* (New York: HarperCollins, 2001), 3–33.

There is an obvious parallel here with Shakespeare's *As You Like It* (1599–1600), in which the good Duke Senior is exiled to the Forest of Arden, where, like Robin Hood, he lives close to nature with his faithful followers. There he reflects that he might be able to learn more from nature than from the corrupt court from which he has been banished:[14]

> And this our life, exempt from public haunt,
> Finds tongues in trees, books in the running brooks,
> Sermons in stones, and good in everything.

Nature is here understood to have the capacity to represent and speak. So how might nature disclose its meaning? Are clues to its significance embedded within its fabric? Yet perhaps such questions need reformulation. Nature, after all, discloses nothing. It does not "speak" because it is mute. The construction of meaning is the creative work of the human mind, as it reflects on what it observes. Nature has "no tongue to plead, no heart to feel"; its role is limited since it can "only be" (Gerard Manley Hopkins).[15] Nevertheless, it might be "instressed" with the signs and symbols that point the wise to its meaning. Yet the identification of that meaning lies with the observer, who must construct a schema, a mental map, in order to make sense of what is observed.

This thought underlies a revealing comment of Sir Isaac Newton (1642–1727), one of the most significant contributors to the scientific revolution of the seventeenth century. Newton's scientific and mathematical breakthroughs—such as the discovery of the laws of planetary motion, his development of calculus, and the theory of optics—placed him at the forefront of the new understanding of nature as a mechanism. For Newton, what could be seen of nature was as a pointer to something deeper, lying beyond it, signposted by what could be seen. Thus he wrote toward the end of his life:[16]

> I seem to have been only like a boy playing on the sea-shore, and diverting myself in now and then finding a smoother pebble or a prettier shell than ordinary, whilst the great ocean of truth lay all undiscovered before me.

The familiarity of both the text and the imagery must not be allowed to detract from the fundamental idea that it expresses: the scientific enterprise often focuses on the empirical, on surface phenomena, passing over the deeper structures and meanings of the world. We play on the shore, unaware of, or unwilling to venture into, the silent depths beyond. The pebble and shell are images of liminality, the awareness of standing on a threshold. What can be seen is a pointer to a greater whole that tantalizingly remains to be discovered.[17]

14. William Shakespeare, *As You Like It*, act 2, scene 1, lines 15–17.
15. Gerard Manley Hopkins, "Ribblesdale" (1883), lines 3–4. For comment, see Alister E. McGrath, *The Open Secret: A New Vision for Natural Theology* (Oxford: Blackwell, 2008), 133–39.
16. David Brewster, *Life of Sir Isaac Newton*, rev. W. T. Lynn, new ed. (London: Tegg, 1875), 303.
17. For an excellent discussiom of this theme in Aquinas, see Lawrence Feingold, *The Natural Desire to See God according to St. Thomas and His Interpreters* (Rome: Apollinare Studi, 2001).

This has long been the concern of natural theology, which is best interpreted as an attempt to find common ground for dialogue between the Christian faith and human culture, based on a proposed link between the everyday world of our experience and a transcendent realm—in the case of the Christian faith, with the "God and Father of our Lord Jesus Christ" (1 Peter 1:3). It represents an "intertwining of knowledge and belief," two habits of thought that are often seen as antithetical in the twenty-first century yet actually have the potential for creative convergence.[18] The growing interest in the dialogue between the natural sciences and Christian theology clearly points to natural theology as a significant conceptual meeting place, capable of stimulating and resourcing enriched visions of reality. Yet natural theology has been curiously sidelined in such discussions, its potential remaining frustratingly untapped.

Why is this so? While several factors have doubtless contributed to this marginalization, it is clear that the predominant concern is that natural theology is a relic from the past, a lost cause, compromised by the ambivalences of its past and tainted by its present associations. If my personal conversations with theologians, philosophers, and natural scientists over the last decade are in any way representative, natural theology is generally seen as being like a dead whale, left stranded on a beach by a receding tide, gracelessly rotting under the heat of a philosophical and scientific sun.

This is a serious issue. In the past, natural theology was seen as mapping out an area with conceptually porous boundaries, allowing dialogue and cross-fertilization between Christian theology, the arts, literature, and especially the natural sciences. The Victorian age, for all its faults, witnessed some remarkably creative discussions of natural theology, as the writings of Charles Kingsley, John Ruskin, and Gerard Manley Hopkins indicate.[19] Yet such conversations are now rare, reflecting, in part, a lack of serious theological engagement with the concept of the "natural."[20] A belief that engagement with nature is theologically sterile has hindered what has the potential for considerable intellectual enrichment. Thus Karl Barth's regrettable failure to engage meaningfully with the natural sciences[21] is clearly linked with his decidedly negative appraisal of natural theology.

Yet the very idea of natural theology designates a method, rather than a settled body of beliefs and assumptions. There is no single continuous narrative of

18. See the sympathetic and informed account in Fernando Vidal and Bernard Kleeberg, "Knowledge, Belief, and the Impulse to Natural Theology," *Science in Context* 20 (2007): 381–400.

19. See the useful analysis in Hilary Fraser, *Beauty and Belief: Aesthetics and Religion in Victorian Literature* (Cambridge: Cambridge University Press, 1986).

20. Note the points made in John Macquarrie, "The Idea of a Theology of Nature," *Union Seminary Quarterly Review* 30 (1975): 69–75. For an excellent account of the "new style" of natural theology that Macquarrie went on to develop, see Georgina Morley, *John Macquarrie's Natural Theology: The Grace of Being* (Aldershot: Ashgate, 2003), esp. 97–120. While I have reservations about some aspects of Macquarrie's approach, I find myself fully in agreement with his suggestion that such a natural theology "does not *prove* anything, but it *lets us see*."

21. Harold P. Nebelsick, "Karl Barth's Understanding of Science," in *Theology beyond Christendom: Essays on the Centenary of the Birth of Karl Barth*, ed. John Thompson (Allison Park, PA: Pickwick Publications, 1986), 165–214.

natural theology within the Christian tradition which defines one approach as normative and others as heterodox or marginal. The styles of engagement between Christian theology and the natural world are shaped, to an ultimately indeterminate and varying extent, by the intellectual and cultural conditions of the age. Thus the styles of natural theology that were developed in fourth-century Alexandria are markedly different from those that predominated in early nineteenth-century England. These are often "local theologies,"[22] reflecting the histories and particularities of their contexts, including highly specific under-standings of the concept of "nature" itself.[23]

In the last fifty years, there has been a growing consensus that "nature" and "the natural," far from being objective, autonomous entities assumed by the Enlightenment, are conceptually malleable notions, patient of multiple inter-pretations, and hence subject to the influence of power, vested interests, ideo-logical agendas, and social pressures.[24] Historical surveys of how humanity has understood and defined "nature" reveal a surprisingly large range of options, most of which lie beyond empirical verification. To note this point is not to lapse into some form of relativism or offer a purely social constructivist account of things. It is to confront the inescapable fact, which can easily be accommodated within a critical realist outlook, that "nature" is now understood to be a con-tested notion.

"Nature" denotes ways in which human observers choose to see, interpret, and inhabit the natural, empirical world. The process of observation is "theory-laden" (N. R. Hanson), involving existing schemas or "mental maps" of reality. There are many concepts of nature, since construals of nature are essentially tractable and indeterminate, highly susceptible to conceptual manipulation by the human mind. Recognition of this point is of critical importance for a renewed "natural theology," especially if undertaken from a critical realist perspective. It acknowledges—contrary to the predominant view of the Enlightenment—that the term "nature" does not designate an objective reality that requires interpreta-tion. It is already an interpreted entity, which requires *reinterpretation*, by being "seen" in a new way.

The notion of "nature" itself is ultimately a social construction.[25] Like all such culturally constructed ideas and worlds, it is an "unstable edifice that generations

22. See Robert J. Schreiter, *Constructing Local Theologies* (Maryknoll, NY: Orbis, 1985).

23. For the importance of the cultural context in shaping such core notions, see Ulf Hannerz, *Cultural Complexity: Studies in the Social Organization of Meaning* (New York: Columbia University Press, 1992), 3–4, 15.

24. See the detailed analysis in Alister E. McGrath, *A Scientific Theology*, vol. 1, *Nature* (London: Continuum, 2001), 81–133.

25. The best analysis of this is Klaus Eder. *Die Vergesellschaftung der Natur: Studien zur sozialen Evolution der praktischen Vernunft* (Frankfurt am Main: Suhrkamp, 1988). For a more accessible exploration of this theme in English, see William Cronon, *Uncommon Ground: Toward Reinventing Nature* (New York: W. W. Norton, 1995). Eder's emphasis upon the importance of power groups in defining master narratives of the natural world is especially evident in a more recent study: Klaus Eder, "The Rise of Counter-Cultural Movements against Modernity: Nature as a New Field of Class Struggle," *Theory, Culture and Society* 7 (1990): 21–47.

constantly labor to build, raze, rebuild, and redesign."[26] The human under-standing of nature has been subject to quite remarkable definitional fluctuations over time,[27] with important consequences for the related idea of natural theol-ogy. Understandings of natural theology are thus often situation-specific, so that they cannot simply be transplanted from one historical community to another, as if any one of them defined or constituted *quod ubique, quod semper, quod ab omnibus creditum est.*

Most recent discussion of natural theology has proceeded on the assumption that this term defines a conceptually stable and epistemologically autonomous style of theology. It is of the very essence of a natural theology, we are told, that it sets out to deduce the existence and at least something of the nature of God from an engagement with nature.[28] Though many would concur with this judg-ment, one must object that it represents an "essentialist" judgment concerning the core identity of natural theology which fails to take account of the impor-tance of the intellectual context in molding its specific forms. Furthermore, this assumes that the temporary historical predominance of one specific approach to natural theology is to be equated with intellectual stability and coherence.

There is an important parallel here with the engagement of science and reli-gion, rapidly emerging as one of the most interesting and productive fields of intellectual inquiry. Yet to speak of the relationship or interaction between sci-ence and religion presupposes that there are certain agreed boundaries between them. For some, those boundaries are defined by the essential natures of the dis-ciplines; others, however, have noted that these boundaries are dependent upon how a given historical era or school of thought chooses to understand the cate-gories of "science" and "religion."[29] "Science" and "religion" alike are socially con-structed notions that reflect the prevailing assumptions of cultural and academic power groups. For the historian, neither science nor religion is reducible to some timeless "essence," even though a series of master narratives have been put for-ward in support of such "essentialist" theses.[30] And since both the categories of "science" and "religion" are molded by their historical locations, it follows that the derivative category of the "relationship between science and religion" is even more greatly shaped by its historical context.

26. David Morgan, *Visual Piety: A History and Theory of Popular Religious Images* (Berkeley: Uni-versity of California Press, 1998), 9.

27. See the penetrating study of Thomas Sören Hoffmann, *Philosophische Physiologie: Eine Systematik des Begriffs der Natur im Spiegel der Geschichte der Philosophie* (Stuttgart: Frommann-Holzboog, 2003). For a detailed analysis of the theological implications of this shifting understand-ing of the concept of "nature," see McGrath, *A Scientific Theology*, vol. 1, *Nature*, 81–133.

28. See, e.g., the excellent account of the cosmological argument found in William Lane Craig, *The Cosmological Argument from Plato to Leibniz* (London: Macmillan, 1980).

29. John Hedley Brooke, *Science and Religion: Some Historical Perspectives* (Cambridge: Cam-bridge University Press, 1991), 52–81; James R. Moore, "Speaking of Science and Religion—Then and Now," *History of Science* 30 (1992): 311–23.

30. The best analysis of this point is the richly documented study of John Brooke and Geoffrey Cantor, *Reconstructing Nature: The Engagement of Science and Religion* (New York: Oxford University Press, 2000), esp. the discussion on 43–72.

So what styles of natural theology have dominated recent discussion of the relation of science and religion? In the following chapter, we shall sketch the development and characteristics of an approach to natural theology which gained the ascendency in the twentieth century, before moving on to propose an alternative vision, more adapted to the explanatory challenges of recent developments in the natural sciences on the one hand, and the distinctive themes of the Christian faith on the other.

A TRINITARIAN
NATURAL THEOLOGY

Chapter 2

The Crisis of Confidence
in Modern Natural Theology

The idea that a transcendent reality can be known or at least intimated through the mundane has a long history and is not a specifically religious idea. Although the idea has found wide (yet not uncritical) acceptance within Christianity and Judaism, contemporary Islam has found the idea uncomfortable and potentially subversive, not least on account of its apparent undermining of the unique authority of the Qur'an to disclose knowledge of God.

Such an approach can be found within the New Testament itself, most notably in Paul's "Areopagus address,"[1] and achieved significant elaboration in the thought of the early Christian fathers.[2] The essential point is that Christian theology provides an interpretative framework by which nature may be "seen" in a way that connects with the transcendent. The enterprise of natural theology is thus one of discernment, of seeing nature in a certain way, of viewing it through a particular and specific set of spectacles, of resolving its ambiguities through an

1. The classic study of this theme is Bertil Gärtner, *The Areopagus Speech and Natural Revelation* (Uppsala: Gleerup / Almqvist & Wiksells, 1955.

2. See esp. Jaroslav Pelikan, *Christianity and Classical Culture: The Metamorphosis of Natural Theology in the Christian Encounter with Hellenism* (New Haven, CT: Yale University Press, 1993).

interpretative framework which on the one hand is grounded in nature, and on the other transcends it.[3] Although nature itself does not possess any autonomous capacity to disclose the transcendent, the Christian faith offers a way of perceiving nature which regards it as an authorized sign of the transcendent. This schema for the interpretation of nature is not given within the natural realm; once discovered, however, it turns out to be consistent with it.[4]

The rise of the "Age of Reason," however, witnessed—and arguably caused—the rise of a family of approaches to natural theology which asserted its capacity to demonstrate the existence of God without recourse to any religious beliefs or presuppositions. This development reflects the Enlightenment's emphasis upon the autonomy and sovereignty of unaided human reason. As used, for example, by the American writer Cotton Mather in his 1715 work *The Christian Philosopher*, natural theology was interpreted as a "theology that seeks to prove the existence and attributes of God from the evidence of purpose and design in the universe."[5]

The term "natural theology" designates a range of attitudes to the relation of science and religion. It is not acceptable to give priority to any one of its historical forms, and then to declare that this determines the "essence" of natural theology. It is certainly true that one specific form of natural theology (or a family of natural theologies) achieved dominance during the period of the Enlightenment and continues to be influential to this day: the idea that natural theology offers a rational demonstration of the existence of God through an engagement with the natural world. Karl Barth's celebrated critique of natural theology actually addresses one specific approach to natural theology, rather than the enterprise in general. Interestingly, both Barth's critique of natural theology and the forms of natural theology to which he objected are by-products of modernism.[6] Yet the enterprise of natural theology itself cannot be judged from any of its historically conditioned manifestations, each of which is adapted and attuned to its own distinctive environment. One of the most important contexts to generate its own version of natural theology was the complex movement that we still designate "the Enlightenment."

At the heart of the Enlightenment lay a quest for a public, invariant, and reliable foundation of knowledge. Recent scholarship has drawn attention to the vulnerability of some accounts of the Enlightenment, which fail to take account of its com-

3. For these themes in Augustine of Hippo, see Roland J. Teske, "Augustine of Hippo on Seeing with the Eyes of the Mind," in *Ambiguity in Western Thought*, ed. Craig J. N. de Paulo, Patrick Messina, and Marc Stier (New York: Peter Lang, 2005), 72–87, 221–26.

4. The point being made is similar to that emphasized by Thomas Aquinas concerning faith and reason: faith is not contrary to reason, but rather transcends it. See Robert Spaemann, "Rationality and Faith in God," *Communio* 32 (2005): 618–36.

5. Cotton Mather, *The Christian Philosopher*, ed. Winton U. Solberg (Urbana: University of Illinois Press, 1994), xliii.

6. Colin Grant, "Why Should Theology Be Unnatural?" *Modern Theology* 23 (2007): 91–106. For the problematic nature of Barth's relationship to the Enlightenment, see Alister E. McGrath, "Karl Barth als Aufklärer? Der Zusammenhang seiner Lehre vom Werke Christi mit der Erwählungslehre," *Kerygma und Dogma* 81 (1984): 383–94.

plex origins and agendas. Both defenders and critics of the Enlightenment have tended to present the movement as essentially homogenous, believing that this intellectual and historical simplification assists their respective agendas.[7] Although the term "the Enlightenment project" is widely encountered in the literature, it is clear that we ought really to speak of a series of such projects.[8] Though there were clearly shared concerns and approaches, scholarship has increasingly recognized that its ideas cannot be treated as "autonomous, discrete objects," but are to be considered as being "deeply embedded in society."[9] It is no criticism of the Enlightenment to concede both its diversity and the historically situated character of some of its leading ideas, since this helps us to understand the historical emergence of the movement, as well as to contextualize at least some of its chief concerns. One primary motivation for this search for objectivity, reflecting the cultural situation of early eighteenth-century Europe, was growing pessimism concerning the capacity of religion or prevailing cultural norms to provide a secure, universal basis for knowledge. Growing suspicion of both the intellectual foundations and ethical consequences of religious belief led many to establish truth on the basis of an appeal to pure human reason, untainted by the foibles of outdated traditions, arbitrary prejudice, or cultural and historical location.[10] Reason was held to transcend all human boundaries, offering the only secure foundation for valid human beliefs and values.

In such an intellectual environment, the church's public defense of the existence of God on the basis of an appeal to tradition or the Bible became increasingly problematic. The emergence of biblical criticism eroded confidence in the text of Scripture, the growing influence of "doctrinal criticism" challenged its traditional interpretations, and the rise of rationalism called the need for divine revelation into question. One apologetic strategy was to attempt to devise arguments for the Christian faith based purely upon reason; the other was to make an appeal to nature itself. These developments took place primarily within England during the late seventeenth century and proved influential subsequently in France and Germany.[11]

The primary motivation for undertaking natural theology within English Christianity during the late seventeenth and eighteenth century was in no small part due to apologetic concerns.[12] The church itself did not reject revelation; it

7. See, e.g., the analysis of the "ruins of the Enlightenment project" in John Gray, *Enlightenment's Wake: Politics and Culture at the Close of the Modern Age* (London: Routledge, 1997). For a critique, see James Schmidt, "Civility, Enlightenment, and Society: Conceptual Confusions and Kantian Remedies," *American Political Science Review* 92 (1998): 419–27.

8. Bernard Yack, *The Fetishism of Modernities: Epochal Self-Consciousness in Contemporary Social and Political Thought* (Notre Dame, IN: University of Notre Dame Press, 1997), esp. 112–19.

9. Dorinda Outram, *The Enlightenment* (Cambridge: Cambridge University Press, 1995), 12.

10. Mark O. Webb, "Natural Theology and the Concept of Perfection in Descartes, Spinoza and Leibniz," *Religious Studies* 25 (1989): 459–75; Frederick C. Beiser, *The Sovereignty of Reason: The Defense of Rationality in the Early English Enlightenment* (Princeton, NJ: Princeton University Press, 1996).

11. The historical importance of English Deism as a catalyst for Enlightenment religious thought is widely conceded. For the broader impact of the English Enlightenment, see Gertrude Himmelfarb, *The Roads to Modernity: The British, French, and American Enlightenments* (New York: Knopf, 2005).

12. Alister E. McGrath, "Towards the Restatement and Renewal of a Natural Theology: A Dialogue with the Classic English Tradition," in *The Order of Things: Explorations in Scientific Theology* (Oxford: Blackwell Publishing, 2006), 63–96.

realized that it needed to relate the gospel to a culture which no longer felt inclined to accept this notion. The church, realizing that it was increasingly difficult to base a dialogue with English academic thought upon the Bible, sought an alternative common ground for its apologetic discourse—and found it in the realm of nature.[13] Natural theology thus rapidly became an apologetic tool of no small importance.

By the early eighteenth century, the concept of "natural theology" was firmly established within English religious culture as a way of demonstrating God's existence without recourse to any religious beliefs or presuppositions.[14] This represented an adaptation of the concept to the realities of the English religious situation, primarily in response to the agenda of the Enlightenment. The abiding influence of the Enlightenment's agenda upon Western theology until relatively recently led to this situation-specific understanding of "natural theology" being assumed to be normative. In fact, it is only one possibility—and one heavily shaped by modernist assumptions, now increasingly being called into question. It is open to revision. There is no compelling reason to defend a modernist vision of natural theology in a postmodern culture.

There is no doubt that contemporary Western theology has been deeply shaped by the ideas of the Enlightenment, both its positive emphasis upon the competency of reason and the possibility of objectivity of judgment, and its negative critiques of the coherence of the concept of revelation, and the capacity of Scripture to disclose truths that allegedly lie beyond reason.[15] The specific understanding of natural theology that arose from this modernist matrix has been so influential that many Christians have come to assume that "natural theology" automatically and necessarily designates the enterprise of arguing directly from the observation of nature to demonstrate the existence of God. In fact, however, this is merely one among many approaches to natural theology, which is best seen as a historically conditioned response to the intellectual and cultural environment of modern Western culture. With the historical erosion of the dominance of these regnant cultural assumptions, there is a clear need to retrieve older approaches or forge new approaches to natural theology which are not trapped by the matrix of Enlightenment assumptions that many now find so problematic.

For natural theology is in crisis. That, it seems, is the dominant—though not necessarily universal—opinion within much of Western theology, particularly

13. For the dangers attending such an appeal to nature, see Peter A. Byrne, *Natural Religion and the Nature of Religion: The Legacy of Deism* (London: Routledge, 1989).

14. For the background, see John Gascoigne, "From Bentley to the Victorians: The Rise and Fall of British Newtonian Natural Theology," *Science in Context* 2 (1988): 219–56.

15. The term "Enlightenment" needs to be used with some caution, because recent scholarship has suggested that this great movement in Western thought is better conceived as a "family of Enlightenments," sharing a common commitment to a core of ideas and values, yet demonstrating diversity at other points. See, e.g., James Schmidt, *What Is Enlightenment? Eighteenth-Century Answers and Twentieth-Century Questions* (Berkeley: University of California Press, 1996).

within Protestantism.[16] It will be helpful to review some of the reasons why natural theology, as this is traditionally understood, has encountered such difficulties in recent years. Without wishing to suggest that these exhaust the issues, I believe that three principal factors have led to the intellectual impoverishment and theological marginalization of natural theology in some theological circles.

First, as already hinted at in the above analysis, the agenda of what is traditionally known as "natural theology" has been so heavily influenced by the agenda of the Enlightenment that the passing of its cultural and intellectual dominance has left this approach stranded. It is so deeply embedded in a web of rationalist assumptions that the erosion of their plausibility has led to its loss of credibility. Postmodernism is, of course, resistant to precise definition; it may, however, reasonably be held to represent the rejection—and occasionally even the total inversion—of some of the fundamental beliefs of modernity, most notably its core belief in a single metanarrative of rationality.

The rise of postmodernism has not necessarily led to the emergence of a new family of natural theologies; it has, however, created a climate of suspicion and distrust for such theologies that are seen to be wedded to a modernist worldview.[17] The ebbing of the rationalist tide has left such approaches beached, with little enthusiasm for their retrieval. The widely held assumption that modernist approaches to natural theology are definitive of the enterprise itself has led some to draw the unfortunate (and clearly inaccurate) conclusion that natural theology itself is now moribund. It is, of course, not necessary to endorse postmodernism in order to critique modernism. Yet a recognition of the intellectual and cultural lineage of certain approaches to natural theology helps us understand something of why they have been found to be so problematic in a postmodern context.

In part, the loss of confidence in this approach to natural theology reflects a growing realization that what Enlightenment thinkers regarded as universal and necessary was actually local and contingent, shaped by social and historical factors as much as by an allegedly universal template of human rationality. One of the most powerful critiques of the rationalist approach to reason and morality is based on the historical observation that an allegedly universal method seemed to deliver quite different intellectual and moral outcomes, depending on the historical and cultural location of its practitioners. As Alasdair MacIntyre points out, "The legacy of the Enlightenment has been the provision of an ideal of rational

16. For representative evaluations of the situation, along with interesting proposals for its transformation, see Christoph Kock, *Natürliche Theologie: Ein evangelischer Streitbegriff* (Neukirchen-Vluyn: Neukirchener Verlag, 2001); Richard Swinburne, "Natural Theology, Its 'Dwindling Probabilities' and 'Lack of Rapport,'" *Faith and Philosophy* 21 (2004): 533–46.

17. I must stress that this judgment is not dependent on any specific view of the merits of the Enlightenment. The point being made is that the ideas of Enlightenment no longer carry the same weight as they did a century ago. For an example of a recent work that is severely critical of the Enlightenment heritage, see James Q. Wilson, *The Moral Sense* (New York: Free Press, 1995), 244–45. The general concerns are helpfully summarized in Outram, *The Enlightenment*.

justification which it has proved impossible to attain."[18] The notion of a universal rationality is an aspiration, he argues, rather than an actually existing entity, capable of being realized. Rationalities, he insists, cannot be detached from the traditions which mediate them. They may have pretensions to universality; nevertheless, the historical record discloses that they are actually specific to traditions.[19] The family of natural theologies developed by Enlightenment thinkers is likewise local in origins and application: they cannot be held to be determinative for all time. Other such theologies are possible and necessary.

For example, the validity of most Enlightenment approaches to the observation of nature was called into question during the twentieth century by philosophers of science such as Norwood Hanson.[20] For Hanson, observation is "theory-laden": that is to say, one observes the world with theoretical preconceptions, which shape what the supposedly neutral and objective observer actually sees.[21] The dominant Enlightenment understandings of the process of human cognition and perception are now widely regarded as resting on outdated and inadequate understandings of the processes of human perception. This has added further to the growing concern about the viability of such styles of natural theology.

A second major concern is the perceived failure of this type of natural theology to provide reliable foundations for belief in God. Its failure to achieve its stated goals has become increasingly evident in recent years, partly through advances in scientific explanation. It is widely agreed that enthusiasm for natural theology—here understood specifically as the attempt to provide a reliable basis for belief in God—reached its zenith in eighteenth-century England. The Boyle lectures, delivered over the period 1692–1732, are widely regarded as the most significant public demonstration of the "reasonableness" of Christianity in the early modern period, characterized by that era's growing emphasis upon rationalism and its increasing suspicion of ecclesiastical authority. English natural theology was given new intellectual energy through William Paley's *Natural Theology* (1802), which rapidly became the most influential defense of the existence of God from the natural world.[22] For Paley, nature showed obvious signs of having been designed and constructed by God, who could be conceived as the cosmological watchmaker.

---

18. Alasdair MacIntyre, *Whose Justice? Which Rationality?* (Notre Dame, IN: University of Notre Dame Press, 1988), 6.

19. Ibid., 334.

20. N. R. Hanson, *Patterns of Discovery: An Inquiry into the Conceptual Foundations of Science* (Cambridge: Cambridge University Press, 1961).

21. For an excellent discussion, see Matthias Adam, *Theoriebeladenheit und Objektivität: Zur Rolle von Beobachtungen in den Naturwissenschafte* (Frankfurt am Main: Ontos Verlag, 2002), esp. 51–97.

22. See, e.g., Aileen Fyfe, "The Reception of William Paley's *Natural Theology* in the University of Cambridge," *British Journal for the History of Science* 30 (1997): 321–35. The Bridgewater Treatises also played an important role in popularizing the themes of natural theology as an apologetic device: see Jon M. Robson, "The Fiat and the Finger of God: The Bridgewater Treatises," in *Victorian Faith in Crisis: Essays on Continuity and Change in Nineteenth-Century Religious Belief*, ed. Richard J. Helmstadter and Bernard Lightman (London: Macmillan, 1990), 71–125.

Yet by about 1860, English natural theology seemed to be in terminal decline, for two main reasons. First, the approach seemed to lead to decidedly heterodox notions of God, rather than the triune God of the Christian faith.[23] Unfortunately, Paley's "watchmaker" was too easily conceptualized as part of the metaphysical furniture of the universe, losing much of its traditional theological depth. This approach to natural theology led to a form of Christianity which seriously distorted the traditional orthodox understanding of the nature of God, and especially the critical issue of God's continuing involvement in the world—in other words, the concept of providence. Natural theology came to be associated with a mechanistic worldview and a significantly reduced conception of God, in which "providence" is evacuated of much, if not all, of its traditional meaning.

Perhaps more significantly, the intellectual case for God associated with natural theology seemed increasingly vulnerable and flimsy as time progressed.[24] The credibility of Paley's natural theology depended heavily on the natural world having been fixed in its present form by an act of special divine creation. The rise of Darwinism destroyed the credibility of Paley's approach at this specific point,[25] thus plunging this form of natural theology into a crisis from which it has never fully recovered. While the rise of Darwinism cannot be regarded as the sole cause of the decline in the intellectual fortunes of natural theology, it was a significant factor in bringing about increasing doubts and suspicions about the viability of the enterprise. When Karl Barth began to express serious misgivings about natural theology on dogmatic grounds, his criticisms resonated with the growing mistrust of natural theology precipitated by advances in science, especially through the rise of Darwinism.

Paley's approach is not, however, totally beyond redemption. After the publication of Darwin's *Origin of Species*, some theistic apologists correctly noted that Paley's arguments could be reformulated in terms of the apparent rationality of the evolutionary process.[26] Yet despite such possibilities of conceptual refurbishment and repristination, many feel that the effort required rather exceeded the somewhat meager rewards offered. For many, Richard Dawkins's incisive dismissal of Paley's approach as "gloriously and utterly wrong" remains both plausible and

---

23. This problem emerged at an earlier stage: see the excellent collection of essays in John Hedley Brooke and Ian Maclean, eds., *Heterodoxy in Early Modern Science and Religion* (Oxford: Oxford University Press, 2005).

24. John Hedley Brooke, "Science and the Fortunes of Natural Theology: Some Historical Perspectives," *Zygon* 24 (1989): 3–22.

25. The classic Darwinian critique of Paley's approach is Richard Dawkins, *The Blind Watchmaker: Why the Evidence of Evolution Reveals a Universe without Design* (New York: W. W. Norton, 1986).

26. See, e.g., James R. Moore, *The Post-Darwinian Controversies: A Study of the Protestant Struggle to Come to Terms with Darwin in Great Britain and America, 1870–1900* (Cambridge: Cambridge University Press, 1979); Frederick Gregory, "The Impact of Darwinian Evolution on Protestant Theology in the Nineteenth Century," in *God and Nature: Historical Essays on the Encounter between Christianity and Natural Science*, ed. D. C. Lindberg and R. L. Numbers (Berkeley: University of California Press, 1986), 369–90; David N. Livingstone, *Darwin's Forgotten Defenders: The Encounter between Evangelical Theology and Evolutionary Thought* (Grand Rapids: Eerdmans, 1987).

persuasive.[27] Nature, many now argue, is religiously ambivalent,[28] leading as much to a natural *a*theology as to a natural theology.[29] Writers such as Dawkins and Daniel Dennett have produced what some have termed "the Bridgewater Treatises of the twentieth century," advocating a natural atheism (or atheology).[30] Where once a scientific account of the world was used to advocate a Christian perspective, the late twentieth century witnessed a growing trend to use it as a weapon against religious belief.[31]

Other approaches are, of course, possible. Richard Swinburne has cogently argued that the basic trajectory of Paley's argument should be shifted from "regularities of copresence," which place the emphasis upon spatial ordering, to "regularities of succession," which emphasize temporal ordering. Once this is done, he suggested, the argument could be reconstructed in a form which does not rely on the premises shown to be false by Darwin. The key to Swinburne's approach is therefore the orderliness of nature, which is ultimately expressed in the basic mathematical laws of the natural sciences.[32] Swinburne offers an inductive and probabilistic approach, which sets out to determine whether theism offers a superior account of such regularities in nature than does its alternatives.

This brings us to the third problem facing this concept of natural theology: the legacy of the theological critique of natural theology by the leading Protestant theologian Karl Barth (1886–1968). Barth's formal critique of natural theology dates from the 1930s and is not, strictly speaking, part of his explicit agenda in his Romans commentary or earlier writings.[33] The polemic which would later be directed against natural theology is initially directed against the category of "religion." In the second edition of his Romans commentary (1922), Barth critiques the idea of "religion" as a human construction erected in opposition to God. This same criticism is later directed against natural theology, although this is not explicitly identified as the target in 1922.[34] Again, in 1927 we find Barth identifying the target of his criticisms as "Schleiermacher's conversion of theol-

---

27. Dawkins, *The Blind Watchmaker*, 5.

28. John Hick, *An Interpretation of Religion: Human Responses to the Transcendent* (London: Macmillan, 1989), 73: Nature "is capable from our present human vantage point of being thought of in both religious and naturalistic ways."

29. See Abigail Lustig, "Natural Atheology," in *Darwinian Heresies*, ed. Abigail Lustig, Robert J. Richards, and Michael Ruse (Cambridge: Cambridge University Press, 2004), 69–83. The term "natural atheology" appears to have been coined by Alvin Plantinga: see Alvin Plantinga, *God and Other Minds: A Study of the Rational Justification of Belief in God*, Cornell Paperbacks (Ithaca, NY: Cornell University Press, 1990), 115–85.

30. John C. Greene, *Science, Ideology, and World View: Essays in the History of Evolutionary Ideas* (Berkeley: University of California Press, 1981), 162.

31. Thomas Dixon, "Scientific Atheism as a Faith Tradition," *Studies in History and Philosophy of Science C* 33 (2002): 337–59.

32. Richard Swinburne, *The Existence of God*, 2nd ed. (Oxford: Clarendon Press, 2004), 167–72.

33. As pointed out by Attila Szekeres, "Karl Barth und die natürliche Theologie," *Evangelische Theologie* 24 (1966): 229–42.

34. Karl Barth, *Der Römerbrief*, 2nd ed. (Munich: Kaiser Verlag, 1922), 213–55.

ogy into anthropology."[35] Yet natural theology is still not identified as the enemy of Barth's theological program. It may be true to suggest that Karl Barth's battle against natural theology was with regard to content a conflict with the theology of the nineteenth century; yet this conflict was not conceptualized in this specific manner until around 1929–30.

While it is entirely proper to stress that the challenging of natural theology is at least implicit in the development of Barth's early dialectical theology,[36] it is not until *Church Dogmatics* II/1 §26 that Barth offers an extended and systematic critique of natural theology. A "natural theology [*natürliche Theologie*]" is here defined as a theology "which comes to humanity from nature," expressing humanity's "self-preservation and self-affirmation" in the face of God. Natural theology is now interpreted as an expression of the human longing for self-justification, forcing a dichotomy between a true theology based upon revelation, and human attempts at self-justification based upon anthropology.[37]

Barth's hostility toward natural theology thus rests on his fundamental belief that it undermines the necessity and uniqueness of God's self-revelation. If knowledge of God can be achieved independently of God's self-revelation in Christ, then it follows that humanity can dictate the place, time, and means of its knowledge of God.[38] Natural theology, for Barth, represents an attempt on the part of humanity to understand itself apart from and in isolation from revelation, serving as a deliberate refusal to accept the necessity and consequences of revelation. One of Barth's central concerns is to expose the myth of human autonomy and identify its consequences for theology and ethics.[39] The human desire to assert itself and take control over things is seen by Barth as one of the most fundamental sources of error in theology, leading to the erection of theological towers of Babel—purely human constructions, erected in the face of God.

Yet Barth's critique is actually directed against a very specific understanding of natural theology, one that is conceived as an attempt to prove God's existence or gain access to knowledge of God under conditions of humanity's own choosing. This is merely one approach to natural theology, in this case shaped by the fundamental assumptions and agendas of the Enlightenment. Yet there are other approaches, such as that adopted and commended in the present volume: the attitude to nature that is mandated and facilitated by the Christian revelation.

---

35. Karl Barth, *Die christliche Theologie im Entwurf* (Munich: Kaiser Verlag, 1927), 82–87. For an excellent account of the reception of Schleiermacher's approach to natural theology within German Protestantism, see Kock, *Natürliche Theologie*, 103–294.

36. Here see Christof Gestrich, *Neuzeitliches Denken und die Spaltung der dialektischen Theologie: Zur Frage der natürlichen Theologie* (Tübingen: Mohr, 1977).

37. See Karl Barth, "Schicksal und Idee in Theologie," in *Theologische Frage und Antworten* (Zurich: Evangelischer Verlag, 1957), 54–92, esp. 85–87.

38. On this general point, see Regin Prenter, "Das Problem der natürlichen Theologie bei Karl Barth," *Theologische Literaturzeitung* 77 (1952): 607–11.

39. On the relevance of the theme of autonomy in Barth's writings at this point, see John Macken, *The Autonomy Theme in the Church Dogmatics of Karl Barth and His Critics* (Cambridge: Cambridge University Press, 1990), esp. 69–80.

What if natural theology is itself seen as a subordinate aspect of revealed theology, legitimated by that revealed theology rather than by natural presuppositions or insights? What if the authorization of natural theology is understood to lie, not in its own intrinsic structures, nor in an autonomous act of human self-justification, but in divine revelation itself? On this approach, found particularly in the writings of Thomas F. Torrance (1913–2007), *theologia revelata* both legitimates *theologia naturalis* and defines its scope.[40] This line of thought points to the possibility of a conceptual relocation of natural theology, with important implications for an understanding of its foundations and its scope.

Natural theology is therefore best understood as the enterprise of engaging and interpreting nature on the basis of the fundamental beliefs of the Christian tradition.[41] It is the way of seeing nature that is made possible and made appropriate by the Christian faith. For this reason, it is a fundamentally Trinitarian and incarnational undertaking. Christian theology provides the theory-laden component of the process of observation and interpretation of the natural order. One cannot therefore speak meaningfully of natural theology "proving" God's existence; it is, however, entirely appropriate to speak of a "resonance" between theory and observation, in which it is confirmed that the fundamental themes of the Christian faith offer the best explanation of what is seen.[42]

Yet this is to run ahead of our argument. We must first turn to consider some of the issues that arise from any attempt to renew and redirect natural theology, on the assumption that it is to be grounded in and legitimated by the Christian tradition.

40. Torrance develops this argument in his assessment of Barth's concerns about natural theology: see Thomas F. Torrance, "The Problem of Natural Theology in the Thought of Karl Barth," *Religious Studies* 6 (1970): 121–35. For an assessment of Torrance's own approach to natural theology, see Alister E. McGrath, *Thomas F. Torrance: An Intellectual Biography* (Edinburgh: T&T Clark, 1999), 175–94.

41. For a detailed defense and exposition of this point, see Alister E. McGrath, *The Open Secret: A New Vision for Natural Theology* (Oxford: Blackwell, 2008), 115–216.

42. This is a major theme in the writings of John Polkinghorne, who speaks of "consonance" between theory and observation, where I prefer "resonance": e.g., see John C. Polkinghorne, "Physics and Metaphysics in a Trinitarian Perspective," *Theology and Science* 1 (2003): 33–49. For reflections on Polkinghorne's approach, see Bernd Irlenborn, "Konsonanz von Theologie und Naturwissenschaft? Fundamentaltheologische Bemerkungen zum interdisziplinären Ansatz von John Polkinghorne," *Trierer theologische Zeitung* 113 (2004): 98–117; Johannes Maria Stenke, *John Polkinghorne: Konsonanz von Naturwissenschaft und Theologie* (Göttingen: Vandenhoeck & Ruprecht, 2006).

Chapter 3

Renewing the Vision
for Natural Theology

"I believe in Christianity as I believe that the Sun has risen, not only because I see it, but because by it I see everything else."[1] These words of C. S. Lewis speak of the binary intellectual virtue of the Christian faith: the conviction that it makes sense in itself, and that it makes sense of everything else. For Lewis, the Christian faith was like an intellectual sun, illuminating and irradiating the rich conceptual landscape of the natural world, enabling the observer to make sense of, and hence appreciate, the intricate patterns of the tapestry of human experience and thought. Cultivating the art of seeing is the key to unlocking the meaning of the world.[2]

Lewis's point is fundamental to my theme in this work. Christian theology is characterized at one and the same time by its intrasystemic elegance and its extrasystemic fecundity. Or to put this more gracefully, the Christian vision of reality

1. C. S. Lewis, "Is Theology Poetry?" in *C. S. Lewis: Essay Collection* (London: Collins, 2000), 1–21, esp. 21.
2. See the elaboration of this point in James Elkins, *How to Use Your Eyes* (London: Routledge, 2000), vii–ix. The importance of this was also noted by my distinguished predecessor as Gifford Lecturer, Stephen Pattison, who delivered these lectures in 2007: see Stephen Pattison, *Seeing Things: Deepening Relations with Visual Artefacts* (London: SCM Press, 2007).

possesses an internal coherence and consistency which is at least matched by its remarkable ability to make sense of what we observe and experience.[3] Christian theology can "fit in"—I here use Lewis's distinctive way of speaking—the natural sciences, art, morality, and other religious traditions. When rightly understood and enacted, natural theology represents the meeting point of the arts and sciences, offering a conceptually rich and productive crucible for the forging of intellectual connections and the exploration of dialogical possibilities.

This comprehensive vision of reality is what underlies a Christian natural theology. We must immediately recognize that the notion of "natural theology" has proved to be conceptually fluid, resistant to precise definition, partly because the notion has been constructed in response to a series of specific agendas. Christian theology provides an interpretative framework by which nature may be "seen" in a specific way that allows it to disclose God. The enterprise of natural theology is thus one of discernment, of seeing nature in a certain way, of viewing it through a particular and specific set of theoretical spectacles.[4] As Bonaventure of Bagnoregio (1221–74) argued, the many features of nature can thus be seen as "shadows, echoes, and pictures" of God its creator, which "are set before us in order that we might know God."[5] The Christian faith thus allows us to see nature through a conceptual matrix that both provides intellectual legitimacy to the enterprise of engaging with nature in the first place, as well as offering a lens through which it may be viewed and understood.

Since about 1750, the term "natural theology" has been used extensively within Western philosophy and theology to designate what can be known or rationally believed about God on the basis of human reason, without recourse to any special or supposedly supernatural revelation.[6] Although the term appears to have been used by continental theologians primarily to refer to an appeal to human reason in theistic apologetics, many English writers came to understand it as referring to an engagement with the world of nature. Writers such as John Ray (1627–1705) and William Derham (1657–1735) developed an extensive and sophisticated defense of belief in God through an appeal to the order and apparent design of the

---

3. For detailed analysis of Christian theology as an internally coherent and externally grounded discipline, see Alister E. McGrath, *A Scientific Theology*, vol. 2, *Reality* (London: Continuum, 2002), 3–54. A similar point was made by Charles Gore in his 1904 sermon "The Permanent Creed," in which he spoke of the "sense of indissoluble coherence" of the themes of the Christian creeds: Charles Gore, *The Permanent Creed and the Christian Idea of Sin* (London: John Murray, 1905).

4. For a detailed account of this approach to natural theology, and evaluation of its alternatives, see Alister E. McGrath, *The Open Secret: A New Vision for Natural Theology* (Oxford: Blackwell, 2008), 115–216.

5. Bonaventure, *Itinerarium mentis in Deum*, 2. See further Clarence J. Glacken, *Traces on the Rhodian Shore: Nature and Culture in Western Thought from Ancient Times to the End of the Eighteenth Century* (Berkeley: University of California Press, 1973), 238–39.

6. For reflections on the importance of Enlightenment rationalism in stimulating the emergence of such a notion of natural theology, see especially Michael Heyd, "Un rôle nouveau pour la science: Jean Alphonse Turrettini et les débuts de la théologie naturelle à Genève," *Revue de théologie et philosophie* 112 (1982): 25–42; Martin Klauber, "Jean-Alphonse Turrettini (1671–1737) on Natural Theology: The Triumph of Reason over Revelation at the Academy of Geneva," *Scottish Journal of Theology* 47 (1994): 301–25.

natural world,[7] which stressed the importance of the providential ordering of nature and the consequent lawful operation of the universe as a proof of divine superintendence and of the power of the divine will. In North America, Cotton Mather (1663–1728) pursued a similar line of thought,[8] arguably anticipating William Paley's masterpiece of integrative natural apologetics. Ralph Waldo Emerson's *Nature* (1834), though comparable to Paley's *Natural Theology* (1802) in terms of its influence, intimated a disconnection between natural theology and the creeds of the church which had no direct parallel in Paley's work.[9]

This approach to natural theology marked a significant move away from older continental approaches which interpreted *theologia naturalis* essentially as philosophical theology.[10] As Ray commented in 1690, Francis Bacon's emphasis upon the importance of the empirical method allowed his generation of natural theologians to anchor their ideas firmly in the natural world.[11] Robert Boyle's work in chemistry and Ray's in biology contributed significantly to the emergence of a new style of natural theology, distinguished by an appeal to the empirical world rather than the truths of reason.[12] The canonical statement of this approach to natural theology in Paley's *Natural Theology* led to the formation of the impression, both at the academic and popular levels, that this specific form of natural theology was normative.

Yet it is essential to appreciate that the concept of "natural theology" is fluid, having been understood in different senses throughout its history.[13] In the classical era, a rational style of natural theology emerged, which is often held to

7. See Neal C. Gillespie, "Natural History, Natural Theology, and Social Order: John Ray and the 'Newtonian Ideology,'" *Journal of the History of Biology* 20 (1987): 1–49; Lisa M. Zeitz, "Natural Theology, Rhetoric, and Revolution: John Ray's Wisdom of God, 1691–1704," *Eighteenth Century Life* 18 (1994): 120–33; Scott Mandelbrote, "The Uses of Natural Theology in Seventeenth-Century England," *Science in Context* 20 (2007): 451–80.

8. Mather's *Christian Philosopher* (1721) is widely regarded as one of the finest American developments of a natural theology: see Winton U. Solberg, "Science and Religion in Early America: Cotton Mather's 'Christian Philosopher,'" *Church History* 56 (1987): 73–92.

9. David Robinson, "Emerson's Natural Theology and the Paris Naturalists: Toward a Theory of Animated Nature," *Journal of the History of Ideas* 41 (1980): 69–88.

10. See the study of John E. Murdoch, "The Analytic Character of Late Medieval Learning: Natural Philosophy without Nature," in *Approaches to Nature in the Middle Ages*, ed. Lawrence D. Roberts (Binghamton, NY: Center for Medieval and Early Renaissance Studies, 1982), 171–213.

11. For an account of Bacon's contribution in these areas, see Stephen Gaukroger, *Francis Bacon and the Transformation of Early-Modern Philosophy* (Cambridge: Cambridge University Press, 2001), 68–100, 132–60.

12. The concept of "natural philosophy" that emerged at this time is best studied from works such as J. F. W. Herschel, *Preliminary Discourse on the Study of Natural Philosophy* (London: Longman, Rees, Orme, Brown & Green, 1830). For the idea in Boyle, see the material assembled by Marie Boas Hall, *Robert Boyle on Natural Philosophy: An Essay with Selections from His Writings* (Bloomington: Indiana University Press, 1965). For the emergence of this important concept as an autonomous discipline, see L. W. B. Brockliss, "Aristotle, Descartes and the New Science: Natural Philosophy at the University of Paris, 1600–1740," *Annals of Science* 38 (1981): 33–69; Heikki Mikkeli, "The Foundation of an Autonomous Natural Philosophy: Zabarella on the Classification of Arts and Sciences," in *Method and Order in Renaissance Philosophy of Nature: The Aristotle Commentary Tradition*, ed. Daniel A. Di Liscia, Eckhard Kessler, and Charlotte Methuen (Aldershot: Ashgate, 1997), 211–28.

13. For the various senses of the term during the patristic period, see Jaroslav Pelikan, *Christianity and Classical Culture: The Metamorphosis of Natural Theology in the Christian Encounter with Hellenism* (New Haven, CT: Yale University Press, 1993).

be the creation of Stoicism, although its origins are in fact to be found in Plato and Aristotle.[14] This later developed into the classic notion of *theologia tripartita*, a threefold division of the domain of theology into the realms of "mythical theology" (*theologia fabulosa*), "civil theology" (*theologia civilis*), and "natural theology" (*theologia naturalis*).[15] This approach is found in the writings of Marcus Terentius Varro (116–27 BCE),[16] and had a significant impact on the manner in which Augustine of Hippo chose to develop his own notion of natural theology.[17] It is clear that Lord Gifford, the distinguished endower of these lectures, entertained some such understanding of natural theology.

As traditionally interpreted, this tripartite approach to theology distinguishes between the religious approaches of the poets, politicians, and philosophers. The first were concerned with *theologia fabulosa*, which characteristically expressed itself in the medium of *mythos*—the often scandalous pagan narratives of gods, as found in the writings of Hesiod and Homer. For Homer, the gods are immortal humans, demonstrating and engaging in the same emotions, vices, and power games as their human counterparts. Sadly, immortality denoted only the infinite extension of existence, not of moral qualities.[18] The deeds of these gods were held to make for good theater and were often enacted in dramatic contexts. Yet their utility for social role models was increasingly regarded to be severely limited. By the time Varro was writing, mythology was seen as being primarily of dramatic rather than moral or intellectual interest.

The second type of theology was concerned with what we might now term "civil religion"—with the civic cults, religious institutions, figureheads, and rites, which offered society social cohesion.[19] *Theologia civilis* can be thought of as "official orthopraxy," defining the cultic norms of a society that were held to be essential for the maintenance of civic unity and identity.[20] It was for this reason

---

14. Günter Pasorek, "Eine historische Notiz zur Scheidung von 'theologia civilis' und 'naturalis,'" in *Symmicta philologica Salisburgensia: Georgio Pfligersdorffer sexagenario oblata*, ed. Joachim Dalfen, Karl Forstner, Maximilian Fussl, and Wolfgang Speyer (Rome: Edizioni dell'Ateneo, 1980), 87–103.

15. Or "tripertita." See the analysis in Hans-Josef Klauck, "Nature, Art, and Thought: Dio Chrysostom and the *Theologia Tripertita*," *Journal of Religion* 87 (2007): 333–54. For earlier studies, see also Godo Lieberg, "Die 'theologia tripartita' in Forschung und Bezeugung," in *Aufstieg und Niedergang der römischen Welt*, vol. 1.4, ed. H. Temporini and W. Haase (New York: de Gruyter, 1973), 63–115; idem, "Die theologia tripartita als Formprinzip antiken Denkens," *Rheinisches Museum für Philologie* 125 (1982): 25–53.

16. See Yves Lehmann, *Varron théologien et philosophe romain* (Brussels: Latomus, 1997), 193–225. For the impact of these ideas on Virgil, see Michael von Albrecht and Gareth L. Schmeling, *A History of Roman Literature: From Livius Andronicus to Boethius with Special Regard to Its Influence on World Literature*, 2 vols. (New York: E. J. Brill, 1996), 1:85–87.

17. As pointed out by Albrecht Dihle, "Die Theologia tripertita bei Augustin," in *Geschichte—Tradition—Reflexion: Festschrift für Martin Hengel zum 70. Geburtstag*, ed. Hubert Cancik, 2 vols. (Tübingen: Mohr Siebeck, 1996), 2:183–202.

18. Jenny Strauss Clay, *The Politics of Olympus: Form and Meaning in the Major Homeric Hymns* (Princeton, NJ: Princeton University Press, 1989).

19. For its importance on the evolution of the Greek city-state, see François de Polignac, *Cults, Territory, and the Origins of the Greek City-State* (Chicago: University of Chicago Press, 1995).

20. For this helpful phrase, see Charles King, "The Organization of Roman Religious Beliefs," *Classical Antiquity* 22 (2003): 275–312.

that the early Christians were regarded as posing such a serious threat to Roman imperial identity through their refusal to take part in the imperial cult.[21] They were a threat to the social cohesion of imperial society.

Yet our concern here is with the third category, *theologia naturalis*, which denotes both physics and metaphysics—the philosophical exploration of nature, and inferring the existence and at least some characteristics of the divine by contemplating the regular movements of the heavenly bodies and the forces of nature.[22] This classic account of "natural theology" is thus understood to be discourse about the divine, grounded not on an appeal to the epistemologically and morally dubious category of "myth," but on a rational engagement with the natural world. An appeal to nature allowed a distinction between ideas which resonated with, or corresponded to, the way things actually were, rather than representing human inventions.[23] The importance of this point was brought out by Antiphon the Sophist, who argued that there is a fundamental distinction between "nature" and "laws": the former is something objective, stable, and immutable; the latter are at best arbitrary constructions or self-serving conventions established by human beings.[24] The study of nature thus provides an objective ground of judgment, counteracting the vested interests of those who forge laws.

Augustine of Hippo can be regarded as playing a major role in the Christianizing of the broad theological approaches of antiquity, weaving them together into a coherent vision of society, undergirded by the Christian revelation. For Augustine, Christian theology was grounded in the narratives of Israel and Jesus of Nazareth, which conformed to the literary style of *mythos*, yet were both historically grounded and theologically significant. Christian theology was able to offer the basis for a civil religion which avoided the errors and moral failings of its classical predecessors,[25] offering a vision for social cohesion. For Augustine, a natural theology offered both the possibility of dialogue with the broader civic culture, and a means for reaffirming the intellectual validity of faith without recourse to revelation.

The types of natural theology that emerged at the time of the Enlightenment in Western Europe are recognized to be essentially continuous with this classic

21. William R. Schoedel, "Christian 'Atheism' and the Peace of the Roman Empire," *Church History* 42 (1973): 309–19. For the background, see S. R. F. Price, *Rituals and Power: The Roman Imperial Cult in Asia Minor* (Cambridge: Cambridge University Press, 1984); Steven J. Friesen, *Twice Neokoros: Ephesus, Asia, and the Cult of the Flavian Imperial Family* (Leiden: Brill, 1993).

22. For this notion in the writings of Dio of Prusa, see Klauck, "Nature, Art, and Thought," 342–45.

23. This involves a distinction between *physis* and *technē*, the former representing a "natural" and the latter an "artificial" realm of existence. For this distinction in Aristotle, see Fred D. Miller, *Nature, Justice and Rights in Aristotle's Politics* (Oxford: Clarendon Press, 1995); Helen S. Lang, *The Order of Nature in Aristotle's Physics: Place and the Elements* (Cambridge: Cambridge University Press, 1998).

24. Gerard Naddaf, *The Greek Concept of Nature* (Albany: State University of New York Press, 2005), 11–35. There is some debate in the literature over whether Antiphon the Sophist is to be identified with Antiphon of Rhamnus (480–411 BCE).

25. See Dihle, "Die Theologia tripertita bei Augustin"; Ernest L. Fortin, *Classical Christianity and the Political Order: Reflections on the Theologico-Political Problem* (Lanham, MD: Rowman & Littlefield, 1996), 85–106.

understanding of *theologia naturalis*. The first significant example of such a work was due to the Catalonian theologian Raymond of Sebonde (died 1436), whose *Theologia naturalis seu liber creaturarum* was completed in the year of his death.[26] There are, of course, some significant differences between the approaches of Augustine and those which emerged in the modern era, of which the most significant is probably the Enlightenment tendency to interpret "reason" as a human faculty that "submitted all reality to the structures of the mind," whereas classical philosophy generally regarded reason to be "an ordering principle inherent in reality."[27] Yet the continuity is obvious: in both cases, natural theology represents a rational engagement with the natural world, with a view to establishing what notion of divinity it discloses. It is therefore appropriate to use the phrase "classic natural theology" to denote a wide range of such theologies, from the classical era to the time of the Enlightenment, which argue for a theology based upon human reflection on the natural world, without presupposing or acknowledging any covert influence of religious ideas.[28]

The concept underwent further development, especially within Protestant circles since the sixteenth century. John Calvin's notion of the *duplex cognitio Domini* led him to posit a distinction between "knowledge of God the creator" and "knowledge of God the redeemer."[29] For Calvin, a generalized knowledge of God was possible, apart from divine revelation, on the basis of reflection on human experience and rationality on the one hand, and on the structure of the external world on the other.[30] Given this theological framework, it was inevitable that use of the term "natural theology" would come to be used to designate both sources of Calvin's *cognitio Dei creatoris*.

The most important recent redefinition of "natural theology" has taken place in response to the agendas and concerns of the Enlightenment.[31] The transmutation of natural theology into an attempt to demonstrate the existence and determine the character of God without recourse to divine revelation reflected two

---

26. Peter Harrison, "'The Book of Nature' and Early Modern Science," in *The Book of Nature in Early Modern and Modern History*, ed. Klaas van Berkel and Arjo Vanderjagt (Leuven: Peeters, 2006), 1–26, esp. 8.

27. Louis K. Dupré, *The Enlightenment and the Intellectual Foundations of Modern Culture* (New Haven, CT: Yale University Press, 2004), 12–17.

28. See, e.g., James Barr's definition: "Traditionally, 'natural theology' has commonly meant something like this: that 'by nature,' that is, just by being human beings, men and women have a certain degree of knowledge of God and awareness of him, or at least a capacity for such awareness; and this knowledge or awareness exists anterior to the special revelation of God made through Jesus Christ, through the Church, through the Bible." See James Barr, *Biblical Faith and Natural Theology* (Oxford: Clarendon Press, 1993), 1.

29. See the classic analysis of this idea in Edward A. Dowey, *The Knowledge of God in Calvin's Theology* (New York: Columbia University Press, 1952). For its later development, see Richard A. Muller, "'Duplex cognitio Dei' in the Theology of Early Reformed Orthodoxy," *Sixteenth Century Journal* 10 (1979): 51–61.

30. Michael Czapkay Sudduth, "The Prospects for 'Mediate' Natural Theology in John Calvin," *Religious Studies* 31 (1996): 53–68.

31. For an analysis of the causes and consequences of this very significant development, see McGrath, *The Open Secret*, 140–70.

central themes of the Enlightenment: the growing rational criticism of the relia-bility of traditional sources of Christian theology (particularly Scripture), and the increasing acceptance of rational criteria of justification of beliefs. As a result of such pressures, "natural theology" has become an autonomous form of theology, essentially detached from the Christian tradition. Karl Barth's criticism of "nat-ural theology" is actually a criticism of *this specific form of natural theology*.[32]

This approach to natural theology clearly represents a historically conditioned response to the specific intellectual agenda of the Enlightenment. With the pass-ing of the hegemony of the Enlightenment in the West, the way has been cleared for the rediscovery of a natural theology which is firmly grounded in a Trinitar-ian vision of God. This offers an enriched and fulfilling engagement with the nat-ural world, transcending the limits of merely making sense of things. The Christian tradition offers a rich conceptual resource for beholding, understand-ing, and appreciating nature, providing an intellectual framework that affirms and legitimates a heightened attentiveness to the world around us.

I set out this vision for a renewed natural theology in some detail in *The Open Secret* (2008). The most significant theological elements of this renewed approach are as follows:

1. The concept of nature is recognized to be conceptually indeterminate.[33] It is an interpreted entity, not autonomous. This opens the way to "seeing" nature in a specifically Christian manner. It involves rejecting the Enlightenment idea of nature as an objective entity, capable of acting as a universal ground of judg-ment.[34] Instead of holding that nature forces its own interpretation upon us, we are free to choose the manner in which we see nature, forcing us to identify the best way of beholding the natural world.

2. Natural theology is understood to be the action of "seeing" nature from a specifically Christian perspective.[35] This involves rejecting the Enlightenment's version of natural theology as a generic attempt to demonstrate the existence and attributes of a putative God from an appeal to the natural world.[36] Instead, nature is viewed from the perspective of the Christian tradition, with its distinct notions of God, nature, and human agency.

32. See the discussion in Alister E. McGrath, *A Scientific Theology*, vol. 1, *Nature* (London: Con-tinuum, 2001), 241–86. Two earlier studies should also be consulted: Regin Prenter, "Das Problem der natürlichen Theologie bei Karl Barth," *Theologische Literaturzeitung* 77 (1952): 607–11; Thomas F. Torrance, "The Problem of Natural Theology in the Thought of Karl Barth," *Religious Studies* 6 (1970): 121–35.

33. McGrath, *The Open Secret*, 7–10, 147–56.

34. For this idea in the early modern period, see Brian W. Ogilvie, "Natural History, Ethics, and Physico-Theology," in *Historia: Empiricism and Erudition in Early Modern Europe*, ed. Gianna Pomata and Nancy G. Siraisi (Cambridge, MA: MIT Press, 2005), 75–103. For its development in the eigh-teenth century, see especially Wolfgang Philipp, "Physicotheology in the Age of Enlightenment: Appearance and History," *Studies on Voltaire and the Eighteenth Century* 57 (1967): 1233–67; Udo Krolzik, "Das physikotheologische Naturverständnis und sein Einfluss auf das naturwissenschaftliche Denken im 18. Jahrhundert," *Medizinhistorisches Journal* 15 (1980): 90–102.

35. McGrath, *The Open Secret*, 1–7, 12–14, 171–216.

36. Ibid., 141–47, 165–70.

3. The specifically cognitive aspects of natural theology are affirmed, since it clearly has to do with making sense of our experience of nature. Yet this is not to be understood as an attempt to deduce the existence of God from observing nature, but as showing the capacity of the Christian faith to make sense of what is observed. Natural theology emphasizes the resonance between the intellectual framework offered by the Christian faith and observation; it does not set out to prove any core element of that faith from an appeal to nature.[37]

4. Since natural theology involves "seeing" nature, the empirical question of how human perception takes place is identified as having considerable theological significance. Natural theology therefore demands an informed understanding of the psychology of human perception, especially its recognition that perception involves thinking about, affective responding to, and enactive interaction with the world.[38] Once more, it requires moving on from the Enlightenment's inadequate and misleading understanding of how the process of perceiving nature takes place.[39]

5. The realization that the process of human perception involves thinking about, affective responding to, and enactive interaction with the world leads to the rejection of purely cognitive approaches to natural theology. The Enlightenment regarded natural theology fundamentally as a sense-making exercise. In place of this inadequate account of perception, I argue that the "Platonic triad" of truth, beauty, and goodness offers a helpful heuristic framework for natural theology.[40] This takes account of the rational, aesthetic, and moral dimensions of the human engagement with nature.

6. Natural theology is therefore to be recognized as representing an important point of contact between the Christian church and secular culture, including the natural sciences, law, the arts, and literature. It can play an important apologetic role, not least in providing a navigable channel from human interest in the beauty of nature or the notion of the "transcendent" to the "God and Father of our Lord Jesus Christ."[41]

At this point, some readers will not unreasonably wish to raise an objection. They will point out that natural theology is commonly understood to mean "the enterprise of providing support for religious beliefs by starting from premises that neither are nor presuppose any religious beliefs."[42] So how can the approach just outlined be considered as natural theology? The shape of my response will, I think, be obvious from what has already been said. I concede that this indeed is how natural theology has been understood since about 1750; I dispute, however,

37. Ibid., 15–18, 232–60.
38. Ibid., 80–110.
39. Ibid., 156–58.
40. For the general principle, see ibid., 221–31; for a more detailed discussion of truth and natural theology, see 232–60; for beauty, see 261–90; for goodness, see 291–312.
41. Ibid., 23–40, 255–60, 282–90.
42. William P. Alston, *Perceiving God: The Epistemology of Religious Experience* (Ithaca, NY: Cornell University Press, 1991), 289.

that this is how it ought to be understood today. Under the influence of the Enlightenment, natural theology was widely interpreted as the defense of the existence of God on the basis of those criteria that the Enlightenment regarded as authoritative and reliable: reason and the natural order.[43] Yet this historical episode in the history of natural theology cannot be regarded as normative or determinative.

Lord Gifford's mandate is that I am to "promote and diffuse the study of Natural Theology in the widest sense of the term—in other words, the knowledge of God." It is therefore my intention to demonstrate and explore how a renewed Christian natural theology has the capacity to make sense of the world, simultaneously reinforcing the intellectual case for the existence of God while offering a way of "seeing nature" that enables us to appreciate and respect it in ways that would otherwise not be possible.

Seeing nature: we must linger momentarily on that pellucid phrase. The fundamental essence of a natural theology is that it allows us to *see* things as they really are. In the third volume of his *Modern Painters* (1856), the great English art critic John Ruskin (1819–1900) declared that "the greatest thing a human soul ever does in this world is to see something, and tell what it saw in a plain way. . . . To see clearly is poetry, prophecy, and religion—all in one."[44] Ruskin here put his finger on what many theologians of his age overlooked, that the Christian mind does not passively receive impressions of nature, but actively interprets it. The process of observation, whether scientific or religious, involves trying to match what is observed with what is believed, and making any necessary adjustments.

Furthermore, we see nature as a whole. One of the more regrettable aspects of eighteenth century natural theology was its tendency to seek explanatory gaps within nature, and attempt to plug them through an appeal to special or covert divine presence or activity. Whatever science could not currently explain, or more exactly, whatever one could make a case for holding that science could never in principle explain, was to be deemed the "special" work of God. Yet the approach to natural theology that I believe arises from within the Christian tradition involves seeing nature as a totality, seeking the explanatory "big picture." How do we account for our capacity to explain things so well? For the "unreasonable effectiveness of mathematics,"[45] the creation of the human mind that seems to be sculpted precisely to the contours of the universe? In no way does a truly Christian natural theology concern itself with the quest for temporary explanatory gaps in the scientific view of the world. It offers an alternative way of viewing nature, which may at

43. Alister E. McGrath. "Towards the Restatement and Renewal of a Natural Theology: A Dialogue with the Classic English Tradition," in *The Order of Things: Explorations in Scientific Theology* (Oxford: Blackwell Publishing, 2006), 63–96.

44. John Ruskin, *Works*, ed. E. T. Cook and A. Wedderburn, 39 vols. (London: Allen, 1903–12), 5:333.

45. Eugene Wigner, "The Unreasonable Effectiveness of Mathematics," *Communications on Pure and Applied Mathematics* 13 (1960): 1–14.

times challenge exaggerated versions of the scientific method,[46] yet welcomes and sees itself as part of the human quest for truth, whether scientific or religious. It expects to find, and does in fact find, a significant explanatory resonance with what is known of nature from other sources, while at the same time insisting on its own right to depict and describe nature in its own special way—as God's creation.

Yet Ruskin's epigrammatic statement also points to the need for natural theology to go far beyond a mere sense-making exercise. As noted earlier, the concept of natural theology that dominated the Victorian age was due to William Paley (1745–1805), whose *Natural Theology* (1802) set out the case for the existence of God on the basis of the observation of nature. For Paley, God was the rational solution to the puzzles of the natural world, offering thinking people an intellectually satisfying solution to such mysteries as the intricacies of the human eye. Some found his approach laudable;[47] others saw it as dangerous, subversive, and destructive of the fundamental themes of the Christian faith. Long before Charles Darwin (1809–82) offered an alternative explanation of the appearance of design in the biological world in his *Origin of Species*,[48] others were distancing themselves from Paley's mechanical vision of God as the divine watchmaker on theological grounds. Why? As it happens, the answers are both theologically and culturally illuminating.

One of the most fundamental concerns was the intellectual integrity of Paley's core argument. How could one speak of observing "design" in nature? One *observes* nature, but one *infers* design in nature. Design is not an empirical datum, but reflects the interpretation of what is observed. This point was perhaps made most forcibly, and certainly most perceptively, by John Henry Newman, who commented: "I believe in design because I believe in God; not in God because I see design."[49] Newman rightly saw that the idea of design was not "given" within the realm of nature, but was acquired by observing and interpreting nature through the inhabitation of the Christian vision of reality.[50]

46. I have in mind here the rather crude "scientism" found in writers such as Richard Dawkins and E. O. Wilson: see the analysis in Frederick A. Olafson, *Naturalism and the Human Condition: Against Scientism* (London: Routledge, 2001); Mikael Stenmark, *Scientism: Science, Ethics and Religion* (Aldershot: Ashgate, 2001).

47. For some examples of the reactions, see Aileen Fyfe, "The Reception of William Paley's *Natural Theology* in the University of Cambridge," *British Journal for the History of Science* 30 (1997): 321–35. William Whewell's approach merits consideration here: Richard R. Yeo, "William Whewell, Natural Theology and the Philosophy of Science in Mid-Nineteenth Century Britain," *Annals of Science* 36 (1979): 493–516.

48. For the best critique of Paley from the standpoint of contemporary evolutionary biology, see Richard Dawkins, *The Blind Watchmaker: Why the Evidence of Evolution Reveals a Universe without Design* (New York: W. W. Norton, 1986).

49. John Henry Newman, letter to William Robert Brownlow, April 13, 1870; in Charles Stephen Dessain et al., eds., *The Letters and Diaries of John Henry Newman*, 31 vols. (Oxford: Clarendon Press, 1963–2006), 25:97. For a careful analysis of this and related points, see Noel Keith Roberts, "Newman on the Argument from Design," *New Blackfriars* 88 (2007): 56–66.

50. Note also Wolfhart Pannenberg's comment about how the doctrine of God as creator "makes possible an ultimate explanation of the world as a whole." See Wolfhart Pannenberg, *Systematic Theology*, 3 vols. (Grand Rapids: Eerdmans, 1991–98), 1:71.

Others found Paley's mechanical conception of nature—and the image of God that it elicited—disturbingly inadequate. Hugh Miller (1802–56), regarded as one of the greatest scientific popularizers of his day, found Paley's argument aesthetically deficient.[51] Machines could be ugly. One might possibly admire the conceptual elegance of a great machine; yet the mechanical principles might be expressed in a creation of hideous proportions and monstrous appearance. Paley's concept of God was aesthetically impoverished.

Newman took this criticism still further, expressing fundamental concerns about the imaginative attenuation of Paley's approach. For Newman, there was clearly a danger that such an excessively rationalist conception of natural theology would conceive the outcome of the human encounter with nature in terms similar to solving a crossword puzzle. Paley's image of God as the divine artificer of the world reduced God to the world's level. Where was any sense of transcendence, mystery, or glory?[52] Paley's approach might appeal to the human reason. But what about the human imagination? For Newman, the most powerful engagement with nature took place at the imaginative rather than the rational level. "The heart," Newman argued, is "commonly reached, not through the reason, but through the imagination, by means of direct impressions, by the testimony of facts and events, by description."[53]

Ruskin's emphasis on the cultural and spiritual importance of "seeing" transcended the rational dissection of nature and extended to an appreciation of its intrinsic beauty and goodness.[54] A natural theology cannot restrict itself to reflecting on the "truth" of nature, on the basis of the impoverished and truncated account of the nature of reality offered by the Enlightenment. It must extend to embrace the totality of the human interaction with nature: that is to say, thinking about (or "knowing"), affective responding to, and enactive interaction with the natural world. The traditional "Platonic triad" of truth, beauty, and goodness offers an excellent framework for facilitating precisely this kind of engagement.

Natural theology is here understood as the enterprise of viewing nature from the standpoint of the Christian tradition. Our inhabitation of the Christian tradition engenders a discipleship of the mind, which leads to an enhanced and deepening grasp of the Christian faith, and consequently results in changes in the way we see and behave toward nature. As we have stressed, there is no "view from nowhere": any attempt to observe nature takes place from a definite social location, which shapes what we see and what we regard as significant. Yet this "viewing" does not take the form of a single glance at nature, but is to be understood

51. See here John Hedley Brooke, "Like Minds: The God of Hugh Miller," in *Hugh Miller and the Controversies of Victorian Science*, ed. Michael Shortland (Oxford: Clarendon Press, 1996), 171–86.

52. John Henry Newman, *The Idea of a University* (London: Longmans, Green & Co., 1907), 450–51, esp. 454.

53. John Henry Newman, *An Essay in Aid of a Grammar of Assent*, 2nd ed. (London: Burns & Oates, 1870), 89–90.

54. Robert Hewison, *John Ruskin: The Argument of the Eye* (Princeton, NJ: Princeton University Press, 1976), 54–64.

as an ongoing interactive process with nature in its totality, leading to modulation of ideas as time proceeds.

So how can we make sense of this process of ongoing interaction between faith and the engagement with nature? There is a helpful analogy here with an aspect of the scientific method that has been overlooked in much theological reflection—the importance of iterative procedures, in which the way of thinking that is initially inferred from an engagement with the empirical world is used as the starting point for a new level of observation and interpretation. This method of engaging with nature was an integral part of my own research in Oxford University's Department of Biochemistry during the years 1975–78 and led me to reflect on its theological potential.[55]

The essential feature of an iterative approach is the successive and incremental revision of how we see or understand something in the light of insights disclosed through the process of engagement itself. We begin by seeing something in a certain way; as the process of inquiry begins, we discover things that make us see it in a quite different way. The "thing" in question remains unchanged; our perception of it, however, undergoes a significant alteration. New levels of appreciation and interpretation emerge within the extended process of observation. The recalibration of theological observation is an integral aspect of the enterprise of natural theology. We begin by seeing nature in one way; we end up seeing it in another.

We must reassert the priority of ontology over epistemology since something may be "seen" in such a way that its true identity is concealed. I give a familiar example. We might begin by "seeing" Jesus of Nazareth as a religious teacher; after due reflection, we "see" him as God incarnate. The one who *is* God incarnate is not initially *perceived as* God incarnate. The incident of Jesus' declaring that a man's sins have been forgiven (Mark 2:1–12) might initially be seen as an example of blasphemy: Jesus, if understood purely as a human being, is seen to do something that only God can do. From the perspective of this schema, this clearly constitutes blasphemy within this Jewish context. Yet from the postresurrection standpoint, this action can be seen as retrospectively validating the schema which the resurrection forced upon the Christian community that Jesus of Nazareth was authorized to act in this manner.[56] The same action can thus be interpreted from two quite different perspectives, with the one giving way to the other as enhanced levels of understanding and disclosure take place. This new perception does not entail a change in the identity of Jesus of Nazareth, but it reflects a change in the schema or intellectual framework through which we view him.

Similarly, in the case of natural theology, nature itself does not change; the way in which we understand it does. We see it in a new way, bringing a new mental map to bear upon its exploration. Theology is here conceived as a dynamic

---

55. See my originally unpublished "position paper" of August 1996, in which I set out my perception of the relevance of this approach for systematic theology: Alister E. McGrath, "A Working Paper: Iterative Procedures and Closure in Systematic Theology," in *The Order of Things*, 194–203.

56. See, e.g., the analysis in Wolfhart Pannenberg, *Jesus, God and Man* (London: SCM Press, 1968), 66–73.

process of exploration, based on iterations. The outcomes of a given iteration are then fed into the next iteration as its presuppositions. The theological insights gained after each iteration are thus fed back into the next iteration, which allows higher levels of understanding to ensue. After a while, a state of equilibrium results, leading to closure of theological reflection. The process can be likened to the ascent of a spiral staircase, in which each cycle of reflection allows the object of theology to be "viewed" in an increasingly sophisticated manner.[57]

On this approach, we might *begin* by seeing natural theology as disclosing simply a creator God; as we begin to follow this through, in the light of the Christian revelation, we realize that this provisional judgment is ultimately unsustainable and requires reworking and reconceptualization. The classic model of natural theology is therefore nothing more than a heuristic starting point, which is developed and modified as the iterative process proceeds. We might begin with a sense of the transcendent—a vague, impersonal, perception which we realize might be the gateway to something greater.[58] Yet when we pass through the threshold of that gateway, we encounter a way of seeing the world which causes us to interpret that initial sense or feeling in a new way. We end with a Trinitarian vision of God, which in one sense was not included in that original perception, and yet in another sense it is. The God, who *is* Trinity, is not initially *perceived as* Trinitarian.

This approach preserves the fundamentally apologetic dimension of many forms of natural theology, including the family of approaches associated with the Enlightenment, and the somewhat different approaches associated with the Cappadocian fathers.[59] It allows nature to be seen as a signpost to the transcendent, without entailing that this God is exhaustively determined, defined, or characterized by being known in this way. Thus the transcendence, glory, and relationality of the triune God are not compromised through being discernible in the natural world. The danger here is that any concept of a God who is known in or through nature is reduced to "the dull catalogue of common things" (Keats).

This, then, is the broad conception of natural theology that I bring to the task of reflecting on anthropic phenomena which are observed within nature. I have no intention of arguing that one may "prove" any aspect of the Christian faith by the perspicuous observation and interpretation of the natural world. Rather, I shall argue that such observation gives rise to the perception that there is a fundamental

---

57. Such imagery is developed in Ray L. Hart, *Unfinished Man and the Imagination: Toward an Ontology and a Rhetoric of Revelation* (New York: Herder & Herder, 1968), 60–68.

58. For the importance of the notion of the transcendent for natural theology, see McGrath, *Open Secret*, 23–79.

59. See the important analysis of the apologetic role of natural theology in Gregory of Nazianzus, Basil of Caesarea, and Gregory of Nyssa, as presented by Jaroslav Pelikan, *Christianity and Classical Culture: The Metamorphosis of Natural Theology in the Christian Encounter with Hellenism* (New Haven, CT: Yale University Press, 1993). Pelikan here explores the interplay between the classic concept of *theologia naturalis* and the dogmatic theology of these Cappadocian writers, noting the subtle interplay of natural theology as *apologetics*, used to refute the views of pagans (such as Libanius) and heretics (such as Eunomius); and natural theology as *dogmatics*, allowing for a systematic presentation of Christian truth.

consonance or resonance between Christian theory and empirical observation. While it is certainly true that Paley and his contemporaries saw their arguments as constituting "proofs" for God's existence, they are perhaps better seen as a retrospective validation of belief in God.

The approach adopted will therefore be to observe the phenomena of the natural world from the standpoint of the Christian tradition, and then to ask whether there is a significant "empirical fit" between the theoretical and empirical. Nature is not studied with any expectation that it will offer a "proof" of the existence of God; rather, Christian theology is proposed as an insightful tool for making sense of what is observed within the world. This has considerable importance in connection with a Christian engagement with the natural sciences, since it opens up the possibility of natural theology as a significant and potentially highly productive interface between theology and the sciences. This approach to natural theology disavows any notion that Christian theology regards itself as the opponent of scientific understanding; instead, I argue that it aims to complement our understanding of the world by setting the natural scientific project within a broader framework of understanding, encouraging dialogue, and offering the hope of mutual enrichment.

This vision for a renewed natural theology raises some important issues about its nature and goals. This leads us to move on and consider some of those concerns and how they might be addressed.

Chapter 4

Challenges to a Renewed Natural Theology

Natural theology is regarded as indefensible by those who choose to define it in indefensible terms. That, as we have seen, appears to have been the sad story of natural theology throughout most of the twentieth century.[1] Yet there is no compelling reason to endorse either the definitions of natural theology that have caused this difficulty, nor the ensuing critical judgments of others who have written on this theme. To no small extent the renewal of natural theology depends on reconceiving and reformulating its vision and goals, either by retrieving older approaches or by developing new ones.

The approach to the engagement with nature, especially the phenomenon of "fine-tuning," as set out in this book, rests on a critical distinction between a "Trinitarian natural theology" and a "classic natural theology." By a "classic natural theology," I mean the way of understanding the natural world, based on a religiously uninformed or neutral stance, which leads to the conclusion that some transcendent entity exists. This is not to suppress or deny the differences which clearly exist between various styles of classic natural theology; it is simply to

---

1. See esp. the somewhat melancholy narrative in Christoph Kock, *Natürliche Theologie: Ein evangelischer Streitbegriff* (Neukirchen-Vluyn: Neukirchener Verlag, 2001).

accentuate their common feature, which serves to distinguish it sharply from a Trinitarian natural theology.

By a "Trinitarian natural theology," I mean the way of understanding both the natural world and the human engagement with that world which results from the Trinitarian vision of reality that is articulated by Christian orthodoxy. This way of looking at things is a consequence of the Christian revelation, and is not entailed by nature itself. I set out a basic sketch of such a Trinitarian approach to natural theology in 2008,[2] and it will be developed further in this volume.

Some might not unreasonably suggest that what is here designated a "Trinitarian natural theology" is really a "Trinitarian theology of nature." I accept that there is merit in this point. However, a Trinitarian natural theology does more than articulate a theology of nature; it also offers an account of the active and constructive role of the human observer of nature. A Trinitarian theology offers a rich ontology which generates and sustains an understanding not merely of nature, but also of *the human engagement with nature* as well. A "natural theology" thus illuminates and shapes both the process of the human engagement with nature and the outcome of that engagement. Given the critical importance of "seeing" nature within the context of a natural theology, it is clearly of no small importance to ensure that due weight is given to a Trinitarian exploration of the process of the human observation and interpretation of nature. A "theology of nature" refers to how humanity interprets nature; a "natural theology" designates both the hermeneutical process and its outcome. The terms "natural theology" and "theology of nature" designate distinct though clearly related notions.

The approach adopted in this work represents a principled and strategic move away from Paleyesque accounts of natural theology, which will perhaps cause some to suggest that it represents an abandonment of natural theology altogether. I do not agree with this judgment. There is no single template or controlling narrative for natural theologies, which are best understood as partially conditioned responses to prevailing scientific understandings of the world, dominant trends in Christian theology, and cultural attitudes to nature. There is no doubt that William Paley's specific approach to natural theology is grounded in an interlocked network of prevailing scientific, cultural, aesthetic, and theological judgments. With the passing of this specific set of historical and social circumstances, new approaches to natural theology are appropriate.

The popular success of Paley's *Natural Theology* (1802) is an important indicator of how deeply it was embedded in its specific cultural milieu. Paley shared many assumptions with his intended audience, allowing him to create a significant degree of intellectual resonance with his readers.[3] Yet subsequent shifts in

---

2. Alister E. McGrath, *The Open Secret: A New Vision for Natural Theology* (Oxford: Blackwell, 2008).

3. Paley's genius for achieving resonance with his presumed audiences was not limited to his *Natural Theology* (1802). His earlier *Principles of Moral and Political Philosophy* (1785), though largely lacking any intellectual originality, was widely read, going through fifteen reprints in Paley's lifetime. Paley's versions of "natural theology" and "utilitarianism" both achieved cultural resonance and

this network of prevailing scientific, cultural, aesthetic, and theological judgments inevitably point to the need for a different style of natural theology. Paley does not define the essence of a Christian natural theology; he simply illustrates one form that natural theology took at an important yet now bygone juncture in cultural history.

Nevertheless, my approach to natural theology will raise concerns of no small importance for at least some readers. In setting out this vision for natural theology, my critics might entirely reasonably raise some or all of the following three points of concern:

1. Natural theology, whether in its traditional form or in the new form set out above, has been seen as offering an explanation of reality. Yet the Christian faith is about the transformation of all things—an idea better explained in terms of "salvation" rather than "explanation." Surely this emphasis upon explanation represents something of a distortion of the fundamental themes and emphases of Christianity, does it not?

2. The proposed approach diverges from the traditional deductive arguments of the philosophy of religion, which generally involve invoking at least one strong a priori causal principle. Richard Swinburne, for example, often defines explanation in terms of causation.[4] In contrast, what is proposed is an understanding of explanation as "a making intelligible" or a "disclosing of the intrinsic rationality of things." It will be argued that Christianity makes better sense of the empirical evidence than any of its alternatives or rivals. This seems a much weaker understanding of "explanation" than that traditionally associated with traditional arguments for God's existence.

3. This approach also seems to encounter difficulties with the natural sciences, potentially an important ally or dialogue partner for natural theology. Writers such as Paul Oppenheim and Carl Hempel have argued for the logical-deductive nature of scientific explanation. Where Hempel argued that deductive-nomological reasoning constituted the basic paradigm for the natural sciences,[5] what is proposed appears to represent a very different form of reasoning, which might be termed "abduction," "inference to the best explanation," or perhaps "inference to the best theory."[6] So how might this obvious tension be resolved?

---

dominance in the early nineteenth century, despite the existence of more rigorous alternatives. For Paley's version of utilitarianism, see Frederick Rosen, *Classical Utilitarianism from Hume to Mill* (London: Routledge, 2003), 131–42.

4. Richard Swinburne, *The Existence of God*, 2nd ed. (Oxford: Clarendon Press, 2004), 23: "What is it to provide a true explanation of the occurrence of a phenomenon *E*? It is to state truly what (object or event) brought *E* about (or caused *E*), and why it was efficacious." His is a perfectly legitimate approach to explanation, which would find much support within the natural sciences: see Paul Humphreys, *The Chances of Explanation: Causal Explanation in the Social, Medical, and Physical Sciences* (Princeton, NJ: Princeton University Press, 1989).

5. Carl Hempel, *Philosophy of Natural Science* (Englewood Cliffs, NJ: Prentice-Hall, 1966), 47–69.

6. Theo A. F. Kuipers, *From Instrumentalism to Constructive Realism: On Some Relations between Confirmation, Empirical Progress, and Truth Approximation* (Dordrecht: Kluwer Academic Publishers, 2000).

Given the importance of these concerns, it is appropriate to consider them individually at this stage, although we shall return to offer further comments on some of them at a later stage in the argument.

CHRISTIANITY, SALVATION, AND EXPLANATION

Does Christianity actually explain anything?[7] Many have pointed out that the emphasis of the New Testament is not upon offering some explanatory account of the world, but upon the transformation of human existence through the life, death, and resurrection of Jesus of Nazareth. The gospel is thus about salvation, the transformation of the human situation, not explanation. Others have appealed to Ludwig Wittgenstein to defend the idea that religious language is at most a reflection of its distinctive *Lebensform* and is not intended to be interpreted as an explanation of anything.[8] Alvin Plantinga makes the reasonable point that we would still believe in God if we believed this was warranted, even if such a belief explained little or nothing.[9] An "epistemically idle" God is, one might reasonably suppose, perfectly capable of existing and is not rendered incapable of saving people by any such explanatory redundancy.

Now an important point is unquestionably being made here. Yet it is fair to point out that, while the emphasis of the Christian proclamation may not be explanatory, there is little doubt that its distinctive intellectual matrix has the capacity to make sense of what is observed. The Christian vision of God turns out to have a remarkably high epistemic value. There is no fundamental objection to postulating explanatory depth to the Christian faith, provided that such explanatory capacity is not made a precondition for postulating the truth or rationality of the Christian faith.[10] It can be thought of as emerging from the rich vision of reality that the gospel engenders. While the New Testament itself tends to hint at such matters, rather than explicitly develop them, it contains the seeds of an explanatory as well as redemptive engagement with nature.

The New Testament speaks of the impact of Jesus of Nazareth in terms of his potential transformation of humanity through faith. While much of this transformation is described in soteriological terms—such as salvation, redemption, or reconciliation—it is already understood to extend to the human mind. To give an obvious example: Paul urges his readers not to "be conformed to this world,"

---

7. The term "explanation" is heavily freighted with associations: for comment, see Robert W. Batterman, *The Devil in the Details: Asymptotic Reasoning in Explanation, Reduction, and Emergence* (Oxford: Oxford University Press, 2002), 23–37. We shall consider this question further in chap. 5.

8. Wilko van Holten, "Does Religion Explain Anything? D. Z. Phillips and the 'Wittgensteinian Objection' to Religious Explanation," *Neue Zeitschrift für Systematische Theologie und Religionsphilosophie* 44 (2002): 199–217.

9. Alvin Plantinga, "The Probabilistic Argument from Evil," *Philosophical Studies* 35 (1979): 1–53, esp. 51–53.

10. See the detailed analysis in Alister E. McGrath, *A Scientific Theology*, vol. 3, *Theory* (London: Continuum, 2003), 133–236.

but rather to "be transformed by the renewing of [their] minds" (Romans 12:2) —thus affirming the capacity of the Christian faith to bring about a radical change in the way in which we understand and inhabit the world.[11] The human mind is not replaced or displaced; rather, it is illuminated and energized through faith. Paul is speaking of a transformed disposition of the knower, which leads to a new way of thinking that enables the discernment of deeper levels of reality than unaided human reason or sight permit.[12] Faith is about the transformation of the human mind to see things in a certain manner, involving the acquisition of certain habits of thinking and perception.

The issue here has to do with the Christian understanding of salvation as a transformative process that has been inaugurated, yet whose final completion has yet to take place. This process of renewal, which is described in the New Testament using a range of soteriological metaphors,[13] clearly entails changed and interconnected patterns of thought and behavior. We come to *see* the world in a new way, and as a result *behave* in a new way. The right interpretation of the "parables of the kingdom" depends upon seeing them in the right way, leading to a change in outlook and action as a result of what is seen.[14] The call to love God "with all your heart, and with all your soul, and with all your mind" (Matthew 22:34–37) clearly envisages a discipleship of the mind, since every aspect of human existence is affected by the gospel.

Augustine of Hippo describes this new way of "seeing" things as the "healing of the eye of the heart" by divine grace: "Our whole business in this life is to heal the eye of the heart [*sanare oculum cordis*], so that God might be seen."[15] While it may be informed and reinforced through the church's ministry of Word and sacrament, Augustine insists that this is to be understood, fundamentally and characteristically, as a divine act of grace, accomplishing something that lies beyond the capacity of unaided human nature. Similarly, Hans Urs von Balthasar speaks of the "light of grace" coming to the aid of humanity's incapacity by "bestowing vision," thus enabling us to discern God's presence and activity within the natural realm.[16]

It can therefore be concluded that, while it would be open to question whether the *primary* focus of the Christian faith is explanatory, there is no doubt that there is an integral explanatory element to the Christian vision of reality.[17] Natural

---

11. John Chrysostom argues that the transformation of humanity by grace leads to believers seeing the world in this new way. See Demetrios Trakatellis, "Being Transformed: Chrysostom's Exegesis of the Epistle to the Romans," *Greek Orthodox Theological Review* 36 (1991): 211–29.

12. Mark McIntosh, "Faith, Reason, and the Mind of Christ," in *Reason and the Reasons of Faith*, ed. Paul J. Griffiths and Reinhart Hütter (New York: T&T Clark, 2005), 119–42.

13. See the impressive collection of studies assembled in J. G. van der Watt, ed., *Salvation in the New Testament: Perspectives on Soteriology* (Leiden: Brill, 2005).

14. For a full discussion, see McGrath, *The Open Secret*, 115–26.

15. Augustine of Hippo, *Sermones* 88.5.

16. Hans Urs von Balthasar, *The Glory of the Lord: A Theological Aesthetics*, 7 vols. (Edinburgh: T&T Clark, 1982–89), 1:175–76.

17. For two studies defending the explanatory dimension of religious belief, see Philip Clayton, *Explanation from Physics to Theology: An Essay in Rationality and Religion* (New Haven, CT: Yale University Press, 1989), 113–45; Michael C. Banner, *The Justification of Science and the Rationality of Religious Belief* (Oxford and New York: Oxford University Press, 1990), 67–118.

theology, understood as the way of interacting with nature that follows from the Christian vision of reality, can therefore be regarded as an entirely appropriate enterprise for Christians. The Christian vision of reality claims both to tell the truth and to possess explanatory power, because it corresponds to the way things really are.

THE DEDUCTION OF GOD FROM NATURE

Traditionally, natural theology has been interpreted as the rational demonstration of the necessity of God through an analysis of the patterns of causality observed within nature. In the past, arguments for the existence of God have been developed that treat God as an agent who intentionally brings about certain phenomena, which are observed to take place. William Lane Craig, for example, deduces the existence of God along such lines:

1. We have good reasons, philosophically and scientifically, to believe that the universe is not eternal in the past, but had an absolute beginning.
2. But something cannot come into being out of nothing.
3. Therefore, there must be a transcendent cause of the origin of the universe—which is God.[18]

Such an approach could have compelling authority. For example, Leibnitz's "principle of sufficient reason," if valid,[19] infers the existence of God with logical certainty. God, on this approach, is ultimately the *sole and total* explanation of what is observed within the world. Thus J. L. Mackie argues that Leibnitz's approach demands a comprehensive explanation of the universe: in other words, it is based on the assumption that "things should be intelligible through and through," and that God is the only ultimate explanation of this intelligible reality.[20] There clearly are difficulties with this approach, not least that it is obliged to invoke at least one strong a priori causal principle as a premise (such as the "principle of sufficient reason" itself). For these and other reasons, many have drawn the conclusion that it is not possible to deduce the existence of God from general principles.[21]

Yet an argument that proves unable to compel assent by demonstrating the existence of God as a necessary inference can nevertheless still be the best explanation

18. See, e.g., William Lane Craig, "The Existence of God and the Beginning of the Universe," *Truth: A Journal of Modern Thought* 3 (1991): 85–96; idem, "Timelessness and Creation," *Australasian Journal of Philosophy* 74 (1996): 646–56. Craig sets out his position with admirable clarity in his dialogue with Quentin Smith: William Lane Craig and Quentin Smith, *Theism, Atheism, and Big Bang Cosmology* (Oxford: Clarendon Press, 1993).

19. Swinburne's concerns must, however, be noted: Swinburne, *Existence of God*, 147–49.

20. J. L. Mackie, *The Miracle of Theism: Arguments For and Against the Existence of God* (Oxford: Clarendon Press, 1982), 85–87.

21. See the detailed analysis in Philip Clayton, *Das Gottesproblem: Gott und Unendlichkeit in der neuzeitlichen Philosophie* (Paderborn: Schöningh Verlag, 1996); and the more succinct statement of the issue in Philip Clayton, "Inference to the Best Explanation," *Zygon* 32 (1997): 377–91.

of what is observed. Its public persuasiveness lies not in its deep logical structures, but in its capacity to bring into harmony the often-conflicting elements in the human experience of reality. The explanatory capacity of the natural sciences and Christian theology rest in part on their ability to discern coherence or unity within what otherwise might seem epistemic turbulence and phenomenological chaos. Indeed, one might go further and make the point that humanity willingly strives for resolution of apparent complexity and chaos, despite knowing that a full resolution will never be achieved. Affirming the importance of a mechanism of resolution does not entail that final resolution is ultimately possible.

Richard Swinburne, widely regarded as one of the most able contemporary exponents of the rationality of theism, points to the strength of this approach as lying in the strength of the logical link between its constituent elements. Consider phenomenon E, which we can all observe. It is argued that E is puzzling, strange, not to be expected in the ordinary course of things; but that E is to be expected if there is a God, since God has the power to bring about E and might well choose to do so. Hence the occurrence of E is reason for supposing that there is a God.[22]

> In the arguments to the existence of God, the theist argues from the existence and order of the world and various features of it to a person, God, who brought these things about, meaning to do so.

Such approaches insist that God can be argued to be the unique sufficient reason for the existence and characteristics of the universe. The existence of God is based upon observation of the world and inferred, using probabilistic approaches, to be the most likely explanation of what is observed.[23]

It is thus important to appreciate that a natural theology has access to other explanatory approaches, which may lack the logical certainty of the necessary inference of deductive approaches, yet avoid some of their difficulties. Chief among these are the problems confronted by any attempt to defend higher-order theories univocally by lower-order data, a problem classically stated in terms of the "underdetermination" of theory by evidence.[24] Whether we consider anthropic phenomena or theories of the origins of ethics, it proves impossible to make any form of deductive argument from what is observed to either naturalism or theism. Yet it remains perfectly fair to ask what the *best* explanation might be of these matters. It is therefore important to note how Swinburne, while rightly stressing the potential importance of deductive arguments for the existence of God as first cause, nevertheless additionally adduces the essentially inductive argument that

22. Swinburne, *Existence of God*, 51. For his discussion of the explanatory power of theism, see 110–32.

23. On Swinburne's use of probabilistic arguments for the existence of God, seen in his use of Bayes's theorem in this context, see Robert Prevost, "Swinburne, Mackie, and Bayes' Theorem," *International Journal for the Philosophy of Religion* 17 (1985): 175–84.

24. Laurie Calhoun, "The Underdetermination of Theory by Data, 'Inference to the Best Explanation,' and the Impotence of Argumentation," *Philosophical Forum* 27 (1996): 146–60.

God may be held to constitute the best and simplest explanation of what is observed in the world.[25]

We must also note the concerns of D. Z. Phillips and other Wittgensteinians, who complain that such approaches treat God as a speculative metaphysical hypothesis, lacking any connection with religious practice, particularly prayer and worship. Indeed, Mackie himself, reviewing the approaches developed by Swinburne and others, suggests that the most interesting and promising arguments in natural theology take the form of inferences to the best explanation rather than deductions.[26]

> [Such] arguments can be seen as resting on one general principle, or as sharing one basic form and purpose: they are arguments to the best explanation. The evidence supports the conclusion, it is suggested, because if we postulate that the conclusion is true—or better, perhaps, that it is at least an approximation to the truth—we get a more adequate overall explanation of that whole body of evidence, in light of whatever considerations are cited, than would be given by any available alternative hypothesis.

In taking this point further, we might take our cue here from Charles Peirce, who draws a distinction between an "argument" (which he defined as "any process of thought reasonably tending to produce a definite belief") and "argumentation" (which is to be understood as a form of structured reasoning "proceeding on definitely formulated premises").[27]

> We should naturally expect that there would be some Argument for [God's] reality that should be obvious to all minds, high and low alike, that should earnestly strive to find the truth of the matter; and further, that this Argument should present its conclusion, not as a proposition of metaphysical theology, but in a form directly applicable to the conduct of life.

According to Peirce, there are excellent arguments for God (including his own "neglected argument"); yet these must be understood to include "processes of thought reasonably tending to produce a definite belief" and not be limited to deductive forms of argumentation. Peirce himself commended "musement"—a form of reflection open to everyone from the metaphysician to the "clodhopper"[28]—on the "homogeneities of connectedness" to be observed within the world of ideas, actualities, and signs.[29] For Peirce, human nature is such that there

---

25. For some comments on Swinburne's approach, especially his appeal to "simplicity" as an epistemic virtue in the natural sciences, see Robert M. Burns, "Richard Swinburne on Simplicity in Natural Science," *Heythrop Journal* 40 (1999): 184–206.

26. Mackie, *Miracle of Theism*, 4.

27. Charles Sanders Peirce, *Collected Papers*, ed. Charles Hartshorne and Paul Weiss, 8 vols. (Cambridge, MA: Harvard University Press, 1960), 6:495–7. For a thoughtful application of Peirce's approach, see John Haldane, "Philosophy, the Restless Heart, and the Meaning of Theism," *Ratio* 19 (2006): 421–40.

28. Peirce, *Collected Papers*, 6:483.

29. "In the Pure Play of Musement the idea of God's reality will be sooner or later to be found an attractive fancy, which the Muser will develop in various ways. The more he ponders it, the more it will find response in every part of his mind, for its beauty, for its supplying an ideal of life, and for

exists a "latent tendency toward belief in God [as] a fundamental ingredient of the soul,"[30] which both occasions and directs this process of "musement." Belief in God thus gives expression to a universal need to acknowledge and respond to an experienced sense of cosmic order and human creatureliness.

On the basis of Peirce's approach, it could be argued that humanity possesses a natural tendency or instinct to draw three conclusions:[31]

1. There is order in the universe, or various universes, for which human beings are not ultimately responsible.
2. The best explanation of this observation is the existence of a transcendent cause or order.
3. This "cause" has bestowed upon us the cognitive powers required for observing evidences of it and for inferring from these its continuing efficacy.

Peirce's "neglected argument" for the existence of God thus appeals to the natural human inclination to believe in God, which he holds to constitute evidence in itself of God's existence, both in respect of the epistemic grounds of that inclination and on account of its very existence.

Peirce, it should here be noted, is emphatic that rational reflection on the world is not limited to what he terms "argumentation." It can take the form of "musement" on the world, wondering about the best explanation of what is observed. Yet the process of inferring explanation is nuanced and complex, and it takes place at a number of levels. Pierce himself distinguished three universes: a primary universe of sensations or raw experience, a secondary universe of reactions to this sensory data, and a tertiary universe of representations or signs used to relate the primary and secondary universes. Rational reflection on these universes, he argues, will lead to "a direct, though darkling perception of God."[32] And precisely because this perception is somewhat unclear, a variety of possible explanations of what is perceived will ensue.

The idea of "abduction" plays a critical role in Peirce's method. Defining abduction as the "provisional adoption of an explanatory hypothesis" as a way of

---

its thoroughly satisfactory explanation of his whole threefold environment." Ibid., 6:465. On this point, see Vincent G. Potter, *Peirce's Philosophical Perspectives* (New York: Fordham University Press, 1996), 169–212, esp. 178–80.

30. Peirce, *Collected Papers*, 6:487. Peirce holds that the capacity of the human mind to make sense of such a vast and often opaque body of material points to it being "adjusted" or "attuned" to this reality. "There is a reason, an interpretation, a logic in the course of scientific advance, and this indisputably proves to him who has perceptions of rational or significant relations, that man's mind must have been attuned to the truth of things in order to discover what he has discovered." Ibid., 6:325.

31. For a contextualization and summary of the argument, see Haldane, "Philosophy, the Restless Heart, and the Meaning of Theism," esp. 426–29.

32. Peirce, *Collected Papers*, 6:430. The term "darkling" here means "indistinct" or "twilight."

making sense of observation,[33] Peirce makes it clear that the empirical evidence may suggest a number of possible abductions, forcing clarification of how the preferred abduction is to be identified. Critically, Peirce argued that abduction was fundamentally innovatory and creative, generating new ideas and insights in response to "surprising facts."[34] Abduction is reasoning by hypothesis—that is, by means of an explanation which arises spontaneously, being motivated by the observation of a "surprising fact," "genuine doubt," and "genuine surprise." It is not merely a logical operation, but is rather to be understood as a spontaneous activity of the mind, which makes the strange familiar, making sense of what has surprised us.

Peirce argues that the human mind appears to have an instinctive capacity to relate to nature. There is an innate attunement between the human mind and nature, because the mind has "a natural bent in accordance with nature."[35] This propensity may be the outcome of nurture as much as nature, representing embedded patterns of thinking as much as inborn instincts. Where others held that the emergence of novel scientific ideas was essentially random, not governed by any discernible logic,[36] Peirce holds that there is some innate human propensity to find its way to the right abduction.

In recent years, Peirce's notion of "abduction" has generally become elided with what Gilbert Harman termed "inference to the best explanation."[37] This general approach recognizes that the engagement with nature may entail or permit a multiplicity of explanations, yet insists that it is perfectly fair to inquire which of these may be regarded as "best."[38] Yet Peirce's concept of abduction can be developed in two slightly different directions, defined by Lorenzo Magnani as *selective* and *creative* abduction.[39] Selective abduction is the process of finding the

33. Ibid., 4:541 n. 1. For a full account of his "logic of abduction," see ibid., 5:180–212. Peirce continually modified his concept of "abduction" throughout his career, occasionally preferring to use the term "retroduction." For a full account, see Douglas R. Anderson, "The Evolution of Peirce's Concept of Abduction," *Transactions of the Charles S. Peirce Society* 22 (1986): 145–64; Lutz Danneberg, "Peirces Abduktionskonzeption als Entdeckungslogik: Eine philosophiehistorische und rezeptionskritische Untersuchung," *Archiv für Geschichte der Philosophie* 70 (1988): 305–26; Berit Brogaard, "Peirce on Abduction and Rational Control," *Transactions of the Charles S. Peirce Society* 35 (1999): 129–55.

34. The creativity of the process of abduction posited by Peirce has led to some fruitful comparisons between this understanding of scientific discovery and creativity in other fields of thought: see, e.g., Paul C. L. Tang, "On the Similarities between Scientific Discovery and Musical Creativity: A Philosophical Analysis," *Leonardo* 17 (1984): 261–68.

35. Peirce, *Collected Papers*, 6:478.

36. See, e.g., Karl R. Popper, *The Logic of Scientific Discovery* (New York: Basic Books, 1959), 20–21.

37. On which see Gilbert Harman, "The Inference to the Best Explanation," *Philosophical Review* 74 (1965): 88–95; Peter Lipton, *Inference to the Best Explanation*, 2nd ed. (London: Routledge, 2004). The contrast between the approaches of Harman and Hanson is instructive here: see Sami Paavola, "Hansonian and Harmanian Abduction as Models of Discovery," *International Studies in the Philosophy of Science* 20 (2006): 93–108.

38. Robert Prevost, *Probability and Theistic Explanation* (Oxford: Clarendon Press, 1990), 1–11.

39. Lorenzo Magnani, *Abduction, Reason, and Science: Processes of Discovery and Explanation* (New York: Plenum Publishers, 2001), 15–29.

correct explanatory hypothesis from a given set of possible explanations, whereas creative abduction *generates* the correct explanatory hypothesis in a creative, innovative manner. We shall consider Peirce's approach in more detail later, noting its nuancing. However, at this stage we notice his view that abduction, to use the words of one of his later interpreters, "is inference to a hypothesis that provides a possible explanation of some puzzling phenomenon."[40]

Natural theology may, it would thus seem, distance itself from any suggestion that it is under an obligation to demonstrate the existence or nature of God through necessary inference. Rather, it takes its cue from the Christian tradition itself, which is grounded in evidence that includes, yet transcends, the outcomes of human reason and reflection on the world. Christian theology presents itself as offering the best explanation of what may be observed, while ultimately deriving at least some of its fundamental ideas from sources that may be mediated through nature, yet ultimately cannot be categorized as purely "natural"—above all, through revelation. Natural theology is the outcome of the process of rational and affective engagement with nature that is motivated and governed by the Christian tradition.

ABDUCTION IN THE NATURAL SCIENCES

It is widely agreed that the natural sciences offer an explanation of reality—for example, the advancing perihelion of the planet Mercury is explained by Einstein's theory of general relativity, and the extinction of the dinosaurs is held to be explained by the "K-T event," usually interpreted as an asteroid hitting Earth at the end of the Cretaceous period, sixty-five million years ago, throwing up a dust layer that encircled Earth.[41] The fundamental question is whether the natural sciences offer a type of explanation that differs from those associated with other disciplines. Does "scientific explanation" represent a distinct discipline, with its own characteristic features? Or is it continuous with other forms of explanation?

Peirce holds that scientific thinking is characterized by a specific form of "abductive inference," which can be set out as follows:[42]

The surprising fact, *C*, is observed.

But if *A* were true, *C* would be a matter of course.

Hence, there is reason to suspect that *A* is true.

40. Paul Thagard, *Computational Philosophy of Science* (Cambridge, MA: MIT Press, 1988), 51–52. See also the comments of Atocha Aliseda, *Abductive Reasoning: Logical Investigations into Discovery and Explanation* (Dordrecht: Springer-Verlag, 2006), 26.

41. S. I. Morehouse and R. S. Tung, "Statistical Evidence for Early Extinction of Reptiles Due to the K/T Event," *Journal of Paleontology* 17 (1993): 198–209.

42. Peirce, *Collected Papers*, 5:189. See further N. R. Hanson, *Patterns of Discovery: An Inquiry into the Conceptual Foundations of Science* (Cambridge: Cambridge University Press, 1961), 86.

The notion of a "surprising fact" clearly plays a critical role in Peirce's thought at this point. Abduction is here presented as a provisional, explanatory type of induction. A "surprising fact" designates an observation which is not covered by expectations arising from or generated by established beliefs. The structure of this style of reasoning is similar to a syllogistic formulation, with some additions; "the surprising fact" as a starting point, "as a matter of course" in the second premise, and "reason to suspect" in the conclusion.

A related approach is found in Norwood Hanson's reflections on the advance of scientific knowledge. While insisting that abductive inference is to be understood as a way of analyzing conceptual issues in discoveries rather than a formulaic or algorithmic device for making these discoveries, Hanson argued for three common features in "the logic of scientific discovery":[43]

1. The observation of some "surprising" or "astonishing phenomena," which represent anomalies within existing ways of thinking. This "astonishment" may arise because the observations are in conflict with existing theoretical accounts.
2. The realization that these phenomena would not seem to be astonishing if a certain hypothesis (or set of hypotheses) H pertained. These observations would be expected on the basis of H, which would act as an explanation for them.
3. There is therefore good reason for proposing that H be considered to be correct.

Like Peirce, thus Hanson identifies astonishing or surprising observations as a fundamental motivation in the enterprise of scientific discovery. Is there a theoretical standpoint from which these observations would not be astonishing, or even merely anomalous, but would be *expected*?

Abduction is thus to be considered as a distinct form of logical inference, which can be thought of as the "only kind of argument which starts a new idea"[44] or as "the process of forming explanatory hypotheses."[45] It consists of an "act of insight" that "comes to us like a flash."[46] Peirce's language here suggests that abduction can be compared to the creative and aesthetic dimensions of human reflection in which the explanatory hypothesis "has to be invented *ex novo*," in an act of creative imagination as much as of rational analysis.[47] Indeed, Peirce himself notes that at times "abductive inference shades into perceptual judgment without any sharp line of demarcation between them."[48] For this reason, we find

43. N. R. Hanson, "Is There a Logic of Scientific Discovery?" *Australasian Journal of Philosophy* 38 (1961): 91–106, esp. 104. For comment, see Kenneth F. Schaffner, *Discovery and Explanation in Biology and Medicine* (Chicago: University of Chicago Press, 1993), 11–13.
44. Peirce, *Collected Papers*, 2:96.
45. Ibid., 5:171.
46. Ibid., 5:181.
47. Umberto Eco, *Semiotics and the Philosophy of Language* (London: Macmillan, 1984), 42–43.
48. Peirce, *Collected Papers*, 5:181.

Peirce using a variety of images and concepts to articulate what he means by abduction—such as *pattern recognition*, in which a confused tangle of things is made intelligible; the *interrogation* of a system in order to disclose its structures; and developing an *instinct* for the best explanation of phenomena.[49]

This merely postpones rather than resolves the question of which specific abductive inference is the best explanation of the scientific data, and what criteria might be appropriate to determine which of these competing abductions is indeed the "best." For example, is the best explanation the *likeliest* (that is, the one best supported by the scientific data) or the *loveliest* (that is, the one which provides the most understanding of the scientific data)?[50] While these questions demand further attention, it will be clear that they move us away from the older positivist understanding of the scientific method, still occasionally encountered in popular accounts of the relation of science and religion,[51] which holds that science is able to—and therefore ought to—offer evidentially and inferentially infallible evidence for its theories. Recognizing that the scientific data are patient of multiple interpretations,[52] rather than the single unambiguous interpretation favored by older positivists, the question of how the best such explanation is to be identified becomes of acute importance.

It should therefore come as no surprise that the question of "inference to the best explanation" has come to the fore in recent discussions of the philosophy of science, both in terms of the analysis of past episodes in scientific advance, and of the application of the scientific method in the present. Older models of the

49. See the analysis in Christopher Hookway, "Interrogatives and Uncontrollable Abductions," *Semiotica* 153 (2005): 101–15; Sami Paavola, "Abduction as a Logic of Discovery: The Importance of Strategies," *Foundations of Science* 9 (2005): 267–83; Sami Paavola, "Peircean Abduction: Instinct or Inference?" *Semiotica* 153 (2005): 131–54. There are also points of importance made in the older study of Thomas A. Sebeok and Jean Umiker-Sebeok, "'You Know My Method': A Juxtaposition of Charles S. Peirce and Sherlock Holmes," in *The Sign of Three: Dupin, Holmes, Peirce*, ed. Umberto Eco and Thomas A. Sebeok (Bloomington: Indiana University Press, 1983), 11–54.

50. Eric Barnes, "Inference to the Loveliest Explanation," *Synthese* 103 (1995): 251–77. For criticism, see Alexander Bird, "Inference to the Only Explanation," *Philosophy and Phenomenological Research* 74 (2007): 424–32. Lipton, *Inference to the Best Explanation*, argues for inference to the loveliest explanation (59): if correct, it provides the most understanding. However, he concedes that if the inferential process is justified, "loveliness" and "likeliness" will tend to be coextensive (61).

51. The idea is regularly encountered in the writings of the British atheist apologist Richard Dawkins, who argues that science is evidence-based, where religion represents a retreat from the evidence. For a discussion, see Alister E. McGrath, *Dawkins' God: Genes, Memes and the Meaning of Life* (Oxford: Blackwell Publishing, 2004). It is a matter for some regret that Dawkins's work is characterized by a virtual absence of engagement with the philosophy of science.

52. A recognition of the multiplicity of potential explanations of a given set of scientific observations underlies the notion of the "underdetermination of theory by evidence." See W. H. Newton-Smith and Steven Lukes, "The Underdetermination of Theory by Data," *Proceedings of the Aristotelian Society* 52 (1978): 71–91; Larry Laudan and Jarrett Leplin, "Empirical Equivalence and Underdetermination," *Journal of Philosophy* 88 (1991): 449–72. The observation of "underdetermination," which is not particularly problematic scientifically, is occasionally interpreted in a strongly relativist manner by social scientists concerned to emphasize the role of social construction in scientific theorizing: see, e.g., Mary Hesse, "What Is the Best Way to Assess Evidential Support for Scientific Theories?" in *Applications of Inductive Logic*, ed. L. Jonathan Cohen and Mary Hesse (Oxford: Clarendon Press, 1980), 202–17.

scientific method, such as Carl Hempel's deductive-nomological explanation, are increasingly being discarded, or subsumed under the general aegis of "inference to the best explanation."[53] This has immense importance for natural theology, as will become clear throughout this volume.

The importance of this approach for the natural sciences can be illustrated from a well-known historical example: Charles Darwin's appeal to the novel concept of natural selection as the "best explanation" of an accumulated body of observations concerning natural history.[54] For Darwin, four features of the natural world in particular seemed to require particularly close attention, in the light of problems and shortcomings with existing explanations, especially the idea of "special creation" offered by religious apologists such as William Paley.[55] While this theory offered explanations of these observations, they seemed increasingly cumbersome and forced. A better explanation, Darwin believed, had to lie to hand. None of these were "proofs" of natural selection; nevertheless, they possessed a cumulative force in suggesting it was the best explanation of observation:

1. Many creatures possess "rudimentary structures" which have no apparent or predictable function, such as the nipples of male mammals, the rudiments of a pelvis and hind limbs in snakes, and wings on many flightless birds. How might these be explained on the basis of Paley's theory, which stressed the importance of the individual design of species? Why should God design redundancies? Darwin's theory accounted for these with ease and elegance.

2. Some species were known to have died out altogether. The phenomenon of extinction had been recognized before Darwin and was often explained on the basis of "catastrophe" theories, such as a "universal flood," as suggested by the biblical account of Noah. Darwin's theory offered a neater account of the phenomenon.

3. Darwin's research voyage on the *Beagle* had persuaded him of the uneven geographical distribution of life-forms throughout the world. In particular, Darwin was impressed by the peculiarities of island populations, such as the finches of the Galápagos Islands. Once more, the doctrine of special creation could account for this, yet in a manner that seemed forced and unpersuasive. Darwin's theory offered a much more plausible account of the emergence of these specific populations.

4. Various forms of certain living creatures seemed to be adapted to their specific needs. Darwin held that these could best be explained by their emergence and selection in response to evolutionary pressures. Paley's theory of special cre-

53. For excellent accounts of "inference to the best explanation" as the core element of the scientific method, see Ernan McMullin, *The Inference That Makes Science* (Milwaukee: Marquette University Press, 1992); Stathis Psillos, "Simply the Best: A Case for Abduction," in *Computational Logic: From Logic Programming into the Future*, ed. Fariba Sadri and Anthony Kakas (Berlin: Springer-Verlag, 2002), 605–25; Lipton, *Inference to the Best Explanation*.

54. For what follows, see Dov Ospovat, *The Development of Darwin's Theory: Natural History, Natural Theology, and Natural Selection, 1838–1859* (Cambridge: Cambridge University Press, 1995).

55. Scott A. Kleiner, "Problem Solving and Discovery in the Growth of Darwin's Theories of Evolution," *Synthese* 62 (1981): 119–62, esp. 127–29. Note that substantially the same issues can be discerned in Johann Kepler's explanation of the solar system: Scott A. Kleiner, "A New Look at Kepler and Abductive Argument," *Studies in History and Philosophy of Science* 14 (1983): 279–313.

ation proposed that these creatures were individually designed by God with those specific needs in mind.

Once more, it must be emphasized that these aspects of the natural order could all be explained on the basis of Paley's theory.[56] Yet the explanations offered seemed more than a little cumbersome and contrived. What was originally a relatively neat and elegant theory began to crumble under the weight of accumulated difficulties and tensions. There had to be a better explanation, which would account for these observations more satisfactorily than the alternatives then available.

Darwin was quite clear that his theory of natural selection was not the only explanation of the biological data which could be adduced. He did, however, believe that it possessed greater explanatory power than its rivals, such as the doctrine of independent acts of special creation. "Light has been shown on several facts, which on the belief of independent acts of creation are utterly obscure."[57] Darwin's theory had many weaknesses and loose ends. Nevertheless, he was convinced that these were difficulties which could be tolerated on account of the clear explanatory superiority of his approach. Yet even though Darwin did not believe that he had adequately dealt with all the problems which required resolution, he was confident that his explanation was the best available:[58]

> It can hardly be supposed that a false theory would explain, in so satisfactory a manner as does the theory of natural selection, the several large classes of facts above specified. It has recently been objected that this is an unsafe method of arguing; but it is a method used in judging the common events of life, and has often been used by the greatest natural philosophers.

While recognizing that it lacked rigorous proof, Darwin clearly believed that his theory could be defended on the basis of criteria of acceptance and justification that were already widely used in the natural sciences, and that its explanatory capacity was itself a reliable guide to its truth.

One of the themes considered in this chapter is the increasing significance of "inference to the best explanation" within the philosophy of science. This naturally leads us to ask what role a natural theology might play in relation to the explanation of what is observed. Can a natural theology legitimately be said to "explain" *anything*?

56. Indeed, further modifications of Paley's theory were proposed in the aftermath of the publication of Darwin's *Origin of Species* (1859), extending it to cope with the new idea of natural selection. Charles Kingsley's adaptation of Paley is of especial interest: see Charles Kingsley, "The Natural Theology of the Future," in *Westminster Sermons* (London: Macmillan, 1874), v–xxxiii.

57. Charles Darwin, *On the Origin of the Species by Means of Natural Selection*, 6th ed. (London: John Murray, 1872), 164.

58. Ibid., 444. This comment is not present in earlier editions of the work.

Chapter 5

Natural Theology and the Explanation of Reality

The human longing to make sense of what we observe in nature and history partly underlies both science and religion.[1] But what sort of explanations can be offered? In particular, in what sense does a natural theology explain anything? To answer this question, we must consider what the term "explain" means and what outcomes arise from alleged "explanations" of things.[2] Three general points need to be made:

1. For the cognitive "naturalness" of religious beliefs as explanations of reality, see Justin L. Barrett, *Why Would Anyone Believe in God?* (Lanham, MD: AltaMira Press, 2004), 21–30. Related arguments were set out earlier by Pascal Boyer, *The Naturalness of Religious Ideas: A Cognitive Theory of Religion* (Berkeley: University of California Press, 1994). Although it is natural to reflect on nature, the methods of the sciences are, in fact, somewhat *unnatural*: see Lewis Wolpert, *The Unnatural Nature of Science* (Cambridge, MA: Harvard University Press, 1993). See also Robert N. McCauley, "The Naturalness of Religion and the Unnaturalness of Science," in *Explanation and Cognition*, ed. F. Keil and R. Wilson (Cambridge, MA: MIT Press, 2000), 61–85. McCauley argues that, while religious belief is "natural," the natural sciences are sufficiently counterintuitive to be "unnatural."
2. For recent discussions of these issues, especially in the natural sciences, see Wesley C. Salmon, "Scientific Explanation: Three Basic Conceptions," *Philosophy of Science Association* 2 (1984): 293–305; Philip Clayton, *Explanation from Physics to Theology: An Essay in Rationality and Religion* (New Haven, CT: Yale University Press, 1989); David-Hillel Ruben, *Explaining Explanation* (London: Routledge, 1990); Gerhard Schurz, "Scientific Explanation: A Critical Survey," *Foundations of*

1. Explanation presupposes that the notions of "knowledge" and "understanding" are not identical. To know that something exists or has happened is not identical with understanding why this is the case. Any account of explanation which is unable to sustain the distinction between "knowing that *A* exists" and "understanding why *A* exists" condemns itself as inadequate. Such explanations are often causal: *A* happened because of *B*. Yet as we shall see later, it is important to emphasize that an appeal to causes is only one type of explanation. The fundamental point is that there is a distinction to be made between knowing that a phenomenon takes place and understanding why this is so.

2. Yet the explanations offered may themselves require explanation. The process of explanation is often regressive, leading to the question of whether there is an ultimate explanation of all things, or whether there exists an infinite chain of explanations. The quest for a "theory of everything" or a "grand unified theory" can be seen as an attempt to offer a comprehensive explanation of explanations.[3] Yet explanations do not themselves require to be explained in order to have explanatory power. Isaac Newton proposed gravity as a general explanation of the motion of terrestrial objects—such as the famous apple dropping from a tree—and of the orbits of the planets in the solar system. Gravity was unquestionably an explanation of these observations. Yet Newton was quite unable to offer an explanation for gravity itself. Indeed, Newton was deeply troubled by the notion of "action at a distance," which he regarded as intrinsically implausible.[4] It is not necessary for a valid explanation of an observation to be explained itself in order to retain its explanatory function.

3. Certain explanations appear circular: what is explained is itself an essential part of our reason for suspecting that the explanation is correct. Following Carl Hempel, these are generally referred to as "self-evidencing explanations."[5] Peter Lipton provides an example of this circularity drawn from modern cosmology, noting that the velocity of recession of a galaxy is held to explain the redshift of its characteristic spectrum, even if the observation of that shift is itself an essential part of the scientific evidence that the galaxy is indeed receding at the specified velocity.[6] Self-evidencing explanations thus exhibit a kind of circularity,

---

Science 1 (1995): 429–65; Lorenzo Magnani, *Abduction, Reason, and Science: Processes of Discovery and Explanation* (New York: Plenum Publishers, 2001); Peter Lipton, *Inference to the Best Explanation*, 2nd ed. (London: Routledge, 2004).

3. An excellent introduction is found in John D. Barrow, *Theories of Everything: The Quest for Ultimate Explanation* (London: Vintage, 1992).

4. In response to Leibniz's criticisms of his idea of gravity, Newton acknowledged in the "General Scholium" to the *Principia mathematica* that he was unable to explain it, tending to favor a theological explanation. See further John Henry, "'Pray Do Not Ascribe That Notion to Me': God and Newton's Gravity," in *The Books of Nature and Scripture: Recent Essays on Natural Philosophy, Theology and Biblical Criticism in the Netherlands of Spinoza's Time and the British Isles of Newton's Time*, ed. James E. Force and Richard H. Popkin (Dordrecht: Kluwer Academic Publishers, 1994), 123–47.

5. Carl G. Hempel, *Aspects of Scientific Explanation* (New York: Free Press, 1965), 370–74. Hempel argues that in these cases the *explicandum* itself contributes to the rationale for believing that the *explicans* is correct.

6. Lipton, *Inference to the Best Explanation*, 24.

which can be set out as follows: *A* explains *B* while *B* justifies *A*. There is nothing invalid or improper about this form of explanatory argument, which is widely encountered in scientific explanation. Good explanations may be self-evidencing, even if this appears to involve at least some degree of self-referential circularity. "Inference to the best explanation" can be seen as an extension of the notion of "self-evidencing explanations," where the explanatory power of an explanation is itself seen as evidence of its correctness.

MODELS OF EXPLANATION

In recent years, three particularly significant discussions of explanation have emerged: Paul Humphreys's model of causal explanation;[7] Peter Lipton's account of the nature of explanatory loveliness, which sets a causal approach to explanation within the framework of "inference to the best explanation";[8] and the account of explanatory unification offered by Michael Friedman and Paul Kitcher.[9] Each of these has potential for illuminating the capacity of natural theology to explain what we observe about the world, and we shall consider their merits in what follows.

In the past, most approaches to natural theology have appealed to causal explanations. To explain something is to give information about its causes.[10] Although the metaphysics of causation remains contested, since no general solution to the issues raised by David Hume has gained general acceptance, this is not generally seen as a fundamental obstacle to the success of this approach. Furthermore, it is widely agreed that there are some explanations that are clearly noncausal, and that not all causes are explanatory.[11] While we possess no adequate account of the nature of causation, most philosophers seem perfectly willing to live with this challenge and to work within its limits.[12] As Lipton's work demonstrates, it is easily incorporated into the general approach of "inference to the best explanation."

Traditional forms of natural theology held that the existence of God provided a causal explanation of what might be observed in the natural world. The approach to natural theology which I develop in this work does not deny causal agency, direct or indirect, to God. It is perfectly possible to affirm God as a causal

7. Paul Humphreys, *The Chances of Explanation: Causal Explanation in the Social, Medical, and Physical Sciences* (Princeton, NJ: Princeton University Press, 1989). See also James Woodward, *Making Things Happen: A Theory of Causal Explanation* (Oxford: Oxford University Press, 2003).

8. Lipton, *Inference to the Best Explanation*, 59–61.

9. See Michael Friedman, "Explanation and Scientific Understanding," *Journal of Philosophy* 71 (1974): 5–19; Paul Kitcher, "Explanatory Unification and the Causal Structure of the World," in *Scientific Explanation*, ed. P. Kitcher and W. Salmon (Minneapolis: University of Minnesota Press, 1989), 410–505.

10. For a classic statement of this approach, see David Lewis, "Causal Explanation," in *Philosophical Papers*, vol. 2 (Oxford: Oxford University Press, 1987), 214–40.

11. One might therefore need to develop a broader notion of "determination" that encompassed such noncausal explanations: Ruben, *Explaining Explanation*, 230–33.

12. Lipton, *Inference to the Best Explanation*, 31–33.

agency within the context of a Trinitarian natural theology. The point I have underscored is that it is more appropriate for such a natural theology to focus on the explanatory virtues of a unificationist approach. In part, this is because Trinitarianism proposes a unitary ontology of the natural world, grounded in the doctrine of creation.

Some might object that Deism represents a more modest and hence more rationally defensible ontology than that proposed by Trinitarianism. Here we see the classic difficulty, which Chris Swoyer has dubbed "the great ontological trade-off" between a "rich, abundant ontology with great explanatory power" on the one hand, and a "more modest ontology with greater epistemological security" on the other.[13] Yet a Trinitarian ontology is an integral aspect of the Christian vision of reality, and it will be defended by theologians not so much on account of its philosophical underpinnings, but in terms of its evangelical integrity and authenticity. Its "rich, abundant ontology" is a gift, and a Trinitarian natural theology is its natural expression.

Yet the ontological vision of reality articulated by a Trinitarian faith is ideally suited to another approach to explanation, which is usually designated "unification." This designates the manner in which theoretical advance takes place by bringing together a group of apparently disparate and disconnected theories, each of which can be accommodated and explained in terms of either a more-advanced theory, or on account of a hitherto unnoticed relationship between existing theories. On this approach, we can be said to understand a phenomenon when we see how it fits together with other phenomena in a unified whole. This resonates strongly with the traditional Christian idea that to understand the world is to see the fundamental reality which underlies its multiple and sometimes apparently disconnected phenomena.

This conception of explanation copes well with the three basic elements of an explanation we noted earlier in this chapter. It clearly articulates a distinction between "knowing" and "understanding," seeing the difference lying in the contextualization or nesting of the observation within a broader vision of reality. It affirms that something can be known without being understood. It also recognizes the importance of explanatory regresses: in showing, for example, how a particular observation fits into a broader pattern, one has not explained why that broader pattern exists in the first place. There is ample room for explanatory regression in such an approach. Perhaps most important, the approach is able to accommodate the phenomenon of "self-evidencing explanations," An individual piece of a pattern may provide evidence for the pattern as a whole, while at the same time disclosing the pattern which allows the piece to be seen in a broader unifying framework.

The unification of scientific theory is a topic of major interest and has been the subject of intense debate in recent literature. Successful unification may

---

13. Chris Swoyer, "How Ontology Might Be Possible: Explanation and Inference in Metaphysics," *Midwest Studies in Philosophy* 23 (1999): 100–131, esp. 103–5.

exhibit connections or relationships between phenomena previously thought to be unrelated, thus offering the possibility of significant advances in scientific understanding. Excellent examples of the unification of explanation are to be found in Descartes's unification of algebra and geometry,[14] Isaac Newton's unification of terrestrial and celestial theories of motion,[15] James Clerk Maxwell's unification of electricity and magnetism,[16] the integration of Darwinian and Mendelian insights in neo-Darwinism,[17] and Einstein's demonstration of the unity of physics.[18] Not all attempts to achieve unification have been successful; to date, for example, the unification of quantum and relativity theory still remains a distant goal.[19]

The heterogeneity of the natural sciences gives rise to a variety of kinds of unification. For example, the creation of a common classificatory scheme or descriptive vocabulary—as in Linnaeus's comprehensive and principled systems of biological classification—where no satisfactory scheme previously existed is clearly an example of unification. Newton's demonstration that the orbits of the planets and the behavior of terrestrial objects falling freely close to the surface of Earth are due to the same gravitational force, and thus conform to the same laws of motion, represents a different form of unification. In this case, phenomena which had previously been seen as unrelated are shown to be the result of a common set of mechanisms or causal relationships. A third type of unification arises when it can be shown that the same mathematical framework or formalism, such as the Lagrange-Hamilton formalism, can be applied to a group of phenomena, once more suggesting that they possess some shared features.

There is also a significant philosophical debate over whether these successful unifications actually demonstrate anything of fundamental importance for such philosophically and theologically significant themes as the ontological unity of nature or the metaphysics of reductive explanation.[20] One may certainly draw the inference that a unified theory implies some ontological unity of nature, and avoid seeing a "successful phenomenological theory as evidence for an ontological interpretation of theoretical parameters."[21] Yet despite this debate about the

---

14. Emily R. Grosholz, "Descartes' Unification of Algebra and Geometry," in *Descartes: Philosophy, Mathematics and Physics*, ed. Stephen Gaukroger (Totowa, NJ: Barnes & Noble, 1980), 156–68. See also her comments about the unification of logic and topology in Emily R. Grosholz, "Two Episodes in the Unification of Logic and Topology," *British Journal for the Philosophy of Science* 36 (1985): 147–57.

15. Malcolm R. Forster, "Unification, Explanation, and the Composition of Causes in Newtonian Mechanics," *Studies in History and Philosophy of Science* 19 (1988): 55–101.

16. Margaret Morrison, "A Study in Theory Unification: The Case of Maxwell's Electromagnetic Theory," *Studies in History and Philosophy of Science* 23 (1992): 103–45.

17. Margaret Morrison, *Unifying Scientific Theories: Physical Concepts and Mathematical Structures* (Cambridge: Cambridge University Press, 2000), 192–206.

18. Ibid., 147–83.

19. Giovanni Battimelli, "Dreams of a Final Theory: The Failed Electromagnetic Unification and the Origins of Relativity," *European Journal of Physics* 26 (2005): S111–S116.

20. Ilpo Halonen and Jaakko Hintikka, "Unification—It's Magnificent But Is It Explanation?" *Synthese* 120 (1999): 27–47; Rebecca Schweder, "A Defense of a Unificationist Theory of Explanation," *Foundations of Science* 10 (2005): 421–35.

21. Morrison, *Unifying Scientific Theories*, 108.

ultimate significance of unification, there is little doubt that the history of science regularly discloses the same pattern: the forging of connections between theories that were initially assumed to have no fundamental connection. The basic point here is that they can be recognized to be part of a bigger picture, which explains them, while they in turn reinforce the plausibility of the bigger picture. In other words, *A* explains *B* while *B* justifies *A*.

This points to the fundamental source of explanatory power lying in *ontology*: an understanding of the way things are, of the fundamental order of things. It is by discovering the "big picture" that its individual elements are able to be both known and understood. Pierre Duhem (1861–1916) argued that to explain something "is to strip the reality of the appearances covering it like a veil, in order to see the bare reality itself."[22] One way of approaching this quest for an ontology would be to suggest, following Mary Hesse, that scientific thinking is best conceived as the construction of a chain of metaphors to describe reality.[23] Scientific explanation can thus be envisaged as a metaphorical redescription of the *explicandum* which allows its properties and behaviors to be correlated. It is, however, also capable of being explored through the use of metanarratives, such as the Christian Trinitarian narrative of creation, fall, redemption, and consummation.

This approach to natural theology does not entertain the idea that the observation of nature can *prove* the existence of God through necessary inference; rather, the vision of nature that is mandated and affirmed by the Christian vision of things is held and found to offer a highly satisfactory degree of consonance with what is actually observed. From its own distinctive point of view, Christian theology offers a map of reality which, though not exhaustive, is found to correspond to the observed features of nature. It makes possible a way of seeing things that is capable of accommodating the totality of human experience and rendering it intelligible through its conceptual schemes. A Christian natural theology is able to explain much of what is observed in nature; that capacity in turn becomes an additional reason for asserting that the Christian tradition, whose fundamental ideas gave rise to this form of natural theology in the first place, is justified in its beliefs.

As we have stressed throughout this work, it does not seem to be appropriate to consider natural theology as developing deductive proofs of God's existence from the natural world, including human reason. So if natural theology is not concerned with "proving" the existence of God, what intellectual purposes does it serve? What are its intellectual virtues? The answer to this question is best framed in terms of "inference to the best explanation," which is increasingly being advocated as a distinctive kind of inductive inference, capable of doing justice to the actual workings of science on the one hand, and the demands for its rational justification on the

22. Pierre Duhem, *The Aim and Structure of Physical Theory* (Princeton, NJ: Princeton University Press, 1954), 7.

23. Mary B. Hesse, *Models and Analogies in Science* (Notre Dame, IN: University of Notre Dame Press, 1966); idem, *Revolutions and Reconstructions in the Philosophy of Science* (Bloomington: Indiana University Press, 1980). See also Michael A. Arbib and Mary B. Hesse, *The Construction of Reality* (Cambridge: Cambridge University Press, 1986).

other. The growing esteem in which the approach is held reflects a belief that it has a plausible claim both to be an accurate description of the inferential processes of actual science, and also to be endowed with the property of conferring epistemic warrant to the conclusions reached by means of it.[24] "Inference to the best explanation," for example, appears to have a significant advantage over Bayesian approaches in being able to illuminate the context of scientific discovery.[25]

EXPLANATION AND EMPIRICAL FIT

Where various traditional forms of natural theology have conceived their tasks of deducing God from the observed characteristics of nature, the approach I adopt argues for the greater "empirical fit" of a Trinitarian worldview with what may be observed of the natural world, human reason and experience, and culture in general. The notion of "empirical fit" was introduced into theological discourse by the Oxford mathematician and philosopher of religion Ian T. Ramsey (1915–72).[26] Ramsey's own formulation of the approach should be studied in full:[27]

> The theological model works more like the fitting of a boot or a shoe than like the "yes" or "no" of a roll call. In other words, we have a particular doctrine which, like a preferred and selected shoe, starts by appearing to meet our empirical needs. But on closer fitting to the phenomena the shoe may pinch. When tested against future slush and rain it may be proven to be not altogether water-tight or it may be comfortable—yet it must not be too comfortable. In this way, the test of a shoe is measured by its ability to match a wide range of phenomena, by its overall success in meeting a variety of needs. Here is what I might call the method of empirical fit which is displayed by theological theorizing.

There are obvious risks of subjectivism in Ramsey's approach, if his imagery is taken at face value. For example, what criterion of epistemological comfort is appropriate to determine the extent of "empirical fit"? Yet Ramsey was clear that his idea of "empirical fit" had significant value for the evaluation of theoretical approaches to nature, where conclusive verification was impossible. It is a fundamentally empirical notion, originating within the natural sciences, which Ramsey believed—rightly, in my view—had considerable theological potential.

24. For defining statements of the approach, see Ernan McMullin, *The Inference That Makes Science* (Milwaukee: Marquette University Press, 1992); Lipton, *Inference to the Best Explanation.*

25. Samir Okasha, "Van Fraasen's Critique of Inference to the Best Explanation," *Studies in History and Philosophy of Science* 31 (2000): 691–710. For some excellent case studies illustrating the importance of the "context of discovery" and its relation to the "context of justification," see Jutta Schickore and Friedrich Steinle, eds., *Revisiting Discovery and Justification: Historical and Philosophical Perspectives on the Context Distinction* (Dordrecht: Springer-Verlag, 2006).

26. For comment, see James W. McClendon Jr. and James M. Smith, "Ian Ramsey's Model of Religious Language: A Qualified Appreciation," *Journal of the American Academy of Religion* 41 (1973): 413–24; Terrence W. Tilley, "Ian Ramsey and Empirical Fit," *Journal of the American Academy of Religion* 45 (1977): 357 (Abstract), G:963–88 (in September Supplement).

27. Ian T. Ramsey, *Models and Mystery* (London: Oxford University Press, 1964), 17.

Its possible subjectivism aside, there are, of course, some difficulties with the notion, as a cursory engagement with the philosophy of science indicates. It might be pointed out, for example, that several "empirically equivalent" theories might be brought forward as explanations of a set of observations, forcing theory choice on other grounds (if, of course, it is possible to make a meaningful adjudication in the first place).[28] Nevertheless, despite his failure to produce a viable general theory of justification of religious beliefs,[29] Ramsey's loose appeal to the idea of "empirical fit" draws attention to the need for a natural theology to possess some conceptual symmetry with what is actually observed.

This, however, might provoke an indignant response from a critic, along the following lines: what you are proposing is simply an ad hoc theology, which is adjusted until a sufficient degree of resonance with experience is achieved. Your theology has simply been invented in response to what is observed. It is a malleable affair, more characterized by intellectual plasticity and apologetic opportunism rather than by conceptual rigor.

The point being made is fair and is undoubtedly significant in regard to some forms of natural theology. However, the approach adopted in this work is *not* to ground a natural theology on an engagement with the purely natural world, but to regard natural theology as the outcome of seeing nature from the standpoint of the Christian tradition. In my view, a Trinitarian reading of the world offers a significant degree of empirical fit with what may be observed, despite the fact that this reading of things rests primarily upon reflection on divine revelation, not on a reading of nature.[30] If N designates the type of natural theology presented and defended in this work, O designates the observation of the world, and T designates Trinitarianism, then we could suggest the following relationship between them, which emphasizes a distinct role for natural theology:

T explains N; N explains O;

O justifies N; N justifies T.

This could, however, be simplified to:

T explains O;

O justifies T.

28. For a more detailed account of the issues associated with the notion, see Bas van Fraassen, *The Scientific Image* (Oxford: Oxford University Press, 1980); idem, *Laws and Symmetry* (Oxford: Clarendon Press, 1989). John Earman, who distinguishes three types of empirical equivalence, argues that empirical indistinguishability implies scientific antirealism: see, e.g., John Earman, "Underdetermination, Realism, and Reason," *Midwest Studies in Philosophy* 18 (1994): 19–38. This is not the case, as pointed out by Igor Deuven and Leon Horsten, "Earman on Underdetermination and Empirical Indistinguishability," *Erkenntnis* 49 (1998): 303–20.

29. McClendon and Smith, "Ian Ramsey's Model of Religious Language," 421–23.

30. For a more detailed account of how revelation is embedded in nature, see Alister E. McGrath, *A Scientific Theology*, vol. 3, *Theory* (London: Continuum, 2003), 138–93.

Here an appeal is made to the notion that the explanatory power of an explanation is itself seen as evidence of its correctness, an assumption that is found in most forms of "inference to the best explanation."

EXPLANATION, PREDICTION AND ACCOMMODATION

In this chapter, we have argued that natural theology, as it is here presented, has considerable explanatory capacity. Yet some might not unreasonably wish to raise an objection here. How can natural theology be said to "explain," when it seems incapable of predicting? The validity of scientific theory, after all, is partly assessed in terms of whether it can predict novelties. Natural theology appears to have somewhat limited potential in this respect. Does not this imply that it represents a deficient and inferior form of "explanation," assuming that it is entitled to be thought of in terms of this category at all?

This issue emerged as important in the debate between William Whewell and John Stuart Mill over the role of induction as a scientific method.[31] Whewell emphasized the importance of predictive novelty within the scientific method; Mill argued that there was nothing more than a psychological distinction between prediction of novel observations and theoretical accommodation of existing observations. It remains important, however, since the issues are far from settled. In their recent discussion of the issue,[32] Hitchcock and Sober argue that while prediction can occasionally be superior to accommodation, this is not always the case. Situations can easily be envisaged where accommodation is superior to prediction. Prediction is neither intrinsically nor invariably to be preferred to accommodation. If a Trinitarian natural theology is able to offer a robust accommodation of known observations, this may in itself be seen as sufficient justification of its ideas, without the necessity of prediction of novel observations.

Historical examples can easily be given of situations in which accommodation played a critically important role in the development of scientific theory. Perhaps the most accessible is Darwin's account of natural selection, which primarily entailed offering a new explanation of a wide range of observational data, some assembled by Darwin himself, others drawn from the works of his predecessors and contemporaries. For Darwin, the all-important question was how these observations could be best accommodated within a grand theory of development. The hypothesis of

31. Laura J. Snyder, "The Mill-Whewell Debate: Much Ado about Induction," *Perspectives on Science* 5 (1997): 159–98. Snyder elsewhere argues that Whewell's views on induction have been misunderstood and merit closer attention as a distinctive approach: Laura J. Snyder, "Discoverers' Induction," *Philosophy of Science* 64 (1997): 580–604.

32. Christopher Hitchcock and Elliott Sober, "Prediction versus Accommodation and the Risk of Overfitting," *British Journal for Philosophy of Science* 55 (2004): 1–34. The "weak predictivism" defended by Hitchcock and Sober has parallels elsewhere: see, e.g., the careful assessment of approaches in Marc Lange, "The Apparent Superiority of Prediction to Accommodation as a Side Effect," *British Journal for Philosophy of Science* 52 (2001): 575–88; David Harker, "Accommodation and Prediction: The Case of the Persistent Head," *British Journal for Philosophy of Science* 57 (2006): 309–21.

natural selection seemed to offer an intellectual vantage point from which the biological landscape could be understood in a more profound manner than before, allowing surprising or puzzling phenomena—such as the continued existence of rudimentary organs—to be accommodated with relative ease.[33] Prediction has a role to play in theory choice; nevertheless, some theories concern entities or situations in which prediction may seem inappropriate or simply impossible. If natural theology rests primarily upon accommodation, it is in good scientific company.

These reflections on how a natural theology makes sense of things suggest that there is a need for a more-detailed discussion of three issues, which are the subject of the chapters which follow.

First, in what sense does the Christian vision of reality unify what is observed? Underlying my approach to natural theology is the conviction that Christianity makes sense in itself and has the capacity to make sense of things as well. So in what ways does a Trinitarian vision of reality correspond to what is actually observed in the natural world? Though any attempt to quantify its successes and failings will be open to challenge, it is important to at least begin this process of exploration, however provisional this process of calibration may turn out to be. This will be discussed in chapter 6.

Second, any attempt to interpret the significance of the natural phenomena regularly described as "anthropic," or held to demonstrate evidence of fine-tuning, requires some framework by which their significance can be evaluated. In chapter 7, an appeal is made to Charles Peirce's notion of "surprising facts" as a way of accounting for the importance of such phenomena. This is supplemented by using counterfactual reasoning to clarify their overall significance for a natural theology.

And third, what theological framework may be proposed for a unificationist attempt to explain the emerging scientific understanding of the world, especially in relation to anthropic phenomena? We will already have discussed some general principles of interpretation that emerge from a Trinitarian approach in chapter 6; it will now be necessary to offer one very specific formulation of such a system as a "lens" through which to view nature. In chapter 8, we shall show how the classic theology of creation developed by Augustine of Hippo during the period 401–15 offers a heuristic for interpreting such phenomena, opening the way to the development of more advanced models.

We begin by considering the relevance of the Christian vision of reality for natural theology. How does a Trinitarian theology affect the way in which we "see" nature? This is a substantial question, requiring detailed consideration. In the next chapter, we shall explore some of the possibilities for engaging the natural world that emerge from this distinctively Christian view of things.

---

33. Unsurprisingly, Darwin's method is regularly cited in the extensive literature dealing with "inference to the best explanation." For an early example, see Paul Thagard, "The Best Explanation: Criteria for Theory Choice," *Journal of Philosophy* 75 (1978): 76–92.

Chapter 6

The Dynamics of a Trinitarian Natural Theology

Christianity is a Trinitarian faith, whether this is explicitly affirmed or implicitly assumed. The twentieth century has seen an enthusiastic reappropriation of the doctrine of the Trinity in Protestant, Catholic, and Orthodox theological discussions.[1] Although the doctrine appears to have been regarded as being of relatively minor importance in the eighteenth and nineteenth centuries, the twentieth century witnessed a renewal of Trinitarian theology of such vigor and range that it seems difficult to envisage how past generations could have neglected it.[2] So what are the implications of such a Trinitarianism, explicit or implicit, for natural theology?

One of the most difficult questions confronting some traditional styles of natural theology, including those developed in response to the agendas of the

---

1. For an excellent account of how the doctrine of the Trinity shapes the way we understand the natural order, see Samuel M. Powell, *Participating in God: Creation and Trinity* (Minneapolis: Fortress, 2003), 61–160.

2. David S. Cunningham, "Trinitarian Theology since 1990," *Reviews in Religion and Theology* 4 (1995): 8–16; Gerald O'Collins, *The Tripersonal God: Understanding and Interpreting the Trinity* (London: Continuum, 2004); Veli-Matti Kärkkäinen, *Trinity and Religious Pluralism: The Doctrine of the Trinity in Christian Theology of Religions* (Aldershot: Ashgate, 2004).

Enlightenment, concerns the relationship of the God whose existence might be inferred from nature, and the rather more specific God of the Christian faith. It is an important question. The forms of natural theology that emerged in the seventeenth and eighteenth centuries have become so influential that we might not unreasonably style them as "classical natural theology." Yet as we emphasized in earlier chapters, these "classical" approaches have what can only be described as an indirect connection with the Christian tradition. Stanley Hauerwas made this point with some force in his 2001 Gifford Lectures: "Natural theology divorced from a full [Christian] doctrine of God cannot help but distort the character of God and, accordingly, of the world in which we find ourselves."[3] So is the somewhat generic divinity of classical natural theology identical to the God who is revealed in the history of Israel, and in the life, death, and resurrection of Jesus Christ? And if not, precisely what relationship does exist between these concepts of divinity?

This is no idle question, which can be easily dismissed. Within the context of a polytheistic or henotheistic worldview,[4] for example, it is perfectly possible to suggest that the "true God" was not involved in the work of creation, which was entrusted to some subordinate divine agency, such as a demiurge. Within this context, a natural theology would thus have an innate tendency to disclose this lesser deity, if it discloses anything at all, rather than the "true" or "ultimate" God. Not all concepts of God are commensurate with a natural theology.[5]

In many traditional accounts of the relationship between natural and revealed theology, a distinction is drawn between the "one God" of nature and the "triune God" of revelation[6]—that is, between a generalized notion of divinity and the specifically Christian construal of God. In medieval works of theology, the section *de deo uno* normally precedes that entitled *de deo trino*, the implication being that the latter amplifies and extends the former.[7] What can be known through nature is thus developed through the grace of revelation. That God is one is a truth of natural theology; that God is three-in-one is a truth of revealed theol-

3. See Stanley Hauerwas, *With the Grain of the Universe: The Church's Witness and Natural Theology* (Grand Rapids: Brazos Press, 2002), 15–16: "The God who moves the sun and the stars is the same God who was incarnate in Jesus of Nazareth."

4. There is a useful discussion of issues relating to Israel's monotheism in Mark S. Smith, *The Origins of Biblical Monotheism: Israel's Polytheistic Background and the Ugaritic Texts* (Oxford: Oxford University Press, 2001), 10–14. The term "henotheism" was introduced by Friedrich Max Müller (1823–1900) to denote the worldview which accepted the existence of many gods, of which only one was the "true God," who was to be worshiped and obeyed.

5. Note the points made about concepts of God and the problem of evil in natural theology in Robert Prevost, *Probability and Theistic Explanation* (Oxford: Clarendon Press, 1990), 152–82.

6. See the comments of John P. Doyle, "*Ipsum Esse* as God-Surrogate: The Point of Convergence of Faith and Reason for St. Thomas Aquinas," *The Modern Schoolman* 50 (1973): 293–96.

7. Much discussion has focused on whether Thomas Aquinas's doctrine of God is fundamentally metaphysical, rather than authentically Trinitarian. Thus Wolfhart Pannenberg suggests that Aquinas derives the doctrine of the Trinity from metaphysical reflection on the notion of *substantia*, rather than through an engagement with the scriptural witness. On this reading of Aquinas, his concept of God is actually non-Trinitarian. For comment on this issue, see Fergus Kerr, *After Aquinas: Versions of Thomism* (Oxford: Blackwell Publishing, 2002), 181–85.

ogy.[8] Similarly, many of the recent philosophical debates about whether the big bang or anthropic phenomena are consistent with the existence of God have posited an essentially Deistic notion of God as the object of debate.[9]

It is a familiar approach, lent dignity by its antiquity. Yet there are difficulties, including the obvious perception that the doctrine of the Trinity tends to be treated as a kind of addendum to the doctrine of God, bolted on without any real attempt at intellectual integration. On this model, nature reveals a certain amount of information about God, which is then supplemented by revelation, which appends additional insights. Nature tells us that there is one God; revelation clarifies and enhances this discernment by adding that God is also threefold. But what if a Trinitarian vision of God forces us to see nature in a very different manner, and in doing so, actually subverts the alleged truths of natural theology?[10]

DEISM, THEISM, AND TRINITARIANISM

In general terms, the intellectual trajectory proposed by the classic forms of natural theology we considered earlier (see chap. 5) can be represented like this:

$$\text{Deism} \rightarrow \text{theism} \rightarrow \text{Trinitarianism}$$

Reflection on nature initially discloses a notion of God which could be described as "Deistic"—for example, the idea of a "supreme intelligence," which brought the world into being and expressed or imposed its ordering upon it. From a Christian perspective, this is a severely attenuated notion of God, which clearly requires amplification and further development. Recognizing that God remains involved with the created order leads from Deism to theism; recognizing that this God chose to become incarnate in Jesus of Nazareth leads from theism to Trinitarianism.

One variant of this approach is found in John Calvin's celebrated notion of *duplex cognitio Dei*, the "twofold knowledge of God" as creator on the one hand and redeemer on the other. As presented by Calvin, this dialectic takes the following form.[11] Humanity is able to arrive at a knowledge of God the creator outside

---

8. For the roots of this idea, see Eric D. Perl, "St. Gregory Palamas and the Metaphysics of Creation," *Dionysius* 14 (1990): 105–30; Wayne J. Hankey, "Dionysian Hierarchy in Thomas Aquinas: Tradition and Transformation," in *Denys l'Aréopagite et sa postérité en Orient et en Occident: Actes du Colloque International Paris, 21–24 septembre 1994*, ed. Ysabel de Andia (Paris: Institut d'Études Augustiniennes, 1997), 405–38.

9. An example is the interesting collection of interacting essays in William Lane Craig and Quentin Smith, *Theism, Atheism, and Big Bang Cosmology* (Oxford: Clarendon Press, 1993). This may be contrasted profitably with the rather-different approach found in John C. Polkinghorne, "Physics and Metaphysics in a Trinitarian Perspective," *Theology and Science* 1 (2003): 33–49.

10. Thomas F. Torrance, *The Christian Doctrine of God: One Being, Three Persons* (Edinburgh: T&T Clark, 1996), 25–31. Torrance suggests that theism may have to be recognized as an alternative to, rather than a deficient or emergent version of, Trinitarianism.

11. See, e.g., Edward A. Dowey, *The Knowledge of God in Calvin's Theology* (New York: Columbia University Press, 1952), 50–220.

the specific framework of the Christian revelation. This knowledge is not saving, and it is confirmed, consolidated, and amplified in Scripture. Knowledge of God the redeemer is only to be had through revelation and is saving. God may thus only be fully known through Jesus Christ, who may in turn only be known through Scripture; the created order, however, provides important points of contact for and partial resonances of this revelation.

It is a neat scheme, providing theological insights of merit and offering a useful starting point for a Christian apologetic.[12] Yet it runs the risk of implying, if not explicitly endorsing, a duality within the economy of salvation, by implying that God can be known as creator without being known as redeemer. This difficulty can be minimized by arguing that such a natural knowledge of God is imprecise and unfocused, taking the form of an awareness that there may indeed be a creator, without being able to name or identify the God in question. This certainly appears to be the apologetic strategy used by Paul in his Areopagus sermon, in which a vague and general awareness of a creator divinity is initially presupposed and subsequently engaged: "What therefore you worship as unknown, this I proclaim to you" (Acts 17:23). The implication is that Paul *names* this unknown divinity, before expanding it into a fully orbed Christian vision of God, such as that set out in his letters. The transition is thus between an *intimated* "unknown God" and a *disclosed* "God and Father of our Lord Jesus Christ" (Romans 15:6).

It would be anachronistic to speak of Calvin's apologetic strategy leading his readers from Deism to theism; we really ought to speak in terms of a transition from a natural or intuitive perception of God to a more biblically grounded understanding of God, which extends and clarifies what can be known through nature.[13] This position is set out with some clarity in later Reformed confessions, which restate the implications of Calvin's approach. For example, the Gallic Confession of Faith (1559) argues that God reveals himself to humanity in two manners: first, through the created order; and second, "and more clearly," in Scripture.[14] The Belgic Confession (1561) expands this brief statement, reaffirming that knowledge of God can come about by two means:[15]

> First, by the creation, preservation, and government of the universe, which is before our eyes as a most beautiful book, in which all creatures, great and small, are like so many characters leading us to contemplate the invisible things of God. . . . Second, God makes himself known more clearly and fully to us by his holy and divine Word; that is to say, to the extent that it is necessary for us to know in this life, to his glory and our salvation.

12. For critical reflections, see Richard A. Muller, "'Duplex cognitio Dei' in the Theology of Early Reformed Orthodoxy," *Sixteenth Century Journal* 10 (1979): 51–61.

13. Calvin's interaction with Cicero's *De natura deorum* is especially important at this point: for a fine commentary, see Emil Grislis, "Calvin's Use of Cicero in the *Institutes* I:1–5: A Case Study in Theological Method," *Archiv für Reformationsgeschichte* 62 (1971): 5–37.

14. *Confessio Gallicana* (1559), art. 2.

15. *Confessio Belgica* (1561), art. 2. Barth's severely critical comment on these two texts should be noted: *Church Dogmatics* II/1:127.

The same fundamental themes that are encountered in Calvin's exposition of the topic recur here: first, there are two modalities of knowing God, one arising through the natural order, and the second through Scripture; second, the biblical mode is clearer and fuller than the first, and leads to salvation. Like many of his contemporaries, Calvin tends to regard the doctrine of the Trinity as an amplification of this understanding of God on the basis of the biblical witness, rather than deriving the notion from speculative argumentation; for example, at no point does Calvin argue that the notion of the "love of God" entails a noncreaturely object, which in turn points to a multiplicity of persons within the Godhead.[16]

Yet the orderly transition Deism → theism → Trinitarianism that we find in Aquinas and Calvin has been called into question through the emergence of more-radical and more-thoroughgoing approaches to the Trinity in the late twentieth century, especially those shaped by reflection on the suffering of God on the cross.[17] Eberhard Jüngel, for example, mounts a sustained and demanding critique of the eliding of "theism" and "Trinitarianism," arguing that the "theistic tradition" transmits a metaphysically distorted notion of God,[18] which easily leads to the emergence of atheism (here conceived as the antithesis of such metaphysical theisms).[19]

While Jüngel's views on the relation between theism and Trinitarianism do not command universal assent, they nevertheless raise some entirely proper questions. For the purposes of natural theology, the most important of these is whether Trinitarianism can indeed be interpreted simply as an amplification of theism.[20] Might it actually represent its modification, or possibly even its denial?

16. See the analysis in Paul Helm, *John Calvin's Ideas* (Oxford: Oxford University Press, 2004), 35–50.

17. Although this way of thinking can be discerned in Luther's *theologia crucis* during the late 1510s, its most powerful statement emerged in Jürgen Moltmann's *Crucified God*. It must be stressed that Christian piety has always recognized the importance of the suffering of Christ: see, e.g., Ellen M. Ross, *The Grief of God: Images of the Suffering Jesus in Late Medieval England* (New York: Oxford University Press, 1997), esp. 67–90. The radical Trinitarian interpretation of this appears to be a late twentieth-century development, not without its difficulties—some of which are outlined in Thomas G. Weinandy, *Does God Suffer?* (Notre Dame, IN: University of Notre Dame Press, 2000).

18. For a useful summary of Jüngel's critique of Descartes, see Paul J. DeHart, *Beyond the Necessary God: Trinitarian Faith and Philosophy in the Thought of Eberhard Jüngel* (Atlanta: Scholars Press, 1999), 43–68.

19. On this see Eberhard Jüngel, *Gott als Geheimnis der Welt: Zur Begründung der Theologie des Gekreuzigten im Streit zwischen Theismus und Atheismus*, 4th ed. (Tübingen: J. C. B. Mohr, 1982). For my reflections on Jüngel's critique of metaphysics, see Alister E. McGrath, *A Scientific Theology*, vol. 3, *Theory* (London: Continuum, 2003), 284–94.

20. Jüngel's own reflections on natural theology reflect his characteristic concerns—e.g., the dangers of metaphysically conceived notions of divinity, the hidden influence of anthropology, the failure to take divine revelation with due seriousness, and especially the absence of the cross from such accounts of nature. See esp. two early essays: Eberhard Jüngel, "Gott—um seiner selbst willen interessant: Ein Plädoyer für eine natürlichere Theologie," in *Entsprechungen: Theologische Erörterungen II* (Munich: Kaiser Verlag, 1980), 193–97; idem, "Das Dilemma der natürlichen Theologie und die Wahrheit ihres Problems: Überlegungen für ein Gespräch mit Wolfhart Pannenberg," in *Entsprechungen: Gott—Wahrheit—Mensch: Theologische Erörterungen* (Munich: Kaiser Verlag, 1980), 158–77. There is obvious importance for natural theology in Jüngel's insight that the incarnational advent of God makes the world even more worldly, and nature even more natural.

Is the metaphysical essence of God actually contrary to God's true divinity?[21] This raises questions very similar to those posed by Stanley Hauerwas in his 2001 Gifford Lectures. Can one undertake the enterprise of natural theology without a full Christian understanding of God, without introducing distortions of the character of God and of the world in which we find ourselves?[22] Can one seriously develop a natural theology without engaging with the cross of Christ?[23]

Both Jüngel and Hauerwas force us to ask whether the end point of natural theology subverts its starting point. Where classic approaches to natural theology tended to assume that a Trinitarian vision of God was the culmination and fulfilment of the natural quest for the divine, Jüngel and Hauerwas (though for slightly different reasons) argue that the Trinitarian vision of God forces us to reconsider the whole enterprise of natural theology. Trinitarianism ultimately renders classic natural theology incoherent. Deism, theism, and Trinitarianism offer quite different "readings" of nature.

The Christian doctrine of God, then, cannot be equated with some "generic" notion of divinity,[24] since it is characterized by a set of specific features that both distinguish this notion of God from its rivals and alternatives and define its attitude toward natural theology.[25] For example, within a monotheistic religious system, the idea of God might be articulated in terms that are not conducive to a viable natural theology. What if the one true God self-disclosed in a fundamentally exclusive manner—as, for example, within Islam, a monotheistic religious belief system which, like Christianity, has a strong doctrine of divine revelation?[26] Nevertheless, Islam understands both what is disclosed and the manner of its disclosure in a fashion very different from that associated with Christianity. In general, Islam recognizes no true knowledge of God outside the Qur'an, thus raising serious difficulties for any notion of natural theology. Since about 1500, most Muslim theologians have followed the general approach of Al-Ghazali, who regarded both natural philosophy and theology as posing significant threats to Islamic orthodoxy.[27] On this view, nature is held to be incapable of disclosing

---

21. For comment on this point in Jüngel's work, see John B. Webster, *Eberhard Jüngel: An Introduction to His Theology* (Cambridge: Cambridge University Press, 1991), 80–82.

22. Hauerwas, *With the Grain of the Universe*, 15–16.

23. Ibid., 17: "The attempt to develop a natural theology prior to or as grounds for subsequent claims about God cannot help but be mistaken to the extent such a project fails to help us see that there can be no deeper reality-making claim than . . . [that] those who bear crosses work with the grain of the universe."

24. For some of the features and implications of such an approach to God, see David T. Morgan, "Benjamin Franklin: Champion of Generic Religion," *Historian* 62 (2000): 723–29.

25. For a detailed analysis, see Alister E. McGrath, *The Open Secret: A New Vision for Natural Theology* (Oxford: Blackwell, 2008), 171–236.

26. William C. Chittick, *The Self-Disclosure of God: Principles of Ibn al-'Arabī's Cosmology* (Albany: State University of New York Press, 1998).

27. Richard M. Frank, *Al-Ghazālī and the Ash'arite School* (Durham, NC: Duke University Press, 1994), 16–17. Islam enjoyed a "golden era" of positive engagement with issues of natural theology and philosophy between the ninth and fifteenth centuries: see Edward Grant, *The Foundations of Modern Science in the Middle Ages: Their Religious, Institutional and Intellectual Contexts* (Cambridge: Cambridge University Press, 1996), 176–86.

anything reliable about God, and it might mislead the faithful into making idol-atrous or blasphemous judgments.

One certainly might respond that natural theology, when undertaken within a monotheistic framework, can only lead to the "God and Father of our Lord Jesus Christ" (1 Peter 1:3). If there is only one God, and nature points to this one God, then the issue of the identity of the divinity intimated by nature would seem to be settled. "The love that moves the sun and the other stars" is identical with the God who became incarnate in Jesus of Nazareth. There is no other God to whom nature can point, lead, or direct.

This apparently promising line of argument, however, encounters serious diffi-culties. The most serious of these is that a distorted conception of God arises from the process of inferring the divine nature and attributes from the natural world, either on account of the assumptions brought to bear by the human interpreter of nature, or on account of distortions or refractions arising from the medium from which God's character is inferred. The problem can be seen emerging in the cele-brated "Boyle Lectures" of the early eighteenth century: many attempts to estab-lish the character of God from the rational analysis of nature ended up yielding a decidedly heterodox vision of God.[28] The importance of this point is given added weight through recent work in the cognitive science of religion, which suggests that humans come to believe in supernatural agents—whether ghosts, goblins, or gods—through essentially the same means.[29] Cognitive approaches appear unable to distinguish between superstition and religion. Justin Barrett proposed a "hyper-active agency detection device" which is inclined to detect agency in the environ-ment, even on the basis of fairly modest evidence.[30] On this model, it proves impossible to avoid placing gods, ghosts, and goblins in the same category, causing difficulty for those who continue to argue that the inference of the existence of God from nature is unproblematic.

History confirms what orthodoxy suspects—that any attempt to render the character of God through the human engagement with nature ultimately leads to a vision of God that is at best Deist, and more probably pagan—a point of no small importance on account of the revival of paganism in many parts of the Western world, although often in somewhat softened and sanitized forms.[31] The

---

28. For a general exploration of this point, see the important collection of studies in John Brooke and Ian McLean, eds., *Heterodoxy in Early Modern Science and Religion* (Oxford: Oxford University Press, 2006). As Maurice Wiles has pointed out, some of the most influential Boyle lecturers were Arians: Maurice Wiles, *Archetypal Heresy: Arianism through the Ages* (Oxford: Oxford University Press, 1996), 62–134.

29. For example, Pascal Boyer and Charles Ramble, "Cognitive Templates for Religious Con-cepts: Cross-Cultural Evidence for Recall of Counter-Intuitive Representations," *Cognitive Science* 25 (2001): 535–64; Scott Atran and Ara Norenzayan, "Religion's Evolutionary Landscape: Counterin-tuition, Commitment, Compassion, Communion," *Behavioral and Brain Sciences* 27 (2004): 713–70; Justin L. Barrett, *Why Would Anyone Believe in God?* (Lanham, MD: AltaMira Press, 2004).

30. Barrett, *Why Would Anyone Believe in God?* 31–33.

31. See the points made in Prudence Jones, "The European Native Tradition," in *Nature Religion Today: Paganism in the Modern World*, ed. Joanne Pearson, Richard H. Roberts, and Geoffrey Samuel (Edinburgh: Edinburgh University Press, 1998), 71–88.

somewhat generic notions of "natural religion" or "religion of nature," which became particularly significant in the eighteenth century, articulate a conception of a remote and detached creator God.[32] This view of God, often dubbed "the divine watchmaker," offers a radically truncated version of the Christian economy of salvation, generally limited to the past action of creation. Yet orthodox Christianity, endorsing the judgment of Irenaeus of Lyons,[33] insists that salvation history does not begin and end with creation, but follows the more complex trajectory of creation, fall, incarnation, redemption, and consummation. This view of salvation history, and the one God whose actions lie behind it, must be seen as an integral aspect of a distinctively and authentically Christian approach to reality that is called "Trinitarianism."[34]

The approach to natural theology that I expound and defend in *The Open Secret* does not base itself upon an allegedly "neutral" reading of nature, which is held to disclose a God who may be known independently of divine revelation. Rather, it interprets natural theology as the process of engagement with nature that has its origins from within the Christian tradition and is guided and nourished by a Trinitarian vision of God. This allows nature to be "seen" as God's creation, which resonates with how empirical reality is observed. The Christian tradition holds that nature possesses a derivative capacity to disclose something of God's wisdom, without undermining or displacing divine revelation itself. It both legitimates and encourages such an engagement in the first place, and in the second offers an intellectual framework through which what is observed may be understood and appreciated.

Furthermore, the Christian vision of God is such that the possible existence of this God cannot be treated as if it were a purely speculative hypothesis. Rather, natural theology emerges and is authorized and resourced from within the matrix of the ideas and habits of the Christian tradition. Thus the discerning reader of Thomas Aquinas notes that his articulation of a natural theology rests on his belief that there exists a propensity for knowledge of God within human nature, as we would expect if we were indeed the creatures of God, created antecedently ignorant of our true origin and end, but with the appetite and capacity to know and to advance in knowledge to the source and goal of all things.[35] Aquinas's rationale for natural theology is thus grounded and nourished by his vision of the

32. Peter A. Byrne, *Natural Religion and the Nature of Religion: The Legacy of Deism* (London: Routledge, 1989); Richard Tuck, "The 'Christian Atheism' of Thomas Hobbes," in *Atheism from the Reformation to the Enlightenment*, ed. Michael Hunter and David Wootton (Oxford: Clarendon Press, 1992), 102–20.

33. Eric F. Osborn, *Irenaeus of Lyons* (Cambridge: Cambridge University Press, 2001), 51–141.

34. For an excellent account of a Trinitarian approach to the doctrine of creation, see Colin E. Gunton, *The Triune Creator: A Historical and Systematic Study* (Edinburgh: Edinburgh University Press, 1998).

35. See the analysis in Lawrence Feingold, *The Natural Desire to See God according to St. Thomas and His Interpreters* (Rome: Apollinare Studi, 2001), which should be seen as a helpful correction to some misreadings in the writings of Henri de Lubac. For further comment, particularly in relation to John Milbank's reading of Aquinas, see Reinhard Hütter, "*Desiderium naturale visionis Dei—Est autem duplex hominis beatitudo sive felicitas*: Some Observations about Lawrence Feingold's and John Millbank's Recent Interventions in the Debate over the Natural Desire to See God," *Nova et vetera* 5 (2007): 81–132.

human desire for knowledge, which leads to reflection on the human situation and its implications.

Engaging with the natural world from a Trinitarian perspective encourages an expectation that nature can, in certain ways and to a certain extent, echo its origins and goal. From a Trinitarian perspective, it is not simply nature itself that is fine-tuned; the believer's perception of nature can also be said to be fine-tuned, since the Christian tradition mandates a certain attentiveness to nature and a heightened anticipation of disclosure, which permits its noise to be heard as a tune.[36]

The grand themes of the Christian faith provide an interpretative framework by which nature may be seen, allowing it to be viewed and read in profound and significant ways. Christian theology is the elixir, the philosopher's stone,[37] which turns the mundane into the epiphanic, the world of nature into the realm of God's creation. Like a lens bringing a vast landscape into sharp focus, or a map helping us grasp the features of the terrain around us, Christian doctrine offers a new way of understanding, imagining, and behaving. It invites us to see the natural order, and ourselves within it, in a special way—a way that might be hinted at, but cannot be confirmed by, the natural order itself. Nature is "seen" as God's creation; the "book of nature" is read as God's story—and ours. It is as if a veil has been lifted, or a bright sun has illuminated a mental landscape. And above all, it allows us to avoid the fatal fundamental error that is so often the foundation or consequence of a natural theology—namely, that divine revelation is essentially reduced to the supreme awareness of an order already present in creation.[38]

It will be clear that this approach to natural theology reflects a nuanced understanding of the "two books" of nature and Scripture.[39] In its more developed form, the image of the "two books" dates from the early modern period and is thought to have played a significant role in encouraging the emergence of the natural sciences,[40] partly on account of its validation of an intellectual engagement with nature. These often tended to be treated as separate entities, each with its own distinctive mode of engagement and interpretation. Yet it is important to

---

36. The image of hearing a noise or a tune, used in chapter 1 (at note no. 10), is due to Michael Polanyi. See the use made of Polanyi's approach in J. J. Sparkes, "Pattern Recognition and Scientific Progress," *Mind* 81 (1971): 29–41.

37. For historical contextualization of the idea of the gospel as the "philosopher's stone" that transmutes life, see Stanton J. Linden, *Darke Hierogliphicks: Alchemy in English Literature from Chaucer to the Restoration* (Lexington: University Press of Kentucky, 1996), 154–92.

38. For an excellent study of this danger, with special reference to recent Jewish writings on natural theology, see David Novak, *Natural Law in Judaism* (Cambridge: Cambridge University Press, 1998), esp. 142–48.

39. For the importance of this image of "two books" for natural theology, see Alister E. McGrath, *A Scientific Theology*, vol. 1, *Nature* (London: Continuum, 2001), 117–21.

40. See Kenneth J. Howell, *God's Two Books: Copernican Cosmology and Biblical Interpretation in Early Modern Science* (Notre Dame, IN: University of Notre Dame Press, 2002); Peter Harrison, "'The Book of Nature' and Early Modern Science," in *The Book of Nature in Early Modern and Modern History*, ed. Klaas van Berkel and Arjo Vanderjagt (Leuven: Peeters, 2006), 1–26. On the development of the image, see William G. Madsen, *From Shadowy Types to Truth: Studies in Milton's Symbolism* (New Haven, CT: Yale University Press, 1968), 124–44; Robert Markley, *Fallen Languages: Crises of Representation in Newtonian England, 1660–1740* (Ithaca, NY: Cornell University Press, 1993), 39–45.

note that they are interactive. How we read the book of Scripture determines how we "see" nature; equally, how we understand the book of nature affects how we interpret the book of Scripture. The rise of evolutionary theories in the nineteenth century, for example, had a significant impact on how the "book of nature" was understood, which in turn led to changes in how the "book of Scripture" was interpreted.[41] William Paley's approach to natural theology rests upon his specific interpretation of both books and of manner in which they interlock to yield a coherent approach to a religious interpretation of the natural order. Yet shifting interpretations of how the Bible (especially the early chapters of the book of Genesis) and nature (especially the origins of the cosmos and our biosphere) are to be read leads to the emergence of other coherent religious approaches to the natural order, such as the Trinitarian approach adopted in the present work.

The emphasis on a specifically Trinitarian vision of God is central to my approach to natural theology. The specifically Christian vision of God, expressed in its fundamental doctrines of the incarnation and the Trinity, articulates a highly precise understanding of the nature of God which affirms that the divine can be known, to a certain extent and in a certain manner, through the mundane.[42] As Colin Gunton has argued, a Trinitarian conception of God forces us to see everything—including nature—in a different way.[43]

> Because God is triune, we must respond to him in a particular way, or rather set of ways, corresponding to the richness of his being. . . . In turn, that means that everything looks—and, indeed, is—different in the life of the Trinity.

The doctrine of the Trinity affirms a "God whose reality as a communion of persons is the basis of a rational universe in which personal life may take shape."[44] As Jürgen Moltmann pointed out in his Gifford Lectures, we must learn to think of the "world of nature as bearing the prints of the Triune God."[45]

So what are the distinctive features of a Trinitarian approach to natural theology? In what follows, we shall outline the contours of the specific form of nat-

41. How the opening chapters of the book of Genesis were interpreted is a case in point: see Charles C. Gillispie, *Genesis and Geology: A Study in the Relations of Scientific Thought, Natural Theology and Social Opinion in Great Britain, 1790–1850* (Cambridge, MA: Harvard University Press, 1996).

42. Rationalist criticism of the doctrine of the Trinity in seventeenth-century England was one factor leading to the emergence of a Deist notion of God, which was a significant influence on the rise of Enlightenment approaches to natural theology. For these developments, see William S. Babcock, "A Changing of the Christian God: The Doctrine of the Trinity in the Seventeenth Century," *Interpretation* 45 (1991): 133–46; Douglas Hedley, "Persons of Substance and the Cambridge Connection: Some Roots and Ramifications of the Trinitarian Controversy in Seventeenth-Century England," in *Socinianism and Arminianism: Antitrinitarians, Calvinists, and Cultural Exchange in Seventeenth-Century Europe*, ed. Martin Mulsow and Jan Rohls (Leiden: Brill, 2005), 225–40.

43. Colin E. Gunton, *The Promise of Trinitarian Theology* (Edinburgh: T&T Clark, 1991), 4.

44. Ibid., 31.

45. Jürgen Moltmann, *God in Creation: An Ecological Doctrine of Creation* (London: SCM Press, 1985).

ural theology that emerges from within a Trinitarian vision of reality, focusing on four points of particular significance.

1. TRINITARIANISM AND A SELF-REVEALING GOD

This is one of the most fundamental insights of the theological vision of Karl Barth.[46] There is the most intimate of relations between the actuality of God's self-revelation and a Trinitarian conception of God.[47] Barth, of course, is here to be seen as representing the characteristic trajectory of Christian thought; where Barth seems idiosyncratic, it is generally on account of the specific historical circumstances associated with Trinitarian theology in the nineteenth century, especially those arising from the revival of the doctrine within the German idealist tradition in response to the somewhat truncated vision of God offered by the Enlightenment.

Most forms of English Deism appear to have proposed a God who could be found and known (though perhaps more cognitively than relationally) through human inquiry and investigation. John Locke (1632–1704), for example, insisted that human beings "have Light enough to lead them to the Knowledge of their Maker, and the sight of their own Duties."[48] For Ralph Cudworth (1617–88), nature is "printed all over with the passive characters and impressions of divine wisdom and goodness."[49] Humans develop the notion of God by observation of, and reflection upon, what they observe in nature. There is no need for God to indulge in self-disclosure; humanity has been created with whatever epistemic capacities might be required to discover God and to discern what moral obligations this imposed upon them. Christianity is thus to be seen as a republication or an elaboration (some argued, a priest-ridden distortion) of the primal religion of nature.[50]

In marked contrast, a Trinitarian vision of God affirms the actuality of divine revelation in "God's two books," Scripture and nature. That God can be known through both (although in different manners and to different extents) is itself understood to be a consequence of God's decision that God is to be known in this manner. The one and only God, who both creates and redeems, has chosen to self-disclose in Scripture and in the natural order, for those who have eyes to see. In both cases, recognition of revelation as such depends upon reading these

---

46. See esp. the analysis in Rowan Williams, "Barth on the Triune God," in *Karl Barth: Studies of His Theological Method*, ed. S. W. Sykes (Oxford: Clarendon Press, 1979), 147–93.

47. One of the best introductions to this theme in Barth's thought is John Webster, *Barth*, 2nd ed. (London: Continuum, 2004), 57–60.

48. John Locke, *Essay concerning Human Understanding*, 1.1.5.

49. See the discussion in Sarah Hutton, "Ralph Cudworth, God, Mind and Nature," in *Religion, Reason, and Nature in Early Modern Europe*, ed. Ralph Crocker (Dordrecht: Kluwer Academic Publishers, 2001), 61–76.

50. Isabel Rivers, *Reason, Grace, and Sentiment: A Study of the Language of Religion and Ethics in England, 1660–1780*, 2 vols. (Cambridge: Cambridge University Press, 1991), 2:7–84.

texts in the right manners—a point echoed in Barth's nuanced idea of "revealed-ness [*Offenbarkeit*]." The same God who reveals is also embedded in the process of interpretation that enables revelation to be recognized as revelation.[51]

The following simplified structure may help an appreciation of the importance of this point. Deism holds that God created the world; theism holds that God created the world and continues to direct it through divine providence; Trinitarianism holds that God created the world, continues to direct it through divine providence, and guides the interpreters of both the books of nature and Scripture through the illumination of the Holy Spirit. This is perhaps seen at its clearest in Karl Barth's theology of the Trinity, where the element of the proper interpretation of God's actions becomes of controlling importance. The extent of God's involvement in the world is thus extended to include the illumination of the human interpreter, whether this is the reader of Scripture or the observer of nature.

Revelation is thus not limited to the divine self-disclosure, but to the matrix of actions and frameworks which enable this self-disclosure to be recognized as such and appropriated as revelation. This matrix includes the social embodiments of the Christian tradition—such as worship, the recital of creeds, and the public reading of Scripture—and the influence of God, whether this is understood to be mediated personally through the Holy Spirit or corporately through the church.[52] A Trinitarian vision of God thus extends, in ways that theology seeks to clarify, to embrace the human activity of interpretation of both the world and Scripture.

2. THE DOCTRINE OF CREATION EX NIHILO

One of the most important points of demarcation between Christianity and Judaism lies in their understandings of the concept of "creation." The canonical texts of the Old Testament typically portray creation in terms of ordering a pre-existing chaos, or defeating chaotic forces which threaten to destabilize the cosmos.[53] The essential point is that creation is understood, not so much as the bringing into existence of a world from nothing, but the ordering or "making good" of an existing chaotic realm, often depicted by using the imagery of the

51. See the points made by Lou Ann Trost, "Theology's Need for a New Interpretation of Nature: Correlate of the Doctrine of Grace," *Dialog: A Journal of Theology* 46 (2007): 246–54.

52. On Barth, see George Hunsinger, "The Mediator of Communion: Karl Barth's Doctrine of the Holy Spirit," in *Cambridge Companion to Karl Barth*, ed. John Webster (Cambridge: Cambridge University Press, 2000), 177–94. More generally, see the points raised in Gavin D'Costa, "Revelation, Scripture and Tradition: Some Comments on John Webster's Conception of 'Holy Scripture,'" *International Journal of Systematic Theology* 6 (2004): 337–50.

53. For a recent survey, see Terence E. Fretheim, *God and World in the Old Testament: A Relational Theology of Creation* (Nashville: Abingdon Press, 2005). Other studies of note here include John Day, *God's Conflict with the Dragon: Echoes of a Canaanite Myth in the Old Testament* (Cambridge: Cambridge University Press, 1985); Bernhard W. Anderson, *From Creation to New Creation: Old Testament Perspectives* (Minneapolis: Fortress, 1994).

sea.[54] In marked contrast, Christianity rapidly developed a notion of creation ex nihilo, largely in response to certain New Testament texts which strongly encouraged such an idea.[55] Judaism, however, retained its emphasis on creation as ordering an existing reality until the sixteenth century.[56] This approach allowed Jewish philosophers and theologians to emphasize the rationality of the world, since God could be thought of as having "impressed" laws which had their origin and character in the uncreated realm of the Godhead itself into the created order.

At one level, this notion of creation could serve as the basis of a type of natural theology. Reflection on an ordered creation naturally evolves into the postulation of an ordering agent, and ultimately (though not without some difficulties) to a creator God. Yet the notion of *creatio ex nihilo* introduces a new element into any approach to natural theology. This point is explored from the standpoint of comparative religious studies by Charles Long. In an important study of the motif of what he terms the "creation-from-nothing myth" within a wide range of religious traditions, Long suggested that such approaches were characterized by four specific features.[57] First, the god who creates is affirmed to be all-powerful. Neither this power nor the work of creation is assigned to an inferior being. Second, this creator god is held to exist before the creation itself. There is no other being, power, or created entity which exists before God. Third, the divine act of creation is to be considered as conscious, ordered, and deliberate. Creation is thus conceived as a purposeful and directed action, revealing a plan of action. Fourth, the Creator is to be regarded as free of limitations imposed by what Long terms the "inertia of a prior reality."

Long is concerned to offer a phenomenological account of this approach and to identify its general religious implications, rather than comment on or defend the distinctive themes of the Christian tradition.[58] Nevertheless, it will be clear that his disinterested analysis highlights the implications of such a theology of creation for a natural theology. This point was made with particular clarity by the English philosopher Michael Beresford Foster (1903–59) during the 1930s. Foster argued that certain themes of a distinctively Christian understanding of nature were of importance, both to the historical question of the evolution of the natural sciences in the West, and to the more general question of the relation of Christian theology and the natural sciences.[59] Although Foster's historical

---

54. David T. Tsumura, *The Earth and the Waters in Genesis 1 and 2: A Linguistic Investigation* (Sheffield: Sheffield Academic Press, 1989).

55. See the analysis in Gerhard May, *Creatio ex Nihilo: the Doctrine of 'Creation out of Nothing' in Early Christian Thought* (Edinburgh: T&T Clark, 1995). The continuity between the New Testament and this early Christian doctrine is, in my view, rather more marked than May allows.

56. Hava Tirosh-Samuelson, "Theology of Nature in Sixteenth-Century Italian Jewish Philosophy," *Science in Context* 10 (1997): 529–70.

57. Charles Long, *Alpha: The Myths of Creation* (New York: George Braziller, 1963), 148–62.

58. Long regards Judaism as representing the "creation-from-nothing myth," which is open to question: see his discussion at ibid., 159–62.

59. Michael B. Foster, "The Christian Doctrine of Creation and the Rise of Modern Science," *Mind* 43 (1934): 446–68; idem, "Christian Theology and Modern Science of Nature (I)," *Mind* 44 (1935): 439–66; idem, "Christian Theology and Modern Science of Nature (II)," *Mind* 45 (1936): 1–27.

explanation of the emergence of the natural sciences in a Christian context is regarded as carrying substantially less weight than he imagined, one of his central theological points remains of crucial importance: the capacity of the created order to render the rationality of God.

Foster explores this point by comparing the Christian doctrine of creation ex nihilo with a Platonic notion of creation through a demiurge. "Because a Demiurge has to work in an alien material," Foster argues, "he never wholly realizes in it the idea which his reason conceives, so that the observer of the product, the object of whose search is to discover the idea of the producer, can never discover in the material product the object of his search."[60] In other words, a creator who is confronted with essentially intractable raw material is limited in terms of the manner in which his own nature can be expressed in the ensuing creation. Nature can only render the character of God to a limited extent. However, Foster points out, "a divine Creator who is not limited by a recalcitrant material can embody his ideas in nature with the same perfection in which they are present to his intellect."

When applied to natural theology, this leads to the notion that the created order is capable of rendering the character of God, especially God's wisdom, goodness, and beauty. This does not mean that one can read such attributes out of the natural order unproblematically and unambiguously. Nevertheless, a theological foundation for such an approach has been laid. It is evident, for example, in the poetry of Gerard Manley Hopkins, who deploys the ultimately *theological* notions of "inscape" and "instress" to refer to the inward identity of created entities and their capacity to signify their creator.[61] Similarly, it leads to Emil Brunner's emphatic assertion that God has bestowed upon his works "a permanent capacity for revelation [*dauernde Offenbarungsmächigkeit*]" which can be discerned through human contemplation of "the traces of his own nature which [God] has expressed and made known in them."[62]

3. HUMANITY AND THE IMAGO DEI

Both Christianity and Judaism share the insight that humanity is the bearer of the "image of God" (Genesis 1:27)[63] and show a propensity to avoid crude inter-

60. Foster, "Christian Theology and Modern Science of Nature (II)," 14–15.

61. Hopkins's notion of "inscape" is best conceived as "the unified complex of those sensible qualities of the object of perception that strike us as inseparably belonging to and most typical of it, so that through the knowledge of this unified complex of sense-data we may gain an insight into the individual essence of the object": William A. M. Peters, *Gerard Manley Hopkins: A Critical Essay towards the Understanding of His Poetry* (London: Oxford University Press, 1948), 1–2. For Hopkins's approach to natural theology, see McGrath, *Open Secret*, 133–40.

62. Emil Brunner, "Natur und Gnade: Zum Gespräch mit Karl Barth," in *Ein offenes Wort*, vol. 1, *Vorträge und Aufsätze 1917–1934*, ed. Rudolf Wehrli (Zurich: Theologischer Verlag, 1981), 333–66, esp. 345.

63. For the interpretation of this text, see James Barr, "The Image of God in the Book of Genesis: A Study of Terminology," *Bulletin of the John Rylands Library* 51 (1968): 11–26; Tryggve N. D. Mettinger, "Abbild oder Urbild? 'Imago Dei' in traditionsgeschichtlicher Sicht," *Zeitschrift für*

pretations of the idea as a "divinized humanity," such as those which gained influence in secular Hellenistic circles in the early Christian era.[64] Jewish interpretation of humanity's creation in the image of God tended to avoid any suggestion that this established a direct correlation with God, perhaps reflecting a fear of some form of anthropomorphism ensuing. Some exegetes argue that God created humanity in the image of the angels, interpreting the context of Genesis 1:27 to imply that God's words are addressed to an angelic audience. Others maintained that the text is to be interpreted as implying that humanity was created according to some image that was specific to it, thus distinguishing humanity from the remainder of creation.[65]

Christian theologians, however, saw no difficulty in interpreting this passage as proposing a direct link between the Creator and the height of the creation. In part, this reflects the New Testament's theological endorsement and christological elaboration of the notion, evident in (though not limited to) the Pauline assertion that Jesus Christ is "the image [*eikon*] of the invisible God" (Colossians 1:15).[66] In the light of this christological reconfiguration of the idea, Christian theologians naturally interpreted the notion of the *imago Dei* in soteriological and incarnational terms, ultimately expressed within a Trinitarian context.[67]

Partly reflecting the influence of Philo,[68] the notion came increasingly to be interpreted as designating human rationality, especially its capacity to discern the divine or transcendent within the world. Philo interprets the biblical idea of the creation of humanity "after the image of God" to mean that humanity itself is not an immediate image of God; rather, it is created after the immediate image, which is the *logos*. This idea was taken up especially within the Alexandrian tradition, which increasingly emphasized the correlation between the "rational [*logikos*]" nature of the created order, the capacity of the human mind to discern this, and the incarnation of the *logos* in Jesus Christ. The same "rational" order

---

Alttestamentlicher Wissenschaft 86 (1974): 403–24; A. Jónsson Gunnlaugur and S. Cheney Michael, *The Image of God: Genesis 1:26–28 in a Century of Old Testament Research* (Stockholm: Almqvist & Wiksell International, 1988).

64. The classic study of this development is Carl R. Holladay, *Theios Anēr in Hellenistic-Judaism: A Critique of the Use of This Category in New Testament Christology* (Missoula, MT: Scholars Press, 1977).

65. See the analysis in Alexander Altmann, "'Homo Imago Dei' in Jewish and Christian Theology," *Journal of Religion* 48 (1968): 235–59. The author's views on the authorship and dating of certain targums almost certainly need revision: see, e.g., Beverly P. Mortensen, *The Priesthood in Targum Pseudo-Jonathan: Renewing the Profession* (Leiden: Brill, 2006).

66. See the detailed analysis in Jacob Jervell, *Imago Dei: Gen 1, 26f. im Spätjudentum, in der Gnosis und in den paulinischen Briefen* (Göttingen: Vandenhoeck & Ruprecht, 1960). For a briefer account, see Herman Ridderbos, *Paul: An Outline of His Theology* (Grand Rapids: Eerdmans, 1997), 68–78.

67. See, e.g., Randall Zachman, "Jesus Christ as the Image of God in Calvin's Theology," *Calvin Theological Journal* 25 (1990): 46–52; F. Leron Shults, "Constitutive Relationality in Anthropology and Trinity: Shaping and *Imago Dei* in Barth and Pannenberg," *Neue Zeitschrift für systematische Theologie und Religionsphilosophie* 39 (1997): 304–22.

68. Stephen M. Wylen, *The Jews in the Time of Jesus: An Introduction* (New York: Paulist, 1996), 40–41.

that was embedded within creation, and the human mind as expressive of the *imago Dei*, was embodied in Christ.

Athanasius of Alexandria is one of the best representatives of this approach. In his *De incarnatione*, Athanasius sets out his *logikos* understanding of humanity:[69]

> God did not create humanity to be like the irrational animals of the earth, but created them according to his own image, and shared with them the power of his own Word, and thus possessing as it were a kind of reflection of the Word, and being made rational, they might be able to remain forever in blessedness, living the true life which belongs to the saints in paradise.

Athanasius's concept of the *imago Dei* is thus strongly shaped by his overarching theology of the *logos* as the agent of creation. While all of nature has been brought into existence by the *logos*, and thus may be said to bear its imprint, humanity alone within the creation possesses the capacity to reason according to that *logos*. Athanasius thus argues that God "made humanity, through His own Word our Savior Jesus Christ, after his own image, and constituted humanity so that it was able to see and know realities by means of this assimilation to Himself."[70]

Although Athanasius is clearly working within an implicitly Trinitarian understanding of the *imago Dei*, the full and explicit articulation of this approach is best seen in the writings of Augustine of Hippo.[71] Since humanity is created in the image of God, and God is Trinitarian, Augustine argues that humanity bears *vestigial Trinitatis*—"footprints of the Trinity."[72] "There is," he comments, "a kind of image of the Trinity in the mind itself." Since humanity has been created by a Trinitarian God, this is reflected in the impression left upon humanity—above all, on its rational character. "The image of its creator is to be found in the rational or intellectual soul of humanity."[73] A Trinitarian God is thus known in a Trinitarian manner.

The implications of such an approach for natural theology will be evident. Athanasius summarizes the central point as follows: humanity was created by God in such a way that, "by looking into the heights of heaven, and perceiving the harmony of creation, they might know its ruler, the Word of the Father, who, by his own providence over all things, makes the Father known to all."[74] Although Athanasius holds that human nature has been corrupted by sin, his understand-

---

69. Athanasius, *De incarnatione* 3.

70. Athanasius, *Contra Gentes* 2. For further comment, see Wolfgang A. Bienert, "Zur Logos-Christologie des Athanasius von Alexandrien in *Contra gentes* und *De incarnatione*," in *Papers Presented to the Tenth International Conference on Patristic Studies*, vol. 2, ed. E. A. Livingstone, Studia patristica 21 (Louvain: Peeters, 1989), 402–19.

71. Roland J. Teske, "The Image and Likeness of God in St. Augustine's *De Genesi ad litteram liber imperfectus*," *Augustinianum* 30 (1990): 441–51.

72. Augustine, *De Trinitate* 9.12.18. For an excellent commentary, see Michael René Barnes, "Rereading Augustine's Theology of the Trinity," in *The Trinity*, ed. Stephen T. Davis, Daniel Kendall, and Gerald O'Collins (Oxford: Oxford University Press, 2001), 145–76.

73. Augustine, *De Trinitate* 16.4.6. For comment, see John Sullivan, *The Image of God: The Doctrine of St. Augustine and Its Influence* (Dubuque, IA: Priory Press, 1963).

74. Athanasius, *De incarnatione* 12.

ing of the dialectic of nature and grace is such that humanity retains a God-given capacity to discern its creator within the created order.[75]

This point is of importance in dealing with one of the most discussed features of the universe: its intelligibility. Scientific advance has disclosed the fundamental explicability of much of the natural world. While some might see this as eliminating any notion of mystery,[76] others have rightly pointed out that it raises a far deeper question: why can we explain things at all? As Albert Einstein pointed out in 1936,[77] "the eternal mystery of the world is its comprehensibility." To speak of "comprehensibility," even in its most modest sense, implies

> the production of some sort of order among sense impressions, this order being produced by the creation of general concepts, relations between these concepts, and by relations between the concepts and sense experience, these relations being determined in any possible manner. It is in this sense that the world of our sense experiences is comprehensible. The fact that it is comprehensible is a miracle.

For Einstein, explicability itself clearly requires explanation. The most incomprehensible thing about the universe is that it is comprehensible. The *intelligibility* of the natural world, demonstrated by the natural sciences, raises the fundamental question as to why there is such a fundamental resonance between human minds and the structures of the universe. From a Trinitarian perspective, this "congruence between our minds and the universe, between the rationality experienced within and the rationality observed without,"[78] is to be explained by the rationality of God as creator of both the fundamental ordering of nature and the human observer of nature.

4. THE ECONOMY OF SALVATION

The notion of the "economy of salvation" is traditionally attributed to Irenaeus of Lyons.[79] Reacting against gnostic interpretations of salvation history, Irenaeus laid

75. Khaled E. Anatolios, *Athanasius* (London: Routledge, 2004), 41–43. The importance of this theme of fallen humanity reflecting on nature is a major theme in Peter Harrison's magisterial study of the early modern period, demonstrating how its approaches to the study of nature were directly informed by theological discussions about the fall of humanity, particularly the extent to which the mind and the senses had been damaged or compromised by that primeval event: Peter Harrison, *The Fall of Man and the Foundations of Science* (Cambridge: Cambridge University Press, 2007), esp. 186–233.

76. Richard Dawkins, *Unweaving the Rainbow: Science, Delusion and the Appetite for Wonder* (London: Penguin Books, 1998), 114–79.

77. Albert Einstein, "Physics and Reality," *Journal of the Franklin Institute* 221 (1936): 349–89, esp. 351.

78. John Polkinghorne, *Science and Creation: The Search for Understanding* (London: SPCK, 1988), 29. See further James F. Moore, "How Religious Tradition Survives in the World of Science: John Polkinghorne and Norbert Samuelson," *Zygon* 32 (1997): 115–24.

79. For an excellent analysis of Irenaeus's statement of the concept, see John Behr, *Asceticism and Anthropology in Irenaeus and Clement* (Oxford: Oxford University Press, 2000), 34–85; Osborn, *Irenaeus of Lyons*, 51–141.

out a panoramic vision of the "economy of salvation," insisting that the entire breadth of history, from creation to consummation, was the work of one and the same triune God. Thus Irenaeus adopts a Trinitarian approach to creation, describing the Son and Spirit as the "two hands of God" in this process.[80] The enterprise of natural theology takes place within the flux of the economy of salvation, not at its points of origination or consummation. This leads to the theologically significant conclusion—which clearly requires scientific comment—that a fallen humanity reflects on a fallen nature.[81]

Hints of the importance of this consideration can be seen within the New Testament. For example, it is well known that Paul makes an appeal to creation as the basis of a knowledge of God. Yet while Paul clearly holds that God can be known through the creation (Romans 1), at other points he qualifies this by referring to the "groaning" of the creation (Romans 8).[82] The created order is to be seen as in transition, from what it once was to what it finally will become. There is a profoundly eschatological dimension to an authentically Christian natural theology, because the natural order should be observed in the light of its goal, not merely of its origination. Paul's statements can thus not only be interpreted in terms of the fall of creation from its original state, but also as an extension of the Old Testament prophetic theme of the hope of the future renewal and restoration of creation.[83]

The importance of contextualizing the enterprise of natural theology within a Trinitarian economy of salvation is perhaps best appreciated by comparing this with the somewhat attenuated alternatives proposed by certain forms of Deism.[84] On this reading of things, God created the world and endowed nature with the appropriate capacity to develop and function without the need for any continuing divine superintendence or interference.[85] There are many difficulties with this view. For example, it encouraged the emergence of a functional atheism, since

---

80. O'Collins, *Tripersonal God*, 194–95.

81. For a theological discussion of the theme of fallenness, see the magisterial study of Julius Gross, *Geschichte des Erbsündendogmas: Ein Beitrag zur Geschichte des Problems vom Ursprung des Übels* (Munich: Reinhardt, 1960); Augustine is of particular importance in this development (69–255). The scientific case for speaking of the "fallenness" of nature or humanity is more complex and is addressed in Timothy Anders, *The Evolution of Evil: An Inquiry into the Ultimate Origins of Human Suffering* (Chicago: Open Court, 1994); Daryl P. Domning and Monika Hellwig, *Original Selfishness: Original Sin and Evil in the Light of Evolution* (Aldershot: Ashgate, 2006), 139–80.

82. Jam Lambrecht, "The Groaning of Creation," *Louvain Studies* 15 (1990): 3–18.

83. Laurie J. Braaten, "All Creation Groans: Romans 8:22 in Light of the Biblical Sources," *Horizons in Biblical Theology* 28 (2006): 131–59.

84. For Deism's rejection of Trinitarianism, see Duncan Reid, *Energies of the Spirit: Trinitarian Models in Eastern Orthodox and Western Theology* (Atlanta: Scholars Press, 1997), 22–25. For Deism's attitude to natural theology, see Peter Harrison, "Natural Theology, Deism, and Early Modern Science," in *Science, Religion, and Society: An Encyclopedia of History, Culture and Controversy*, ed. Arri Eisen and Gary Laderman (New York: Sharp, 2006), 426–33.

85. For reflection on the changing role of previously fixed theological assumptions in the seventeenth-century development of natural science, see Peter Harrison, "Physico-Theology and the Mixed Sciences: The Role of Theology in Early Modern Natural Philosophy," in *The Science of Nature in the Seventeenth Century*, ed. Peter Anstey and John Schuster (Dordrecht: Springer-Verlag, 2005), 165–83.

God was, to all intents and purposes, absent from the world.[86] From the stand-point of natural theology, however, this approach encourages the idea that a direct equivalence, or at least a near equivalence, may be posited between the empirical reality designated "nature" and the primordial creation that God declared to be "good" (Genesis 1:12).

The plausibility of this idea would be fatally eroded through scientific advance. In the eighteenth century, it became increasingly clear that, whatever the expla-nation might be, the surface of Earth had changed significantly over time. Geol-ogy proposed a history of Earth which could only be reconciled with some difficulty with traditional readings of the Christian Bible. It was little wonder that John Ruskin found his childhood evangelical beliefs being shattered by the geol-ogists' hammers: "If only the Geologists would let me alone, I could do very well, but those dreadful Hammers! I hear the clink of them at the end of every cadence of the Bible verses."[87]

More significant, however, the rise of Darwinism destroyed the plausibility of any traditional "argument from design" which presupposed that empirical nature—what is presently observed—can be equated with God's primordial cre-ation.[88] William Paley's *Natural Theology* proved vulnerable at this point, pre-cisely because Paley assumed that the natural world had remained more or less constant since its creation.

The theological notion of the "economy of salvation" does not entail the phys-ical alteration of the natural world over time, although it can easily be stated in forms that are entirely consistent with an evolutionary perspective, whether cos-mological, geological, or biological. The relevance of the notion for natural the-ology is that it acknowledges that both the human observer and the natural world observed are located *in hoc interim saeculo* (Augustine of Hippo)[89]—in other words, at a point that is theologically distant and removed from the creation that was declared to be "good." That creation now groans, and those groanings are observed by those whose judgments are clouded and obscured by sin.[90] From this perspective, it is a theological inevitability that a naïve observer will interpret the natural world in such a way that may lead to idolatry, heterodoxy, or some form of paganism. Nature must be "seen" in the right way for it to act as a wit-ness to, or conduit for, the Trinitarian God of the Christian tradition.[91] Like any

86. For this idea of God being absent in Hobbes, see Richard Tuck, "The 'Christian Atheism' of Thomas Hobbes," in *Atheism from the Reformation to the Enlightenment*, ed. Michael Hunter and David Wootton (Oxford: Clarendon Press, 1992), 102–20.

87. John Ruskin, *Works*, ed. E. T. Cook and A. Wedderburn, 39 vols. (London: Allen, 1903–12), 36:115.

88. For an excellent study of these developments, see John Hedley Brooke, "Science and the For-tunes of Natural Theology: Some Historical Perspectives," *Zygon* 24 (1989): 3–22; idem, *Science and Religion: Some Historical Perspectives* (Cambridge: Cambridge University Press, 1991).

89. Augustine, *De civitate Dei* 11.1.

90. For this point in Augustine, see Gillian R. Evans, *Augustine on Evil* (Cambridge: Cambridge University Press, 1990), 73–74; in Calvin, see Paul Helm, "John Calvin, the *Sensus Divinitatis* and the Noetic Effects of Sin," *International Journal of Philosophy of Religion* 43 (1998): 87–107.

91. This is the central theme of my 2008 Riddell Memorial Lectures, published as *The Open Secret*.

text, nature can be translated and interpreted in a multiplicity of manners; the question of how it is *rightly* to be interpreted cannot be overlooked or marginalized, as older approaches to natural theology tended to do.

Our insistence that a natural theology is shaped by an ontology within which the notion of the "economy of salvation" is firmly embedded allows us to address the specific concerns raised by Stanley Hauerwas and Eberhard Jüngel. Where, they ask (though in their different ways), is the cross of Christ to be found in a natural theology? Both correctly discern that a traditional natural theology— such as that criticized by Karl Barth—has severe difficulties with the inclusion of any reference to the cross.[92] Yet a Trinitarian natural theology brings to the observation and interpretation of nature an understanding of God that is deeply shaped by the revelational and soteriological implications of the cross. A Trinitarian engagement with nature is already marked with the sign of the cross and is thus especially attentive to the problem of suffering in nature.

Undertaking natural theology within the Trinitarian framework of the economy of salvation thus allows the Christian interpreter of nature to accommodate the moral and aesthetic ambivalence of nature by contextualizing its observation. The force of this point is considerable. Unless constrained by an excessive cognitive bias, the observer of nature will observe what can only be interpreted as beauty and ugliness, joy and pain, good and evil. To adapt a theological slogan from Martin Luther, nature is *simul bona et mala*. A naive natural theology can only reflect this ambiguity. How can the existence of a good God be inferred from such ambivalence? When all is said and done, there are really only two options at our disposal: turn a blind eye to the aspects of nature that cause us moral or aesthetic discomfort; or develop a theological framework that allows us to account for evil, while affirming the primordial goodness of nature. The first approach, in addition to being intellectually disreputable, causes considerable psychological discomfort, giving rise to a potentially destructive "cognitive dissonance" between theory and observation.[93] We are thus left with only one viable way of handling the issue: developing a framework which allows this moral ambiguity to be observed, honored, and interpreted.[94]

A Trinitarian "economy of salvation" offers such a framework. Christian theology holds that its vision of reality offered a compelling imaginative resource, fully capable of confronting the spectrum of complexities of human existence and experience without intellectual evasion or misrepresentation. It affirms that God

92. See Christoph Kock, *Natürliche Theologie: Ein evangelischer Streitbegriff* (Neukirchen-Vluyn: Neukirchener Verlag, 2001), 5–8, 400–410.

93. For the original statements of the theory, see Leon Festinger, *A Theory of Cognitive Dissonance* (Stanford, CA: Stanford University Press, 1957).

94. For this theme in Augustine, see Roland J. Teske, "Augustine of Hippo on Seeing with the Eyes of the Mind," in *Ambiguity in Western Thought*, ed. Craig J. N. de Paulo, Patrick Messina, and Marc Stier (New York: Peter Lang, 2005), 72–87, 221–26. Teske has also written with insight on Augustine's views on original human nature and its implications for an understanding of the economy of salvation: see Roland J. Teske, "St. Augustine's View of the Human Condition in *De Genesi contra Manichaeos*," *Augustinian Studies* 22 (1991): 141–55.

created all things good and that they will finally be restored to goodness. Yet at the present, it insists that good and evil coexist in the world, as wheat and weeds grow together in the same field (Matthew 13:24–43). Without collapsing one into the other, it allows us to locate good and evil within the context of the theological trajectory of creation, fall, incarnation, redemption, and consummation.

To explore the potential of such an approach, let us consider a passage from the final volume of John Ruskin's *Modern Painters* (1860), in which he reflects on a landscape in the Scottish Highlands.[95] Ruskin insists that God does not wish us to see only the "bright side" of nature. God has given us "two sides" of nature and intends us to see them both. Those who see nature only in positive terms are failing to see it as it actually is. To make this point, Ruskin points to an unnamed "zealous" Scottish clergyman who was determined to see the landscape as a witness to the "goodness of God." And so he described it in terms of "nothing but sunshine, and fresh breezes, and bleating lambs, and clean tartans, and all kinds of pleasantness."

Yet Ruskin dismisses this as inept. The zealous clergyman has chosen to see what he wishes to see, not to see what is actually there. For Ruskin, "to see clearly" lies at the heart of poetry, prophecy, and religion.[96] How can one live with such a blatant failure to see clearly? How can nature be sunlit without there being shadows? Ruskin offers an alternative viewing of a Highland landscape, stressing its moral and aesthetic ambivalence:

> It is a little valley of soft turf, enclosed in its narrow oval by jutting rocks and broad flakes of nodding fern. From one side of it to the other winds, serpentine, a clear brown stream, drooping into quicker ripple as it reaches the end of the oval field, and then, first islanding a purple and white rock with an amber pool, it dashes away into a narrow fall of foam under a thicket of mountain-ash and alder. The autumn sun, low but clear, shines on the scarlet ash-berries and on the golden birch-leaves, which, fallen here and there, when the breeze has not caught them, rest quiet in the crannies of the purple rock.

Up to this point, Ruskin echoes the somewhat one-sided sentiments of the Scottish parson. Yet the shadows, he now insists, must be seen. Ruskin's mood alters as he describes the less-attractive aspects of the scene:

> Beside the rock, in the hollow under the thicket, the carcase of a ewe, drowned in the last flood, lies nearly bare to the bone, its white ribs protruding through the skin, raven-torn; and the rags of its wool still flickering from the branches that first stayed it as the stream swept it down. . . . At the turn of the brook, I see a man fishing, with a boy and a dog—a picturesque

---

95. Ruskin, *Works*, 7:268. For comment on Ruskin's growing sense of the fallenness or chaos of natural landscapes around this time, see Charles T. Daugherty, "Of Ruskin's Gardens," in *Myth and Symbol: Critical Approaches and Applications*, ed. Northrop Frye and Bernice Slote (Lincoln: University of Nebraska, 1963), 141–51, esp. 142–44.

96. Ruskin, *Works*, 5:333.

and pretty group enough certainly, if they had not been there all day starving. I know them, and I know the dog's ribs also, which are nearly as bare as the dead ewe's; and the child's wasted shoulders, cutting his old tartan jacket through, so sharp are they.

Ruskin's point cannot be challenged, and there is nothing to be gained by gilding his lily through further comment. There is a shadowy side to nature, which cannot be denied or softened by even the most zealous romantic imagination. Yet this is the "nature" that a natural theology must address—a harsh empirical reality, not the idealized fiction of an armchair theologian. Nature must be observed and interpreted from a Trinitarian perspective, which allows us to see the natural world as decayed and ambivalent—as a morally and aesthetically variegated entity whose goodness and beauty are often opaque and hidden, yet are nevertheless irradiated with the hope of transformation. Such an approach does not filter out theological inconveniences, but seeks to contextualize them within an overall vision of the history of the natural order.

There is much more that needs to be said, both about the moral and aesthetic complexity of nature in particular, and about the characteristics of a Trinitarian approach to nature in general. What has been said is intended to illustrate, not exhaust, such an account of things, pointing to its potential to illuminate and thus allow us to "see clearly" (Ruskin).

Yet sometimes the process of "seeing" nature leads to the realization that something is not quite what was expected. In what follows, we shall consider Charles Peirce's notion of "surprising facts" and their importance for scientific explanation, especially in relation to anthropic phenomena.

Chapter 7

Surprising Facts

Counterfactuals and Natural Theology

The great American pragmatic philosopher Charles Peirce held that the observation of "surprising facts" was the stimulus that catalyzed the process of "forming explanatory hypotheses" that he termed "abduction." This sense of "puzzlement" appears to be envisaged as something intuitive, rather than deductive. Abduction, for Peirce, "comes to us like a flash," as an "act of insight." It is, nevertheless, elicited by observation and the process of reflection that it stimulates—above all, when something that is observed is held to be puzzling. It must be understood that Peirce is not suggesting that the only valid forms of abduction derive from the observation of surprising phenomena. The abductive process is as valid for surprising as it is for routine observations. Rather, Peirce is making the entirely reasonable point that it is things that surprise us that often trigger off lines of thought that lead to new discoveries or perspectives.

Historical illustrations of this point are legion. An excellent example lies to hand in the work of Charles Darwin, whose theory of evolution can be seen as an attempt to explain observations that were "surprising" when viewed in the context of prevailing theories of biological origins, such as those associated with William Paley or the Bridgewater Treatises. Darwin's son later recalled his father's habit of not allowing such anomalies (or "exceptions") to pass, believing that their accumulated significance pointed to the need, and even the form, of a new theory.[1]

> There was one quality of mind which seemed to be of special and extreme advantage in leading him to make discoveries. It was the power of never letting exceptions pass unnoticed. Everybody notices a fact as an exception when it is striking or frequent, but he had a special instinct for arresting an exception. A point apparently slight and unconnected with his present work is passed over by many a man almost unconsciously with some half-considered explanation, which is in fact no explanation. It was just these things that he seized on to make a start from.

The importance of this point was appreciated by William Paley, even if he did not frame the issue quite in Peirce's terms. The central image that defined Paley's approach to natural theology is that of a "surprising" observation: a watch found lying on a heath. The presence of the watch, Paley argues, clearly needs to be explained in a way that the presence of a stone does not.[2] One expects to find stones and other natural objects in such a context; the watch, however, stands out as being different. Paley is perfectly prepared to accept that an account might be given of how the stone came to be there; his point is that the corresponding account of how the watch came to be present involves actors and agencies that do not need to be invoked to explain the presence of a stone.

Paley's approach to natural theology is now widely (though not universally) regarded as outmoded and unhelpful.[3] Yet its controlling image points to the capacity of the human imagination to identify counterintuitive presences and phenomena—things that surprise us because they are counter to normal expectations, and hence force us to ask whether there is another way of looking at them. Might they seem "surprising" because we view them through a predetermined filter or lens, which cannot adequately accommodate them, and hence might require revision, if not abandonment? Is there a standpoint from which they would *not* seem strange or surprising? Is there another way of looking at the same things, which might even

---

1. Francis Darwin, "Reminiscences of My Father's Everyday Life," in *Charles Darwin: His Life Told in an Autobiographical Chapter*, ed. Francis Darwin (London: John Murray, 1892), 66–103.

2. Paley's own account of the distinction may be noted: "In crossing a heath, suppose I pitched my foot against a *stone*, and were asked how the stone came to be there: I might possibly answer, that, for any thing I knew to the contrary, it had lain there for ever; nor would it perhaps be very easy to show the absurdity of this answer. But suppose I had found a *watch* upon the ground, and it should be inquired how the watch happened to be in that place; I should hardly think of the answer which I had before given,—that, for any thing I knew, the watch might have always been there. Yet why should not this answer serve for the watch as well as for the stone?" *The Works of William Paley* (London: William Orr, 1844), 25.

3. There is a significant yet generally overlooked critique of Paley's approach in Dorothy L. Sayers, "Creative Mind," in *Letters of a Diminished Church* (Nashville: W Publishing, 2004), 35–48. Although not referring to Paley specifically, Sayers makes the general point that certain conceptual difficulties which arise "if one thinks of God as a mechanician" disappear if God is conceived as a "creative artist" (41). For a fuller outworking of this model of God, see the classic work by Dorothy L. Sayers, *The Mind of the Maker* (London: Methuen, 1941).

lead to them being expected or anticipated? Resonance between theory and observation does not prove that a theory is true; it is, however, highly suggestive.

This work is concerned with identifying and exploring a series of such "surprising facts," observed within the natural world, which force further discussion of some of the most fundamental questions of life. The heavily freighted vocabulary of "fine-tuning" is widely used to express the idea that the universe appears to have possessed certain qualities from the moment of its inception which were favorable to the production of intelligent life on Earth at this point in cosmic history, life capable of reflecting on the implications of its existence. Nature's fundamental constants turn out to have been fine-tuned to reassuringly life-friendly values. The existence of carbon-based life on Earth depends upon a delicate balance of physical and cosmological forces and parameters, which are such that were any one of these quantities to be slightly altered, this balance would have been destroyed and life would not have come into existence.[4] Stephen Hawking sets out the basic problem in the following way:[5]

> Why is the universe so close to the dividing line between collapsing again and expanding indefinitely? In order to be as close as we are now, the rate of expansion early on had to be chosen fantastically accurately. If the rate of expansion one second after the Big Bang had been less by one part in 10^{10}, the universe would have collapsed after a few million years. If it had been greater by one part in 10^{10}, the universe would have been essentially empty after a few million years. In neither case would it have lasted long enough for life to develop. Thus one either has to appeal to the anthropic principle or find some physical explanation of why the universe is the way it is.

For theologians and philosophers unfamiliar with the mathematical annotation, Hawking is suggesting that a difference of *one part in ten billion* in the rate of primal cosmic expansion would be sufficient to prohibit the emergence of life.

Others have stressed the extraordinary sensitivity of the universe's fundamental characteristics or original conditions for the origins of cosmic life. Sir Martin Rees, Britain's Astronomer Royal and President of the Royal Society, has argued that the emergence of human life in the aftermath of the big bang is governed by a mere six numbers, each of which is so precisely determined that a minuscule variation in any one would have made both our universe and human life, as we now know them, impossible.[6] Roger Penrose also speaks of an "extraordinary degree of precision (or 'fine-tuning')" required for life.[7]

4. For standard discussions of these ideas, see John D. Barrow and Frank J. Tipler, *The Cosmological Anthropic Principle* (Oxford: Oxford University Press, 1986); George Greenstein, *The Symbiotic Universe: Life and Mind in the Cosmos* (New York: Morrow, 1988); John Gribbin and Martin Rees, *Cosmic Coincidences: Dark Matter, Mankind, and Anthropic Cosmology* (New York: Bantam Books, 1989); Paul Davies, *The Goldilocks Enigma: Why Is the Universe Just Right for Life?* (London: Allen Lane, 2006).

5. Stephen W. Hawking and Roger Penrose, *The Nature of Space and Time* (Princeton, NJ: Princeton University Press, 1996), 89–90.

6. Martin J. Rees, *Just Six Numbers: The Deep Forces That Shape the Universe* (London: Phoenix, 2000).

7. Roger Penrose, *The Road to Reality: A Complete Guide to the Laws of the Universe* (London: Jonathan Cape, 2004).

These observations are unquestionably surprising, save to those who have become so used to them that their power to astonish and evoke wonder has evaporated through overfamiliarity. Peirce would, not without reason, suggest that they call out for an explanation. So what may be inferred about the world in the light of these observations? And what criteria are to be used to establish which is the best such inference? These questions lie at the heart of this book.

So how might we go about exploring this question? What intellectual context is appropriate for the discussion of these issues? One of the most productive ways of engaging such questions is to employ counterfactual thinking—the envisaging of an alternative situation, in which fundamental parameters are altered. In an act of informed imagination, the scholar attempts to evaluate how this counterfactual world might appear, not in any hope of creating or inhabiting it, but in the expectation of clarifying the role of the altered parameter. In what follows, we shall consider the increasing importance being attached to counterfactual thinking, especially in history, its potential relevance for natural theology in general, and the theological evaluation of anthropic phenomena in particular.

COUNTERFACTUAL THINKING
AND THE NATURAL SCIENCES

Counterfactual thinking is an act of imagination—the construction and inhabitation of a world that did and does not exist, as a means of achieving a better understanding of the forces that shape the empirical world. An appeal to the "counterfactual imagination" is a normal part of social discourse and is widely perceived to be a normal, natural, and justified way of thinking.[8] In the New Testament, we find a classic example of such an approach in the account of the death of Lazarus found in John's Gospel: "Martha said to Jesus, 'Lord, if you had been here, my brother would not have died'" (John 11:21). Martha here creates a counterfactual alternative to actual situations by altering a single factor, which she believes to be mutable on the one hand and significant on the other.

The starting point for counterfactual thinking is the belief that things need not be as they actually are (or have been as they actually were). By conducting "thought experiments," it is possible to construct alternative scenarios, which allow the roles of specific actors, factors, and agencies and the generalities of happenstance in bringing about an existing situation to be better understood.[9] What would have happened if Charles I had won the English Civil War? If the Confederates had won the American Civil War? If Nazi Germany had defeated the Soviet Union

---

8. See Ruth M. J. Byrne, *The Rational Imagination: How People Create Alternatives to Reality* (Cambridge, MA: MIT Press, 2007), 3–14.

9. Denis J. Hilton, John I. McClure, and Ben R. Slugowski, "The Course of Events: Counterfactuals, Causal Sequences, and Explanation," in *The Psychology of Counterfactual Thinking*, ed. David R. Mandel, Denis J. Hilton, and Patrizia Catellani (London: Routledge, 2005), 44–60.

during the Second World War?[10] Or, to consider a more specifically theological issue, what difference would it have made to the religious history and intellectual development of the European church if the young Martin Luther had died—rather than merely been emotionally shaken—when thrown from his horse during the thunderstorm at Storterheim in June 1505? The question allows us to assess the importance of Luther as an individual to the emergence and shaping of the movement that is now retrospectively designated "the Reformation."[11]

Although counterfactual thinking has increasingly found a role in historical studies, the same is not yet true of the philosophy of science. Indeed, at first sight it might seem that counterfactual thinking has little role to play in the natural sciences, since these disciplines focus on the actual, observed world. The key issue concerns the explanation of what is observed, rather than speculation about what might have been observed. However, on reflection, the situation is not quite as straightforward as this naive empiricism might suggest.

Olbers's Paradox is a useful point at which to begin exploring this point.[12] In 1826, Heinrich Wilhelm Olbers formulated the question that proved such a powerful catalyst to thinking about some fundamental questions of astronomy. Why is the sky dark at night?[13] Olbers pointed out that a highly plausible counterfactual situation could easily be imagined, emphasizing the strangeness of what was actually observed. In what follows, we shall set out this paradox, highlighting the critical role played by counterfactual considerations.

The paradox arises, Olbers argues, precisely because the observed situation is seen to be unusual. So how does this perception of strangeness arise when there is no alternative observed reality? Because, Olbers argued, we are able to imagine a counterfactual situation which turns out to be highly theoretically plausible. The strangeness of what is observed is only appreciated when this is compared with its imaginary counterfactual counterpart, yet the process of comparison is both helpful and legitimate.

So how does Olbers construct his imaginary counterfactual scenario? Olbers followed a line of argument developed by Jean-Philippe Loys de Cheseaux of Lausanne (1718–51). Olbers assumed that the universe is static, uniform, and infinite. This means that Earth will be bombarded with light emitted from stars

10. For an extended range of possibilities, see Geoffrey Hawthorn, *Plausible Worlds: Possibility and Understanding in History and the Social Sciences* (Cambridge: Cambridge University Press, 1993), 1–37.

11. For an assessment of the scholarly debates over the inevitability of the Reformation, see Alister E. McGrath, *The Intellectual Origins of the European Reformation*, 2nd ed. (Oxford: Blackwell, 2003), 182–89.

12. For a basic introduction to the paradox, see Edward R. Harrison, *Cosmology: The Science of the Universe*, 2nd ed. (Cambridge: Cambridge University Press, 2000), 491–513.

13. The paradox was known before Olbers. For example, in his *Perfect Description of the Celestial Spheres* (1576), Thomas Digges argues that, contrary to Aristotle, the stars are randomly distributed throughout space. Noting that this implied that the night sky should be bright, he suggested that most of the stars were simply too distant to have any impact on terrestrial observations. For an excellent historical account of the emergence of the paradox, see Edward R. Harrison, *Darkness at Night* (Cambridge, MA: Harvard University Press, 1987).

throughout the galaxy. The more distant the stars, the fainter their light. Yet the greater the distance from Earth, the greater the number of stars that exist at this distance. The two factors cancel each other out, meaning that the light emission received from a set of stars at any given distance is independent of that distance—and hence that every point in the sky should appear equally bright. And if our sun can be considered to be an "average" star, then every point in the sky should appear as bright as the sun, overwhelming its brilliance. There should therefore be no significant difference between the brightness of the sky at night and during the day.

We can express this more precisely. Imagine that Earth stands at the center of a series of imaginary concentric shells, each of the same thickness. If the thickness of each shell is much smaller than its radius, then the number of stars contained within that shell is proportional to the square of its radius. Yet the intensity of the light received on Earth is *inversely* proportional to the square of the distance from the star to Earth. If we assume a uniform distribution of stars and that one can speak of an "average" brightness, this means that each of these hypothetical shells will emit the same amount of light. Every line of sight will receive equal levels of illumination. The night sky should therefore be bright.

Except it isn't. So what explanations might be offered? The obvious answers lie in challenging the fundamental assumptions on which the paradox rests. As stated by Hermann Bondi, Olbers's paradox rests on four such assumptions:[14]

1. The universe is homogeneous, so that both the location and luminosity of stars are uniform.
2. The universe does not change significantly over time.
3. Stars are relatively fixed within the universe and not subject to any form of motion that might affect their emission of light or how this light is received elsewhere.
4. All known laws of physics apply throughout the universe.

Counterfactual thinking suggested that at least one of these beliefs was incorrect. But which?

Here we see the emergence of a pattern of no small significance for any attempt to undertake natural theology: the use of counterfactual thinking to identify what is "strange" and the quest for the best explanation of this observation. As Peirce pointed out, a "strange fact" is identified, opening up the question of how this is to be accounted for. Which of a number of possibly empirically equivalent abductions is to be preferred? Two factors can be identified as being of particular importance: the finite age of the universe, which means that the amount of stellar light that has been emitted is insufficient to have the predicted impact; and the expansion of the universe increases the volume of space, while at the same time red-

14. Hermann Bondi, *Cosmology*, 2nd ed. (London: Cambridge University Press, 1960), 19–26.

shifting the spectral emission of stars, and thus leading to a reduction in their overall luminosity.[15] (In other words, the second and third of the four assumptions undergirding Olbers's paradox are now regarded as being incorrect.) In this respect it is also important that stars have finite lifetimes and thus do not emit light permanently.

The recognition that things might not be the way they are is an important catalyst to reflection on what has caused them to be as they are. The use of counterfactual arguments in history suggests that the areas of scientific inquiry most likely to be amenable to counterfactual approaches are those with significant historical components, such as biological evolution. The study of the past raises a number of issues of difficulty for the scientific method. How, for example, can a unique event be studied when the achievement of controlled replicability of results—widely regarded as an integral aspect of the scientific method—is by definition impossible? Can the scientific method actually be applied to the study of the past?

In 1976, Karl Popper expressed significant hesitations over whether the Darwinian theory of natural selection could strictly be said to fall within the scope of a scientific method and hence be deemed to be genuinely "scientific" in character.[16] He later revised this view,[17] holding that the historical sciences, such as the history of the evolution of life on Earth, possessed a genuine "scientific character" because their hypotheses could in many cases be tested. This is now widely accepted within the scientific community.

Nevertheless, the biological sciences remain particularly problematic when it comes to the predictive power that some regard as integral to the scientific method. Ernst Mayr (1904–2005) pointed out that certain aspects of biology—most notably, evolutionary biology—were influenced by the contingencies of history to an extent that made prediction difficult.[18] Biology is shaped by history and is dependent upon critical random events and entities whose properties cannot be predicted. Furthermore, biological development arises through the interaction of unique individuals with a complex, variable, and changing environment. Yet although biology cannot be said to predict novel developments, it is able to offer retrospective accounts of what has been observed, thus laying a strong claim to scientific character.

Yet the difficulties arising from the historical development of the universe remain. History is shaped partly by physical forces and partly by the happenstance

15. For an early statement of these factors, see Paul S. Wesson, "Olbers's Paradox and the Spectral Intensity of the Extragalactic Background Light," *Astrophysical Journal* 367 (1991): 399–406.

16. Karl R. Popper, *Unended Quest: An Intellectual Autobiography* (London: Fontana, 1976). For a survey of the issues, see David N. Stamos, "Popper, Falsifiability, and Evolutionary Biology," *Biology and Philosophy* 11 (1996): 161–91.

17. Karl R. Popper, "Natural Selection and the Emergence of Mind," *Dialectica* 32 (1978): 339–55. See further his letter to *New Scientist* 87 (August 21, 1980): 611.

18. See especially Ernst Mayr, *This Is Biology: The Science of the Living World* (Cambridge, MA: Belknap Press, 1997), 64–78. His earlier study also includes some important reflections: Ernst Mayr, *The Growth of Biological Thought* (Cambridge, MA: Belknap Press, 1982), 58–59.

of contingencies. Whether we are concerned with the questions of the origins of the universe or of the origins and extinction of biological species, we are forced to ask questions that are ultimately historical in nature. This immediately creates an opening for counterfactual reasoning. Those inclined to doubt the veracity of this suggestion might like to consider the following thoroughly counterfactual question: what would have happened if the K-T meteorite had missed? Or to expand this somewhat terse question, what would have happened if the meteorite which is widely believed to have been responsible for the Cretaceous-Tertiary extinction event 65 million years ago had missed Earth?[19]

Theological readers might appreciate amplification of the scientific background to this question before we begin analysis of the issues it raises. Although most evolutionary biologists like to think of the process of evolution as essentially continuous, it is clear that there are discontinuities within that process, as determined by the fossil record. A study of the fossil record points to a series of significant "mass extinctions" in the past,[20] the largest of which is the Permo-Triassic extinction, which took place between the Permian and Triassic periods, roughly 250 million years ago. It is thought that up to 95% of all marine life on Earth was destroyed, while 70% of all land families became extinct. The causes of this mass extinction are not known, although both catastrophic and gradualistic explanations have been advanced.[21]

It is widely known that dinosaurs became extinct between 64 and 66 million years ago. In fact, about 60% of all species that are present below (after) the Cretaceous-Tertiary boundary are not present above (before) the line that divides the so-called "Age of Dinosaurs" and the "Age of Mammals." Although the dinosaurs are the best-known group to become extinct, virtually all the large vertebrates on Earth, whether on land, in the sea, or in the air (including all dinosaurs, plesiosaurs, mosasaurs, and pterosaurs) became extinct, along with many forms of terrestrial and oceanic plant life, especially plankton.[22] Others, however, survived. Insects, mammals, birds, and flowering plants on land; and fishes, corals, and mol-

19. For the original hypothesis, see L. W. Alvarez, W. Alvarez, F. Asaro, and H. V. Michel, "Extraterrestrial Cause for the Cretaceous-Tertiary Extinction," *Science* 208 (1980): 1095–1108. The International Commission on Stratigraphy recently recommended that the term "Tertiary" be abandoned. The event in question should now be referred to as the "Cretaceous-Paleogene" extinction. The older term is so familiar that it is unlikely to be abandoned for some considerable time. Throughout this section we retain traditional terminology.

20. See the useful studies of Vincent Courtillot, *Evolutionary Catastrophes: The Science of Mass Extinction* (Cambridge: Cambridge University Press, 1999); and Michael J. Benton, *When Life Nearly Died: The Greatest Mass Extinction of All Time* (London: Thames & Hudson, 2003).

21. Gradualist explanations include deoxygenation of the oceans; catastrophist explanations include meteorite impact: see, e.g., K. Kaiho et al., "End-Permian Catastrophe by a Bolide Impact: Evidence of a Gigantic Release of Sulfur from the Mantle," *Geology* 29 (2001): 815–18; L. R. Kump, A. Pavlov, and M. A. Arthur, "Massive Release of Hydrogen Sulfide to the Surface Ocean and Atmosphere during Intervals of Oceanic Anoxia," *Geology* 33 (2005): 397–400.

22. N. R. Ginsburg, "An Attempt to Resolve the Controversy over the End-Cretaceous Extinction of Planktic Foraminifera at El Kef, Tunisia Using a Blind Test; Introduction: Background and Procedures," *Marine Micropaleontology* 29 (1997): 67–68.

luscs in the ocean—these went on to experience considerable growth and diversification soon after the end of the Cretaceous era.[23]

So what caused this mass extinction? How are we to explain this unusual event? It must be immediately conceded that a multiplicity of explanations can be devised, many lying beyond the scope of the scientific method, as strictly interpreted. Most recent work on the K-T extinction has focused on the theory that a meteorite, or even a small asteroid, collided with Earth at this time. The Chicxulub Crater, named after the nearby village of Puerto Chixulub, is widely regarded as resulting from such a massive bolide collision with Earth.[24] The impact of an item approximately 12.5 miles wide left an egg-shaped crater of between 90 and 125 miles across the undersea Yucatan platform of Mexico. This impact, reckoned to be equivalent to an explosion of 100 million megatons of conventional explosive, would have caused a massive tsunami, with massive expulsion of dust and debris into Earth's atmosphere, possibly preventing photosynthesis from taking place. This vaporized and molten debris, including glass spherules and iridium, would have risen high above the atmosphere to be deposited across the entire globe as it slowly drifted downward. Acid rain might have resulted from the sulfur-rich rock of the impact site. Yet although the evidence for a massive impact on Earth at this time is strong, it is impossible to determine whether it was the cause of the extinction event, or whether it arrived, coincidentally, during an established extinction process. The patterns of extinction cannot all be explained by the impact of a meteorite.[25]

It is not our intention to comment further on possible explanations for the K-T mass extinction event. Rather, we use this event as a way of highlighting the importance of counterfactual approaches within the natural sciences, especially where there is a significant historical dimension to the issues under consideration—as is unquestionably the case in the fields of cosmology and evolutionary biology. The counterfactual question that needs to be asked is this: What would have happened if the meteorite had missed Earth? Would life have been very different from what we now know?

Our exploration of the importance of counterfactual thinking in the natural sciences, though interesting, has really been a preface to considering its role in relation to natural theology, and above all to anthropic phenomena. As we shall

23. See, e.g., David Jablonski, "Geographic Variation in the Molluscan Recovery from the End-Cretaceous Extinction," *Science* 279 (1998): 1327–30; Joel Cracraft, "Avian Evolution, Gondwana Biogeography and the Cretaceous-Tertiary Mass Extinction Event," *Proceedings of the Royal Society B* 268 (2001): 459–69.

24. Charles Frankel, *The End of the Dinosaurs: Chicxulub Crater and Mass Extinctions* (Cambridge: Cambridge University Press, 1999).

25. A second factor which may be involved is massive volcanic eruptions. The Deccan Traps are often cited as a rival to the bolide theory as the cause of K-T extinction; see S. Bhattacharji et al., "Indian Intraplate and Continental Margin Rifting, Lithospheric Extension, and Mantle Upwelling in Deccan Flood Basalt Volcanism near the K/T Boundary: Evidence from Mafic Dike Swarms," *Journal of Petrology* 104 (1996): 379–98. The Deccan Traps would have discharged poisonous gases into the atmosphere, thus causing acid rains, depleting the biosphere, and increasing the concentration of acidic gases in the atmosphere. Once more, the volcanic hypothesis proves helpful in explaining some observations, but not others.

see, counterfactual thinking offers a highly productive framework for beginning to assess the theological significance of such anthropic phenomena.

COUNTERFACTUAL THINKING AND ANTHROPIC PHENOMENA

The approaches to anthropic phenomena that have emerged in recent years have emphasized the significance of certain fundamental constants which, if varied slightly, would have significant implications for the emergence of human existence. This understanding of "fine-tuning," it must be stressed, is quite distinct from speculation concerning "mathematical fine-tuning," which is generally thought to originate with Hermann Weyl in 1919, and was subsequently speculatively amplified by Arthur Eddington.[26] In this case, interest focused on three numbers: 10^{40}, the ratio of the strengths of the electromagnetic and gravitational forces between two protons; 10^{80}, the total number of protons believed to lie within the observable universe; and 10^{120}, the action of the universe, expressed in terms of multiples of Planck's constant. Although Paul Dirac in 1937 suggested that these "coincidences" reflected some not-yet-understood feature of the deep structure of the universe,[27] Robert Dicke in effect put an end to such numerological speculation by showing that it was a form of observation selection effect in 1961.[28] Human observers are located at a point in cosmic history after the formation yet before the death of the stars. Our concern is not with such alleged mathematical fine-tuning, but with cosmological fine-tuning, evident in a number of phenomena to be discussed in the second part of this work.

Examples of canonical statements of the astrophysical fine-tuning of fundamental cosmological constants include the following:

1. If the strong coupling constant were slightly smaller, hydrogen would be the only element in the universe. Since the evolution of life as we know it is fundamentally dependent on the chemical properties of carbon, that life could not have come into being without some hydrogen being converted to carbon by fusion. On the other hand, if the strong coupling constant were slightly larger (even by as much as 2%), the hydrogen would have been converted to helium, with the result that no long-lived stars would have been formed. Since such stars are regarded as essential to the emergence of life, such a conversion would have led to life as we know it failing to emerge.

26. For the distinction and its importance, see Mark A. Walker and Milan M. Cirkovic, "Astrophysical Fine Tuning, Naturalism, and the Contemporary Design Argument," *International Studies in the Philosophy of Science* 20 (2006): 285–307. For an accessible discussion of "large number coincidences," see John D. Barrow, *The Constants of Nature: From Alpha to Omega* (London: Vintage, 2003), 97–118.

27. P. A. M. Dirac, "The Cosmological Constants," *Nature* 139 (1937): 323–24.

28. Robert H. Dicke, "Dirac's Cosmology and Mach's Principle," *Nature* 192 (1961): 440–41.

2. If the weak fine constant were slightly smaller, no hydrogen would have formed during the early history of the universe. Consequently, no stars would have been formed. On the other hand, if it was slightly larger, supernovae would have been unable to eject the heavier elements necessary for life. In either case, life as we know it could not have emerged.

3. If the electromagnetic fine-structure constant were slightly larger, the stars would not be hot enough to warm planets to a temperature sufficient to maintain life in the form in which we know it. If smaller, the stars would have burned out too quickly to allow life to evolve on these planets.

4. If the gravitational fine-structure constant were slightly smaller, stars and planets would not have been able to form, on account of the gravitational constraints necessary for coalescence of their constituent material. If stronger, the stars thus formed would have burned out too quickly to allow the evolution of life.

The important point to appreciate is that each of these four statements is framed *counterfactually*. We are asked to envisage alternative worlds in which these constants have different values, and compare these worlds with that which we actually know. Small variations in any of these constants would have led to very different outcomes. For a theist, the implications of such points are obvious: "God would need to be careful which physics he chose."[29] Yet at this stage, we are not concerned with offering explanations of unusual observations—or even considering whether it is possible or necessary to offer any explanation in the first place—but with identifying features of the cosmos which appear to stand out as being significant, since *they could have been different*—and a very different universe would have emerged as a result. Perhaps most intriguingly of all, there might have been no observers able to reflect on the significance of their observations.

We are now in a position to take our reflections on the theological significance of anthropic phenomena further, by asking what explanatory framework might be used to assess them.

29. John Leslie, *Universes* (London: Routledge, 1989), 63.

Chapter 8

Augustine of Hippo on Creation

A Theological Lens

"I believe in Christianity as I believe that the Sun has risen, not only because I see it, but because by it I see everything else."[1] These words of C. S. Lewis, cited earlier, serve as a highly appropriate motto to any Christian natural theology, which is to be understood not as an attempt to deduce the existence of God from a cold, detached observation of nature, but rather as the enterprise of seeing nature from the standpoint of the Christian tradition, so that it is viewed, interpreted, and appreciated with Trinitarian spectacles. Events and entities within nature are thus not held to "prove," but to be consonant with, the existence of God. What is observed within the natural order resonates with the core themes of the Christian vision of God.

This approach is strongly consonant with the unification model of explanation, noted in chapter 5. While not in any way denying God's direct or indirect causality in relation to the natural world, the particular style of explanation offered by a Trinitarian natural theology is that of offering a unitary vision of reality, which allows the correlations and interconnections of the natural world with

1. C. S. Lewis, "Is Theology Poetry?" in *C. S. Lewis: Essay Collection* (London: Collins, 2000), 1–21.

itself and with God to be grasped and appreciated. The capacity of this kind of natural theology to explain things in this way, while important in itself, also represents an important justification of a Trinitarian metaphysic itself.

The approach to natural theology that I set out earlier in *The Open Secret* emphasizes how such an approach to nature is able to engage with its truth, beauty, and goodness, offering a conceptual framework which allows the rational, aesthetic, and moral aspects of nature to be affirmed, critically yet positively. While this understanding of natural theology has the potential to reveal and value the aesthetic and moral dimensions of nature, the present work concentrates on only one aspect of natural theology: its important role as a sense-making enterprise, capable of offering an account of the rationality and explicability of the universe. Natural theology is able to engage with, and offer explanations of, a number of significant features of the world, including the following:[2]

1. The apparent ordering of the universe, which is accessible and intelligible to the human mind
2. A fruitful cosmic history, including the suggestion that it is fine-tuned for the emergence of life
3. The interconnectedness of the universe, which resists reduction to its individual parts
4. The coexistence of disorder and order within the world
5. A generalized human awareness of the transcendent

We have already noted how the Christian doctrine of creation, set within the context of the "economy of salvation," has an explanatory elegance and fecundity (see chap. 6). On the basis of a Christian doctrine of creation, the universe can be considered to be both "inherently intelligible and inherently contingent, not intelligible without being contingent and not contingent without being intelligible."[3] So how does this way of seeing nature enable us to engage with the complexities of the natural world?

In the second part of this work, we set out to identify and assess some "surprising facts" which need to be accommodated within any view of reality, religious or secular. Since this work is likely to be read primarily by theologians and philosophers, I shall try to present the scientific analysis in as accessible a manner as possible, often including some introductory or explanatory material that those familiar with the scientific literature can safely disregard. Nevertheless, readers need to be warned that there are limits to legitimate simplification, which must be respected.

But before embarking on a substantial engagement with possible examples of fine-tuning in nature, we must offer at least a provisional interpretative frame-

2. See, e.g., John Polkinghorne, "Trinitarian Physics and Metaphysics," *Theology and Science* 1 (2003): 33–49, who outlines six slightly different features of the universe which call for explanation and briefly indicates how Trinitarianism accounts for them.

3. Thomas F. Torrance, "Divine and Contingent Order," in *The Sciences and Theology in the Twentieth Century*, ed. A. R. Peacocke (Notre Dame, IN: University of Notre Dame Press, 1981), 81–97.

work which allows these phenomena to be "seen" in a properly Christian light. We have already emphasized the importance and fecundity of a Trinitarian natural theology, which is able to offer a rich conceptual resource for accounting for the complex variegations of the natural world. So what specific form of Trinitarian theology is to be preferred? In what follows, I propose to outline some basic features of a classic Trinitarian vision of reality, which has the potential for development and enrichment for an engagement with the natural sciences. Augustine of Hippo (354–430) is unquestionably the most respected and widely cited theologian in Western Christianity, serving both as a major intellectual stimulus and resource to virtually every subsequent period of theological reflection and activity.[4] Augustine's doctrine of creation is classic, both in the sense of establishing a norm and offering a resource for future generations.[5] While Augustine's successors have felt free to modify and develop as much as endorse his ideas,[6] it is clear that they have been one of the most productive and significant influences on the shaping of Christian theology in the West, and seem set to remain so.

Yet my reason for setting out Augustine's conceptually rich approach goes beyond its historical influence and potential fruitfulness. I have deliberately chosen a classic Christian writer who developed his system in the light of a close reading of Scripture and the Christian tradition long before the emergence of modern scientific revolution—the period, usually identified as 1500–1700, which is often seen as the historical moment when "modern science" and its attendant institutions emerged[7]—to avoid any suggestion that these systems were somehow accommodated or adapted to conform with modern scientific knowledge. There is a widespread suspicion that certain theories, philosophical and theological, are merely constructed ad hoc in order to accommodate data. As Peter Lipton has pointed out, such theories are often "forced" and "fudged."[8] Though there is a sense in which every theory is a response to observation, many are rightly suspicious of a theory which appears to have been developed opportunistically as a matter of intellectual convenience rather than integrity. For this reason many philosophers of science have stressed the importance of prediction, holding this to be of greater intellectual virtue than accommodation, even though some have

4. For the best account of Augustine's influence, see the magisterial survey in Allan D. Fitzgerald, ed., *Augustine through the Ages: An Encyclopedia* (Grand Rapids: Eerdmans, 1999).

5. See here T. S. Eliot, "The Idea of a Classic," in *Selected Prose of T. S. Eliot*, ed. Frank Kermode (London: Faber, 1975), 115–31.

6. Thomas Aquinas's use of Augustine illustrates this point: see the classic study of Étienne Gilson, "Pourquoi Saint Thomas a critiqué Saint Augustin," *Archives d'histoire doctrinale et littéraire du Moyen Age* 1 (1926–27): 5–127.

7. There is, of course, considerable debate over both the periodization and the significance of the "scientific revolution": see the perspectives adopted in David C. Lindberg and Robert S. Westman, eds., *Reappraisals of the Scientific Revolution* (Cambridge: Cambridge University Press, 1990); Margaret Osler, ed., *Rethinking the Scientific Revolution* (Cambridge: Cambridge University Press, 2000). In fact, almost all of the ideas to be discussed in the next six chapters date from after the first edition of Darwin's *Origin of Species* (1859), which is later than the traditional period of this "scientific revolution."

8. Peter Lipton, *Inference to the Best Explanation*, 2nd ed. (London: Routledge, 2004), 164–77.

rightly pointed out that this distinction ultimately seems to rest more on the psychology of dramatic discovery rather than the epistemology of confirmation.[9]

My point here is that Augustine offers us theological paradigms which are deeply rooted in the Christian faith, offering us a way of engaging with modern scientific knowledge without being constituted or determined by that knowledge in the first place. If Augustine's approach is capable of accommodating modern scientific insights, this undoubted epistemic virtue would have been unknown to him. If we accept Musgrave's distinction between "historical" and "logical" approaches to confirmation,[10] then it is of no small significance that Augustine's approach has merits which he himself could not have known or anticipated at the time of writing. In the final part of this work, we shall consider how Augustine's approach might be expanded and extended; at this stage, we shall simply present it on its own terms.

AUGUSTINE ON CREATION:
THE COMMENTARY ON GENESIS

The basic aspects of Augustine's doctrine of creation have been carefully studied and are reasonably well understood.[11] It represents a set of beliefs that are rigorously grounded in the biblical witness on the one hand, yet which are also subtly textured by prevailing trends in both philosophy and the natural sciences.[12] Although Augustine wrote no fewer than four commentaries on the creation narratives of Genesis,[13] the most significant and influential of these is entitled *On the Literal Meaning of Genesis*, written between 401 and 415.[14] As the title makes clear, Augustine intended this to be a "literal" commentary on the text—not, however, in the modern sense of the term, but in contrast to the then popular "allegorical" mode of interpretation, which saw the Old Testament as prefiguring the New. Augustine understood the term "literal" to mean something like "in the sense intended by the author." In what follows, I shall offer a close reading of this

---

9. Christopher Hitchcock and Elliott Sober, "Prediction versus Accommodation and the Risk of Overfitting," *British Journal for Philosophy of Science* 55 (2004): 1–34. Hitchcock, Sober, and Lipton (see no. 8) all endorse "weak" forms of predictivism.

10. Alan Musgrave, "Logical versus Historical Theories of Confirmation," *British Journal for Philosophy of Science* 25 (1974): 1–23.

11. For an excellent overview, see Simo Knuuttila, "Time and Creation in Augustine," in *The Cambridge Companion to Augustine*, ed. Eleonore Stump and Norman Kretzmann (Cambridge: Cambridge University Press, 2001), 103–15.

12. Joseph T. Lienhard, "Reading the Bible and Learning to Read: The Influence of Education on St. Augustine's Exegesis," *Augustinian Studies* 27 (1996): 7–25.

13. For Augustine's developing understandings of these passages, see Yoon Kyung Kim, *Augustine's Changing Interpretations of Genesis 1–3: From "De Genesi contra Manichaeos" to "De Genesi ad litteram"* (Lewiston, NY: Edwin Mellen Press, 2006).

14. It is important to distinguish the complete, mature work *De Genesi ad litteram libri duodecim* (401–15) from the incomplete earlier work *De Genesi ad litteram imperfectus liber* (393–94). All references in this chapter are to the complete, mature work.

text, considering the importance of its ideas in engaging with the phenomenon of fine-tuning.

Augustine is widely credited with playing a major role in the shaping of the Western theological tradition, especially in relation to the doctrines of the Trinity, church, and grace. Yet his signal contribution to the formulation of a Christian doctrine of creation is often overlooked. Augustine's highly important formulation of the concept of creation distinguishes the emerging views of the Christian tradition, grounded in the biblical narratives, from those of contemporary Greek science and the prevailing cultural trends. Whereas most Neoplatonic thinkers regarded the world as an eternal entity, Augustine categorically affirms that it is a created entity. God created the universe ex nihilo as an act of freedom.[15] The universe is neither eternal nor necessary but is a contingent entity which had its origins at a specific moment in time.

This distinctively Christian belief, found in the New Testament and given systematic expression during the patristic era, was regarded as ludicrous by the pagan critics of Christianity. One such critic was Claudius Galen (ca. 129–ca. 200), who served as court physician to the emperor Marcus Aurelius.[16] Galen objected to the idea, which he held to be implicit in the Genesis creation account, that the world was created out of what did not already exist, regarding this as both a logical and metaphysical absurdity.[17] His concern here appears to have been the idea that God should bring things into being solely by an act of will, without regard to any prior act of reasoning or foresight, so that God has to be thought of as creating the world in an essentially arbitrary act of volition.[18]

In insisting that the world came into being from nothing, Augustine was therefore adopting a profoundly countercultural position, which distanced him from the prevailing wisdom of contemporary classical science. Yet Augustine distances himself further from contemporary science by arguing that time itself is part of the created order. Augustine does not hold to a temporal continuum, as if there were a continuous time line along which the origins of the universe may be located. Time is itself an integral aspect of the created order. God, Augustine insists, cannot be considered to have brought the creation into being at a certain definite moment in time, as if "time" itself existed before creation, or as if creation took place at a definite moment in a chronological continuum.[19] For Augustine, time itself must be seen as an element of the created order, to be contrasted with the

15. N. Joseph Torchia, *Creatio ex Nihilo and the Theology of St. Augustine* (New York: Peter Lang, 1999). For the emergence of this patristic consensus, see Gerhard May, *Creatio ex Nihilo: The Doctrine of "Creation out of Nothing" in Early Christian Thought* (Edinburgh: T&T Clark, 1995).

16. Heinrich Schlange-Schöningen, *Die römische Gesellschaft bei Galen: Biographie und Sozialgeschichte* (Berlin: de Gruyter, 2003).

17. Roger K. French, *Medicine before Science: The Rational and Learned Doctor from the Middle Ages to the Enlightenment* (Cambridge: Cambridge University Press, 2003), 53–54.

18. Galen, *De usu partium* 11.14. For further comments, see Robert L. Wilken, *The Christians as the Romans Saw Them*, 2nd ed. (New Haven, CT: Yale University Press, 2003), 83–93.

19. Augustine, *De Genesi ad litteram* 5.5.12. For a similar idea elsewhere, see Augustine, *Confessions* 11.30.40. More generally, see Gilles Pelland, *Cinq études d'Augustin sur les débuts de la Genèse* (Paris: Desclée, 1972).

timelessness which he held to be the essential feature of eternity. Augustine thus speaks of the creation of time (or "creation with time"), rather than envisaging the act of creation as taking place in time.[20] Time is a constituent characteristic of the domain of the created, which remains dependent upon its creator. "We speak of 'before' and 'after' in the relationship of creatures, although everything in the creative act of God is simultaneous."[21] There is no concept of a period intervening before creation, nor an infinitely extended period which corresponds to "eternity." Eternity is timeless; time is an aspect of the created order. Time must therefore be thought of as one of God's creatures and servants. Augustine thus answers the question "What was God doing before he created the universe?" by pointing out that there is no temporal "before" in relation to the creation of the universe. God does not exist *in* time, which is a characteristic feature of the created order.[22]

The term "created" also needs comment. Augustine does not limit God's creative action to the primordial act of origination. God's creation of things is understood to embrace both the origination of the world and the direction of the subsequent unfolding and development of the causalities which were embedded within the created order by that act of creation. There are thus two "moments" in creation, corresponding to a primary act of origination and a continuing process of providential guidance.[23] While conceding that there is a natural tendency to think of creation as a past event, he insists that God must be recognized to be working even now, in the present, sustaining and directing the unfolding of the "generations that he laid up in creation when it was first established."[24]

Augustine takes the view that the biblical creation accounts must be interpreted in the light of Ecclesiasticus (Sirach) 18:1 (Latin Vulgate), which states that God created "all things together" in one initial, all-inclusive, and instantaneous act of creation.[25] "God made all things together, disposing them in an order based not on intervals of time, but on causal connections."[26] So what of the six days of creation?[27] Declining to interpret these as periods of extended time, Augustine in effect treats these as a heuristic device, a textual accommodation to the text's readers, thus eliminating the notion of a temporal sequence within the divine process

20. For more detailed exploration of this point, see Charlotte Gross, "Augustine's Ambivalence about Temporality: His Two Accounts of Time," *Medieval Philosophy and Theology* 8 (1999): 129–48. For useful comments on patristic critiques of the notion of a temporal eternity, see Harry A. Wolfson, "Patristic Arguments against the Eternity of the World," *Harvard Theological Review* 59 (1966): 351–67.

21. Augustine, *De Genesi ad litteram* 4.35.56.

22. Michael Lockwood, *The Labyrinth of Time: Introducing the University* (Oxford: Oxford University Press, 2005), 92.

23. Augustine, *De Genesi ad litteram* 5.4.11.

24. Ibid., 5.20.41–42.

25. Ibid., 4.33.52. See Ecclesiasticus (= Sirach) 18:1, "qui vivit in aeternum creavit omnia simul" (Latin Vulgate).

26. Augustine, *De Genesi ad litteram* 5.5.12: "operatus est omnia simul, praestans eis etiam ordinem, non intervallis temporum, sed connexione causarum."

27. For earlier patristic discussion of this question, see Louis J. Swift, "Basil and Ambrose on the Six Days of Creation," *Augustinianum* 21 (1981): 317–28; Rainer Henke, *Basilius und Ambrosius über das Sechstagewerk* (Basel: Schwabe, 2001).

of creation. Since all things were, at least in some sense, already present in the first instant of the universe's temporal appearance, there was no need for a six-day sequence of supplemental additions on the part of the Creator.[28]

> In this narrative of creation, Holy Scripture states of the Creator that he completed his work in six days; elsewhere, without contradicting this, it states that he created all things together [simul]. It therefore follows that he who created all things together also created these six or seven days—or rather the one day, repeated six or seven times. So why was there any need to set out six distinct days, one after the other, in the narrative? The reason is that those who cannot understand the meaning of the phrase "he created all things together" will not understand the meaning of Scripture as a whole, unless the narrative proceeds slowly, in this stepwise manner.

For Augustine, creation is a Trinitarian action, in which each of the persons of the Trinity has a distinct role to play,[29] both in the creation of the universe in general and in the creation of humanity in particular.[30] This theme underlies one of the most distinctive ideas of Augustine's natural theology: the *vestigia Trinitatis*.[31] The created order, Augustine argues, bears witness to its creator; the human mind, on account of its Trinitarian origins, has the capacity both to reflect and to discern its creator.[32]

AUGUSTINE'S NOTION OF THE *RATIONES SEMINALES*

Perhaps the most significant aspect of Augustine's account of creation lies in his notion of "seminal reasons" (*rationes seminales* or *rationes causales*).[33] We have already noted how Augustine's interpretation of Genesis is partly shaped by his knowledge of the natural science of his day; note, for example, his respectful recognition of the authority of contemporary medical opinion in his discussion of aspects of the human body, as created by God.[34] In elaborating his idea of instantaneous creation, Augustine argued that certain principles of order were embedded within the creation, which developed as appropriate at later stages.

28. Augustine, *De Genesi ad litteram* 4.33.52.
29. Ibid., 1.6.12.
30. Ibid., 3.19.29–20.32.
31. Augustine's fullest treatment of this question is to be found in *De Trinitate* 15.5.7–8; see the excellent discussion in Rowan Williams, "Sapientia and Trinity: Reflections on the *De Trinitate*," in *Mélanges T. J. Van Bavel*, ed. Tarsicius J. van Bavel, Bernard Bruning, and Mathijs Lamberigts (Leuven: Uitgeverij Peeters, 1990), 317–32.
32. The theme is found in Greek patristic writers: e.g., see David Bentley Hart, "The Mirror of the Infinite: Gregory of Nyssa on the *Vestigia Trinitatis*," *Modern Theology* 18 (2002): 541–61. For the idea in the English Renaissance, see Dennis R. Klinck, "*Vestigia Trinitatis* in Man and His Works in the English Renaissance," *Journal of the History of Ideas* 42 (1981): 13–27.
33. For one of the best accounts of this notion, including discussion of its intellectual provenance and fecundity, see Ernan McMullin, "Introduction," in *Evolution and Creation*, ed. Ernan McMullin (Notre Dame, IN: University of Notre Dame Press, 1985), 1–58, esp. 8–16.
34. Augustine, *De Genesi ad litteram* 7.13.20.

The idea was not new. Earlier Christian writers had observed how the first Genesis creation narrative spoke of the earth and the waters "bringing forth" living creatures, and had drawn the conclusion that this pointed to God endowing the natural order with a capacity to generate living things.[35] Augustine's contribution to the further development of this notion was a powerful metaphor, almost certainly borrowed from Stoic writers: *rationes seminales*, or seedlike principles that are present from the cosmic beginning, in each of which is contained the potential for the later development of a specific living kind.[36] Augustine exploits this notion in his interpretation of Genesis 1:12, which he holds to mean that the earth has received the power or capacity to produce things by itself:[37]

> Scripture has stated that the earth brought forth the crops and the trees causally [*causaliter*], in the sense that it received the power of bringing them forth. God created what was to be in times to come in the earth from the beginning, in what I might call the "roots of time."

The image of a seed provided Augustine with a suitable analogy on which he could draw to support his more-general thesis about the role of potential existing entities within the earth before their appearance in mature form when the conditions were right: "There is, indeed, in seeds some likeness to what I am describing because of the future developments stored up in them."[38] This also allowed him to maintain his emphasis on the simultaneous creation of all things, while additionally insisting that God, through his providence, was able to direct the subsequent actualization of the potentialities thus created.[39] What some might attribute to chance, the believer attributes to providence.[40] Yet Augustine was emphatic that these *rationes seminales* are not "seeds" in the normal sense of the term. The notion of the seed is heuristic, providing an inexact, though helpful, means of visualization for the theologically difficult notion of a hidden force within nature through which latent things are enacted.[41]

---

35. McMullin, "Introduction," 12.

36. For comment, see Maryanne Cline Horowitz, "The Stoic Synthesis of the Idea of Natural Law in Man: Four Themes," *Journal of the History of Ideas* 35 (1974): 3–16.

37. Augustine, *De Genesi ad litteram* 5.4.11.

38. Ibid., 6.6.11.

39. Ibid., 5.23.44–46. Note especially his emphasis upon the seed as a force and causal power: "in semine ergo illa omnia fuerunt primitus, non mole corporeae magnitudinis, sed vi potentiaque causali." For the appeal to both creation and conservation in medieval theological arguments against the eternity of the world, see Richard Cross, "The Eternity of the World and the Distinction between Creation and Conservation," *Religious Studies* 42 (2006): 403–16.

40. Augustine, *De Genesi ad litteram* 5.21.42–22.43. Alvin Plantinga argues that views of evolution through natural processes are "semi-Deist," in that God is excluded from directing those processes. It is clear that Augustine is not affected by such a criticism. See Alvin Plantinga, "When Faith and Reason Clash: Evolution and the Bible," *Christian Scholar's Review* 21 (1991): 8–33. For a perceptive critique of this essay, especially in relation to (1) its presentation of evolutionary theory and (2) its philosophical implications, see Ernan McMullin, "Plantinga's Defense of Special Creation," *Christian Scholar's Review* 21 (1991): 55–79.

41. Augustine, *De Genesi ad litteram* 6.6.10–11; 4.16.27: "alia quadam notitia colligitur inesse in natura quiddam latens."

Augustine's basic argument is that God created the world complete with a series of dormant multiple potencies, which were actualized in the future through divine providence. Where some might think of creation in terms of God's insertion of new kinds of plants and animals ready-made, as it were, into an already-existing world, Augustine rejects this as inconsistent with the overall witness of Scripture. Rather, God must be thought of as creating in that very first moment the potencies for all the kinds of living things that would come later, including humanity. Augustine illustrates this by considering how one might speak of the creation of a tree.[42]

> In the seed then, there was present invisibly everything that would develop in time into a tree. And we must visualize the world in the same way, when God made all things together, as having all things that were made in it and with it. . . . [This] includes also the beings which earth produced potentially and causally [*potentialiter atque causaliter*] before they emerged in the course of time.

It will be clear that the explanatory appeal of this analogy for Augustine lies primarily in its notion of potentiality. The image of the "seed" implies that the original creation contained within it the potentialities for all the living kinds that would later emerge. Augustine does not press this analogy to its limits, suggesting that these seeds are to be understood as distinct physical entities that were embedded within the original creation, as seeds lie in the ground. Rather, Augustine seems to have conceived of them as dormant "virtual" entities, enabling the natural world to emerge in its own way and in its own time.[43]

This does not mean that God created the world incomplete or imperfect, since "what God originally established in causes, he subsequently fulfilled in effects."[44] God's creation extends from actualities to potentialities, all of which were bestowed in the primordial act of origination.[45]

> These were made by God in the beginning, when he made the world, and simultaneously created all things, which were to be unfolded in the ages to come. They are perfected, in that in their proper natures, by which they achieve their role in time, they possess nothing that was not already present in them causally. They have, however, just begun, since in them are the seeds, as it were, of the future perfections that would arise from their hidden state, and which would be manifested at the appropriate time.

This process of development, Augustine declares, is governed by fundamental laws, which reflect the will of their creator: "God has established fixed laws governing the

42. Ibid., 5.23.45.
43. Ibid., 6.10.17: "Sed etiam ista secum gerunt tamquam iterum seipsa invisibiliter in occulta quadam vi generandi, quam extraxerunt de illis primordiis causarum suarum, in quibus creato mundo, cum factus est dies, antequam in manifestam speciem sui generis exorerentur, inserta sunt."
44. Ibid., 6.11.19.
45. Ibid., 6.11.18.

production of kinds and qualities of beings, and bringing them out of concealment into full view."[46]

While Augustine's doctrine of the *rationes seminales* may well rest primarily on his biblical exegesis, shaped at least to some extent by previous philosophical reflection on the issue, his understanding of how these "seeds" develop is determined by the natural science of his day. Unsurprisingly, we find Augustine is firmly committed to what we would now term the "fixity of species."[47]

> The elements of the physical world have a fixed power and quality which determine what each thing can and cannot do, and what can be done, or not done, with it. From these elements, all things which come about in due course have their origin and development, as well as their end and dissolution, according to their kind. Thus a bean does not emerge from a grain of wheat, nor does wheat emerge from a bean, or human beings from cattle, or cattle from human beings.

Intellectual alternatives were simply denied to Augustine on account of his historicity. Only when Augustine borrows ideas from the scientific outlook of the culture within which he was embedded does he make mistakes that his successors need to correct.

Augustine approached his text with the culturally prevalent presupposition of the fixity of species and found nothing in the text to challenge him on this point.[48] Yet the ways in which he interacts with his scientific authorities and personal experience suggest that, on this point at least, his views would be open to correction in the light of prevailing scientific opinion.[49] Augustine was emphatic that the interpreter of Scripture must not become frozen or locked into a specific pattern of biblical interpretation:[50]

> In matters that are obscure and beyond our vision, even those we find in Holy Scripture, different interpretations are sometimes possible without prejudice to the faith we have received. In this case, we should not rush in impetuously and adopt a position on one side with such commitment that, if further progress in the search of truth should undermine this position, we too should fall with it. That would be to contend, not for the teaching of Holy Scrip-

---

46. Ibid., 6.13.23.

47. Ibid., 9.17.32.

48. Similar comments apply to Aristotle. Revisionist readings of his biological works suggest that his notion of the "fixity of species" (to use a modern term) or "eternity of kinds" (to use his own phrase) was open to at least certain forms of evolutionism, even though Aristotle saw no evidence of it in the world around him: see the discussion in James G. Lennox, *Aristotle's Philosophy of Biology: Studies in the Origins of Life Science* (Cambridge: Cambridge University Press, 2001), 131–59.

49. This is not, however, to avoid Augustine's major discussion about the identity of humanity being linked to its possession of a God-given soul: see, e.g., Augustine, *De Genesi ad litteram,* 7.1.1. For an excellent account of Augustine's views, see Robert J. O'Connell, *The Origin of the Soul in St. Augustine's Later Works* (New York: Fordham University Press, 1987).

50. Augustine, *De Genesi ad litteram* 1.18.37. See the comments in Tarsicius van Bavel, "The Creator and the Integrity of Creation in the Fathers of the Church," *Augustinian Studies* 21 (1990): 1–33, esp. 1–2.

ture, but for our own teaching. We would wish its teaching to conform to ours, when we ought to wish ours to conform to that of Holy Scripture.

Clearly concerned about the possibility of becoming locked into fixed patterns of biblical interpretation, when the evidence required several possibilities to be kept open, Augustine emphasized the importance of exegetical restraint, lest personal commitment to an existing interpretation of Scripture might prejudice its future correction.[51]

Augustine himself was not entirely consistent in the application of his own principle, incorporating what he clearly regarded as sound contemporary science into his psychological analogies of the Trinity,[52] as well as accepting the fixity of species. Yet the principle is sound. This approach to biblical interpretation, if applied responsibly, would do much to ensure that Christian theology never became trapped in a prescientific worldview. For example, it is sometimes suggested that the controversies over the views of Copernicus and Galileo arose partly because biblical exposition took no account of the natural sciences. A more-plausible interpretation is that the controversy arose precisely because early generations of theologians and philosophers gave far too much weight to provisional scientific accounts of nature; they failed to update their thinking with scientific advance. Many medieval writers had become locked into certain Aristotelian readings of Scripture, which they treated as if they were part of a sacred tradition that lay beyond challenge. Scientific advance sometimes cruelly exposes how earlier generations of exegetes had incorporated provisional scientific theories into their biblical interpretation, thus unintentionally giving those theories the status of religious dogma.

Augustine's idea of *rationes seminales* is thus a theologically productive answer to a series of troublesome issues that emerged as he engaged with the Genesis creation narratives. How could the two narratives be reconciled with each other? And with other biblical statements? Augustine's approach allowed him to interpret the first Genesis creation narrative as describing the instantaneous bringing into existence of primal matter, which already contained within it the causal resources for further development. The second narrative then sets out the subsequent history of the chronological actualization of these causal possibilities from the earth. His use of the notion of *rationes seminales* allowed Augustine to declare both that God made all things simultaneously, while also stating that the various sorts or kinds of living things made their appearance only gradually over unspecified (and presumably extended) periods of time.[53] Furthermore, this approach allowed Augustine to formulate a distinctive account of cosmic origins, based on the analogy of seeds and their dormant potentiality, which envisaged the natural realm as having a God-given capacity to develop.

---

51. Augustine, *De Genesi ad litteram* 2.18.38.

52. See Boghos Levon Zekiyan, *L'interioriso Agostiniano: La struttura onto-psicologica dell'interioriso Agostiniano e la "Memoria sui"* (Genoa: Studio Editoriale di Cultura, 1981).

53. Augustine, it must be appreciated, saw time as an aspect of God's creation and was thus able to integrate the role of time in the actualization of potentiality within his overall doctrine of creation.

The imaginative power and intellectual fecundity of this approach is obvious, and later in this work we shall turn to explore it further. At this stage, it is offered simply as a lens through which to view the theme which will dominate this second section of this book, that the cosmos appears to have come into existence with the potentiality for human existence, which we will explore in greater detail in subsequent chapters.

THE RECEPTION OF AUGUSTINE'S APPROACH

Yet the relevance of Augustine to evolutionary approaches to the natural world can hardly be overlooked. Historically, Augustine's approach was generally eclipsed, partly on account of the rise of Aristotelianism during the Middle Ages, which led to the notion of embedded causalities within the natural order being reinterpreted primarily in terms of God operating through secondary natural causes.[54] The emphasis upon the physical and biological fixity of nature,[55] evident in William Paley's *Natural Theology* (1802), meant that any notion of biological development, emergence, or evolution—which can actually be accommodated relatively easily within Augustine's scheme—was regarded as implausible. Yet Augustine's notion remained a significant intellectual option for many throughout the Renaissance and found expression in a variety of manners.[56] Although the idea of the *rationes seminales* was incorporated in various alchemical and mystical works, some of which adopted vitalist approaches to biology,[57] it proved capable of development

54. For the development of this idea in Thomas Aquinas and its potential as a framework for evolutionary approaches to biology, see William E. Carroll, "Creation, Evolution, and Thomas Aquinas," *Revue des questions scientifiques* 171 (2000): 319–47. Aquinas did not abandon the notion of *rationes seminales* but limited its application: see, e.g., Vivian Boland, *Ideas in God according to Saint Thomas Aquinas: Sources and Synthesis* (Leiden: Brill, 1996), 264–66. The scholastic discussion of secondary causality was rendered complex by the problem of occasionalism: see the excellent paper by Alfred J. Freddoso, "Medieval Aristotelianism and the Case against Secondary Causation in Nature," in *Divine and Human Action: Essays in the Metaphysics of Theism*, ed. Thomas V. Morris (Ithaca, NY: Cornell University Press, 1988), 74–118. Yet other medieval writers, such as Bonaventura of Bagnioregio (1221–74), retained Augustine's doctrine of *rationes seminales*, holding that matter contains within itself, in an undeveloped and imperfect state of being, the roots of the forms it could later assume. See further José de Vinck, "Two Aspects of the Theory of the *Rationes Seminales* in the Writings of Bonaventure," in *S. Bonaventura 1274–1974*, vol. 3, *Philosophia* (Grottaferrata: Collegio S. Bonaventurae, 1973), 307–16.

55. This idea underlies the taxonomy of the Swedish botanist Linnaeus (1707–78), although Linnaeus later abandoned the idea that species were fixed and invariable; he suggested that at least some, and perhaps most, species in a genus might have arisen after the creation of the world, through the process of hybridization. For reflections on Linnaeus's theoretical difficulties with the notion of hybrids, see Brian G. Gardiner, "Linnaeus's Species Concept and His Views on Evolution," *The Linnean* 17 (2001): 24–36.

56. See the exhaustive study of Hiro Hirai, *Le concept de semence dans les théories de la matière à la Renaissance: De Marsile Ficin à Pierre Gassendi* (Turnhout: Brepols, 2005).

57. See, e.g., William R. Newman, *Atoms and Alchemy: Chymistry and the Experimental Origins of the Scientific Revolution* (Chicago: University of Chicago Press, 2006), 146–48.

in more-orthodox scientific directions. The idea thus played a significant role in English natural philosophy of the seventeenth and eighteenth centuries.[58]

Augustine interweaves biblical interpretation, an appeal to "right reason," and a knowledge of contemporary science in his theological reflections concerning creation,[59] which can be summarized as follows.

1. God brought everything into being at a specific moment.
2. Part of that created order takes the form of embedded causalities which emerge or evolve at a later stage.
3. This process of development takes place within the context of God's providential direction, which is integrally connected to a right understanding of the concept of creation.[60]
4. The image of a dormant seed is an appropriate but not exact analogy for these embedded causalities.
5. The process of generation of these dormant seeds results in the fixity of biological forms.

The first four of these points are all derived from Augustine's reading of Scripture; the fifth represents what seemed to be a self-evident truth to Augustine, in the light of his personal experience and the contemporary scientific consensus. Augustine's espousal of the fixity of species is best seen as a provisional judgment of experience, not a fixed statement of theological interpretation. As Augustine himself constantly and consistently emphasized, there is a danger of making biblical interpretation dependent on contemporary scientific opinion, leaving its outcome vulnerable when today's provisional scientific consensus is replaced with tomorrow's.[61] The Darwinian controversies partly arose over this inadvertent incorporation of Aristotelian science into Christian biblical interpretation, so that a scientific challenge to Aristotle was misread as a scientific challenge to the Bible. It was the lens through which Scripture was read, not Scripture itself, that was challenged by Darwin's notion of the evolution of species.

Augustine thus offers a theological account of creation which is capable of scientific transcription. The nature and level of scientific and theological descriptions

58. See Peter R. Anstey, "Boyle on Seminal Principles," *Studies in History and Philosophy of Science C* 33 (2002): 597–630. The unhelpful link that emerged between *rationes seminales* and vitalism needlessly discredited this notion: see Justin E. H. Smith, ed., *The Problem of Animal Generation in Early Modern Philosophy* (Cambridge: Cambridge University Press, 2006).

59. For reflections on Augustine's approach, see Lienhard, "Reading the Bible and Learning to Read"; Michael C. McCarthy, "'We Are Your Books': Augustine, the Bible, and the Practice of Authority," *Journal of the American Academy of Religion* 75 (2007): 324–52.

60. This point can be restated in terms of God being the cause of things both *in fieri* and *in esse*. For this distinction in Descartes, see Daniel Garber, "How God Causes Motion: Descartes, Divine Sustenance, and Occasionalism," *Journal of Philosophy* 84 (1987): 567–80.

61. A similar point was made by the conservative Protestant theologian Benjamin B. Warfield, widely regarded as being of defining importance within modern American evangelicalism: see David N. Livingstone and Mark A. Noll, "B. B. Warfield (1851–1921): A Biblical Inerrantist as Evolutionist," *Isis* 91 (2000): 283–304.

are quite different; nevertheless, it is quite misleading to think of these as noninteracting magisteria,[62] which are intellectually isolated and disengaged. Even though the natural sciences and Christian theology do not speak the same language, they clearly possess overlapping domains of interest, leading to the potential for intellectual enrichment on the one hand and conflict on the other. Where some see boundaries as barriers, I see them as places of dialogue and exploration. Augustine does not translate his theological principles into explicit scientific statements, even though at times his statements reflect the prevailing consensus of his era. Rather, Augustine bequeathed to his successors a set of theological principles concerning the Christian doctrine of creation that are capable of provisional correlation with the scientific worldview of our own day. As I hope to indicate, that correlation proves remarkably positive and helpful.

Our attention now turns to recent understandings of the rich panorama of the history of the universe, which has considerable significance for any account of natural theology. Augustine's fifth-century interpretative framework offers a helpful heuristic for further reflection on the apparent evidence of fine-tuning that we shall consider in what follows. We begin by considering recent reflections on the origins of the universe.

62. The view of Stephen Jay Gould, "Nonoverlapping Magisteria," *Natural History* 106 (1997): 16–22. A fuller exposition may be found in Stephen Jay Gould, *Rocks of Ages: Science and Religion in the Fullness of Life* (London: Jonathan Cape, 2001).

FINE-TUNING
Observations and Interpretations

Chapter 9

In the Beginning

The Constants of the Universe

Cosmology is one of the most fascinating areas of the natural sciences, not least on account of the philosophical and theological questions that arise from its speculations. It is an unusual science in certain ways, not least because its central concerns relate to a singularity: the origins of the universe. We are unable to manipulate its originating conditions in any way, as in normal forms of scientific experimentation, and there are limitations on our ability to observe phenomena relating to either very distant regions or to very early times in the universe.[1] Furthermore, a careful distinction must be drawn between "the universe" and "the observable" universe, not least on account of the problem of *selection effects* which interfere with observations.[2] For example, some kinds of matter both emit very little radiation and are not easy to detect by absorption, giving rise to the famous *dark matter problem*. The "dark matter" is not "seen"; its existence is rather inferred

---

1. A related question concerns how our local situation relates to the universe as a whole: see the analysis in George Ellis, "Cosmology and Local Physics," *International Journal of Modern Physics* A17 (2002): 2667–72.
2. Chung-Pei Ma and Edmund Bertschinger, "A Cosmological Kinetic Theory for the Evolution of Cold Dark Matter Halos with Substructure: Quasi-Linear Theory," *Astrophysical Journal Letters* 612 (2004): 28–49.

from its gravitational effects, as in the rotation curves of galaxies. So is what we can see actually typical of the universe? To answer this question, we need to know both the characteristics of dark matter and its extent, neither of which are currently well understood.

These considerations raise difficulties for certain formulations of the scientific method. For example, how can science hope to deal with a singularity—a unique, never-to-be-repeated event? And what about the fundamental principle that some hold to underlie methodological naturalism, that all events have natural causes? In 1965, Milton Munitz argued that the scientific method presupposed that all spatiotemporal events are caused by other spatiotemporal events.[3] The scientific method, he concluded, was thus inconsistent with an initial singularity. "Any conception of the beginning of the universe," he therefore argued, "is an indefensible notion." This, however, represents a slightly confused account of the scientific method, in which metaphysical preconceptions appear to have been allowed to assume a controlling role. An empirical scientific method will always seek to inquire about natural causes; only a nonempirical metaphysical naturalism will insist that they can always be found.[4] As might be expected, the discussion of the origins of the universe has been intensely controversial precisely because of the challenges or reinforcements that it is seen to offer various metaphysical positions, whether theistic or atheistic.

THE EMERGENCE OF THE BIG BANG THEORY OF COSMIC ORIGINS

The twentieth century saw dramatic changes in our understanding of the origins and development of the universe.[5] The first two decades were dominated by the assumption that the universe was static. This led Albert Einstein to make what he later came to regard as one of the greatest blunders of his life. In 1915, Einstein published his ten coupled, nonlinear, partial differential equations, now known as the "Einstein field equations," which set out some fundamental features of his theory of general relativity.[6] The solution of his equations indicated that the universe

3. Milton K. Munitz, *The Mystery of Existence: An Essay in Philosophical Cosmology* (New York: Appleton-Century-Crofts, 1965). See further Michael F. Martin, *Atheism: A Philosophical Justification* (Philadelphia: Temple University Press, 1990), 105–6; Quentin Smith, "Causation and the Logical Impossibility of a Divine Cause," *Philosophical Topics* 24 (1996): 169–91.

4. This is correctly noted by Rem B. Edwards, *What Caused the Big Bang?* (Amsterdam: Rodopi, 2001), 112–13.

5. Works which survey the history of our understanding of the origins of the universe include Martin J. Rees, *New Perspectives in Astrophysical Cosmology*, 2nd ed. (Cambridge: Cambridge University Press, 2000); Edward R. Harrison, *Cosmology: The Science of the Universe*, 2nd ed. (Cambridge: Cambridge University Press, 2000). For the historical background, see Helge Kragh, *Conceptions of Cosmos: From Myths to the Accelerating Universe; A History of Cosmology* (Oxford: Oxford University Press, 2007).

6. For an accessible introduction, see Amir D. Aczel, *God's Equation: Einstein, Relativity and the Expanding Universe* (London: Piatkus, 2000).

was not static, but expanding. Alarmed by an apparent inconsistency with the prevailing model of a static universe, Einstein brought his theories into line with it by adding an artificial term—now known as the *cosmological constant*—to his field equations, stabilizing his model of the universe against expansion or contraction.[7] Yet if Einstein had possessed sufficient confidence in his original equations, on the basis of his theory he would have *predicted* that the universe was expanding or contracting, long before there was any observational evidence for any such expansion.[8]

During the 1920s, evidence began to emerge suggesting that the universe was indeed expanding.[9] Up to this point, it had been generally (though not universally) assumed that the nebulae observed in the night sky—such as M31 in Andromeda or M42 in Orion—were part of the Milky Way, the galaxy within which our solar system is located. On the basis of observations at the newly constructed 100-inch telescope on Mount Wilson (California), Edwin Hubble (1883–1953) proposed that these objects were galaxies in their own right, lying far beyond our own. Developing work on the spectral redshifts of these galaxies, Hubble was able to propose that the greater the distance between any two galaxies, the greater their relative speed of separation. The universe was expanding, with increasing speed and apparently irreversibly.

It was a difficult idea to accept at the time, since it seemed to suggest that the universe must have evolved from a very dense initial state—in other words, that the universe had a beginning. But this was merely a suggestion, one way of making sense of the observations. Other ways of thinking were certainly possible. In 1948, Fred Hoyle and others developed a "steady state" theory of the universe, which held that the universe, although expanding, could not be said to have had a beginning. Matter was continuously created in order to fill in the voids arising from cosmic expansion.

Opinion began to shift in the 1960s, chiefly on account of the discovery of the cosmic background radiation. In 1965, Arno Penzias and Robert Wilson were working on an experimental microwave antenna at the Bell Laboratories in New Jersey. They were experiencing some difficulties: irrespective of the direction in which they pointed the antenna, they found that they picked up an unwanted and obtrusive background hissing noise which they simply could not eliminate. Their initial explanation of this phenomenon was that the pigeons roosting on

7. Einstein himself actually referred to the "cosmological term." More recently, this has been interpreted in terms of the vacuum energy density.

8. The question of whether the cosmological constant has a nonzero value remains open: see, e.g., Martin J. Rees, *Just Six Numbers: The Deep Forces That Shape the Universe* (London: Phoenix, 2000), 95–99. Einstein might well have been surprised to learn that his banished cosmological constant has found a new lease of life, not on account of the universe being static, but to account for an accelerating universe. Expanding solutions of the Einstein field equations had been found by Alexander Friedmann and Abbé Georges Lemaître before Hubble's observations. For an accessible account of Friedmann's work, see Eduard A. Tropp, Viktor Y. Frenkel, and Arthur D. Chernin, *Alexander A. Friedmann: The Man Who Made the Universe Expand* (Cambridge: Cambridge University Press, 1993).

9. For an excellent study, see Robert W. Smith, *The Expanding Universe: Astronomy's "Great Debate," 1900–1931* (Cambridge: Cambridge University Press, 1982).

the antenna were interfering with it. Yet even after the enforced removal of the offending birds, the hiss remained.[10]

It was only a matter of time before the full significance of this irritating background hiss was appreciated. It could be understood as the "afterglow" of a primal cosmic explosion—a hot "big bang"—which had been proposed in 1948 by Ralph Alpher and Robert Herman.[11] This thermal radiation corresponded to photons moving about randomly in space, without any discernible source, at a temperature of 2.7 K (Kelvin). Taken alongside other pieces of evidence, this background radiation served as significant evidence that the universe had a beginning, and it caused severe difficulties for the rival steady state theory.[12]

Since then, the basic elements of the standard cosmological model have become clarified and have secured widespread support within the scientific community. Although there remain significant areas of debate, this model is widely agreed to offer the best resonance with observational evidence.[13] Scientists now believe that the universe originated some 14 billion years ago and that it has been expanding and cooling ever since. The two most significant pieces of evidence in support of this theory are the cosmic microwave background radiation and the relative abundance of light nuclei (such as hydrogen, deuterium, and helium) synthesized in the immediate aftermath of the big bang.[14] This entails the recognition that the origins of the universe must be recognized to be a singularity—a unique event, something which can never be repeated, and hence never subjected to the precise experimental analysis that some hold to be characteristic of the scientific method.

THE STANDARD COSMOLOGICAL MODEL

In general terms, the standard cosmological model takes the following form, often expressed in terms of "eras" or "epochs." The first dramatic moment of the universe's history is termed the "Planck era," lasting about 5×10^{-44} seconds. During this extraordinarily short period of time, the temperature of the universe was 1.4×10^{32} K. At this point, the universe was intensely compact and dense, caus-

10. The story is told in Jeremy Bernstein, *Three Degrees above Zero: Bell Laboratories in the Information Age* (New York: Scribner's, 1984).

11. The big bang was essentially what Abbé Georges Lemaître had called the "primordial atom" in 1927. The realization that a "*hot* big bang" would give rise to the background radiation was due to Ralph Alpher, Robert Herman, and George Gamow in 1948. The term "big bang" itself was coined by Fred Hoyle, the leading proponent of the hitherto dominant "steady state" theory, as a term of abuse for the new approach.

12. For an excellent discussion, see Steven Weinberg, *The First Three Minutes: A Modern View of the Origin of the Universe* (New York: Harper, 1993).

13. Douglas Scott, "The Standard Cosmological Model," *Canadian Journal of Physics* 84 (2006): 419–35.

14. On this theory see R. B. Partridge, *3K: The Cosmic Microwave Background Radiation* (Cambridge: Cambridge University Press, 1995).

ing difficulties for theoretical representations of what actually happened.[15] String theory suggests that there may have been 10 or 11 dimensions, of which only four were expanded into our four-dimensional space-time, the remainder retaining their original minuscule Planck dimensions. During this short epoch, quantum gravitational effects dominated, and there was no distinction between what would later be the four fundamental forces of nature: gravity, electromagnetism, the strong nuclear force, and the weak nuclear force. (Other forces, such as friction, arise from electromagnetic interactions between atoms and therefore are not considered to be fundamental forces of physics.)

As the universe expanded and cooled, various processes began to take place. In a period of rapid inflation, the universe grew by a factor of 10^{35} in 10^{-32} seconds, from being smaller than a subatomic particle to roughly the size of a grapefruit. As the universe evolved, structure formation on the scale of galaxies emerged out of gravitational growth of small primeval departures from homogeneity. Matter started to form clumps, including stars, allowing the process of nucleosynthesis to take place within stellar cores, leading to the chemical enrichment of the interstellar medium.

An important observation needs to be made at this stage. The big bang generated little chemical diversity. The conditions that prevailed in the early universe led to the production of hydrogen, helium, and small amounts of lithium—the three lightest elements.[16] Yet the thermonuclear processes which would lead to the formation of heavier elements could not occur under these conditions. The production of oxygen, magnesium, silicon, iron, and sulfur—the chemicals that make up 96% of Earth's mass—could not take place until and unless the vast amount of stellar material coalesced to form stars, which were able to initiate thermonuclear reactions in their cores.[17]

THE FINE-TUNING OF THE COSMOS

Close examination of the cosmic narrative just outlined suggests that its shape and outcome was determined by some critically important factors. It is clear that there exist certain invariant properties of the natural world and its elementary components which make the gross size and structure of almost all its composite objects inevitable. The size of bodies such as stars and planets are neither random nor the result of any progressive selection process, but simply manifestations of the different strengths of the various forces of nature. We can thus imagine a

15. See Alfio Bonanno and Martin Reuter, "Cosmology of the Planck Era from a Renormalization Group for Quantum Gravity," *Physics Review D* 65 (2002): 043508 (20 pages).

16. Small amounts of deuterium, a heavier isotope of hydrogen, are also known to have been formed at this stage.

17. Peter D. Ward and Donald Brownlee, *Rare Earth: Why Complex Life Is Uncommon in the Universe* (New York: Copernicus, 2003), 38–43.

mental experiment in which someone designs a machine that allows us to vary the values of some of the fundamental properties of the universe—such as the weak nuclear force—and see what would happen (at least theoretically) if they were significantly different from what is actually observed. The term "fine-tuning" is often—and it must be said, somewhat controversially—used to refer to the often-narrow window of possibilities that emerges from such mental experiments. The values of certain fundamental cosmological constants and the character of certain initial conditions of the universe appear to have played a decisive role in bringing about the emergence of a particular kind of universe, within which life is capable of developing. Although the term is clearly supportive of God as fine-tuner, it will be used throughout the present work in a neutral sense, referring simply to the surprisingly restricted range of values that certain fundamental constants must take to bring about our universe.

Some landmarks along the way should be noted. In 1973 Barry Collins and Stephen Hawking pointed out that, out of all the possible values of the physical constants, only a relatively narrow range of initial conditions could give rise to the observed isotropy of the actual universe.[18] A quite extraordinary degree of constraint would have to be imposed on the initial cosmic energy density to give rise to the universe as we know it. They found this result puzzling since accepted theories did not offer any explanation for the fact that the universe turned out this way rather than another. Collins and Hawking reasoned along what would now be considered to be anthropic lines in their discussion of the "flatness problem." Basing themselves on the clearly anthropic assumption that galaxies and stars are necessary for life, they argued that a universe beginning with too much gravitational energy would recollapse before it could form stars, and a universe with too little energy would not permit the gravitational condensation of galaxies and stars. Thus, out of many different possible initial values of Ω (the ratio of the actual average density of the universe to the critical density), human life could only have emerged in a universe where the initial value of Ω was almost precisely 1.

A year later, Brandon Carter published a paper in which he introduced the term *anthropic principle*, which he stated in two forms.[19] The *weak* anthropic principle states that "what we can expect to observe must be restricted by the conditions necessary for our presence as observers." The *strong* anthropic principle holds that "the universe (and hence the fundamental parameters on which it depends) must be such as to admit the creation of observers within it at some stage."

These speculative explorations culminated in 1986 with the publication of John Barrow and Frank Tipler's landmark book *The Anthropic Cosmological Principle*, which propelled the "anthropic principle" from the pages of obscure jour-

18. C. B. Collins and Stephen Hawking, "Why Is the Universe Isotropic?" *Astrophysical Journal Letters* 180 (1973): 317–34.
19. Brandon Carter, "Large Number Coincidences and the Anthropic Principle," in *Confrontation of Cosmological Theories with Observational Data*, ed. M. S. Longair (Boston: Reidel, 1974), 291–98.

nals to popular culture.[20] In doing so, it raised many theological questions, including the apologetic value of the anthropic principle. Barrow and Tipler provided a comprehensive yet relatively accessible account of the fundamental role played by the constants of nature, and the astonishing great implications of seemingly small variations in their magnitude. *The Anthropic Cosmological Principle* set out the extraordinary, seemingly fortuitous coincidences that appear to have made life possible. Barrow and Tipler went on to present three possible ways of making sense of apparent fine-tuning of the world for biological life: the "weak," "strong," and "final" forms of the principle.[21] Although each of these models was already known within the scientific community, Barrow and Tipler made them intelligible and accessible to a much-wider readership. It rapidly became the "Bible of anthropic reasoning" (Robert Klee).

It was, some felt, a risky book for both authors to write. By raising questions about design, Barrow and Tipler were breaking scientific taboos that might have had a major detrimental impact upon their careers. For example, nearly two hundred pages of text were devoted to a rigorous exploration of the notion of "purpose" and "design." Yet the intellectual range and sheer brilliance of their exposition disarmed their critics. The book represents a landmark in the acceptance of "science and religion" as a legitimate, proper, and even necessary adjunct to scientific reflection, prompting some to suggest that it might be the greatest work of natural theology since William Paley.[22] It has catalyzed a new debate within Christian apologetics—and beyond—over the evidential basis of faith.

By setting the discussion about design in its proper intellectual framework, Barrow and Tipler challenged the popular secular myth that talk about "design" of the world was a recent innovation, associated with intellectual arrivistes such as William Paley. As they rightly pointed out, it is one of the oldest and most fundamental questions of all, deriving its legitimacy partly from its antiquity and partly from its sheer intellectual importance.[23] "Aristotelian science was based

20. John Barrow and Frank J. Tipler, *The Anthropic Cosmological Principle* (Oxford: Oxford University Press, 1986).

21. For critical analysis of these statements of the principle, see works such as John Earman, "The SAP Also Rises: A Critical Examination of the Anthropic Principle," *American Philosophical Quarterly* 24 (1987): 307–17; William Lane Craig, "Barrow and Tipler on the Anthropic Principle versus Divine Design," *British Journal for Philosophy of Science* 38 (1988): 389–95; Joseph Silk, *The Infinite Cosmos: Questions from the Frontiers of Cosmology* (Oxford: Oxford University Press, 2006), 14–18; Mark A. Walker and Milan M. Cirkovic, "Astrophysical Fine Tuning, Naturalism, and the Contemporary Design Argument," *International Studies in the Philosophy of Science* 20 (2006): 285–307.

22. See the comments in Craig, "Barrow and Tipler on the Anthropic Principle versus Divine Design." The influence of the book is evident from recent literature, both academic and popular: see, e.g., Gilbert Fulmer, "Faces in the Sky: The Anthropic Principle Design Argument," *Journal of American Culture* 26 (2003): 485–88.

23. For a more recent discussion, endorsing their judgment, see Milan M. Cirkovic, "Ancient Origins of a Modern Anthropic Cosmological Argument," *Astronomical and Astrophysical Transactions* 22 (2003): 879–86.

upon presupposition of an intelligent natural world that functions according to some deliberate design." The debate may have taken a specific form in the hands of William Paley in the early nineteenth century, yet Paley's intellectual and theological misadventures, which are clearly specific to his age, cannot be allowed to negate the question of why things are the way they are—or indeed, why there is anything at all.

Barrow addressed such issues in subsequent writings,[24] making the fair point that two quite different forms of the design argument are used by theologians and philosophers. The first is that which is encountered in the larger, biological section of Paley's *Natural Theology*, based on "nice outcomes of the laws of nature." The argument, though easily grasped, is severely vulnerable. God can easily be eliminated from the argument (a development which began long before Darwin published his theory of natural selection.) In my view, it amounts to little more than Deism, positing a somewhat attenuated notion of God, rather than the somewhat richer Trinitarian vision of God associated with Christianity.

Barrow's second approach is based on "nice laws." Where do the laws of nature come from? If the universe sprang into existence in an astonishingly short time *already possessing the laws that would govern its development*, the question of the origin and character of those laws becomes of major apologetic importance. As Barrow rightly points out, this latter version of the design argument is much harder to explain without reference to God. After all, the laws of nature clearly did not come into being by a gradual process of cumulative selection. The universe that emerged out of the big bang, on an anthropic reading of things, was already governed by laws that were fine-tuned to encourage the rise of carbon-based life-forms.[25] The apparent fine-tuning of the universe has been considered in a large number of relatively accessible works[26] and does not require detailed exegesis in this chapter. For our purposes, it is enough to note several features that are illustrative of this phenomenon, rather than provide a more-extended analysis. The debate in the literature mainly concerns the *interpretation* of these phenomena, whose existence is generally conceded. The essential point is that if the values of certain fundamental constants which govern the development of the universe had been slightly different, its evolution would have taken a different course, leading to a cosmos in which life would not have been possible. The element of surprise in this analysis relates to the impact on cosmic evolution of even a small variation of some of these constants.

24. For example, see John D. Barrow, *Theories of Everything: The Quest for Ultimate Explanation* (London: Vintage, 1992), 118–21; John D. Barrow, *Between Inner Space and Outer Space: Essays on Science, Art, and Philosophy* (Oxford: Oxford University Press, 2000), 61–63.

25. For a more recent statement of a similar position, see Paul Davies, *The Goldilocks Enigma: Why Is the Universe Just Right for Life?* (London: Allen Lane, 2006), 147–71.

26. In addition to Barrow and Tipler, *The Anthropic Cosmological Principle*, see also John Leslie, *Universes* (London: Routledge, 1989); John R. Gribbin and Martin J. Rees, *The Stuff of the Universe: Dark Matter, Mankind and Anthropic Cosmology* (London: Penguin, 1995).

FINE-TUNING AND THE CONSTANTS OF NATURE:
A SUMMARY

A canonical statement of the importance of the fine balancing of the fundamental constants of the universe was provided recently by Martin Rees.[27] We may summarize his analysis as follows:

1. The ratio of the electromagnetic force to the force of gravity, which can also be expressed in terms of the electrical (coulomb) force between two protons divided by the gravitational force between them. This measures the strength of the electrical forces that hold atoms together, divided by the force of gravity between them. If this were slightly smaller than its observed value, "only a short-lived miniature universe could exist: no creatures could grow larger than insects, and there would be no time for biological evolution."

2. The strong nuclear force, which defines how firmly atomic nuclei bind together. This force, which has a value of 0.007, "controls the power from the Sun and, more sensitively, how stars transmute hydrogen into all the atoms of the periodic table." Once more, the value of this constant turns out to be of critical importance. If it "were 0.006 or 0.008, we could not exist."

3. The amount of matter in the universe. The cosmic number Ω (omega) is a measure of the amount of material in our universe—such as galaxies, diffuse gas, and so-called "dark matter" and "dark energy." Thus Ω tells us the relative importance of gravity and expansion energy in the universe. "If this ratio were too high relative to a particular 'critical' value, the universe would have collapsed long ago; had it been too low, no galaxies or stars would have formed. The initial expansion speed seems to have been finely tuned."

4. Cosmic repulsion. In 1998, cosmologists became aware of the importance of cosmic antigravity in controlling the expansion of the universe, and in particular its increasing importance as our universe becomes ever darker and emptier.[28] "Fortunately for us (and very surprisingly to theorists), λ is very small. Otherwise its effect would have stopped galaxies and stars from forming, and cosmic evolution would have been stifled before it could even begin."

5. The ratio of the gravitational binding force to rest-mass energy, Q, is of fundamental importance in determining the "texture" of the universe. "If Q were even smaller, the universe would be inert and structureless; if Q were much larger, it would be a violent place, in which no stars or solar systems could survive, dominated by vast black holes."

6. The number of spatial dimensions, D, which is three. String theory argues that, of the 10 or 11 original dimensions at the origins of the universe, all but

27. Rees, *Just Six Numbers*, 2–4. This terse synopsis is amplified in the remainder of the work.
28. For an excellent account of this development, and especially its implications for Einstein's cosmological constant, see Alexei V. Filippenko, "Einstein's Biggest Blunder? High-Redshift Supernovae and the Accelerating Universe," *Publications of the Astronomical Society of the Pacific* 113 (2001): 1441–48.

three were compactified. Time, of course, is to be treated as a fourth dimension. "Life," Rees comments, "couldn't exist if D were two or four."[29]

These six points can easily be expanded to include a series of observations about the values of fundamental constants, or the initial boundary conditions of the universe.[30] As Freeman Dyson once remarked, "the more I examine the universe and study the details of its architecture, the more evidence I find that the universe in some sense must have known that we were coming."[31]

So how are these observations to be explained? For the theist, unsurprisingly, these observations point to the inherent potentiality with which the Creator has endowed creation. The relatively recent and unexpected discovery of anthropic phenomena has led to considerable discomfort on the part of some cosmologists, who are uneasy that a new lease on life has been given to discussion of apparent design in the cosmos. This has led to intense discussion of possible explanations of these observations, sometimes driven as much by the hope of eliminating the new styles of natural theology that have emerged in recent years as by the yearning to understand the cosmos better.

It is quite clear that anthropic phenomena fit easily and naturally into a theistic framework, especially its Trinitarian forms.[32] Theologians do not hold that the Christian doctrine of God allows us to predict the specifics of the universe; the general view has always been that, since God made the cosmos with no constraining influences other than the divine will and nature, it could have been created in a variety of manners. René Descartes (1596–1650) thus argued that we must use empirical evidence to determine the structure of the world. There is no question of predicting the form of the world on theological grounds; rather, the form of the world is a contingency which is to be determined empirically and then shown to be consistent with the known will of God.[33]

> We cannot determine by reason how big these pieces of matter are, how quickly they move, or what circles they describe. God might have arranged

29. The classic statement of this argument is found in Max Tegmark, "On the Dimensionality of Spacetime," *Classical and Quantum Gravity* 14 (1997): L69–L75. Dr. Rodney Holder kindly drew my attention to William Paley's significant argument that the inverse square law of gravitation is needed for life. For comment, see John D. Barrow, *The Constants of Nature: From Alpha to Omega* (London: Vintage, 2003), 218–20.

30. See, e.g., the classic paper of Roger Penrose, "Difficulties with Inflationary Cosmology," in *Proceedings of the 14th Texas Symposium on Relativistic Astrophysics*, ed. E. J. Fergus (New York: New York Academy of Sciences, 1989), 249–64. Penrose here explores the extraordinarily large array of theoretical possibilities for the shape of the universe, noting that only one of them would resemble that which we know and inhabit. Penrose's main interest is the initial entropy of the universe and the asymmetry between the original big bang and the final big crunch.

31. Freeman J. Dyson, *Disturbing the Universe* (New York: Harper & Row, 1979), 250.

32. For an excellent statement of the explanatory superiority of theism in relation to anthropic phenomena, see Robin Collins, "A Scientific Argument for the Existence of God: The Fine-Tuning Design Argument," in *Reason for the Hope Within*, ed. Michael J. Murray (Grand Rapids: Eerdmans, 1999), 47–75. For a more-popular account, see Michael A. Corey, *The God Hypothesis: Discovering Design in Our "Just Right" Goldilocks Universe* (Lanham, MD: Rowman & Littlefield, 2001).

33. René Descartes, *Principles of Philosophy* 3.46, translation from Elizabeth Anscombe and Philip T. Geach, *Descartes: Philosophical Writings* (London: Nelson, 1969), 225.

these things in countless different ways; which way he in fact chose rather than the rest we must learn from observation. Therefore, we are free to make any assumptions we like about them, as long as all the consequences agree with experience.

The observation of anthropic phenomena is thus situated within a long tradition of theological and metaphysical reflection on *theologia naturalis*. It holds that the general phenomenon of fine-tuning is consonant with Christian belief in a creator God, arguing that the nature of things is such that the most appropriate outcome for a natural theology is to demonstrate that observation of the natural world furnishes conceptual resonance with, not deductive proof of, the Christian vision of God. On this approach, theism offers the best "empirical fit" of the various theories which set out to account for anthropic phenomena. Yet it must be emphasized that Christian theology has never seen itself as charged with the task of inventing an explanation for these observations; rather, they fit within, and resonate with, an *existing* way of thinking, which proves capable of satisfactorily incorporating such observations.[34]

ON MAKING SENSE OF ANTHROPIC PHENOMENA

God, then, unquestionably represents a plausible explanation of anthropic phenomena. But is this the *best* explanation? Alternative perspectives certainly exist, even if they are generally of very recent origin. For example, some argue that apparent cosmic fine-tuning is nothing more an interesting happenstance. The fundamental constants in question had to have *some* value—so why not these ones? They need possess no further significance. To give an example: the population of the United States of America is (over) 300 million. There is only one president. The odds of any one American becoming president are thus 1 in 300 million. But so what? Someone has to be president. It may be highly improbable that any given individual should be president, but it is a certainty that someone will be. At one level, it is impossible to refute this argument. Yet it is clearly inadequate to account for the actualization of a highly improbable scenario: the emergence of a universe adapted for life.

A second and much-more-significant approach argues that anthropic phenomena appear significant on account of the bias or location of the observer. In 1937, the distinguished theoretical physicist Paul Dirac became interested in what are known as "large number coincidences."[35] By that time it was well known that the ratio of the electrostatic attraction between the proton and the electron

34. However, I would concur entirely with the caveats noted by Ernan McMullin in a significant essay of some years ago: Ernan McMullin, "Natural Science and Belief in a Creator," in *Physics, Philosophy, and Theology*, ed. Robert J. Russell, William R. Stoeger, and George V. Coyne (Rome: Vatican Observatory, 1988), 49–79.
35. P. A. M. Dirac, "The Cosmological Constants," *Nature* 139 (1937): 323–24.

in the hydrogen atom to the gravitational force between the same two particles is about 10^{39}. Dirac found other combinations of fundamental constants with approximately the same value and suggested that this coincidence was to be explained by some hitherto unknown link between the fundamental constants and the age of the universe. Since the age of the universe increases with time, the fundamental constants of physics in the universe would also have to change with time, in order to preserve this relationship. In particular, the value of the gravitational constant G should therefore decrease with time.

Dirac's idea of a variable gravitational constant, already treated with skepticism within the scientific community, was finally laid to rest in 1961, when Robert Dicke put forward a simpler explanation, framed in terms of the "selection effect" on possible values of the constants which arises from the existence of human observers.[36] As Dicke pointed out, the Hubble time T which had elapsed since the big bang was "not a 'random choice' from a wide range of possible choices, but is limited by the criteria for the existence of physicists." The values of T are thus constrained by the elementary requirement that the universe should have aged sufficiently to allow biochemically necessary elements to have formed. As Dicke wittily remarked, "It is well known that carbon is required to make physicists."

This carbon is produced by nuclear fusion of helium inside red giant stars, a process which can take several billion years in the case of small or medium-size stars, or a few million years in the case of large stars. After this, the star can explode as a supernova, scattering the newly formed elements throughout space, where they can eventually coalesce to form planets, on which life could evolve. Dicke therefore pointed out that, in order to be able to produce carbon-based life, the universe must be between several million and a trillion years old (a rather generous range of possibilities, it may be noted). On the other hand, if the universe were much older, the stellar processes necessary to produce the radiation energy upon which known life-forms ultimately depend would have terminated. This, Dicke insisted, was the true reason for the coincidences noticed by Dirac, which could therefore be explained without any need for the notion of a variable gravitational constant. Dirac had failed to appreciate the importance of this biotic window in the history of the universe.

A related approach is taken by Nick Bostrom, who argues that any special features of the universe which we might observe are ultimately illusory, a necessary consequence of our restricted viewpoint.[37] Since we could not exist in other situations (for example, those in which there is no resonance in ^{12}C nucleus, enabling formation of elements heavier than helium), we will not observe those places, no matter how real and common they are. Bostrom thus argues that the central error of much anthropic thinking concerns a failure to appreciate that it represents nothing other than an *observational selection effect*.

36. Robert H. Dicke, "Dirac's Cosmology and Mach's Principle," *Nature* 192 (1961): 440–41.
37. Nick Bostrom, *Anthropic Bias: Observation Selection Effects in Science and Philosophy* (New York: Routledge, 2002), 11–58. See also Nick Bostrom, "Self-Locating Belief in Big Worlds: Cosmology's Missing Link to Observation," *Journal of Philosophy* 99 (2002): 607–23.

A third approach has generated considerable interest: the multiverse. On this view, there exists a multiplicity of universes, so that the one we inhabit is an inevitability. We happen to live in a universe with these biologically friendly properties; we do not observe other universes, where these conditions do not pertain. Our insights are restricted by observation selection effects, which means that our location within a biophilic universe inclines us to propose that the entire cosmos possesses such properties, when in fact other universes will exist which are inimical to life. Indeed, such biophobic universes are predicted to be the norm. We happen to exist in an exceptional universe.

So how did this intellectually challenging idea arise? The basic idea of an inflationary universe was first proposed by Alan Guth in 1981 in order to solve two key cosmological puzzles within standard big bang cosmology.[38] According to this model, an enormous inflation of the universe took place within an astonishingly short period of time,[39] perhaps as small as 10^{-35} seconds, in which the size of the universe increased by an astonishing factor of as much as 10^{50}. Although the existing model had been extremely successful in correlating the observable properties of our universe, two major difficulties remained, generally known as the "flatness problem" and the "horizon problem." The former concerned the question of why the curvature of the universe is so small; the second, how the temperature of the cosmic microwave background can have a temperature uniform to better than one part in 30,000. The isotropy of the cosmic microwave radiation had been a significant problem for Collins and Hawking, as noted above. Guth's approach seemed to open the way to resolving these explanatory difficulties.

Yet this model had significant implications for our understanding of the universe.[40] As a consequence of this enormous initial cosmic inflation, all of space has expanded to colossal proportions, many times larger than our observable universe. We are therefore in a position in which we cannot observe these other spatial regions simply because there has not been enough time for light to travel from these regions into our universe. Furthermore, there is a growing body of data implying an accelerated expansion of the universe, which indicates that the light from these distant regions will never reach us. They are not, and never will be, observable.

On this model, the observable universe is therefore to be conceived of as a minuscule region or "bubble" within this vast spatial structure, consisting of multiple universes. This multiverse consists of a vast ensemble of existent universes, in different spatial domains of varying sizes and structures. Within each domain, the constants of nature could take on distinct values as a consequence of the different ways that inflation begins and ends in that cosmic region. Current interpretations

38. Alan Guth, "Inflationary Universe: A Possible Solution to the Horizon and Flatness Problems," *Physical Reviews* D23 (1981): 347–56.

39. Alan Guth, *The Inflationary Universe: The Quest for a New Theory of Cosmic Origins* (Reading, MA: Addison-Wesley Publishing Co., 1997), 167–88; a lower factor is suggested earlier (175).

40. For details of these implications and their theoretical justification, see ibid. further; Alex Vilenkin, *Many Worlds in One: The Search for Other Universes* (New York: Hill & Wang, 2006); Bernard Carr, ed., *Universe or Multiverse?* (Cambridge: Cambridge University Press, 2007).

of string theory suggest that the multiverse may consist of as many as 10^{500} sets of constants.[41] In most of these domains, the set of values inherited would be expected to be biophobic. However, on probabilistic grounds, there will be some region in which the set of values are biophilic. We happen to live in one such universe. It may be fine-tuned for life. But what of the 10^{500} others?

It is important to appreciate that at present the multiverse hypothesis remains little more than a fascinating yet highly speculative mathematical exercise. It has, perhaps unwisely, been adopted by atheists anxious to undermine the potential theological significance of fine-tuning in the universe. Thus part of the attraction of the multiverse hypothesis to atheist physicists such as Steven Weinberg and Leonard Susskind is that it appears to avoid any inference of design or divinity.[42] In fact, however, it seems that substantially the same arguments can be brought to bear for the existence of God in the case of a multiverse as in the case of a universe, with the multiverse hypothesis being consistent with, not the intellectual defeater of, a theistic understanding of God.[43] Yet the multiverse, at the time of writing, remains an immature and speculative scientific theory, raising some difficulties in its own right,[44] suggesting that a more-detailed theological response should await further clarification of its status within the scientific community.

So how are we to assess these new developments in cosmology, which are clearly of considerable theological significance? Though there are dissenting voices, it is widely agreed that the "new cosmology" is consonant with theism.[45] Some would go further and argue that the phenomenon of fine-tuning gives new life to more rigorous forms of inductive or deductive argumentation for the existence of God, such as the teleological and cosmological arguments.[46] The real-

---

41. Michael R. Douglas and Shamit Kachru, "Flux Compactification," *Reviews of Modern Physics* 79 (2007): 733–96.

42. Bernard Carr, "Introduction and Overview," in *Universe or Multiverse?* ed. Bernard Carr (Cambridge: Cambridge University Press, 2007), 3–28, esp. 16.

43. See John Leslie, *Universes* (London: Routledge, 1989), 198: "My argument has been that the fine tuning is evidence, genuine evidence, of the following fact: that God is real, and/or there are many and varied universes." See further Robin Collins, "The Multiverse Hypothesis: A Theistic Perspective," in Carr, *Universe or Multiverse?* 459–80, esp. 464–65. For the idea of an intellectual "defeater," see Alvin Plantinga, "Reliabilism, Analyses and Defeaters," *Philosophy and Phenomenological Research* 55 (1995): 427–64.

44. For some of these, see Rodney D. Holder, *God, the Multiverse, and Everything: Modern Cosmology and the Argument from Design* (Aldershot: Ashgate, 2004), 113–29; Anthony Aguirre, "Making Predictions in a Multiverse," in Carr, *Universe or Multiverse?* 367–86. Holder, like Richard Swinburne, argues for a "more rigorous inductive" argument for God's existence, based on the phenomena described in this chapter. William Lane Craig adopts a more deductive approach, based on the belief that the universe has an origin.

45. For an excellent statement of this position, see John Polkinghorne, *Belief in God in an Age of Science* (New Haven, CT: Yale University Press, 1998), 1–24.

46. For example, see William Lane Craig, "The Existence of God and the Beginning of the Universe," *Truth: A Journal of Modern Thought* 3 (1991): 85–96; Richard Swinburne. *The Existence of God*, 2nd ed. (Oxford: Clarendon Press, 2004). For a useful collection of essays representing all sides of this debate, see Neil A. Manson, ed., *God and Design: The Teleological Argument and Modern Science* (London: Routledge, 2003).

ization that the universe as a whole, and not simply life on Earth, has a history has major implications for our understanding of the emergence of life, often ignored in biological works. For example, Richard Dawkins's account of biological evolution often seems to assume that it is utterly unproblematic, and perhaps even uninteresting, that the critical chemical materials required for life are present in the universe, with physical properties that facilitate both the emergence and development of living forms. We shall be considering this point in further detail in subsequent chapters.

In chapter 8 we proposed Augustine of Hippo's model of creation as a heuristic for exploring anthropic phenomena. The fundamental picture that emerges from the contemporary view of the origins and development of the universe is that of an entity which came into existence and was virtually instantaneously endowed with potentialities for anthropic development. Augustine had little interest in the chronology of the creation and its subsequent development; his primary concern was to emphasize the total dependence of all things upon God, and the continuing divine involvement in the guidance of the emergence of living forms from the causalities embedded in the fabric of the universe. Augustine's model elegantly enfolds the broad features of modern cosmology; though weak on detail, as one might expect, the broad brushstrokes of his approach resonate strongly with contemporary understandings of the origin and development of the cosmos. The intellectually capacious notion of *rationes seminales* is consonant with a universe that evolves and, as time progresses and conditions change, unfolds potentialities that were present early, though not yet actualized. There is no fundamental difficulty in affirming the autonomy of nature to develop on the one hand, and providential divine agency on the other. As William Carroll points out, "God's causality is such that he causes creatures to be the kind of causal agents which they are."[47]

Yet the issue of fine-tuning is no longer being limited to a discussion of cosmology. Since about 1990, there has been growing awareness that other scientific disciplines are generating material that is open to a similar interpretation. In particular, there has been a growing realization of the interconnections between certain fundamental principles of biology and astrophysics. As we have already seen, the early universe produced nearly nothing other than hydrogen and helium, yet biochemistry requires and uses almost all of the chemically active, reasonably abundant elements in the upper half of the periodic table. The time required to manufacture abundant biological elements and stars with Earthlike planets is determined by the formation and evolution times of galaxies and stellar populations, setting a minimum age of billions of years.[48] It is widely believed that the origins of life require the formation of small planet-like bodies, with chemistries

47. William E. Carroll, "Divine Agency, Contemporary Physics, and the Autonomy of Nature," *Heythrop Journal* 49 (2008): 1–21, esp. 14.

48. Craig J. Hogan, "Why the Universe Is Just So," *Review of Modern Physics* 72 (2000): 1149–61.

and surface temperatures that are capable of supporting living organisms. Earth is believed to have been formed by a process of accretion from the solar nebula, leading to a series of defining characteristics—such as its chemical composition, atmosphere, and distance from the sun—which made it suitable for life.[49] The significance of these observations is a matter of intense discussion at present.

So how did life begin? In the next chapter, we shall consider some of the questions surrounding this significant development.

49. Ward and Brownlee, *Rare Earth*, 35–54.

Chapter 10

Can These Bones Live?

The Origins of Life

In 1913, Lawrence J. Henderson (1878–1942), professor of biological chemistry at Harvard University, made the suggestion that "the whole evolutionary process, both cosmic and organic, is one, and the biologist may now rightly regard the universe in its very essence as biocentric."[1] Henderson's bold statements can be seen as an example of biologically focused anthropic thinking,[2] which asserted both the biocentric properties of the universe and the need to clarify their mechanism. Although Henderson was emphatic that he did not wish to invoke

1. Lawrence J. Henderson, *The Fitness of the Environment: An Inquiry into the Biological Significance of the Properties of Matter* (New York: Macmillan, 1913; repr., Boston: Beacon Press, 1958), 312. On Henderson's approach, see John Parascandola, "Organismic and Holistic Concepts in the Thought of L. J. Henderson," *Journal of the History of Biology* 4 (1971): 63–113; Iris Fry, "On the Biological Significance of the Properties of Matter: L. J. Henderson's Theory of the Fitness of the Environment," *Journal of the History of Biology* 29 (1996): 155–96. For similar ideas to be set out more recently, see Michael Denton, *Nature's Destiny: How the Laws of Biology Reveal Purpose in the Universe* (New York: Free Press, 1998). Note the references to "biocentric adaptations in the design of the cosmos" (14), and the assertion that "the universe is profoundly biocentric and gives every appearance of having been specially designed for life" (16).
2. See John Barrow and Frank J. Tipler, *The Anthropic Cosmological Principle* (Oxford: Oxford University Press, 1986), 143–47; John R. Gribbin and Martin J. Rees, *Cosmic Coincidences: Dark Matter, Mankind, and Anthropic Cosmology* (New York: Bantam Books, 1989), 270.

a divine designer,[3] the possible implications of his approach for theistic views of reality could hardly be ignored.

Henderson taught at Harvard University from 1904 until his death in 1942 and was one of the leading lights in the movement to establish a Department of Physical Chemistry at Harvard Medical School. His research into the physical chemistry and biochemistry of physiological systems, especially regulatory mechanisms of respiration in the blood, led him to the view that the chemical environment was adapted to life. Through his work on the interdependence and self-regulation of the various factors constituting the physiochemical system of the blood, Henderson came to realize the intricate nature of biological organization. He was instrumental in the establishment of the concept of the living organism as a self-regulating system that maintains a complex system of dynamic equilibria.

Henderson's general conclusion resulting from his research on biological buffers was that the physiological mechanisms involved in the maintenance of neutrality possessed "a remarkable and unsuspected degree of efficiency." So what explanation could be offered?[4]

> If it shall appear that the fitness of the environment to fulfil these demands of life is great, we may then ask whether it is so great that we can not reasonably assume it to be accidental, and finally we may inquire what manner of law is capable of explaining such fitness of the very nature of things.

In particular, Henderson pointed out how the organic chemistry of carbon and physical chemistry of water were unusually adapted to life.[5] He thus suggested that the unique fitness of carbon and water for life was a consequence of deep natural laws that ultimately led to life under the right types of circumstances. "If life has originated by an evolutionary process from dead matter, that is surely the crowning and most wonderful instance of teleology in the whole universe." Yet Darwinian evolution could not account for these properties, which had to be seen as a "natural result of the properties of matter and the characteristics of energy in the course of cosmic evolution."[6] These were already there, embedded in the deeper structure of things. In some sense, the origins of life were dependent upon them.

To some of Henderson's critics, his concept of "environmental fitness" was little more than a self-evident truth.[7] The fitness of an organism to its environment, they argued, necessarily entails the fitness of the environment for organisms. This point was made in an early review of Henderson's work by the biologist R. S. Lillie, who claimed "that the universe must show itself, on examination, to be a fit

---

3. He nevertheless cites appreciatively from the Bridgewater Treatises: Henderson, *Fitness of the Environment*, 5–7.

4. Ibid., 37.

5. Ibid., 65–110.

6. Ibid., 275.

7. On Henderson's concept of "fitness" and its relevance for fine-tuning, see Everett Mendelsohn, "Locating 'Fitness' and L. J. Henderson," in *Fitness of the Cosmos for Life: Biochemistry and Fine-Tuning*, ed. John D. Barrow et al. (Cambridge: Cambridge University Press, 2007), 3–19.

environment for living beings, since they continue to exist in it."[8] Yet Henderson was not actually guilty of such a tautology. Rather, he was trying to imagine what kind of material properties a hypothetical cosmic architect might choose a priori, if charged with the task of designing a world similar to ours, characterized by the evolution of diversity of physicochemical systems, including living systems. For Henderson, those properties concerned primarily the ability to maintain stable conditions in which systems can evolve; most of these specifications, he argued, are met by "the ensemble of properties of the elements hydrogen, carbon, and oxygen."[9]

While Henderson's arguments are open to challenge at a number of points, his contention that the fundamental characteristics of certain elements of the universe are fine-tuned (if this anachronistic way of speaking may be permitted) for life remains scientifically and philosophically significant. Evolution is a contextualized process, dependent upon environmentally available resources.[10] Long before Darwinian evolution took place, Henderson pointed out, the essential chemical preconditions for life were in place. This line of argument clearly merits further exploration, just as it equally requires amendment in the light of more recent developments.

WHAT IS LIFE?

An appropriate starting point for this discussion is to ask how "life" is to be defined.[11] What determines whether something can be said to "live"?[12] Since the nineteenth century, there has been a clear recognition that the capacity to metabolize is an integral aspect of life. Metabolism (the total of all chemical reactions occurring in a cell) has two components: catabolism, the breakdown of larger, more-complex molecules into smaller, simpler ones, during which energy is released, trapped, and made available for work; and anabolism, the synthesis of complex molecules from simpler precursors, requiring the input of energy. It was therefore appropriate that the *Viking* mission to search for life on Mars in 1976 contained a biology package which allowed it to undertake experiments designed to detect signs of microbial metabolism.

8. R. S. Lillie, "Review of *The Fitness of the Environment*," *Science* 38 (1913): 337.

9. Lawrence J. Henderson, *The Order of Nature: An Essay* (Cambridge, MA: Harvard University Press, 1917), 181.

10. Note the helpful and suggestive imagery deployed in G. Evelyn Hutchinson, *The Ecological Theater and the Evolutionary Play* (New Haven, CT: Yale University Press, 1965).

11. Henderson's view was that life had three fundamental characteristics: complexity, durability through self-regulation, and metabolic activity: Henderson, *Fitness of the Environment*, 31–32.

12. For surveys of the problems of definition, see Martino Rizzotti and André E. Brack, eds., *Defining Life: The Central Problems in Theoretical Biology* (Padua: University of Padua, 1996); Carol E. Cleland and Christopher F. Chyba, "Defining 'Life,'" *Origins of Life and Evolution of the Biosphere* 32 (2002): 387–93; Gyula Pályi, Claudia Zucchi, and Luciano Caglioti, eds., *Fundamentals of life* (Paris: Elsevier, 2002); T. M. Fenchel, *The Origin and Early Evolution of Life* (Oxford: Oxford University Press, 2002).

One obvious definition of life would thus focus on the capacity of living organisms to sustain themselves metabolically. Yet a simple definition of life as "a self-sustaining system" runs into immediate difficulties, due to the high degree of interconnectedness evident within the biosphere. Animals feed on plants or other animals; plants require microorganisms to be present in their root systems if they are to absorb nutrients; bacteria often live inside other organisms, relying on the internal environment of their host for their survival. This definition of life would seem to restrict it unintentionally to relatively rare chemolithotrophs and photolithotrophs.[13]

The real difficulty, however, is that attempts to address the definition of living systems have often led to nothing more than phenomenological characterizations of life, which are then reduced to a mere list of observed (or inferred) properties.[14] These inventories are not only unsatisfactory from an epistemological viewpoint, since they lack conceptual rigor and fail to provide determinative criteria by which "life" may be defined. For example, one might define life in terms of a capacity to reproduce; this encounters serious difficulties on account of mules and other sterile living entities which are not able to replicate structurally. A definition of life which includes reproduction as a prerequisite for life leads to the deeply problematic conclusion that mules, children, worker ants—to mention some obvious examples—cannot be considered to be alive, whereas crystals, fire, and cells removed from a dead person can be thought of as "living."

This difficulty can be largely avoided by considering life as being an autopoietic system—in other words, as an entity defined by an internal process of self-maintenance and self-generation. Cells and organisms made of cells are fundamentally autopoietic. They metabolize continuously, and in doing so affect the chemical composition of their surroundings. Nevertheless, there are difficulties here. For example, a number of physical and chemical analogues have been argued to show autopoietic behavior, mimicking at least some of the basic properties of life. One of the most interesting examples is that of the self-replicating micelles and liposomes, such as synthetic vesicles formed by caprylic acid containing lithium hydroxide and stabilized by an octanoic acid derivative. These have been shown to catalyze the hydrolysis of ethyl caprylate. The resulting caprylic acid is incorporated into the micelle walls, leading to their growth and, eventually, to their fragmentation over a period of several "generations."[15] Yet though exhibiting some features of living entities, these replicative micelles and liposomes do not exhibit genealogy or phylogeny. A good case can thus be made that Darwinian evolution is essential

13. Lansing M. Prescott, John P. Harley, and Donald A. Klein, *Microbiology*, 4th ed. (Boston, MA: McGraw-Hill, 1999), 179–87, 193–95.

14. Joan Oliver and Randall S. Perry, "Definitely Life but Not Definitively," *Origins of Life and Evolution of Biospheres* 36 (2006): 515–21.

15. Pascale Angelica Bachmann, Pier Luigi Luisi, and Jacques Lang, "Autocatalytic Self-Replicating Micelles as Models for Prebiotic Structures," *Nature* 357 (1992): 57–59. The same is true of prions, whose multiplication involves only the transmission of phenotypes due to self-perpetuating changes in protein conformations: see Leslie E. Orgel, "Molecular Replication," *Nature* 358 (1992): 203–9.

for understanding the nature of life itself. Accordingly, life could be defined as a "self-sustaining chemical system," able to transform resources into its own building blocks, that is "capable of undergoing Darwinian evolution."[16] This definition of life, though not without its difficulties, is certainly consistent with the observation that cyanobacteria, plants, and other autotrophs are not only self-sustaining, but also very much alive.

So how did life arise? What conditions are required for it to emerge? Before addressing this issue, we must note the limitations of the Darwinian paradigm in explaining the origins of life.[17] Present-day life reproduces using a biochemical template, a set of replication instructions robustly encoded in RNA or DNA.[18] Since these two acronyms for biochemicals are of immense significance for the origins of life and the process of genetic transmission, a little more needs to be said about them for the benefit of theologians new to the field.

First, RNA is ribonucleic acid, the molecule that carries out DNA's instructions for making proteins. It consists of one long chain made up of nucleotides. Each nucleotide contains one base, one phosphate molecule, and the sugar ribose. The bases in RNA nucleotides are adenine, uracil, guanine, and cytosine. There are three main types of RNA: messenger RNA, transfer RNA, and ribosomal RNA.

Second, DNA is deoxyribonucleic acid, the molecule that contains the genetic code. It consists of two long, twisted chains (a double helix) made up of nucleotides. Each nucleotide contains one base, one phosphate molecule, and the sugar deoxyribose. The bases in DNA nucleotides are adenine, thymine, guanine, and cytosine, traditionally abbreviated as A, T, G, and C.

Both RNA and DNA (particularly the latter) are complex structures, whose very existence, not to mention their biological significance, clearly require explanation. The probability of such a complex biochemical structure arising spontaneously is widely conceded to be vanishingly small. As Fred Hoyle suggested in 1981, this scenario raises formidable difficulties. "The chance that higher life forms might have emerged in this way is comparable with the chance that a tornado sweeping through a junk-yard might assemble a Boeing 747 from the materials therein."[19] Hoyle's statistical argument is a little misleading: it fails to take account of the apparent capacity for self-organization within the biochemical world. Nevertheless, the implausibility of the spontaneous appearance of a self-assembly code has led to the widespread acceptance of what are sometimes known as "metabolism-first" theories, which hold that life originally began with an ensemble of simple, collectively replicating molecules, such as an array of autocatalytic polymers. Where natural selection is a highly constrained process based on a self-assembly code, this is

16. Gerald F. Joyce, "Foreword," in *Origins of Life: The Central Concepts*, ed. D. W. Deamer and G. R. Fleischaker (Boston, MA: Jones & Bartlett, 1994), xi–xii.

17. For a discussion of the limits of the natural selection in accounting for the origins of life, see Liane M. Gabora, "Self-Other Organization: Why Early Life Did Not Evolve through Natural Selection," *Journal of Theoretical Biology* 241 (2006): 443–50.

18. Andreas Wagner, *Robustness and Evolvability in Living Systems* (Princeton, NJ: Princeton University Press, 2005), 13–61.

19. Fred Hoyle, "Hoyle on Evolution," *Nature* 294 (1981): 105.

increasingly being recognized to have been preceded by a more haphazard process involving *autopoiesis*.[20] On this model, self-replication is a piecemeal process, rather than a unified mechanism of replication based upon a self-assembly code. Although no one molecule can strictly be said to replicate itself, the whole is regenerated through the interactions and transformations of its parts. Genetically mediated template replication subsequently emerged from the dynamics of these molecular systems,[21] which can be thought of as an autopoietic ensemble.

It is widely agreed that the existence of life, as we know it, is dependent upon the emergence of a complex and not fully understood hierarchy of structures.[22] One of the core difficulties in speaking about biological fine-tuning is that it is unclear whether the DNA-based forms of life on Earth reflect a universal pattern, or whether other chemistries of life might be possible elsewhere in the solar system or in the universe in general. What may be said with confidence, however, is that all living organisms on Earth are made up of the same fundamental chemical building blocks consisting chiefly of amino acids, fatty acids, sugars, and nitrogenous bases. The core elements of these core biochemical compounds are hydrogen, carbon, nitrogen, and oxygen. So where did these come from? And what would have happened if they had not been available?

This is no idle question. If the fundamental constants of the universe had been different, these elements could not have appeared. Why not? Because they originate only in the cores of stars, a later and thoroughly contingent development in the history of the universe. Since this point is so important, we shall consider it in more detail. Hydrogen was the first element to be synthesized. Atomic hydrogen began to form when the temperature of the universe dropped to about 4000 K (Kelvin), about 100 seconds after the origins of time, followed rapidly by the emergence of heavier nuclei, such as deuterium and helium. Yet by then, the very high temperatures required for the nucleosynthesis of heavier elements no longer existed. The universe was in the process of cooling.

THE STELLAR NUCLEOSYNTHESIS OF ESSENTIAL ELEMENTS

At this point, we must return to one of the points made in chapter 9, when we considered the importance of the fundamental constants of nature: the essential role of certain elements, whose origins take place in stellar interiors, for both the

20. For one of the earliest statements of such an approach, see Humberto Maturana and Francisco Varela, *Autopoiesis and Cognition: The Realization of the Living* (Dordrecht: Reidel, 1973).

21. Kalin Vetsigian, Carl Woese, and Nigel Goldenfeld, "Collective Evolution and the Genetic Code," *Proceedings of the National Academy of Sciences* 103 (2006): 10696–701.

22. Bernard J. Carr and Martin J. Rees, "Fine-Tuning in Living Systems," *International Journal of Astrobiology* 3 (2003): 79–86. More generally, see Peter Ulmschneider, *Intelligent Life in the Universe: From Common Origins to the Future of Humanity* (Berlin: Springer-Verlag, 2004). For an attempt to use information theory to illuminate this question, see Radu Popa, *Between Necessity and Probability: Searching for the Definition and Origin of Life* (Berlin: Springer-Verlag, 2004).

origination and development of life. Biochemically critical elements such as carbon, nitrogen, and oxygen did not form and could not have formed in the early history of the universe. Their existence is the consequence of the "clumping" or "accretion" of material into stars, with the subsequent initiation of nuclear fusion reactions. The ratio of the gravitational binding force to rest-mass energy is such that it permitted the gradual "clumping" of material into larger bodies—the stars. Stars form as a result of turbulence in giant clouds of matter within the tenuous interstellar medium.[23] All the heavier elements of the universe, from carbon upward, are believed to be the result of nuclear fusion within stars, and not to be a direct outcome of the primordial fireball.[24] Without the formation of stars, the universe would have been limited to hydrogen and helium, with only a tiny percentage of other elements, such as lithium and beryllium.

The nucleosynthesis of carbon, nitrogen, and oxygen must therefore be regarded as essential to the emergence of life. The formation of carbon requires the fusion of three helium nuclei (or alpha-particles), through a twofold process involving beryllium as an intermediate:

$$^4He + {}^4He \rightarrow {}^8Be$$
$$^8Be + {}^4He \rightarrow {}^{12}C$$

This fusion process occurs rapidly only at temperatures above 10^8 K and in stellar interiors having a high helium abundance. The probability of such a double fusion is very low, because ^8Be is a very unstable nucleus, with a half-life of 10^{-17} seconds. This could lead to a "beryllium bottleneck," preventing the production of heavier nuclei, including oxygen, which would result from the fusion with a further helium nucleus:[25]

$$^{12}C + {}^4He \rightarrow {}^{16}O$$

Yet if all the ^{12}C were converted to ^{16}O, carbon would not be produced in sufficient quantities to allow for the emergence of life.

In what is recognizably an anthropic argument, Fred Hoyle argued during the 1950s that there had to be a yet-undiscovered aspect of the nuclear chemistry of carbon that would allow the production of carbon and oxygen in comparable biophilic quantities. This critically important carbon-forming reaction could occur more rapidly only if there is a excited 0^+ state in ^{12}C just about the threshold at

23. For an excellent summary of present theories of stellar formation, see Michael D. Smith, *The Origin of Stars* (London: Imperial College Press, 2004), esp. 31–136.
24. Donald D. Clayton, *Principles of Stellar Evolution and Nucleosynthesis* (New York: McGraw-Hill, 1968), 70–72.
25. The production of nitrogen in stellar cores takes place through the Bethe-Weizsäcker cycle, also known as the CNO (carbon-nitrogen-oxygen) cycle: see G. Gervino, A. Lavagno, and P. Quarati, "Modified CNO Nuclear Reaction Rates in Dense Stellar Plasma," *Nuclear Physics A* 688 (2001): 126–29.

7.65 MeV that would make a resonance reaction possible. This mechanism was subsequently discovered by William Fowler, who investigated the matter at Hoyle's request.[26] It also turned out that a resonance reaction did *not* take place in the case of the ^{16}O level at 7.12 MeV, since this is just below the combined energies of ^{12}C and ^4He at 7.19 MeV. The resonance level which assisted the formation of ^{12}C thus did not exist in the case of ^{16}O, preventing the immediate conversion of carbon to oxygen through alpha-capture. In a later reflection, Hoyle mused about the theological implications of this remarkable observation:[27]

> From 1953 onward, Willy Fowler and I have always been intrigued by the remarkable relation of the 7.65 Mev energy level in the nucleus of ^{12}C to the 7.12 Mev level in ^{16}O. If you wanted to produce carbon and oxygen in roughly equal quantities by stellar nucleosynthesis, these are the two levels you would have to fix, and your fixing would have to be just where these levels are actually found to be. Another put-up job? Following the above argument, I am inclined to think so. A common sense interpretation of the facts suggests that a superintellect has monkeyed with physics, as well as with chemistry and biology, and that there are no blind forces worth speaking about in nature.

THE ORIGINS OF LIFE ON EARTH

There remains a massive gap between the origination of carbon, nitrogen, and oxygen in stellar cores and the origins of life itself. Yet it is clear that some form of cosmic chemistry led to the production of hundreds of organic molecules in the universe. The evidence for this comes from a number of sources, including radio astronomical spectroscopy and the detailed chemical analysis of meteorites that have fallen onto Earth, such as the famous Murchison meteorite of 1969.[28] These point to the key building blocks of life being present, to varying degrees of complexity, within interstellar space, on comets and asteroids, and on the surfaces of planets and their moons.[29] These range from the chemically simple hydroxyl radical, through hydrogen cyanide and water, and on to more complex amino acids and sugars. The Murchison meteorite, for example, was found to contain certain

---

26. Hoyle and Fowler collaborated in the production of the famous "B²FH paper," which laid the foundations for modern understandings of stellar nucleosynthesis: E. Margaret Burbidge et al., "Synthesis of the Elements in Stars," *Review of Modern Physics* 29 (1957): 547–650.

27. Fred Hoyle, "The Universe: Past and Present Reflections," *Annual Review of Astronomy and Astrophysics* 20 (1982): 1–35; esp. 16.

28. See the exhaustive survey in P. Ehrenfreund et al., "Astrophysical and Astrochemical Insights into the Origin of Life," *Reports on Progress in Physics* 65 (2002): 1427–87. On the Murchison meteorite, see Keith A. Kvenvolden et al., "Evidence for Extraterrestrial Amino-Acids and Hydrocarbons in the Murchison Meteorite," *Nature* 228 (1970): 923–26.

29. For example, it is suggested that spectroscopic evidence points to the existence of complex carbon compounds in protoplanetary nebulae: see Uma P. Vijh, Adolf N. Witt, and Karl D. Gordon, "Discovery of Blue Luminescence in the Red Rectangle: Possible Fluorescence from Neutral Polycyclic Aromatic Hydrocarbon Molecules?" *Astrophysical Journal Letters* 606 (2004): L65–L68.

common amino acids such as alanine, glycine, and glutamic acid, in addition to more unusual ones such as isovaline and pseudoleucine.[30] These could not be due to terrestrial contamination as a result of the impact of the meteorite.

The presence of such significant chemical building blocks in comets and meteorites might be taken to suggest that life on Earth arose from extraterrestrial sources.[31] While the notion that life itself, or biotic precursors, arrived on Earth during early eras of its history, particularly during periods of intense meteorite bombardment, is not to be dismissed lightly, alternatives certainly exist. This was suggested by the famous experiment of 1953 at the University of Chicago, in which Stanley Miller and Harold Urey simulated hypothetical conditions then thought to prevail on Earth around the time that life first appeared.[32] The experiment involved the passing of electrical discharges, simulating lightning, through a mixture of water vapor (H_2O), ammonia (NH_3), methane (CH_4), and hydrogen (H_2)—a mixture believed to reflect the primitive molecules present on Earth at that time. After a week, Miller and Urey found that about 10–15% of the carbon within the system had been converted into organic compounds, and 2% of the carbon had formed amino acids, including thirteen of the twenty-two required to make proteins in living cells. Sugars, lipids, and some of the building blocks for nucleic acids, though not nucleic acids themselves, were also formed. Although some of their working assumptions are now known to require modification,[33] Miller and Urey succeeded in showing that natural processes had the capacity to generate some of the key building blocks of life without recourse to extraterrestrial sources.[34]

Yet their production of prebiotic chemicals is only one stage in the emergence of life. As Lynn Margulis dryly remarked, "To go from a bacterium to people is less of a step than to go from a mixture of amino acids to a bacterium."[35] As we noted earlier, two fundamental characteristics of any living system are the ability to metabolize and the capacity to undergo Darwinian evolution. Yet both of these capacities require immensely complex systems to be in place.

Metabolism takes place through complex systems, resulting from a collection of enzyme reactions and transport processes that convert metabolites into molecules

30. Michael H. Engel and Bartholomew Nagy, "Distribution and Enantiomeric Composition of Amino Acids in the Murchison Meteorite," *Nature* 296 (1982): 837–40.

31. A theory often designated "panspermia" or "exogenesis," probably best known through the idea of "directed panspermia," was proposed in Francis Crick, *Life Itself: Its Origin and Nature* (London: Macdonald, 1982). The idea was also supported by Fred Hoyle in Fred Hoyle and N. C. Wickramasinghe, *Astronomical Origins of Life: Steps towards Panspermia* (Dordrecht: Kluwer Academic Publishers, 2000).

32. Stanley L. Miller, "Production of Amino Acids under Possible Primitive Earth Conditions," *Science* 117 (1953): 528.

33. See Antonio Lazcano and Jeffrey L. Bada, "The 1953 Stanley L. Miller Experiment: Fifty Years of Prebiotic Organic Chemistry," *Origins of Life and Evolution of Biospheres* 33 (2004): 235–42.

34. Important theoretic work on the possible origins of "molecules of life" was subsequently carried out by Fritz Lipmann, "Projecting Backward from the Present Stage of Evolution of Biosynthesis," in *The Origin of Prebiological Systems and of Their Molecular Matrices*, ed. S. W. Fox (New York: Academic Press, 1965), 259–80.

35. Cited in John Horgan, *The End of Science: Facing the Limits of Knowledge in the Twilight of the Scientific Age* (Reading, MA: Addison-Wesley Publishing Co., 1996), 140–41.

capable of supporting cellular life. So what happened before these metabolic pathways and systems evolved? The host of metabolic reactions that sustain life would not take place at all, or would occur at a very slow rate, unless they were catalyzed by enzymes. While a few biological reactions are catalyzed by RNA, the dominant trend is for them to be catalyzed by enzymes, most of which are proteins. These enzymes are widely believed to have been created by RNA, which is thought to have carried genetic information before the evolution of DNA.

The first enzymatic takeover of an ancient biochemistry or prebiotic chemistry involved processes related to the synthesis of nucleotides for a world in which RNA was the only genetically encoded catalyst. In 1986 Harvard molecular biologist Walter Gilbert invented the idea of an "RNA World" to designate a period in the evolution of life in which RNA played a number of roles, later to be taken up by other agents.[36]

> The first stage of evolution proceeds by RNA molecules performing the catalytic activities necessary to assemble themselves from a nucleotide soup. The RNA molecules evolve in self-replicating patterns, using recombination and mutation to explore new niches. . . . They then develop an entire range of enzymic activities. At the next stage, RNA molecules began to synthesize proteins, first by developing RNA adaptor molecules that can bind activated amino acids and then by arranging them according to an RNA template using other RNA molecules such as the RNA core of the ribosome. This process would make the first proteins, which would simply be better enzymes than their RNA counterparts.

Once DNA appeared, however, the multiple roles of RNA became redundant. "RNA is then relegated to the intermediate role it has today—no longer the center of the stage, displaced by DNA and the more effective protein enzymes." So how did metabolism take place before the emergence of RNA and proteins? One suggestion is that this may have taken place through peptides, short polymers of amino acids.[37]

There is no consensus within the scientific community concerning how precellular life emerged or how it supported itself by using some form of metabolism to draw resources from its environment.[38] Some are tempted to follow Stuart Kauffman, who concedes that the direct synthesis of nucleotides from prebiotic

---

36. Walter Gilbert, "The RNA World," *Nature* 319 (1986): 618. For a more recent reflection on this theory, see Gustavo Caetano-Anollés, Hee Shin Kim, and Jay E. Mittenthal, "The Origin of Modern Metabolic Networks Inferred from Phylogenomic Analysis of Protein Architecture," *Proceedings of the National Academy of Sciences* 104 (2007): 9358–63.

37. André E. Brack, "La chimie de l'origine de la vie," in *Les traces du vivant*, ed. M. Gargaud et al. (Pessac: Presses Universitaires de Bordeaux, 2003), 61–81.

38. This is not to say that there is any shortage of ideas: see, e.g., the ideas put forward in Freeman J. Dyson, *Origins of Life* (Cambridge: Cambridge University Press, 1985); Graham Cairns-Smith, *Seven Clues to the Origin of Life* (Cambridge: Cambridge University Press, 1985); Manfred Eigen, *Steps towards Life: A Perspective on Evolution* (Oxford: Oxford University Press, 1992). The possible role of chemically simpler "midwife" systems in bringing about the RNA world has also been discussed: Nicholas V. Hud and Frank A. L. Anet, "Intercalation-Mediated Synthesis and Replication: A New Approach to the Origin of Life," *Journal of Theoretical Biology* 205 (2000): 543–62.

precursors in reasonable yield and unaccompanied by larger amounts of unrelated molecules could not be achieved by presently known chemical reactions; he nevertheless suggests that "whenever a collection of molecules contains enough different kinds of molecules, a metabolism will crystallize from the broth."[39]

The mechanism of transition from living to nonliving matter has been the subject of considerable speculation.[40] One possible scenario for this process of emergence is the formation of "protoorganisms" with three fundamental components. This "protoorganism" can be thought of as a single cooperative aggregate consisting of a protocontainer, a protometabolism, and protogenes. This physicochemical network derives energy from oxidation-reduction processes or photochemical reactions—a simple form of metabolism—and carries encoded information about the metabolic processes in a protogene, which together with the metabolic complexes are integrated in a lipid aggregate. This aggregate can thus self-replicate, use energy and nutrients available from its environment, and undergo evolutionary change over time.

It will be clear that one of the most fundamental questions that emerges from a consideration of biochemical evolution concerns how the evolutionary process got under way. Since the Darwinian process of natural selection depends upon some form of replicator, there is a genuine question of how the necessary biochemical and biophysical systems necessary to support even a primitive form of evolution could have emerged, without presupposing some earlier evolutionary process. The emerging sciences of molecular paleobiology and paleobiochemistry enable the history of at least some gene and protein sequences to be investigated, casting some light on the present situation.[41] Yet this may tell us more about the contingencies of history than the necessities of biophysics. For example, what was the effect of lunar tides on the cyclic replication of early biomolecules?[42] There are so many historical contingencies, often incapable of being reproduced under laboratory conditions, that speculation on these matters is often of limited value.

So can one speak of "biological fine-tuning"? Certainly in some sense of the term: for example, one can speak of an enzyme being fine-tuned for its metabolic task. Yet this is an emergent property, whose emergence can be argued to reflect the processes of natural selection. As Graham Cairns-Smith puts it, "That kind of engineering can only happen in nature through the trial and error processes of natural selection."[43] Thus it is not clear that natural selection has led to the "best"

39. Stuart A. Kauffman, *At Home in the Universe: The Search for Laws of Complexity* (Harmondsworth: Penguin, 1995), 45.

40. For what follows, see Steen Rasmussen et al., "Bridging Nonliving and Living Matter," *Artificial Life* 9 (2003): 269–316.

41. See the excellent survey in Steven A. Benner, Slim O. Sassi, and Eric A. Gaucher, "Molecular Paleoscience: Systems Biology from the Past," *Advances in Enzymology and Related Areas of Molecular Biology* 75 (2007): 1–132.

42. For this point, see Richard Lathe, "Fast Tidal Cycling and the Origin of Life," *Icarus* 168 (2004): 18–22.

43. Graham Cairns-Smith, "Fine-Tuning in Living Systems: Early Evolution and the Unity of Biochemistry," *International Journal of Astrobiology* 2 (2003): 87–90. See also his comment: "Biology has its own mechanism for fine-tuning, found in the long-term processes of evolution through natural selection. How such an evolution became established on the Earth is still unknown" (87).

or a "necessary" outcome, in terms of the biochemistry of life. Why, for example, are only twenty amino acids used in the synthesis of proteins? A range of other amino acids, not found in nature, has been synthesized and incorporated into proteins, with no obvious deleterious effects.[44] The selection of the existing palette of amino acids seems to be a contingency of history, rather than a biochemical necessity. Similarly, why are the two nucleic acids so heavily involved in the transmission of genetic information—RNA and DNA—based on the pentoses ribose and deoxyribose? Why not a hexose or tetrose? In other words, why do RNA and DNA use a monosaccharide with five carbon atoms, when there seems no particular reason not to use those with six or four carbon atoms?[45] Or why are they using adenine rather than aminoadenine? Alternatives are certainly possible. The answer would seem to be that evolution builds on the available.

These lines of reflection would seem to raise questions about the legitimacy of speaking of fine-tuning in relation to the origins of life on Earth. Evolution, many would argue, tunes itself. Yet the situation is actually rather more complex than this. The emergence of evolutionary pathways, though clearly reflecting the influence of the process of natural selection, still requires that certain elements of the universe possess certain properties in order for these pathways to work; the unusual properties of carbon are an obvious example. A point that has not been sufficiently emphasized in the biological literature, perhaps because it is so obvious biochemically, is that the entire evolutionary process depends upon the unusual chemistry of carbon, which allows it to bond to itself as well as to other elements, creating highly complex molecules that are stable over prevailing terrestrial temperatures and are capable of conveying genetic information (especially DNA). The only element which is believed to possess anything approaching a similar capacity is silicon. Although 29.4% of Earth's surface by weight is made up of silicon, it plays an insignificant role in metabolic processes; carbon, in marked contrast, makes up only 0.032% of Earth's surface and is of central importance. Evolution has bypassed silicon as a potential scaffolding for life.[46]

It is not difficult to see why. Some chemists have pointed to the capacity of silicon to act as scaffolding for complex molecules, noting that oligosilanes

44. C. J. Noren et al., "A General Method for Site-Specific Incorporation of Unnatural Amino Acids into Proteins," *Science* 244 (1989): 182–88; André R. O. Cavalcanti and Laura F. Landweber, "Genetic Code: What Nature Missed," *Current Biology* 13 (2003): R884–R885; S. Ye et al., "Site-Specific Incorporation of Keto Amino Acids into Functional G Protein-Coupled Receptors Using Unnatural Amino Acid Mutagenesis," *Journal of Biological Chemistry* 283 (2008): 1525–33. However, see also the comments of Albert Eschenmoser, "Chemical Etiology of Nucleic Acid Structure," *Science* 284 (1999): 2118–24.

45. A point stressed by Steven A. Benner, Alonso Ricardo, and Matthew A. Carrigan, "Is There a Common Chemical Model for Life in the Universe?" *Current Opinion in Chemical Biology* 8 (2004): 672–89.

46. This is not to deny that silicon has any role in biology. Some sea creatures, for example, incorporate silicon dioxide in their exoskeletons. Nor is it to deny a possible role for clays (which contain silicates) as possible inorganic matrices or replication platforms for the emergence of complex organic molecules: see Graham Cairns-Smith, *Genetic Takeover and the Mineral Origins of Life* (Cambridge: Cambridge University Press, 1982).

(chemically similar to hydrocarbons) having up to twenty-six consecutive Si—Si bonds are known, able to support a variety of functionalized and nonfunctionalized side chains.[47] Though this is true, it fails to take account of several points of major importance in relation to the origins of life:

1. Many oligosilanes are unstable owing to the larger atomic radius of silicon and the correspondingly weaker silicon-silicon bond. In particular, silanes decompose rapidly in the presence of oxygen, severely reducing their biotic potential in oxygen-rich environments. In marked contrast, carbon is able to form five-, six-, and seven-membered rings by a variety of pathways, even when oxygen is present.[48]

2. Silicon does not have carbon's capacity to form double or triple bonds, or the biologically significant form of "delocalized" bonding found in aromatic structures.[49]

3. Carbon dioxide plays a critical role in metabolism, being absorbed from the atmosphere in photosynthesis and discharged through various forms of metabolism. Carbon dioxide is a gas, soluble in water. Silicon dioxide is an insoluble solid. There is no silicon equivalent to the "carbon cycle," for example, which plays such a major role in terrestrial life.[50]

These observations point to the biological significance of some signature characteristics of carbon and are clearly open to anthropic interpretation. Although one might argue that nature creates its own fine-tuning, this can only be done if the primordial constituents of the universe are such that an evolutionary process can be initiated. The unique chemistry of carbon is the ultimate foundation for the capacity of nature to tune itself.

The critical importance of carbon chemistry can thus be seen in anthropic terms. Yet this requires supplementation with many other considerations. To illustrate this point, we may consider the biological role of phosphates. One of the most remarkable features of living systems is that virtually all depend upon ATP (adenosine triphosphate) to circulate energy.[51] The central reaction is the reversible conversion of ATP to ADP (adenosine diphosphate), with the release of a phosphate group. The conversion of ATP to ADP releases energy for work, whereas energy created from catabolism can be used to bring about the conversion of ADP to

47. Benner, Ricardo, and Carrigan, "Is There a Common Chemical Model for Life?" 675.

48. The chemical properties of oxygen also merit close attention. It is important to note that O_2 provides the highest *feasible* energy release per electron transfer for carbon-based life, a universal property set by the limits of the periodic table. See D. C. Catling et al., "Why O_2 Is Required by Complex Life on Habitable Planets and the Concept of Planetary 'Oxygenation Time,'" *Astrobiology* 5 (2005): 415–38.

49. See the detailed analysis in Dirk Schulze-Makuch and Louis N. Irwin, *Life in the Universe: Expectations and Constraints* (Berlin: Springer-Verlag, 2006), 82–93.

50. For an excellent analysis of the elements of this cycle and their interconnections, see D. R. Cameron et al., "A Factorial Analysis of the Marine Carbon Cycle Controls on Atmospheric CO_2," *Global Biogeochemical Cycles* 19 (2005): 1–12.

51. For an excellent account of the uniqueness and importance of this mechanism, see Christian de Duve, *Singularities: Landmarks on the Pathways of Life* (Cambridge: Cambridge University Press, 2005), 25–40.

ATP.[52] Yet the role of phosphates in biology is not limited to energy conversion; their role extends to the biosynthesis of nucleic acids and phospholipids, the former being essential to the transmission of genetic information, and the latter to the formation of stable cell membranes.[53] Interestingly, phosphate is not common on Earth, being mostly concentrated in insoluble mineral deposits.[54] The concentration of phosphate in the world's oceans is very low—so low, in fact, that some researchers have suggested that it could not have played a significant role in early prebiotic chemistry.[55]

So why did nature choose phosphates? This was the question posed by the Harvard chemist Frank Westheimer (1912–2007) in 1987.[56] "Phosphate esters and anhydrides," Westheimer pointed out, "dominate the living world."[57] For Westheimer, the question that required discussion was not *how* nature selected phosphates for such a critical role; the biosynthetical mechanisms in which it was involved were relatively well understood at that time. The point was that the chemical characteristics of the phosphate group (PO_4^{3-}) enable it to play certain key biological roles.

We have already noted the importance of ATP in energy transfer within metabolism. Westheimer further pointed out the importance of phosphates in maintaining a dynamic chemical environment within cells by which metabolites might be conserved. Phosphate is itself ionized at neutral pH in aqueous environments; it can link up to two groups, as esters (as in nucleic acids), and still remain ionized. All these ionized species are retained within cells because of the inability of charged species to traverse nonpolar cell membranes readily.[58] Furthermore, phosphate esters and their anhydrides, such as ATP, are thermody-

---

52. For an introduction to the discovery and significance of this mechanism, see Fritz Lipmann, "Metabolic Generation and Utilization of Phosphate Bond Energy," *Advances in Enzymology and Related Areas of Molecular Biology* 1 (1941): 99–162; Herman M. Kalckar, "Origins of the Concept Oxidative Phosphorylation," *Molecular and Cellular Biochemistry* 5 (1974): 55–62.

53. On which see Maw-Shung Liu and K. Joe Kako, "Characteristics of Mitochondrial and Microsomal Monoacyl- and Diacyl-Glycerol 3-Phosphate Biosynthesis in Rabbit Heart," *Biochemical Journal* 138 (1974): 11–21; Timothy Soderberg, "Biosynthesis of Ribose-5-Phosphate and Erythrose-4-Phosphate in Archaea: A Phylogenetic Analysis of Archaeal Genomes," *Archaea* 1 (2005): 347–52.

54. These deposits are generally in the form of $Ca_3(PO_4)_2$ in minerals such as apatite. The incorporation of this mineral in vertebrate skeletons is evolutionarily significant: H. Catherine W. Skinner, "In Praise of Phosphates; or Why Vertebrates Chose Apatite to Mineralize Their Skeletal Elements," in *Frontiers in Geochemistry: Organic, Solution, and Ore Deposit Geochemistry*, ed. W. G. Ernst (Columbia, MD: Geological Society of America, 2002), 41–49.

55. Anthony D. Keefe and Stanley L. Miller, "Are Polyphosphates or Phosphate Esters Prebiotic Reagents?" *Journal of Molecular Evolution* 41 (1995): 693–702. But see Yukio Yamagata, "Prebiotic Formation of ADP and ATP from AMP, Calcium Phosphates and Cyanate in Aqueous Solution," *Origins of Life and Evolution of the Biosphere* 29 (1999): 511–20.

56. Frank H. Westheimer, "Why Nature Chose Phosphates," *Science* 235 (1987): 1173–78.

57. As Skinner points out, Westheimer forgot to mention the critical role of calcium phosphate in the vertebrate world: without it, there would be no bones or teeth. See Skinner, "In Praise of Phosphates," 41.

58. For an early appreciation of the biochemical importance of the ionization of metabolites, see the seminal paper of Bernard D. Davis, "On the Importance of Being Ionized," *Archives of Biochemistry and Biophysics* 78 (1958): 497–509. For more recent discussion of this point in metabolism, see Peter W. Hochachka and George N. Somero, *Biochemical Adaptation: Mechanism and Process in Physiological Evolution* (Oxford: Oxford University Press, 2002), 351–53.

namically unstable with respect to hydrolysis. However, their negative charge repels nucleophiles (such as the hydroxyl ion, OH^-), and thus renders them kinetically stable.

The DNA and the RNA contain purines and pyrimidines linked together by phosphate groups. A stable molecular configuration results through nucleoside pairing with phosphate groups on the outside of the biomolecule. Once more, the overall negative charge of the phosphate groups limits the rate of nucleophyllic attack by nucleophiles and thus protects the molecule against hydrolysis. The combination of phosphate and nucleosides assures a stable biomolecule, necessary for long-term transmission and maintenance of genetic material. This point has been recently emphasized by Benner and Hutter, who point out the importance of the phosphodiester backbone for the proper functioning of DNA as a genetic molecule.[59] This polyanionic backbone appears to be critical to prevent the single strands from folding, thus permitting molecular recognition to follow simple rules.

Phosphate also plays a key role in biosynthesis. This can be seen from the Calvin cycle,[60] a glycolytic pathway for the synthesis of ribulose and other sugars, regarded as one of the first steps in biomolecular construction by autotrophic photosynthetic organisms. Phosphate is also an essential cofactor in electron transport and oxidation reduction reactions as part of the molecule NADP.[61] Westheimer's list can easily be expanded.[62]

So what conclusions might be drawn about the notion of biological fine-tuning from this brief analysis? We have already made the point that nature tunes itself.[63] "Evolution is cleverer than you are" (Leslie Orgel). Yet far from eliminating the notion of biological fine tuning, this merely focuses our attention on one critical aspect of the biochemical processes that are thought to have led to life. The fundamental properties of the chemical elements, which are exploited *but not created* by biological processes, have to be such that these metabolic pathways are possible in the first place. Equally, if Darwinian evolution is to take place and is to be regarded as essential to a definition of life, the chemistry of nature must be such that replication is possible—in other words, such that DNA or its functional equivalent may exist. We have briefly noted the unusual properties of

59. Steven A. Benner and Daniel Hutter, "Phosphates, DNA, and the Search for Nonterrean Life: A Second Generation Model for Genetic Molecules," *Bioinorganic Chemistry* 30 (2002): 62–80. For similar suggestions concerning RNA, see Christoph Steinbeck and Clemens Robert, "The Role of Ionic Backbones in RNA Structure: An Unusually Stable Non-Watson-Crick Duplex of a Nonionic Analog in an Apolar Medium," *Journal of the American Chemical Society* 120 (1998): 11576–80.

60. James A. Bassham, "Mapping the Carbon Reduction Cycle: A Personal Retrospective," *Photosynthesis Research* 76 (2003): 25–52.

61. The molecule NADP is nicotinamide adenine dinucleotide phosphate.

62. See the further comments in Andrew J. Pratt, "The Curious Case of Phosphate Solubility," *Chemistry in New Zealand* 70 (2006): 78–80; Giovanna Costanzo et al., "Nucleoside Phosphorylation by Phosphate Minerals," *Journal of Biological Chemistry* 282 (2007): 16729–35.

63. As we shall see, this has particular relevance in any discussion of the molecular mechanisms of evolution: see, e.g., Rong Wu, Prim B. Singh, and David M. Gilbert, "Uncoupling Global and Fine-Tuning Replication Timing Determinants for Mouse Pericentric Heterochromatin," *Journal of Cell Biology* 174 (2006): 185–94.

carbon and phosphorus to illustrate these points. This approach, it may be noted, resonates strongly with Barrow's idea of "nice laws" (chap. 9).

The origins of life are thus unquestionably anthropic. They depend upon the fundamental values of constants of nature being such that the universe is able to progress beyond the formation of atomic hydrogen and bring about the nucleosynthesis of biologically critical elements. Had they been otherwise, this process might never have begun. No life-forms are known that are based solely upon hydrogen, helium, or lithium—the three lightest elements, all of which were created in the primordial big bang. In itself and of itself, the big bang was not capable of producing carbon, nitrogen, or oxygen. The formation of stars depends upon the value of the gravitational constant, which is regularly cited as an example of fine-tuning. Similarly, the strong nuclear force, whose value is 0.007, defines how firmly atomic nuclei bind together and hence the extent to which stars can transmute hydrogen into atoms of the heavier elements. Its value is of critical importance if nucleosynthesis is to take place in stellar interiors. "If ε were 0.006 or 0.008, we could not exist."[64] It is thus beyond reasonable doubt that the origins of life depend upon the fundamental constants of the universe.

It will also be clear that Augustine's notion of *rationes seminales* plays an important heuristic role in engaging with the complex chemical phenomena that have been briefly described in this chapter. The emergence of chemical complexity precedes that of biological complexity and is generally ignored in accounts of biological evolution. Yet the importance of this point is clear: without an inherent capacity for chemical complexification, the foundations for biological development would not have been in place.[65] These chemical properties must be regarded as emergent. Augustine's image of the dormant seed, awaiting the right environmental conditions for germination, is a helpful analogue for understanding how certain chemical properties emerge under appropriate circumstances.

It may, of course, be objected at this point that this argument overlooks the vastness of chemical space, much of which remains unexplored. Might there not be pockets within this chemical space within which alternative viable chemical systems might arise? The point must be conceded, yet must be seen in context. On the basis of known biochemical systems, biological evolution remains dependent upon chemical properties which were ultimately determined in the primordial state of the universe.

Yet we have only begun to reflect on aspects of nature that are of relevance to natural theology. In the following chapter, we shall move on to consider the unusual properties of water and their potential importance for a natural theology.

64. Martin J. Rees, *Just Six Numbers: The Deep Forces That Shape the Universe* (London: Phoenix, 2000), 2. For further discussion, see chap. 9. See further Michael L. Graesser et al., "Anthropic Distribution for Cosmological Constant and Primordial Density Perturbations," *Physics Letters B* 600 (2004): 15–21.

65. For reflections on the potentiality of chemical systems for complexification and its broader significance, see Achim Müller, "Die inhärente Potentialität materieller (chemischer) Systeme," *Philosophia naturalis* 35 (1998): 333–58.

Chapter 11

The Matrix of Life

The Curious Chemistry of Water

Water is the matrix of life.[1] Unsurprisingly, it has thus received attention from physicists, chemists, biochemists, and biologists—and also from those inclined to theological speculation. As H. J. Paton pointed out in his Gifford Lectures of 1949–50, in the eighteenth century "hydrotheology" joined an exotic group of specialist forms of natural theology, including "pyrotheology" and "ornithotheology," which somewhat unpersuasively sought to identify the wisdom of God in the behavior of water, fire, and birds.[2] As Paton reminds us, these somewhat implausible approaches show how "natural theology may become highly artificial." For Paton, they were best left behind, replaced with an appeal to the tried and tested methods of philosophy. Yet water proves to raise some interesting philosophical questions of its own, not least what the term properly designates.[3]

---

1. As pointed out by Felix Franks, *Water: A Matrix of Life*, 2nd ed. (Cambridge: Royal Society of Chemistry, 2000).

2. H. J. Paton, *The Modern Predicament: A Study in the Philosophy of Religion* (London: Allen & Unwin, 1955), 20–21. Paton presumably has in mind Johann Albert Fabricius's *Hydrotheologia* (1734) and the erudite though ultimately slightly baffling trilogy of works penned by Friedrich Christian Lesser: *Lithotheologia* (1735), *Insectotheologia* (1738), and *Testaceotheologia* (1747).

3. See Barbara Abbott, "Water = H₂O," *Mind* 108 (1999): 145–48.

While I can understand Paton's desire to turn aside from the ambiguities of nature to the safer ground of philosophical argument, I must nevertheless raise some concerns about his understandable dismissal of such seeming aberrations as "hydrotheology." First, only the most conceptually impoverished theology lacks the will and the intellectual resources to engage with the natural world, which is in any case mandated by the Christian vision of reality. Second, Paton is perhaps unduly optimistic about the resources of philosophy to engage with the questions raised by the natural world—or, indeed, anything. The Polish philosopher and cultural critic Leszek Kolakowski's disarmingly frank critique of philosophical certitudes merits recollection at this point:[4]

> For centuries philosophy has asserted its legitimacy by asking and answering questions inherited from the Socratics and pre-Socratics: how to distinguish the real from the unreal, true from false, good from evil. . . . There came a point, however, when philosophers had to confront a simple, painfully undeniable fact: that of the questions which have sustained European philosophy for two and a half millennia, not a single one has been answered to general satisfaction. All of them, if not declared invalid by the decree of philosophers, remain controversial.

In proposing that we return to contemplate the properties of water, I am suggesting that natural theology should indeed engage the natural world, although not in any expectation of developing a deductive argument in favor of God's existence. Rather, I shall argue that our increasing awareness of the unusual chemical and physical properties of water resonate with the Christian vision of reality, pointing to the inherent potentiality with which God, as creator, has endowed the creation. In this chapter, we shall therefore deal with two questions. First, just what is so special about water? And second, how do these properties relate to the emergence of life?[5]

But we shall begin by posing a counterfactual question: what would have happened if there were no liquids at all? It is not an idle question. Victor Weisskopf (1898–2002), director general of CERN (the Geneva-based European Organization for Nuclear Research) from 1961 to 1965, pointed out that, from a purely theoretical perspective, liquids are something of an anomaly:[6]

> The existence and general properties of solids and gases are relatively easy to understand once it is realized that atoms or molecules have certain typical properties and interactions that follow from quantum mechanics. Liquids

4. Leszek Kolakowski, *Metaphysical Horror* (Chicago: University of Chicago Press, 2001), 1–2.

5. For an excellent review of the issues, see John L. Finney, "Water? What's So Special about It?" *Philosophical Transactions of the Royal Society B* 359 (2004): 1145–65. One of the best extended discussions is found in Philip Ball, *Life's Matrix: A Biography of Water* (New York: Farrar, Straus & Giroux, 2000).

6. The following quotation, dating from 1977, is widely cited in the literature concerning the utility and properties of the liquid state: see, e.g., Daan Frenkel, "Introduction to Colloidal Systems," in *Soft Condensed Matter Physics in Molecular and Cell Biology*, ed. Wilson C. K. Poon and David Andelman (New York: Taylor & Francis, 2006), 21–47, esp. 35.

are harder to understand. Assume that a group of intelligent theoretical physicists had lived in closed buildings from birth such that they never had occasion to see any natural structures. Let us forget that it may be impossible to prevent them to see their own bodies and their inputs and outputs. What would they be able to predict from a fundamental knowledge of quantum mechanics? They probably would predict the existence of atoms, of molecules, of solid crystals, both metals and insulators, of gases, but most likely not the existence of liquids.

The point lying behind Weisskopf's comment is that the existence of the liquid state is actually somewhat fragile, depending upon a certain specific degree of intermolecular attraction (generally known as the van der Waals force).[7] Even the existence of the liquid state itself reflects certain constants of nature. Yet water turns out to be quite a remarkable liquid.

THE CURIOUS PROPERTIES OF WATER

Early attempts to explore the significance of water for life were somewhat hampered by a lack of understanding of the chemical and physical properties of water. William Whewell (1794–1866) penned perhaps the most successful of the Bridgewater Treatises "on the power, wisdom, and goodness of God, as manifested in the creation." In it he argues that a series of mainly heat-related properties of water— such as the insulating capacity of snow and ice, and the expansion of water on freezing—were clearly "selected with a beneficent design."[8] These themes were amplified by Lawrence Henderson in 1913, who asserted that the distinctive physical properties of water were integral to a biocentric world.

Since then, the debate has moved on considerably and has opened up new and important questions, of no small relevance to our theme. Perhaps the most important of these concerns the universality of terrestrial biochemistry. There is no doubt that water is essential to life on Earth. But is this characteristic feature of terrestrial biology universal? Can Darwinian processes take place in alternative chemical environments?[9] It is certainly correct that other planetary environments may point to alternative solvent systems. Liquid ammonia is a possible solvent for life and is often cited as an alternative to water in biotic systems. There are important chemical analogies between water and ammonia. Ammonia, like water, dissolves many organic compounds. Ammonia, like water, is liquid over a wide range of temperatures and is known to exist in the clouds of the planet

7. For a review of the issues, see Wilson C. K. Poon, "The Physics of a Model Colloid-Polymer Mixture," *Journal of Physics: Condensed Matter* 14 (2002): R859–R880.

8. William Whewell, *Astronomy and General Physics Considered with Reference to Natural Theology,* 5th ed. (London: William Pickering, 1836), 80–95.

9. Steven A. Benner, Alonso Ricardo, and Matthew A. Carrigan, "Is There a Common Chemical Model for Life in the Universe?" *Current Opinion in Chemical Biology* 8 (2004): 672–89. See also Norman R. Pace, "The Universal Nature of Biochemistry," *Proceedings of the National Academy of Sciences* 98 (2001): 805–8.

Jupiter.[10] Sulfuric acid, known to be present in the upper atmosphere of Venus, is also a reasonably good solvent that supports chemical reactivity.[11]

Others, however, have been more skeptical, pointing out that water has a series of highly unusual properties which must be seen systematically, not individually. Water is a physical, chemical, and biological system, not a mere collection of individual properties.[12] These remarkable physical characteristics of water include the following.

1. The liquid range of water at normal atmospheric pressure is 0°C–100°C, which results in its being present in a liquid form over most of Earth's surface. (This, of course, is as much a statement about the ambient temperature of the earth as about the usual properties of water.)

2. The density of liquid water does not change rapidly with temperature and has a maximum near 4°C.

3. As a result of this anomalous density behavior, ice floats on water, so that there is often liquid water below solid water in colder environments.

4. The latent heat of water is unusually high, which means that it is less easy to evaporate than "normal" liquids.

5. Water exhibits an anomalously high specific heat capacity, thermal conductivity, and surface tension.

6. The dielectric constant of water exceeds that of all pure liquids except hydrogen cyanide and formamide, so that water has an exceptional capacity for stabilizing polar and ionic species in solution.

7. The high polarity of water as a solvent forms the basis for the intricate interplay of hydrophobic and hydrophilic interactions that shape biochemical macromolecules, such as enzymes and nucleic acids, into their biologically active forms. The water-lipid disparity in polarity drives the self-organization of cell membranes that provide essential compartmentalization of biological processes.

8. The solvent properties of water also engender CO_2 acid-base chemistry that serves effectively both to distribute carbon atoms and to buffer living tissues near pH neutrality.

While certain individual properties of water may have parallels with alternative solvents, the ensemble of properties of water remains unique and of considerable significance to the origins and development of life. Water designates a system,

10. Katia I. Matcheva et al., "The Cloud Structure of the Jovian Atmosphere as Seen by the Cassini/CIRS Experiment," *Icarus* 179 (2005): 432–48.

11. Marc A. Kolodner and Paul G. Steffes, "The Microwave Absorption and Abundance of Sulfuric Acid Vapor in the Venus Atmosphere Based on New Laboratory Measurements," *Icarus* 132 (1998): 151–69.

12. A failure to give due weight to this point weakens the argument of some recent speculation on this point—as, e.g., found in William Bains, "Many Chemistries Could Be Used to Build Living Systems," *Astrobiology* 4 (2004): 137–67.

not a collection of individual isolated chemical and physical properties. While other solvent systems may at points appear superior to water, it is the sum total of their properties that ultimately matters. Water possesses a suite of distinctive features that mark it out from its alternatives.

Water has many properties which seem to be indispensable for the functioning of proteins and biological cells. It is an excellent solvent for ions, which play a crucial role in nerve signaling, enzymatic processes, biomineralization, and some aspects of the behavior of DNA. Water permits intermolecular interactions such as hydrogen bonds and hydrophobic forces, the former playing an important role as bridges between protein-binding sites and their substrates, and the latter in protein folding and protein-protein interactions. The well-known ability of water to absorb and lose heat without undergoing a large temperature change provides thermal cushioning, shielding cells and organisms from wild temperature swings. No other known liquid combines all of these properties in this systemic manner.

So why is water so special and important for the origins of life on Earth? To do justice to the unique chemical and physical properties of water would require a book in its own right; in what follows, we shall offer a brief account of some of those features and an indication of their biological importance.

WHAT IS WATER?

The chemical composition of water is H_2O. The ratio of two parts hydrogen to one part oxygen was discovered about 1781 by the London scientist Henry Cavendish (1731–1810). Yet this simple description of water is inadequate, since it fails to do justice to the complex interactions that take place within its liquid state. We have already noted the importance of van der Waals forces (commonly known as dispersion forces), which are quantum mechanical in origin, in determining the properties of liquids. Yet other forces also operate, including strong "hydrogen bonds" which allow each water molecule to link with up to four others, thus giving liquid water a far-higher degree of internal ordering than might be expected, leading in turn to its unusually high boiling point, melting point, and viscosity compared with similar substances in which hydrogen bonding is not such a significant phenomenon.[13] Were it not for hydrogen bonding, water would be a gas, not a liquid, at normal temperatures. The boiling point of water is actually about 200°C higher than would be expected for a molecule of such low molecular weight in comparison with the closely related compounds H_2S, H_2Se, and H_2Te.

Hydrogen bonding also plays an important role in determining and stabilizing the three-dimensional structures adopted by proteins, such as enzymes and nucleic

13. José Teixeira, Alenka Luzar, and Stéphane Longeville, "Dynamics of Hydrogen Bonds: How to Probe Their Role in the Unusual Properties of Liquid Water," *Journal of Physics: Condensed Matter* 18 (2006): S2353–62.

bases. The double helical structure of DNA is largely due to hydrogen bonding between the base pairs.[14] The specific shape of proteins, which is known to be of critical importance in determining their physiological or biochemical role, is also the outcome of hydrogen bonding.[15] Older studies of the structures of proteins, such as the pioneering work of Linus Pauling,[16] tended to treat these biological structures as existing without the need for a solvation matrix. Over the past two decades or so, it has become increasingly clear that water cannot simply be regarded as a solvent for significant biomolecules and reactions; rather, it acts as a matrix which actively engages and interacts with biomolecules in complex, subtle, and essential ways. For example, there are now good reasons for thinking that we must speak of the "active volume" of biomolecules such as proteins as extending beyond their formal boundary to include the structured shell of water which surrounds them and is involved in their biological functions, which depend upon a delicate interplay between what we have formally regarded as the molecule and its environment. Thus many proteins make use of bound water molecules as functional units which mediate interactions with other proteins or with substrate molecules, or transport protons rapidly to locations deep within the folded protein.

The bond angle in the H_2O molecule is $104.5°$, close to the angle of an ideal tetrahedron, $109.47°$. Computer simulations to model changes in the properties of water suggest that if the bond angle in H_2O were $90°$, rather than the actual $104.5°$, or if the hydrogen bond were 15% weaker than what is actually observed, the three-dimensional network of hydrogen bonds which give water its unique solvation properties would collapse.[17] These solvation properties appear to play a particularly important role within cell membranes, in which highly concentrated solutions of biologically active agents are gathered.[18]

The phenomenon of protein folding, through which genetic information is converted into biological activity, is of especial interest. In this process, a polypeptide chain, newly synthesized from the information contained within the cellular DNA, is transformed into a native and functional protein. It is thought that protein folding is driven primarily by a balance between two factors: intramolecular hydrogen

14. Andrew J. Dingley and Stephan Grzesiek, "Direct Observation of Hydrogen Bonds in Nucleic Acid Base Pairs by Internucleotide $^2J_{NN}$ Couplings," *Journal of the American Chemical Society* 120 (1998): 8293–97.

15. For an excellent survey of these issues, see Martin F. Chaplin, "Water: Its Importance to Life," *Biochemistry and Molecular Biology Education* 29 (2001): 54–59. For some specific examples of the importance of hydrogen bonding in relation to protein folding, see Kazufumi Takano et al., "The Contribution of Polar Group Burial to Protein Stability Is Strongly Context-Dependent," *Journal of Biological Chemistry* 278 (2003): 31790–95.

16. Linus Pauling, Robert B. Corey, and Herman R. Branson, "The Structure of Proteins: Two Hydrogen-Bonded Helical Configurations of the Polypeptide Chain," *Proceedings of the National Academy of Sciences* 37 (1951): 205–11. For comment on this achievement, see David Eisenberg, "The Discovery of the α-Helix and β-Sheet, the Principal Structural Features of Proteins," *Proceedings of the National Academy of Sciences* 100 (2003): 11207–10.

17. Ruth M. Lynden-Bell and Pablo G. Debenedetti, "Computational Investigation of Order, Structure, and Dynamics in Modified Water Models," *Journal of Physical Chemistry B* 109 (2005): 6527–34.

18. For reflection on the cellular role of water, see Gilbert Ling, "What Determines the Normal Water Content of a Living Cell?" *Physiological Chemistry and Physics and Medical NMR* 36 (2004): 1–19.

bonding and hydrophobic interactions which lead to the burial of hydrophobic residues within the protein interior. While it may be helpful to think of globular proteins as a kind of "polymer micelle" that is wholly hydrophobic inside and wholly hydrophilic on the surface, this is a simplification of the situation.

It is now well accepted that small proteins can fold under laboratory conditions without the assistance of any other protein, indicating that the information for the folding process is contained in the protein sequence itself. The question of how this information is encoded is one of the most intriguing as well as difficult problems in contemporary structural biology.[19] It is thought that water actively participates in molecular recognition in a highly specific manner by mediating the interactions between binding partners and contributing to either enthalpic or entropic stabilization of the folded protein structure.[20] The unique solvent and hydrogen-bonding properties of water thus provide the entropic driving force for the spontaneous acquisition of the three-dimensional structures of biological macromolecules and supermolecular assemblies.[21]

While water is important for the structure, stability, dynamics, and function of biological macromolecules, nevertheless at least some of the biological functions of proteins, such as enzymes, can be replicated to some limited extent by using polar solvents other than water. For example, it has been shown that unfolded and reduced hen egg-white lysozyme can be refolded and reoxidized in glycerol containing varying amounts of water, achieving up to 30% of its correct refolding in 99% glycerol. Its level of biological activity, however, was found to be much less (by a factor of 600) than that observed in water.[22] Other studies, however, suggest a more-specific role for water in protein folding, particularly in relation to triggering the burying of the hydrophobic regions of the protein internally.[23]

WATER AND BIOLOGICAL CELLS

Water also plays a major role in the emergence of biological cells, a phenomenon that is essential to life as we know it. The cell is the fundamental building block of life, the basic structural and functional unit of all known living organisms on

19. Fabrizio Chiti et al., "Development of Enzymatic Activity during Protein Folding," *Journal of Biological Chemistry* 274 (1999): 20151–58.

20. For a detailed analysis, see Yaakov Levy and José N. Onuchic, "Water Mediation in Protein Folding and Molecular Recognition," *Annual Review of Biophysics and Biomolecular Structure* 35 (2006): 389–415.

21. On this process see Yehuda Snir and Randall D. Kamien, "Entropically Driven Helix Formation," *Science* 307 (2005): 1067; Jayanth R. Banavar et al., "Structural Motifs of Biomolecules," *Proceedings of the National Academy of Sciences* 104 (2007): 17283–86.

22. Roman V. Rariy and Alexander M. Klibanov, "Correct Protein Folding in Glycerol," *Proceedings of the National Academy of Sciences* 94 (1997): 13520–23.

23. Young Min Rhee et al., "Simulations of the Role of Water in the Protein-Folding Mechanism," *Proceedings of the National Academy of Sciences* 101 (2004): 6456–61; Gerard Hummer, "Water Pulls the Strings in Hydrophobic Polymer Collapse," *Proceedings of the National Academy of Sciences* 104 (2007): 14883–84.

Earth.[24] The discovery of the cell took place in 1663, when Robert Hooke (1635–1703) examined a piece of cork through his microscope and found that it was divided into tiny compartments, which he termed "cellulae," or cells.[25] It was not until the nineteenth century that their biological importance came to be appreciated. In 1839, the botanist Matthias Jakob Schleiden (1804–81) and zoologist Theodor Schwann (1810–82) recognized the fundamental similarities between plant and animal cells, and proposed that they were the basic components of all living things. Some organisms, including bacteria, consist only of a single cell (unicellular); other organisms, including human beings, are multicellular. Perhaps the most important component of the cell is the membrane, which provides a physical means of enclosing the cell contents and preventing them from being dispersed, keeping unwanted viruses out, and especially partitioning the cell into functional and segregated compartments. An intact and healthy membrane is selectively permeable since it allows substances needed for cell metabolism to enter, while it attempts to prevent the entrance of unwanted or potentially hazardous substances. Yet this all-important membrane consists of a thin molecular skin a mere two molecules wide, often described as a "lipid bilayer," which turns out to be truly remarkable in its properties.[26]

Lipids (more strictly, phospholipids) are complex biological models with two basic components. At one end, lipids possess long carbon chains, typically based on a biologically optimal skeleton of 16–18 carbon atoms. These are strongly hydrophobic (or lipophilic). At the other, we find a highly polar phosphate group which is hydrophilic. When lipids are physically dispersed in water, they show a remarkable property, first noticed in the 1960s.[27] They form vesicles, small spheres consisting of two layers of lipid molecules. In this lipid bilayer, the polar phosphate groups (the "heads") maintain contact with the water, whereas the hydrophobic hydrocarbon groups (the "tails") are attracted to each other and thus orientate themselves toward the interior of the bilayer. The hydrophobic tails always try to avoid water and face the inside of the bilayer, whereas the hydrophilic head faces the exterior and the interior of this chemical cell.

This lipid bilayer is the essential element of all biological membranes. Its formation is determined by its physical chemistry: its basic elements adopt the con-

24. For comment, see Christian de Duve, *Singularities: Landmarks on the Pathways of Life* (Cambridge: Cambridge University Press, 2005), 118–32.

25. Howard Gest, "The Remarkable Vision of Robert Hooke (1635–1703): First Observer of the Microbial World," *Perspectives in Biology and Medicine* 48 (2005): 266–72. For a useful summary of the history of cell biology, see Paolo Mazzarello, "A Unifying Concept: The History of Cell Theory," *Nature Cell Biology* 1 (1999): E13–E15.

26. My own doctoral research at Oxford University back in the 1970s focused on the biophysics of cell membranes, just after the emergence of the "fluid mosaic" model stimulated a battery of new investigations of their properties: S. J. Singer, "The Molecular Organization of Biological Membranes," in *Structure and Function of Biological Membranes*, ed. L. I. Rothfield (New York: Academic Press, 1971), 145–222; S. J. Singer and G. L. Nicolson, "The Fluid Mosaic Model of the Structure of Cell Membranes," *Science* 175 (1972): 720–31.

27. Ching-Hsien Huang, "Studies on Phosphatidylcholine Vesicles: Formation and Physical Characteristics," *Biochemistry* 8 (1969): 344–52.

figuration of lowest free energy. In living cells, the lipids act as a fluid mosaic which is enriched by a variety of additional molecules, bound by van de Waals forces. The molecules which embed themselves in the cell membrane include proteins, which help to hold the membrane in a regular, identifiable structure for easy bonding. These proteins also function as receptors and receptor sites for attachment to the appropriate raw materials needed for cellular functions, such as metabolism.

The essential point to appreciate here is that the basic structure of the cell membrane is determined by the fundamental forces of physical chemistry. On account of their intrinsic chemical nature, phospholipids will naturally and spontaneously form such membranes in an aqueous environment. It is now known that such micelles, vesicles, and lipsomes can develop the capacity to replicate themselves.[28] This has led some researchers to argue that cells could have formed in the prebiotic environment from chemical precursors of phospholipids, providing a matrix for future biotic development.[29] If such vesicles are able to embed or entrap biologically active molecules involved in significant biosynthetic processes, a relatively simple mechanism for the origins of cellular life could be proposed.[30] Once more, it reflects the fundamentals of chemistry. If the prebiotic environment was aqueous, and lipids or their immediate precursors were present in that environment, the fundamental forces of physical chemistry would lead to the formation of structures that are emergent cell membranes.

THE ORIGIN OF WATER ON EARTH

So how did water come to be present in such large quantities on Earth? Earth seems to have substantially more water present than some contemporary theories of the origins of the solar system predict. Furthermore, many geochemists argue that water has not permeated the deep structure of Earth, being more of a veneer on the planet's surface. This points to terrestrial water coming largely from extraterrestrial sources. Some have suggested that comets were the most likely source of this water.[31] As the planet Jupiter formed by the process of accretion, its growing gravitational pull would have deflected many icy comets originating

28. Pascale Angelica Bachmann, Pier Luigi Luisi, and Jacques Lang, "Autocatalytic Self-Replicating Micelles as Models for Prebiotic Structures," *Nature* 357 (1992): 57–59.

29. Gianluca Pozzi et al., "Single-Chain Polyprenyl Phosphates Form 'Primitive' Membranes," *Angewandte Chemie International Edition* 35 (1996): 177–80; Andrea Veronese and Pier Luigi Luisi, "An Autocatalytic Reaction Leading to Spontaneously Assembled Phosphatidyl Nucleoside Giant Vesicles," *Journal of the American Chemical Society* 120 (1998): 2662–63.

30. For exploration of this possibility, see Pier Luigi Luisi, "Some Open Questions about the Origin of Life," in *Fundamentals of Life*, ed. Gyula Pályi, Claudia Zucchi, and Luciano Caglioti (Paris: Elsevier, 2002), 289–301.

31. See esp. Armand H. Delsemme, "An Argument for the Cometary Origin of the Biosphere," *American Scientist* 89 (2001): 432–42. Note also Kevin Zahnle and Norman H. Sleep, "Impacts and the Early Evolution of Life," in *Comets and the Origin and Evolution of Life*, ed. P. J. Thomas, C. F. Chyba, and C. P. McKay (New York: Springer-Verlag, 1997), 175–208.

from its region onward toward Earth. Over a billion years, hundreds of millions of comets might have collided with Earth, the bombardment being especially heavy just after Earth formed. Others have suggested carbonaceous chondrites, meteorities originating from beyond the planet Mars which carry up to 10 percent of their mass in ice, as possible sources of Earth's ample supply of water.[32]

The theory is certainly plausible. Comets and carbonaceous chondrites are known to contain substantial amounts of frozen water. The cometary or meteoric origin of terrestrial water would explain how water, widely regarded as originating at the outer edges of the solar system, found its way to one of the inner planets, and also how water arrived late enough in Earth's formation for the planet to have sufficient gravity to retain it. However, recent studies of the spectral analyses of the chemical compositions of three comets during near-Earth passes—Halley (1986), Hyakutake (1996), and Hale-Bopp (1997)—showed that they were much richer in "heavy water" (based on the isotope deuterium, rather than simple hydrogen), suggesting that Earth's water could not be accounted for in this manner.[33]

So where does this brief account of the significance of water leave us? Several highly significant points clearly emerge from even this short discussion. Water plays a quite remarkable role as a biological solvent—evident in, for example, the phenomenon of protein folding, which is essential if a protein is to assume the specific shape required to fulfill certain biological functions, such as enzymatic activity. These properties, some of which we have enumerated in this chapter, play a crucial role in life as we know it and are widely seen as representing a possible instance of an anthropic phenomenon.

Yet we must emphasize that the fact that water contains oxygen is enormously significant. Speculation about the origins of life has generally been based upon three potential biotic solvents: methane (CH_4), ammonia (NH_3), or water (H_2O). However, the former two have significant drawbacks. For example, the hydrogen bonds between ammonia molecules are significantly weaker than those in water, causing the surface tension of liquid ammonia to be three times smaller than that of water, and in particular reducing its ability to concentrate nonpolar molecules through a hydrophobic effect. This raises questions about how well ammonia could hold prebiotic molecules together in order to allow the emergence of a self-reproducing system. Yet in each of these three cases, the core elements of potential biotic solvents remain elements which required stellar nucleosynthesis for their existence: carbon, nitrogen, and oxygen. The very existence of water, or any other biotic solvent, thus again depends upon the fine-tuning of the fundamental con-

32. Alessandro Morbidelli et al., "Source Regions and Timescales for the Delivery of Water to the Earth," *Meteoritics and Planetary Science* 35 (2000): 1309–20; Jörn Müller and Harald Lesch, "Woher kommt das Wasser der Erde?—Urgaswolke oder Meteoriten," *Chemie in unserer Zeit* 37 (2003): 242–46.

33. The ratio of xenon to krypton on typical carbonaceous chondrites is also significantly different from that found on Earth. For comment, see Michael J. Drake and Kevin Righter, "Determining the Composition of the Earth," *Nature* 416 (2002): 39–44. Drake and Righter consider three options for the origins of water, favoring the view that Earth could have accreted "wet" from both hydrous and anhydrous materials, with no significant addition of water from exogenous sources.

stants of the universe. The importance of this point cannot be overstated, yet it is frequently overlooked by those who assume that the relative abundance and availability of these elements requires no explanation.

Yet water is only one of a number of factors leading to the emergence and consolidation of life. We must now turn to reflect on the growing interest in bioinorganic chemistry and its implications for the chemical catalysis of the processes on which life is dependent.

Chapter 12

Chemical Catalysts and
the Constraints of Evolution

A central argument of this section of the book is that the emergence of life cannot be studied in isolation from the environment that creates the conditions and provides the resources making this possible. While Lawrence Henderson can rightly be criticized at certain points for his views on the "biocentricity" of the environment, his approach may be stated in terms that make it unproblematic, while at the same time highlighting its importance: if the fundamental properties of the universe were such that life could not come about, then life would never have emerged. In other words, the fundamental conditions of the universe are such that life is able to emerge. This minimalist statement, which to some is little more than a truism, nevertheless invites us to consider the remarkable properties of the universe and appreciate how, had they been different, life might never have emerged.

It is generally agreed that living systems require two fundamental components: a self-maintaining metabolic system and a genetic system capable of transmitting biological information.[1] Yet surprisingly little attention has been paid to the question of the fundamental chemical requirements for both these processes.

---

1. See the analysis in Freeman J. Dyson, *Origins of Life*, rev. ed. (Cambridge: Cambridge University Press, 1999); John Maynard Smith and Eörs Szathmáry, *The Origins of Life: From the Birth of Life to the Origin of Language* (Oxford: Oxford University Press, 1999), 1–36.

What if terrestrial chemistry had taken a very different form? In recent years, there has been a growing appreciation of constraints imposed by chemistry on the evolutionary process. While fully conceding the role of contingencies in evolutionary development, some researchers are emphasizing that evolution was resourced, guided, and constrained by the changing chemistry of the environment, with many inevitable results. These arguments are to be seen as part of a broader paradigm shift within evolutionary biology, in which the randomness of traditional neo-Darwinism is being supplanted by a more-scientific law-regulated emergence of life. The basic principles of thermodynamics and chemical assembly thus give evolution a strong directionality. Hence, evolution is not to be seen as a purely random process, since it appears to have been channeled along a predictable progression from single-celled organisms to plants and animals by chemical constraints.[2] In this chapter, we shall begin to explore some aspects of chemical fine-tuning, indicating its importance for our broader theme.

THE BIOCHEMICAL ROLE OF TRANSITION METALS

As we saw earlier, certain lighter elements are of fundamental importance to life—above all, hydrogen (H), carbon (C), nitrogen (N), and oxygen (O), but also sulfur (S). The elements carbon, nitrogen, and oxygen—with atomic numbers 6, 7, and 8 respectively—are found early on in the periodic table of the elements. The fundamental chemicals on which life depends are constituted primarily from these elements. It is also known that four light metal ions are also essential to life: sodium (Na), magnesium (Mg), potassium (K), and calcium (Ca).

Yet it is now widely accepted that nature employs a series of what are often termed "first-row transition metal ions"—such as manganese (Mn), iron (Fe), nickel (Ni), copper (Cu), and zinc (Zn)—to mediate a variety of fascinating single- and multi-electron reduction and oxidation (redox) transformations that are critical to all life.[3] These metals generally have atomic numbers between 25 and 30. Examples of the transformations which depend upon the electronic properties of these metal ions include the following: the oxidation of water to evolve O_2 and the storage of sunlight as chemical fuel in the process of photosynthesis, which is catalyzed by manganese; proton reduction and H_2 oxidation as critical metabolic reactions in bacteria (catalyzed by iron and nickel); and partial methane oxidation to methanol by O_2 (catalyzed by iron and copper).[4] The metalloenzymes

2. See the important analysis in R. J. P. Williams and J. J. R. Fraústo da Silva, "Evolution Was Chemically Constrained," *Journal of Theoretical Biology* 220 (2003): 323–43.

3. Transition metals are now defined as those elements whose distinguishing feature is an incomplete *d* subshell, or which can give rise to positively charged ions (cations) with an incomplete *d* subshell. No actinides or lanthanides appear to be essential to life: see A. J. Borovik, "Characteristics of Metals in Biological Systems," in *Heavy Metal Tolerance in Plants: Evolutionary Aspects*, ed, A. Jonathan Shaw (Boca Raton, FL: CRC Press, 1990), 3–6.

4. See further Richard H. Holm, Pierre Kennepohl, and Edward I. Solomon, "Structural and Functional Aspects of Metal Sites in Biology," *Chemical Reviews* 96 (1996): 2239–2314.

that bring about these difficult reactions are embedded in biological matrices with highly organized inorganic components that facilitate each of the key reaction steps. For example, the use of hybrid density functional theory has allowed quantum mechanical modeling of some aspects of the role of transition metals in enzymes, increasing our understanding of their important biological roles.[5] Recent studies have also clarified the mechanisms by which transition metal ions are transported from the environment to specific reaction sites.[6]

We have already examined some of the fundamental properties of the universe in our quest to understand something of its unusual character. In recent years, a new field of research has opened up, exploring the remarkable role played in the development of life by metal ions.[7] The term "bioinorganic chemistry" is sometimes used to refer to the exploration of the remarkable biological significance of small traces of metal ions in critical processes, such as photosynthesis and oxygen transport. This field was pioneered in the 1950s by R. J. P. Williams at Oxford University[8] and has since become a leading area of scientific research.[9] In the present chapter, we shall explore the significance of this field for the question of fine-tuning for life, focusing on the critical role played by a small group of metal ions in critical biochemical processes: iron, magnesium, manganese, and vanadium. What is the anthropic significance of these chemicals for life?[10]

There is still considerable debate about the composition of the early Earth's atmosphere. For a substantial part of early history of Earth—about 1.5 billion years—the atmosphere is thought to have been composed mostly of carbon dioxide, methane, sulfur dioxide, and nitrogen. Oxygen made up only a very small part of the atmosphere. Due to its high reactivity with other elements, primarily hydrogen and carbon, oxygen was toxic to most existing life-forms at this time.[11] Life

5. Per E. M. Siegbahn and Margareta R. A. Blomberg, "Transition-Metal Systems in Biochemistry Studied by High-Accuracy Quantum Chemical Methods," *Chemical Reviews* 100 (2000): 421–37; Per E. M. Siegbahn and Tomasz Borowski, "Modeling Enzymatic Reactions Involving Transition Metals," *Accounts of Chemical Research* 39 (2006): 729–38.

6. J. L. Hall and Lorraine E. Williams, "Transition Metal Transporters in Plants," *Journal of Experimental Botany* 54 (2003): 2601–13.

7. See esp. R. J. P. Williams and J. J. R. Fraústo da Silva, *The Chemistry of Evolution: The Development of Our Ecosystem* (Boston: Elsevier, 2006); idem, *The Natural Selection of the Chemical Elements: The Environment and Life's Chemistry* (Oxford: Clarendon Press, 1996).

8. For the article that is often seen as the manifesto of this movement, see R. J. P. Williams, "Metal Ions in Biological Systems," *Biological Reviews* 28 (1953): 381–412. For Williams's views on the matter fifty years later, see R. J. P. Williams, "The Inorganic Chemistry of Life," in *The New Chemistry*, ed. Nina Hall (Cambridge: Cambridge University Press, 2000), 259–99; see also R. J. P. Williams and B. Abolmaali, *Bioinorganic Chemistry: Trace Element Evolution from Anaerobes to Aerobes* (Berlin: Springer-Verlag, 1998).

9. The best introduction is Rosette M. Roat-Malone, *Bioinorganic Chemistry: A Short Course*, 2nd ed. (Hoboken, NJ: Wiley-Interscience, 2007).

10. The term "anthropic" is often used in the literature dealing with the biological significance of metal ions with the alternative meaning "caused by human presence or action": see, e.g., Emilio Marengo et al., "Investigation of Anthropic Effects Connected with Metal Ions Concentration, Organic Matter and Grain Size in Bormida River Sediments," *Analytica Chimica Acta* 560 (2006): 172–83.

11. These combinations led to the production of water and carbon dioxide, respectively. For an excellent discussion of the evolutionary significance of the atmosphere, see James F. Kasting and Janet L. Siefert, "Life and the Evolution of Earth's Atmosphere," *Science* 296 (2002): 1066–68.

on Earth existed primarily in the form of anaerobic bacteria—in other words, bacteria that could metabolize without the need for any oxygen. Over an extended period of time, two major developments took place which radically altered the nature of life on Earth, making possible the development of new life-forms: the evolution of photosynthesis and the "Great Oxidation."

THE BIOCHEMISTRY OF PHOTOSYNTHESIS

The first major development was the evolution of photosynthesis: a biochemical means of converting light into chemical energy, capable of being stored, that could be used to power cell growth and activity. This complex process takes place in photosynthetic membranes in plants, which contain two photosystems, known as photosystems I and II.[12] Photosystem I depends upon a family of chemicals known as chlorophylls, which absorb visible light in the blue and red regions of the spectrum, thus giving rise to its characteristic green appearance. The chlorophyll molecule has two parts: a substituted porphyrin ring and a phytol chain. The former is a complex structure, based on four heterocyclic carbon rings, that is capable of enfolding a metal ion and is found regularly in nature.[13] In hemoglobin, the metal ion is iron; in vitamin B_{12}, it is cobalt; in chlorophyll, it is magnesium (Mg).

The fundamental process involved in photosynthesis can be set out as follows:[14]

1. Light energy is trapped by chlorophyll to make ATP (a process known as photophosphorylation).

2. Water is split into oxygen, hydrogen ions, and free electrons:

$2H_2O \rightarrow 4H^+ + O_2 + 4e^-$ (the process of photolysis)

3. The free electrons then react with nicotinamide adenine dinucleotide phosphate (NADP, a carrier molecule), changing it from its oxidized state (NADP$^+$) to its reduced state (NADPH):

$NADP^+ + 2e^- + 2H^+ \rightarrow NADPH + H^+$

The whole process depends upon the capacity of chlorophyll to absorb light, causing its electrons to gain energy and move to higher energy levels in the mol-

---

12. For these two processes, see Wei-Zhong He and Richard Malkin, "Photosystems I and II," in *Photosynthesis: A Comprehensive Treatise*, ed. A. S. Raghavendra (Cambridge: Cambridge University Press, 1998), 29–43. For details of the chloroplasts and their biochemical role, see L. Andrew Staehelin, "Chloroplast Structure: From Chlorophyll Granules to Supra-Molecular Architecture of Thylakoid Membranes," *Photosynthesis Research* 76 (2003): 185–96.

13. For some of the chemical issues, see Anthony Harriman and Jean-Pierre Sauvage, "A Strategy for Constructing Photosynthetic Models: Porphyrin-Containing Modules Assembled around Transition Metals," *Chemical Society Reviews* 25 (1996): 41–48.

14. For a detailed study of our present understanding of these processes, see the review by Gernot Renger, "Oxidative Photosynthetic Water Splitting: Energetics, Kinetics and Mechanism," *Photosynthesis Research* 92 (2007): 407–25.

ecule (a process known as "photoexcitation"). This energy in turn ionizes the molecule (a process called photoionization), leading to the liberation of an electron, leaving a positively charged chlorophyll ion, which can then accept a pair of electrons from a neighboring electron donor such as water.

Photosynthesis is not a particularly efficient process; perhaps 1% of the light falling on chloroplasts is converted into chemical energy. However, evolution finds its ways to workable, not necessarily the best, solutions, and this solution was good enough. The evolutionary importance of this process cannot be overstated. The metabolism of living organisms constantly dissipates energy in a non-reusable form. If life is to be sustained, this lost energy has to be replenished. The only significant available external energy source is the sun, requiring that a means of using sunlight to fuel all metabolic demands had to be developed. This process depends upon a source of high potential electrons which are electromagnetically excited by the absorption of light by chlorophyll. The electrons are energized in the magnesium center of chlorophyll molecules. This process depends upon the energy levels of magnesium electrons. In photosystem II, a critical role is played by a tetranuclear core of manganese ions, a complex of four precisely arranged manganese ions which are successively oxidized to higher and higher states by light in a process that is still not well understood.[15] This system becomes the most powerful oxidizing agent in any known biological system, capable of splitting water molecules to draw off electrons and allow the production of molecular oxygen. Its efficacy rests upon the quantum mechanical properties of the excited states of manganese electrons, without which this process could not take place.[16]

Photosynthesis, as we noted, led to an increase in the presence of oxygen in the atmosphere, possibly in a series of steps. This leads us to consider the second major development of importance to our reflections: the emergence of mechanisms for dealing with the increased presence of oxygen on Earth.

TRANSITION METALS AND OXYGEN

This development took place about 2.2 billion years ago, during the Paleoproterozoic era, when oxygenic photosynthesis slowly began to evolve in a form of blue-green algae known as cyanobacteria. Cyanobacteria could convert sunlight, carbon dioxide, and water into carbohydrates, producing free oxygen as a waste product. All three of these fundamental resources were plentiful, and the cyanobacteria population thrived. As a result, the oxygen content of the atmosphere began to rise.

15. For recent research, see Holger Dau, Peter Liebisch, and Michael Haumann, "The Manganese Complex of Oxygenic Photosynthesis: Conversion of Five-Coordinated Mn(III) to Six-Coordinated Mn(IV) in the S2–S3 Transition Is Implied by XANES Simulations," *Physica Scripta* T115 (2005): 844–46.
16. For further comments on the biological role of manganese, see T. Rajendiran et al., "Evaluating Hydrogen Bond Interactions in Enzymes Containing Mn(III)-Histidine Complexation Using Manganese-Imidazole Complexes," *Journal of Biological Inorganic Chemistry* 8 (2003): 283–93.

The first significant increase in atmospheric oxygen levels on Earth (the Great Oxidation) is thought to have occurred at least 300 million years after the evolution of oxygenic photosynthesis, but the reason for this time lag remains clear.[17] The impact of this development was not simply to increase the atmospheric amount of dioxygen (O_2), but also of its highly reactive derivatives, such as superoxide anions, hydrogen peroxide, and hydroxyl radicals.

The increasing oxygenation of the atmosphere caused severe difficulties for many life-forms. Oxygen was toxic for anaerobic organisms. Initially, atmospheric oxygen appears to have been absorbed by "oxygen sinks." The oceans were rich in soluble forms of iron, which reacted with the oxygen to produce insoluble iron oxide. Great deposits of hematite and magnetite began to be laid down on the ocean floors.[18] Yet there were limits to how much oxygen could be absorbed in this way. Once the iron content of the oceans had been exhausted in this way, there was nothing to prevent oxygen from entering the atmosphere. All the gaseous oxygen in the present atmosphere is believed to have had a biological origin, suggesting that a by-product of one life-form turned out to force the development of its successor.

Over a period of some 300 million years, significant changes emerged in response to the growing presence of oxygen in the atmosphere. Cyanobacteria, the cause of this oxygen surge, ended up being a victim of its own success, unable to prosper in the oxygen-rich environment which it had created. Some organisms retreated into anoxic environments, safe from the presence of oxygen.[19] Others were able to adapt to the oxygen surge by developing enzymes and processes which neutralized oxygen's toxicity.[20] Indeed, what was initially a threat turned into an opportunity for growth.[21] The presence of oxygen offered organisms opportunities for respiration and the biosynthesis of entirely new classes of molecules. The presence of oxygen, especially the need for mechanisms of oxygen metabolism, was thus a key to evolutionary development, most notably in relation to the evolution of multicellular forms of life. The chemistry of oxygen thus proved fruitful to stimulating the emergence of more complex life-forms. Three major chemical routes for oxygen transport developed:[22] hemocyanins (metalloproteins containing cop-

17. The Great Oxidation may have been triggered by a relatively small environmental change, as argued by Colin Goldblatt, Timothy M. Lenton, and Andrew J. Watson, "Bistability of Atmospheric Oxygen and the Great Oxidation," *Nature* 443 (2006): 683–86.

18. For a useful account, see Steve Kershaw, "Evolution of the Earth's Atmosphere and Its Geological Impact," *Geology Today* 6 (1990): 55–60.

19. Robert Rye and Heinrich D. Holland, "Paleosols and the Evolution of Atmospheric Oxygen: A Critical Review," *American Journal of Science* 298 (1998): 621–72.

20. There is some evidence that biological mechanisms originally developed to remove oxygen from biological systems subsequently evolved into means of transporting oxygen within systems to allow aerobic respiration. This is thought to be the case with certain copper oxygen-binding proteins: see Heinz Decker and Nora Terwilliger, "Cops and Robbers: Putative Evolution of Copper Oxygen-Binding Proteins," *Journal of Experimental Biology* 203 (2000): 1777–82.

21. Jason Raymond and Daniel Segré, "The Effect of Oxygen on Biochemical Networks and the Evolution of Complex Life," *Science* 311 (2006): 1764–67.

22. Donald M. Kurtz, "Oxygen-Carrying Proteins: Three Solutions to a Common Problem," in *Essays in Biochemistry*, ed. David P. Ballou (London: Portland Press, 1999), 85–100.

per as a prosthetic group at their oxygen-binding site), which are found in mollusks and arthropods; hemerythrins (metalloproteins containing iron as a prosthetic group at their oxygen-binding site), found only in a few marine worms;[23] and the much more common hemoglobins, which are found in all kinds of species from microorganisms and vegetables to human beings.

Some have suggested that this rise in oxygen was a triggering factor for the "Cambrian explosion."[24] The Cambrian period is sometimes described as "evolution's big bang" because the animal kingdom underwent explosive growth at some point around 560 million years ago, for reasons that are still not fully understood. The length of the Cambrian explosion is ambiguous and uncertain, but most regard up to thirty million years (560–530 million years ago) as a reasonable estimate for its duration. Over this period, the animal phyla underwent rapid, significant, and irreversible diversification, during a period of such rapid development that it causes difficulties for "gradualist" theories of evolution.[25] Whether organismal heterogeneity is measured in terms of phylogenetic diversity or morphological disparity, it is generally recognized that the fossil evidence indicates that most inclusive groups of metazoan organisms, including arthropods, made their first unambiguous appearance around this time. Before this period, all existing animals were soft-bodied creatures, not dissimilar to worms.[26] During the Cambrian period, most animal groups developed hard body parts, making possible the preservation of their fossils.

Our concern in this chapter, however, is with chemical changes and their biological impact. Two of these shifts are of particular interest. First, the transition from a chemically reducing to a chemically oxidizing environment had a significant

23. Note Stenkamp's comment that hemerythrin represents "an evolutionary development that failed to provide the best means of solving the reversible oxygen-binding problem": Ronald E. Stenkamp, "Dioxygen and Hemerythrin," *Chemical Reviews* 94 (1994): 715–26, esp. 724.

24. A. L. R. Thomas, "The Breath of Life—Did Increased Oxygen Levels Trigger the Cambrian Explosion?" *Trends in Ecology and Evolution* 12 (1997): 44–45. More generally, see the excellent overview in Nick Lane, *Oxygen: The Molecule That Made the World* (Oxford: Oxford University Press, 2002), 29–74.

25. The most accessible introductions to this important development are Stephen Jay Gould, *Wonderful Life: The Burgess Shale and the Nature of History* (New York: W. W. Norton, 1989); Simon Conway Morris, *The Crucible of Creation: The Burgess Shale and the Rise of Animals* (Oxford: Oxford University Press, 1998). The Burgess Shale fossils were discovered by Charles Doolittle Walcott in the Canadian Rockies in 1909.

26. The abrupt appearance of such fossils implies only the origin of biological or geological factors that enhance fossilization and does not, in itself, necessarily indicate Cambrian accelerations in either the formation of new protostome lineages or major body plans. Indeed, a phylogenetically and morphologically diverse soft-bodied fauna may have existed long before the Cambrian, yet only acquired paleontological "visibility" with the evolution of body armor, large body size, or extensive ecological or geographical ranges. For discussion of this important point, see Simon Conway Morris, "A Palaeontological Perspective," *Current Opinion in Genetics and Development* 4 (1994): 802–9; Jerome C. Regier and Jeffrey W. Schultz, "Molecular Phylogeny of Arthropods and the Significance of the 'Cambrian Explosion' for Molecular Systematics," *American Zoologist* 38 (1998): 918–28; James W. Valentine, David Jablonski, and Douglas H. Erwin, "Fossils, Molecules and Embryos: New Perspectives on the Cambrian Explosion," *Development* 126 (1999): 851–59. The argument set out by Richard Fortey, "Evolution: The Cambrian Explosion Exploded?" *Science* 293 (2001): 438–39, seems logically flawed.

impact on the availability of certain elements now essential for life. For example, sulfur, previously available in the form of easily assimilated sulfides (typically in the form of the HS⁻ radical), had to be extracted from sulfates (SO_4^{2-}). More important, nitrogen—an essential component of amino acids, the building blocks of life—was formerly available to biological organisms in the form of ammonia, NH_3, which was relatively easily converted to biologically accessible forms. The oxygen surge caused ammonia to be oxidized to nitrogen gas, N_2, which rapidly became the predominant component of Earth's atmosphere. Yet nitrogen is an extremely stable molecule and very difficult to convert to chemical forms that can be biologically assimilated. Unless this conversion could take place, the growth of living organisms would be severely impeded. Second, as an oxygen-rich atmosphere developed, life adapted by evolving forms of aerobic metabolism. As more-complex life-forms emerged, a need arose for oxygen transport systems.[27] In the event, both of these mechanisms were able to evolve, yet both depended upon the fundamental chemical properties of certain transition metals. We shall consider them both briefly.

How could atmospheric nitrogen be converted into a biologically useful form? The triple nitrogen-nitrogen bond in atmospheric dinitrogen is strong and difficult to break. Three first-row transition metals turned out to have the properties necessary to catalyze this development: iron, molybdenum, and vanadium.[28] Only one family of biological enzymes have developed to allow this conversion to take place: the nitrogenases. The chemical reaction that nitrogenases catalyze can be represented as follows:

$$N_2 + 8H^+ + 8e^- \rightarrow 2NH_3 + H_2$$

This reaction, which requires a substantial amount of chemical energy derived from ATP, can be seen as a re-creation of an earlier phase in the history of Earth, in which ammonia (NH_3) was plentiful and accessible, thus allowing existing biosynthetic mechanisms to convert ammonia to amino acids. The critically important component of any nitrogenase is the unique metal center which is thought to be the locus of the conversion of nitrogen.[29] This efficacy appears to depend partly on its electron configuration and partly on the geometry of the enzyme complex. In vitro studies of molybdenum, one of the three metals used

27. For an excellent analysis, see Peter D. Ward and David W. Ehlert, *Out of Thin Air: Dinosaurs, Birds, and Earth's Ancient Atmosphere* (Washington, DC: Joseph Henry Press, 2006), 51–80.
28. See the review of the present state of knowledge in John W. Peters and Robert K. Szilagyi, "Exploring New Frontiers of Nitrogenase Structure and Mechanism," *Current Opinion in Chemical Biology* 10 (2006): 101–8.
29. For theoretical considerations of possible mechanisms of nitrogen fixing, see Uwe Huniar, Reinhart Ahlrichs, and Dimitri Coucouvanis, "Density Functional Theory Calculations and Exploration of a Possible Mechanism of N_2 Reduction by Nitrogenase," *Journal of the American Chemical Society* 126 (2004): 2588–2601.

in natural nitrogen fixation processes, suggest that this capacity is partly due to its stereochemistry and partly to its wide range of oxidation states.[30] The unusual properties of molybdenum are paralleled by those of vanadium, which also plays a significant (though not fully understood) role in biology.[31]

Oxygen transport is of critical importance to many living organisms. The best-known example of such a system is found in blood, which uses hemoglobin to transport oxygen. However, it should be noted that leguminous plants use hemoglobin to keep oxygen away from the nitrogenase reduction centers in the root nodules. In other plants, such as rice, hemoglobin seems to play a role in stress management for nitrous oxide.[32] Not only do plants create oxygen during the process of photosynthesis; they also require it for respiration and use forms of hemoglobins to bind and transfer that oxygen. The first plant hemoglobins (now known as "leghemoglobins") were discovered in the root nodules of legumes. The fixing of nitrogen consumes large amounts of energy, and leghemoglobin facilitates the diffusion of oxygen to the respiring bacteroids in the root nodule. The functional center of hemoglobins is very similar to that already noted in chlorophyll and vitamin B_{12}; in this case, an iron atom is enclosed within four heterocyclic carbon rings, set within a protein scaffolding. The capacity of such complexes to transport oxygen is dependent upon the unusual properties of these transition metals, particularly their capacity to bond to gases.

Many other examples of biological activities that are critically dependent upon the properties of metal ions could be given. For example, metal ions are essential to the stabilization of the tertiary structure of RNA, enabling its folding and catalysis.[33] These positively charged metal ions neutralize the negatively charged RNA phosphate backbone, trigger collapse of its polynucleotide chain, and mediate highly specific conformational rearrangements within the active sites of RNA catalysts.[34] The point being made here is that these critically important biological roles of metal ions are ultimately dependent upon their fundamental properties. Furthermore, certain biologically essential properties only emerge under certain conditions—as, for example, when a metal ion is coordinated very tightly within a protein. To note an especially luminous situation, the properties of copper and iron in aqueous solution are markedly different from those which emerge when

30. Dmitry V. Yandulov and Richard R. Schrock, "Catalytic Reduction of Dinitrogen to Ammonia at a Single Molybdenum Center," *Science* 301 (2003): 76–78. For more recent analysis, see Liam P. Spencer et al., "Inner-Sphere Two-Electron Reduction Leads to Cleavage and Functionalization of Coordinated Dinitrogen," *Proceedings of the National Academy of Sciences* 103 (2006): 17094–98.

31. Enrique J. Baran, "Model Studies Related to Vanadium Biochemistry: Recent Advances and Perspectives," *Journal of the Brazilian Chemical Society* 14 (2003): 878–88.

32. Ross C. Hardison, "A Brief History of Hemoglobins: Plant, Animal, Protist, and Bacteria," *Proceedings of the National Academy of Sciences* 93 (1996): 5675–79.

33. Martha J. Fedor, "The Role of Metal Ions in RNA Catalysis," *Current Opinion in Structural Biology* 12 (2002): 289–95; David E. Draper, "A Guide to Ions and RNA Structure," *RNA* 10 (2004): 335–43.

34. Sarah A. Woodson, "Metal Ions and RNA Folding: A Highly Charged Topic with a Dynamic Future," *Current Opinion in Chemical Biology* 9 (2005): 104–9.

these metals are enfolded in a complex organic scaffolding.[35] The electrostatic field of the enzyme proteins plays, a crucial role in fine-tuning the redox potential of these metals to permit electron transfer to take place,[36] thus enabling a biological process which would otherwise not be possible.

THE FINE-TUNING OF BIOLOGICAL PROCESSES

All of this serves to emphasize—though not to explain—the remarkable fine-tuning of biological processes. This point is not negated by suggesting that evolution can fine-tune itself. Chemical reality constrains evolution; these processes can occur only because the chemistry of certain metals, predetermined by quantum mechanical parameters, permits them to do so. If this were not the case, evolution could not have found its way to such solutions as photosynthesis, nitrogen fixing, or oxygen transport. Evolution can only fine-tune itself because of the predetermined properties of chemical elements. Had they been significantly different, this fine-tuning within nature could not take place.

This leads us to reiterate a further point of importance. In chapter 10, we emphasized how the nucleosynthesis of carbon, nitrogen, and oxygen clearly depended on the critical values of the constants of nature which facilitated the formation of stars. Without stars, these biologically critical elements would not have formed. The same point applies with even greater force to higher elements, such as transition metals, which require extraordinarily dense environments if nucleogenesis is to take place. The production of elements up to and including iron takes place by fusion. The synthesis of elements heavier than iron takes place by neutron capture processes that are typically found in supernovae.[37] In the case of copper, which plays a significant biological role in terrestrial situations, there is a debate as to whether the origins of this metallic element are primarily found in massive stars or in type 1a supernovae.[38] Nevertheless, the critical dependence of these processes upon the values of certain constants will be obvious. Counterfactual situations can easily be imagined, in which stars did not form. In that sit-

35. The case of the active copper sites in nitrous oxide reductase is a case in point: see the review by Walter G. Zumft, "Cell Biology and Molecular Basis of Denitrification," *Microbiology and Molecular Biology Reviews* 61 (1997): 533–616.

36. For example, see the significant redox potential shift of copper in the coordination polyhedron of the protein azurin with respect to copper in water: Michele Cascella et al., "Role of Protein Frame and Solvent for the Redox Properties of Azurin from Pseudomonas Aeruginosa," *Proceedings of the National Academy of Sciences* 103 (2006): 19641–46. As these writers point out, the reorganization of free energy (λ) for the redox process is much smaller than copper ions in aqueous solution, allowing a much-higher electron transfer rate than the aqueous chemistry of copper would suggest.

37. For a review of what is known of these neutron capture processes, see Marcel Arnould, Stephane Goriely, and Kohji Takahashi, "The R-Process of Stellar Nucleosynthesis: Astrophysics and Nuclear Physics Achievements and Mysteries," *Physics Reports* 450 (2007): 97–213.

38. Donatella Romano and Francesca Matteucci, "Contrasting Copper Evolution in Ω Centauri and the Milky Way," *Monthly Notices of the Royal Astronomical Society: Letters* 378 (2007): L59–L63.

uation, it is impossible to see how any elements essential to life could be formed. No stars, no life.

In this chapter, we have considered the significance of certain chemical catalysts which are essential for biological processes. We shall now move on and consider how Darwinian mechanisms came into play and their implications for our theme.

Chapter 13

The Origins of Complexity

The Mechanism of Evolution

The concept of "fine-tuning" is widely recognized within biology;[1] the manner of its interpretation, however, raises some important difficulties for any natural theology. Though these difficulties are ultimately positive and productive, they must be confronted from the outset. It is a fundamental axiom of Darwinism that nature is capable of tuning itself through evolutionary mechanisms, even though that fine-tuning may only lead to a workable, rather than the best, solution. If it could be demonstrated that fine-tuning is to be observed in evolved biological systems, many would argue that this observation could be explained reductively, generally without undue difficulty, by Darwinian orthodoxy. William Paley's discussion of what we might now call the fine-tuning of the human eye is an excellent example of a phenomenon of this kind for which a plausible evolutionary explanation can be advanced.[2]

1. Bernard J. Carr and Martin J. Rees, "Fine-Tuning in Living Systems," *International Journal of Astrobiology* 3 (2003): 79–86.
2. For useful recent surveys, see Timothy H. Goldsmith, "Optimization, Constraint, and History in the Evolution of Eyes," *Quarterly Review of Biology* 65 (1990): 281–322; Georg Halder, Patrick Callaerts, and Walter J. Gehring, "New Perspectives on Eye Evolution," *Current Opinion in Genetics and Development* 5 (1995): 602–9. Vertebrate eyes are often cited as showing suboptimal functionality

Yet the concept of biological fine-tuning does not lose its potential to stimulate and inform a natural theology in the light of these observations. As the English theologian Charles Kingsley (1819–75) argued in his landmark 1871 lecture "The Natural Theology of the Future," older natural theologies, including Paley's, rested on the belief that God made all things—whereas a modern natural theology pointed to a God who was "much wiser than even that," since God chose to "make all things make themselves."[3] Kingsley's new-style natural theology evaded the static account of creation inherited, perhaps rather uncritically, by Paley and replaced it with a notion of divine providence and causality that affirmed God's continuing presence and action within the slowly evolving natural order.[4] On Kingsley's approach, the created order is such that it possesses a given or "instressed" capacity to evolve, in which new structures may legitimately be said to "emerge."

Kingsley's new approach to natural theology can be seen as part of the Christian tradition's episodic reformulation of its fundamental conceptual contents to meet the religious needs of differing historical and cultural epochs—in this case, occasioned by both the publication of Darwin's *Origin of Species* in 1859 and a growing sense of frustration with the rigidities of Paley's highly static approach to the natural world. Kingsley's intellectual frustration and his proposal for its alleviation resonated with the cultural mood. The adoption of this approach by Frederick Temple (1821–1902), future Archbishop of Canterbury, secured its cultural acceptance.[5] For Temple, the unity of the evolutionary process bore more eloquent testimony to the unity of its creator than a series of separate (and potentially unrelated) creations. Even "Darwin's bulldog," Thomas Henry Huxley, conceded that there was no reason, in principle, why the evolutionary process should not have been incorporated into an initial design of the universe.

As we noted earlier (see chap. 8), the approach of Augustine of Hippo is easily adapted to this evolutionary scenario. While Kingsley probably did not appre-

---

on account of "many functionally arbitrary or maladaptive features"; see George C. Williams, *Natural Selection: Domains, Levels, and Challenges* (New York: Oxford University Press, 1992), 73. For example, blood vessels and nerves must pass through the retina, thus creating a "blind spot." It is not clear that this really is maladaptive, since the high sensitivity of the photoreceptors needs to be maintained by the removal of spent membranes, for which the vertebrate arrangement appears superior.

3. Charles Kingsley, "The Natural Theology of the Future," in *Westminster Sermons* (London: Macmillan, 1874), v–xxxiii. See further David M. Levy and Sandra J. Peart, "Charles Kingsley and the Theological Interpretation of Natural Selection," *Journal of Bioeconomics* 8 (2006): 197–218. Kingsley is the author referred to by Darwin in an important passage inserted in the second edition of *The Origin of Species*: "A celebrated author and divine has written to me that 'he had gradually learnt to see it is just as noble a conception of the Deity to believe that He created a few original forms capable of self-development into other and needful forms, as to believe that He required a fresh act of creation to supply the voids caused by the action of His laws.'" Charles Darwin, *On the Origin of the Species by Means of Natural Selection*, 2nd ed. (London: John Murray, 1860), 481.

4. For the significance of this approach and its historical influence, see John Hedley Brooke, "Darwin and Victorian Christianity," in *The Cambridge Companion to Darwin*, ed. Jonathan Hodge and Gregory Radick (Cambridge: Cambridge University Press, 2003), 192–213, esp. 206.

5. See Arthur McCalla, *The Creationist Debate: The Encounter between the Bible and the Historical Mind* (London: T&T Clark International, 2006), 166–17.

ciate the fact, his neat slogan about God choosing to "make all things make themselves" is nothing more than a creative reworking of Augustine's notion of *rationes seminales*, designed to accentuate its convergence with the evolutionary paradigm. Augustine, we must emphasize, did not himself adopt or envisage such an evolutionary position; his own view, as we noted, relies on the scientific consensus of his age, which Augustine had no reason to challenge.

Yet there is no fundamental reason why Augustine's fundamental theological insights cannot be detached from their temporary and provisional coupling to fifth-century natural science, which has no divine endorsement, and be coupled instead to more recent natural scientific ideas. The historical provisionality of any such coupling, whether ancient or modern, must be conceded. As Augustine himself wished to make clear, any attempt to bind biblical interpretation to the prevailing scientific worldview will create difficulties for future exegetes, who find themselves locked into an earlier generation's perspectives.

Even a cursory reading of contemporary works in evolutionary biology shows how theological or antitheological agendas repeatedly intrude into what are supposed to be neutral, objective scientific discussions. What is presented as an empirical account of reality often turns out to be infested with nonempirical assumptions, often involving covert metaphysical dogmas. To explore this point further, we may consider a statement made by Oxford zoologist Richard Dawkins in *The Selfish Gene*. Dawkins here sets out the "gene's-eye" view of evolution, which was then dominant in biological circles.[6]

> [Genes] swarm in huge colonies, safe inside gigantic lumbering robots, sealed off from the outside world, communicating with it by tortuous indirect routes, manipulating it by remote control. They are in you and me; they created us, body and mind; and their preservation is the ultimate rationale for our existence.

Dawkins here offers an empirical statement—genes "are in you and me"—surrounded by a thicket of interpretative statements, which a casual reader might interpret as straightforward observation, unaware that they are actually heavily metaphysically freighted.

The extent to which such a nonempirical approach has intruded can be judged by comparing this paragraph with an alternative version, devised by the celebrated Oxford physiologist and systems biologist Denis Noble. What is proved empirical fact—that genes "are in you and me"—is retained; the interpretative elements have been rewritten, offering a radically different account of the role of the gene.[7]

6. Richard Dawkins, *The Selfish Gene*, 2nd ed. (Oxford: Oxford University Press, 1989), 21. For an account of the rise and fall of this approach, see the comprehensive analysis in Kim Sterelny and Paul E. Griffiths, *Sex and Death: An Introduction to Philosophy of Biology* (Chicago: University of Chicago Press, 1999), esp. 55–76.

7. Denis Noble, *The Music of Life: Biology beyond the Genome* (Oxford: Oxford University Press, 2006), 11–15.

> [Genes] are trapped in huge colonies, locked inside highly intelligent beings, moulded by the outside world, communicating with it by complex processes, through which, blindly, as if by magic, function emerges. They are in you and me; we are the system that allows their code to be read; and their preservation is totally dependent on the joy that we experience in reproducing ourselves. We are the ultimate rationale for their existence.

These two statements are empirically equivalent: both have equally good grounding in observation and experimental evidence. Yet they express totally different views concerning the role of the gene. So which is right? Which is more scientific? How could we decide which is to be preferred on scientific grounds? As Noble rightly observes,"no-one seems to be able to think of an experiment that would detect an empirical difference between them."[8]

This digression indicates how easily metaphysical presuppositions intrude into what is meant to be an objective scientific account of things. This is perhaps most evident in the case of writers wishing to argue that evolutionary naturalism eliminates either (or both) belief in God or (and) in divine involvement in natural processes.[9] There is no question of a theologian such as myself artificially and unnecessarily introducing theological agendas into a discussion about the broader themes of contemporary biology where they are clearly out of place. Quite the reverse; it is impossible to reflect on the metaphysical implications of contemporary evolutionary biology without becoming involved in a debate about God. Even seemingly neutral or objective discussions about teleological judgments are often metaphysically freighted, occasionally making them functionally indistinguishable from theology.[10] Given the prevalence of theological judgments within contemporary evolutionary biology, there is no need to offer a defense for continuing reflection on the theological significance of its themes and concerns, focusing particularly on the mechanisms and directions of evolution.

We begin by considering how contemporary understandings of evolutionary biology relate to ideas of fine-tuning, a subject which is as important as it is neglected. We shall explore this in two stages in consecutive chapters, this chapter dealing with the mechanism of evolution, and chapter 14 with its outcomes. Since some readers of this work may not be familiar with the basics of neo-Darwinian evolutionary theory, we shall begin by exploring the historical emergence of its core themes, before focusing on the critical issues of relevance to this work.[11]

---

8. Ibid., 13.

9. Paul A. Nelson, "The Role of Theology in Current Evolutionary Reasoning," *Biology and Philosophy* 11 (1996): 493–517.

10. Nelson provides a rich range of examples for those wishing to take this further, especially in relation to the theological significance of alleged "imperfections" in nature. On this specific point, see further Timothy Shanahan, "Darwinian Naturalism, Theism, and Biological Design," *Perspectives on Science and Christian Faith* 49 (1997): 170–78.

11. Readers wanting a fuller introduction should consult the standard textbooks, including John H. Gillespie, *The Causes of Molecular Evolution* (New York: Oxford University Press, 1991); Mark Ridley, *Evolution*, 3rd ed. (Malden, MA: Blackwell Science, 2004).

AN INTRODUCTION TO NEO-DARWINISM

Charles Darwin's *Origin of Species* (1859), rightly regarded as a landmark in nineteenth-century science, identified a series of features of the natural world which seemed to require particularly close attention, in the light of problems and shortcomings with existing explanations, especially Paley's doctrine of "special creation."[12] These aspects of the natural order could all be explained on the basis of Paley's theory, in much the same way that Ptolemy's geocentric model of the solar system could accommodate observations if sufficient arbitrary epicycles were added to the model. Yet in each case, the explanations offered seemed cumbersome and strained. What was originally a relatively neat and elegant theory began to crumble under the weight of accumulated difficulties and tensions. There had to be a better explanation. And just as Ptolemy gave way to Kepler, so Paley gave way to Darwin.

Darwin's *Origin of Species* offered a wealth of evidence in support of the idea of biological evolution and proposed a mechanism by which it might work: *natural selection*. The basic idea lying behind this approach is that in any population, there is descent with modification due to natural selection. Changes thus occur over many generations, reflecting the "pressure" which the environment places on the various genetic varieties in terms of their ability to cope and survive. The approach can be summarized under four main points:

1. *Variation.* Individuals, even siblings, in a population vary.
2. *Inheritance.* These variations can somehow be passed to offspring.
3. *Competition.* More offspring are produced than the environment can support, so there is competition for limited resources (a point that Darwin borrowed from Thomas Malthus).
4. *Survival.* Those individuals whose characteristics make them best suited to the environment live and reproduce and have more offspring.

The *Origin of Species* set out to demonstrate, by the sheer weight of observational evidence, why the idea of "natural selection" is the best mechanism to explain how the evolution of species took place and how it is to be understood. The key point is that natural selection is proposed as nature's analogue to the process of "artificial selection" in stockbreeding.[13] Darwin argues that the process

---

12. For a detailed account, see Dov Ospovat, *The Development of Darwin's Theory: Natural History, Natural Theology, and Natural Selection, 1838–1859* (Cambridge: Cambridge University Press, 1995). For the specific issues, see Peter J. Bowler, "Darwinism and the Argument from Design: Suggestions for a Reevaluation," *Journal of the History of Biology* 10 (1977): 29–43; John Hedley Brooke, "Science and the Fortunes of Natural Theology: Some Historical Perspectives," *Zygon* 24 (1989): 3–22.

13. Darwin was familiar with these issues, especially as they related to the breeding of pigeons: James A. Secord, "Nature's Fancy: Charles Darwin and the Breeding of Pigeons," *Isis* 72 (1981): 163–86.

of "domestic selection" or "artificial selection" offers a model for a mechanism for what happens in nature: the process of "natural selection."

Darwin's theory had considerable explanatory force, a point recognized by many at the time, even those who were anxious about the implications of his ideas for the place of humanity within nature. Yet there was a serious problem with the theory. How did nature "remember" and "transmit" these new developments? What mechanism could be proposed by which these new developments could be passed on to future generations? Darwin's contemporaries generally believed that characteristics of the parents were "blended" when they were passed to the offspring. But if this was the case, how could a single mutation be spread throughout a species? It would be diluted to the point of insignificance, like a drop of ink in a bucket of water. Darwin put forward the idea of "pangenesis," based on hypothetical "gemmules"—minute particules which somehow determine all characteristics of the organism.[14] These "gemmules" had never been observed; nevertheless, Darwin argued that it was necessary to propose their existence to make sense of the observational data at his disposal. It was an ingenious solution, yet it was not right. Darwin's theory faltered, lacking a plausible theory of genetics.[15]

The answer to this problem would emerge from the detailed observations of Gregor Mendel (1822–84), a monk at the Augustinian monastery of St. Thomas in the Austrian town Brünn (now the Czech town of Brno). Mendel had been encouraged by his teachers at the University of Vienna and by the abbot of his monastery to explore his interest in hybridization in plant populations. He set up a series of experiments involving some twenty-eight thousand pea plants over the period 1856–63 and was observing how characteristics were transmitted from one generation to the next. He chose to focus on seven easily determined characteristics of his peas. Two of the best known of these are the color of their flowers (purple or white?) and the color of their seeds (yellow or green?). As he observed the patterns of inheritance of these characteristics, Mendel noticed some significant recurring features. In cross-pollinating plants that produce either yellow or green peas exclusively, Mendel found that the first offspring generation always has yellow peas. However, the following generation consistently has a 3:1 ratio of yellow to green. Certain characteristics, such as yellow seeds, were found to be "dominant" over other "recessive" characteristics, such as green seeds.

From his research, Mendel was able to formulate three fundamental principles which seemed to govern inheritance:[16]

14. Charles Darwin sets out the theory in *The Variation of Animals and Plants under Domestication*, 2 vols. (London: John Murray, 1868).

15. For the issues linked with this, see Marjorie Grene and David Depew, *The Philosophy of Biology: An Episodic History* (Cambridge: Cambridge University Press, 2004), 221–46.

16. Peter J. Bowler, *The Mendelian Revolution: The Emergence of Hereditarian Concepts in Modern Science and Society* (London: Athlone Press, 1989).

1. The inheritance of each trait—such as the color of the flower or seed—seems to be determined by certain units or factors that are passed on to descendants.

2. An individual plant inherits one such unit from each parent for each of these traits.

3. Traits which do not show up in an individual may nevertheless be passed on to a later generation.

Mendel thus proposed a theory of "particulate inheritance," in which characteristics were determined by discrete units of inheritance that were passed intact from one generation to the next. Adaptive mutations could spread slowly through a species and never be "blended out," as some contemporary theories of genetics held. The evolutionary implications of this were considerable. Darwin's theory of natural selection, building on small mutations over long periods of time, suddenly became much more plausible.

Yet Mendel had shown that inheritance seemed to be determined by certain "units" or "factors." But what where they? In the end, the solution was set out in a seminal paper published by the American geneticist Thomas Hunt Morgan (1866–1945) in 1926. The solution? The gene.[17] Excited by Mendel's ideas, Morgan had exploited the short reproductive cycle of the fruit fly *Drosophila melanogaster* to explore the transmission of heritable characteristics. Like Mendel, he chose to focus on some well-defined characteristic traits that occurred in pairs, such as the color of the flies' eyes. Morgan's most important conclusion concerned how these traits were transmitted. It had been known for some time that the division of biological cells was accompanied by the appearance of tiny rod-shaped, threadlike structures, known as chromosomes. Some had speculated that these chromosomes might be responsible for transmitting hereditary information. Morgan was able to provide overwhelming evidence that this was the case. The "genes" responsible for transmitting this information were physically located on the chromosomes. As microscopes with increasing resolution were developed, it eventually became possible to confirm this visually.

The principles of hereditary transmission were now known to be based on the Mendelian notion of discrete hereditary factors ("genes"). What is known as the "neo-Darwinism" synthesis was now possible: Mendelian genetics was the basic explanation of evolutionary change, linked with the process of Darwinian natural selection as determining its outcome. Yet further clarification was needed concerning the molecular basis of genetics. A decisive step forward was made in the United States during the Second World War—to which we now turn.

Morgan's discovery of the critical role of the chromosomes in genetics sparked off new interest in their chemical composition. What were these threadlike fibers actually made of? The Swiss biochemist Friedrich Miescher (1844–95) established

17. Thomas H. Morgan, *The Theory of the Gene* (New Haven: Yale University Press, 1926).

the chemical composition of cell nuclei in 1868. He determined that they contained two basic components: a nucleic acid (now known as deoxyribonucleic acid, and universally known by its acronym DNA), and a class of proteins (now known as histones).[18] These nucleic acids were not regarded as particularly important biologically. Chemical studies suggested they were not complex, having only a small number of components.

In 1919, Phoebus Levene (1869–1940), working at the Rockefeller Institute in New York, discovered that DNA existed as a remarkably long polymer.[19] However, he took the view that this long polymer simply consisted of repeated units of four basic nucleotides: adenine (A), guanine (G), thymine (T), and cytosine (C). For this reason, many (including Levene himself) regarded DNA as highly unlikely to have any major role in the transmission of inherited characteristics. It was too simple chemically to encode genetic information. Many believed that the ultimate key to the molecular basis of genetics would lie in proteins found within the chromosomes.

The key to solving this riddle came when an English medical worker, Fred Griffith (1879–1941), was involved in investigating a pneumonia epidemic in London in 1928. While investigating the pneumococcus responsible for this outbreak, Griffith made the surprising discovery that live pneumococci could acquire genetic traits from other, dead pneumococci in a process he termed "transformation." But how could this be? All that the dead pneumococci could transmit were chemicals. These were two types of nucleic acid, ribonucleic acid (RNA) and deoxyribonucleic acid (DNA), and protein. But how could these apparently dead chemicals bring about genetic change in living cells?

The importance of Griffith's work was not appreciated until a research team headed up by Oswald Avery replicated his findings at the Rockefeller Institute in New York, founded in 1901 by John D. Rockefeller as the nation's foremost biomedical research center. Avery and his team began detailed studies of how genetic information was transmitted to living pneumococci. They conducted a series of experiments which demonstrated that genetic information was not mediated by proteins, or by RNA, but specifically by DNA. This was a momentous discovery, even if it would be some time before its full implications were appreciated. If DNA—and no other substance—was the carrier of hereditary information, it must have a much more complex structure than had previously been appreciated.[20] Yet nobody knew what this structure was nor how DNA was able to play such a critical genetic role.

18. Ralf Dahm, "Friedrich Miescher and the Discovery of DNA," *Developmental Biology* 278 (2005): 274–88.

19. Phoebus A. Levene, "The Structure of Yeast Nucleic Acid," *Journal of Biological Chemistry* 40 (1919): 415–24.

20. Oswald Avery, Colin MacLeod, and Maclyn McCarty, "Studies on the Chemical Nature of the Substance Inducing Transformation of Pneumococcal Types: Induction of Transformation by a Deoxyribonucleic Acid Fraction Isolated from *Pneumococcus* Type III," *Journal of Experimental Medicine* 79 (1944): 137–58.

This gave new impetus to a remarkable series of studies. Rosalind Franklin (1920–58) undertook pioneering X-ray crystallography work on DNA, which did much to facilitate the groundbreaking work of the English physicist Francis Crick (1916–2004) and the American geneticist James Watson (b. 1928), demonstrating a double helix structure for DNA. This achievement opened the way to understanding how DNA could pass on genetic information. Watson and Crick immediately realized that the pairing of the bases in this double-stranded DNA had to be the key to its function as a replicator and as the transmitter of genetic information. They wrote: "It has not escaped our notice that the specific pairing we have postulated immediately suggests a possible copying mechanism for the genetic material." In other words, a knowledge of the physical structure of DNA suggested a mechanism by which it could replicate itself.[21]

On the basis of this research, Crick proposed what he called the "Central Dogma": DNA replicates, acting as a template for RNA, which in turn acts as a template for proteins. The long and complex DNA molecule contains the genetic information necessary for transmission "encoded" by using the four basic nucleotides: adenine (A), guanine (G), thymine (T), and cytosine (C), arranged in sequences of "base pairs" (in the double helix structure of DNA, adenine is always linked to thymine, and guanine to cystosine), attached to a sugar and phosphate spine. It is the sequence of these base pairs which determines the genetic information transmitted.[22]

So why is this so important for an understanding of evolutionary biology? The most important point to emphasize is that Darwin's theory of natural selection required variation to take place *and* to be transmitted, rather than diluted, to following generations. Natural selection would then take place, determining whether or not the genetic code for this variation would ultimately survive. The neo-Darwinian synthesis is grounded in the assumption that small random genetic changes (mutations) over long periods of time occasionally have positive survival value. Organisms possessing these favorable mutations should have relative advantage in survival and reproduction, and they will tend to pass their characteristics on to their descendants. Assuming that there are differential rates of survival, it is easy to see how a favorable characteristic can become established and transmitted.

There is, of course, considerably more to the contemporary understanding of evolution than this brief sketch. For example, a fuller account would note how the modern evolutionary synthesis owed much to the work of R. A. Fisher, J. B. S. Haldane, and Sewall Wright during the 1920s and 1930s, who were able to provide a firm theoretical foundation for the reconciliation of Darwinism and Mendelism through mathematical population genetics. Furthermore, there are difficulties with the concept of "natural selection"—an idea introduced by

21. Francis H. C. Crick and James D. Watson, "Molecular Structure of Nucleic Acids: A Structure for Deoxyribose Nucleic Acid," *Nature* 171 (1953): 737–38.
22. For a basic introduction, see Mary K. Campbell and Shawn O. Farrell, *Biochemistry*, 5th ed. (Pacific Grove, CA: Brooks / Cole, 2006), 240–329.

Darwin to explain evolutionary change, but which really explains the maintenance of adaptation. This "dynamic stabilization" (to use a helpful rephrasing of "natural selection") does not explain the origin of species or adaptations, though it is helpful in accounting for their spread.[23] However, this concise sketch of the development of the core ideas of Darwinian theory is simply intended to highlight the critical importance of DNA as a genetic replicator; it allows us to begin to look at the issue of fine-tuning in biology with this molecular agenda in mind.

FINE-TUNING IN BIOLOGY

At first sight, the neo-Darwinian model seems to undercut any possible appeal to the biological domain as evidence of design or fine-tuning. Just as William Paley's belief that aspects of nature—such as the structure of the human eye—showed clear evidence of "contrivance" was eroded by Darwinism,[24] so most Darwinists would exclude, as a matter of principle, any idea that biological entities have been created in such a way that they are fine-tuned for their environments. This fine-tuning, it is argued, emerges through the evolutionary process, in which an organism adapts to environmental factors.[25] Nature fine-tunes itself.

This approach can be expanded to include an analysis of the structure of significant biomolecules, such as enzymes, widely agreed to be of critical importance to metabolism. How does their functional precision arise? The standard Darwinian answer to such questions makes an appeal to two significant factors: fitness and history. These can be combined to give three different approaches to the question of explanation of biological structures.[26]

The first approach places an emphasis upon "functional" considerations and holds that a specific biomolecular structure is found in life because it offers the best solution to a particular biological problem. It is here assumed that, in terms of the Darwinian paradigm, "best" means "confers the greatest degree of fitness," or that it at least confers more fitness than potentially available yet ultimately unused alternatives. This approach assumes that living systems had access to alter-

23. For comment on these difficulties and their possible resolution, see Robert G. B. Reid, *Biological Emergences: Evolution by Natural Experiment* (Cambridge, MA: MIT Press, 2007), 1–22.
24. See Richard Dawkins, *The Blind Watchmaker: Why the Evidence of Evolution Reveals a Universe without Design* (New York: W. W. Norton, 1986).
25. The phenomenon of "melanism" in ladybirds or rock pocket mice is often cited as an example of such an adaptation to environments: see Michael E. N. Majerus, *Melanism: Evolution in Action* (Oxford: Oxford University Press, 1998); Hopi E. Hoekstra, Kristen E. Drumm, and Michael W. Nachman, "Ecological Genetics of Adaptive Color Polymorphism in Pocket Mice: Geographic Variation in Selected and Neutral Genes," *Evolution: International Journal of Organic Evolution* 58 (2004): 1329–41.
26. See the landmark review of Steven A. Benner and Andrew D. Ellington, "Interpreting the Behavior of Enzymes: Purpose or Pedigree?" *Critical Reviews in Biochemistry and Molecular Biology* 23 (1988): 369–426. The lines of thought developed in this article are reflected in the remainder of this chapter.

native solutions and that the process of natural selection filtered out solutions that were poorly adapted.

The second approach to biological explanation considers the historical dimensions of the evolutionary process. It notes, for example, that the universe of chemical possibilities is huge. One obvious example illustrates this notion of "chemical space":[27] the number of different proteins 100 amino acids long that can be constructed from the standard set of 20 amino acids is larger than the number of atoms in the universe. The chemical compounds used by biological systems represent an astonishingly small fraction of the total possible number of small carbon-based compounds with molecular masses in the same range as those of living systems. Some estimates of this number are in excess of 10^{60}. Yet the simplest living organisms can function with just a few hundred different types of such molecules, and fewer than 100 account for nearly the entire molecular pool. Terrestrial life simply did not have time to sample all possible sequences to find the best protein, the best form of genetic replicator, and so forth. What exists in modern terrestrial life must therefore reflect contingencies, chance events in history that led to one choice over another, whether or not the choice was optimal.

The third approach to biological explanation draws on the concept of vestigiality, familiar to readers of Darwin's *Origin of Species*. Here it is recognized that some features of contemporary terrestrial biochemistry may reflect ancient selective pressures that no longer exist. Contemporary features of biological structures or systems may therefore not represent optimization for the present situation, but are rather to be thought of as vestiges of optimization in the past. Such models explain not only the human appendix and male nipples, but also many of the biochemical details found in modern life.[28]

These three classes of biological explanation are neatly illustrated by possible answers to a biochemical question about the structure of DNA: Why does DNA use adenine, which forms only two hydrogen bonds with thymine, when the chemically related structure aminoadenine can form three, thus leading to pairing for a much-stronger nucleobase pair?[29] Are double helices not better if they are more stable? Would not aminoadenine be better than adenine as a component of DNA?[30] So how might the presence of adenine, rather than aminoadenine, in DNA be explained?

27. For a useful review, see Christopher M. Dobson, "Chemical Space and Biology," *Nature* 432 (2004): 824–28.

28. An obvious example would be the RNA component of many cofactors used in contemporary metabolism. For a fuller discussion of such vestigial chemistries, see Steven A. Benner, Slim O. Sassi, and Eric A. Gaucher, "Molecular Paleoscience: Systems Biology from the Past," *Advances in Enzymology and Related Areas of Molecular Biology* 75 (2007): 1–132.

29. C. Ronald Geyer, Thomas R. Battersby, and Steven A. Benner, "Nucleobase Pairing in Expanded Watson-Crick-like Genetic Information Systems: The Nucleobases," *Structure* 11 (2003): 1485–98. But see also the comments in Albert Eschenmoser, "Chemical Etiology of Nucleic Acid Structure," *Science* 284 (1999): 2118–24.

30. See Y. Lebedev et al., "Oligonucleotides Containing 2-Aminoadenine and 5-Methylcytosine Are More Effective as Primers for PCR Amplification Than Their Nonmodified Counterparts," *Genetic Analysis: Biomolecular Engineering* 13 (1996): 15–21.

The functional approach might hold that genomes are optimal when they have access to *both* a weak (AT) *and* strong (GC) nucleobase pair. According to this explanation, biological systems need to modulate the melting temperature of its DNA to achieve an optimum, which may not be the maximum melting temperature. If it has both a strong and weak base pair, it can do so by adjusting the ratio of AT and GC nucleobase pairs. An organism that has both a strong base pair (GC) and a weak base pair (AT) has, according to this explanation, a competitive advantage over an organism that uses aminoadenine, does not have a weak base pair, and therefore does not have the opportunity to modulate the melting temperature of its DNA by choosing between a strong and a weak base pair.

The historical approach might argue that adenine was arbitrarily chosen over other available candidates for reasons of historical contingency. This presumed historical accident, once it had taken place, led to cascade effects which reinforced the privileged role of adenine. Once adenine is incorporated into DNA, polymerases evolve which accept adenine (not aminoadenine), and biosynthetic pathways to adenine (not aminoadenine) are developed. The originally chosen molecule soon becomes difficult to replace. Yet no particular reason can be given for the original selection of adenine, other than that it is consistent with general principles and was constrained by the environment.

A approach to biological explanation which focuses on vestigiality might argue that adenine, not aminoadenine, is made from ammonium cyanide under conditions presumed to have been present in the cosmos before life emerged. This might be argued to make adenine a preferential starting point for life, based on the assumption that compounds which initiate life must be available before life starts. In the contemporary biological world, metabolic pathways provide access to many molecules that are not prebiotically accessible. This explanation is clearly consistent with the possibility that adenine no longer has an advantage over aminoadenine. In other words, biological systems making the choice today might well be indifferent with respect to the two and might even prefer aminoadenine over adenine in certain respects and contexts.

The mechanisms of evolutionary biology are thus sufficiently adaptive to allow a degree of fine-tuning within nature. This clearly precludes a simple, direct appeal to apparent design or fine-tuning in biological organisms as evidence that they have been directly created with such properties by God. William Paley's admirable descriptions of the remarkable adaptations of plants and animals to their environments no longer require us to draw his original conclusion that the only plausible explanation is that they were "contrived" (that is, designed and constructed) with those environments in mind. They may well be consistent with it; they do not, however, compel us to accept it.

The outcome of our brief reflections on evolutionary mechanisms to date is thus inconclusive, allowing little to be drawn in the way of secure conclusions for any natural theology. Yet by reframing the issue slightly in terms of a related idea, a more-sophisticated and intellectually interesting question begins to emerge, with obvious and significant implications for a natural theology. The idea in question is *evolvability*, which we may define as "an organism's capacity to generate herita-ble phenotypic variation."[31] As Kirschner and Gerhart define this notion in a land-mark study: "The capacity of a lineage to evolve has been termed its evolvability, also called evolutionary adaptability. By evolvability, we mean the capacity to gen-erate heritable, selectable phenotypic variation." Evolvability depends upon a number of critical factors. We have already noted the importance of the long-term stability of DNA as a decisive factor in the evolutionary process. The stability of other evolutionary components such as proteins is also of importance in fostering evolvability.[32] Recognition of this point has led to increasing interest in exploring whether the propensity to evolve can itself be an object of Darwinian natural selec-tion. It has long been recognized that one of the major riddles of evolutionary biol-ogy is the mechanism which enables the generation and maintenance of sufficient phenotypic variation to allow adaptive responses to novel environments, includ-ing both challenges and opportunities. There is little doubt that much available observational evidence could be explained if it is assumed that evolvability is itself a selectable trait.[33] The traditional concept of a stable genome is evolving: genomes are increasingly being seen as plastic and responsive to environmental changes. There is growing evidence which suggests that a variety of environmental stresses induce genomic instability in bacteria, yeast, and human cancer cells, generating occasional fitter mutants and potentially accelerating adaptive evolution.[34] This emphasizes the importance of the biological capacity to adapt to circumstances, and hence the importance of evolvability.[35]

Until the 1990s, most biologists were more concerned about the outcomes of variation rather than its origins, tacitly assuming that the origin and maintenance of variability was somehow intrinsic to the Darwinian paradigm, as if it were somehow an automatic outcome. It is now clear that this is not the case and that an explanation is required for how evolvability emerged and is maintained. Evolv-ability is not well understood and is increasingly being seen as an area for further

31. Marc Kirschner and John Gerhart, "Evolvability," *Proceedings of the National Academy of Sci-ences* 95 (1998): 8420–27. This question can be developed further by considering how genetic changes are to be interpreted in terms of their capacity to allow future evolution, rather than merely present adaptation. For further discussion of the issues, see Marc W. Kirschner and John C. Gerhart, *The Plausibility of Life: Resolving Darwin's Dilemma* (New Haven, CT: Yale University Press, 2005), 219–43.

32. Jesse D. Bloom et al., "Protein Stability Promotes Evolvability," *Proceedings of the National Academy of Sciences* 103 (2006): 5869–74. Note especially the comment that "a protein's capacity to evolve is enhanced by the mutational robustness conferred by extra stability."

33. See the case made by David J. Earl and Michael W. Deem, "Evolvability Is a Selectable Trait," *Proceedings of the National Academy of Sciences* 101 (2004): 11531–36; and Joanna Masel, "Evolu-tionary Capacitance May Be Favored by Natural Selection," *Genetics* 170 (2005): 1359–71.

34. See Rodrigo S. Galhardo, P. J. Hastings, and Susan M. Rosenberg, "Mutation as a Stress Response and the Regulation of Evolvability," *Critical Reviews in Biochemistry and Molecular Biology* 42 (2007): 399–435.

35. For the argument that nature may have selected particular enzymes for evolvability, rather than for catalytic efficiency or substrate specificity, see Taryn L. O'Loughlin, Wayne M. Patrick, and Ichiro Matsumura, "Natural History as a Predictor of Protein Evolvability," *Protein Engineering, Design and Selection* 19 (2006): 439–42.

exploration within which Darwinian evolutionary theory might require expansion or modification. How is the capacity to achieve an optimal solution acquired and effected?

The critical question for natural theology is this: is evolvability itself fine-tuned? In other words, is the capacity for Darwinian evolution, which many hold to be essential to any definition of life (chap. 10), itself an anthropic phenomenon? Life is fundamentally a *physicochemical phenomenon*,[36] and as such it depends upon the fundamental laws of physics and chemistry, as well as the availability of fundamental materials required to achieve certain biologically necessary outcomes. As we emphasized earlier, there is a very strong case for arguing that evolution is chemically and physically constrained. Is the very phenomenon of evolvability itself dependent upon certain fundamental predetermined parameters which, if these were to have been significantly different, would have prevented or subverted this critical faculty?

This point is consistently overlooked in many accounts of evolution, which seem to treat physics and chemistry as essentially irrelevant background information to a discussion of evolution. Yet this biological process requires the availability of a stable planet, irradiated by an energy source capable of chemical conversion and storage, and the existence of a diverse array of core chemical elements, with certain fundamental properties, before life can begin, let alone evolve. Biology has become so used to the existence and aggregation of highly organized attributes that they are seen primarily as core assumptions of evolutionary theory, rather than something that requires explanation in its own right. There is an implicit assumption that life would adapt to whatever hand of physical and chemical cards were dealt to it. Yet this is untested and intrinsically questionable.

In chapter 10, we explored some questions about the origins of life, noting in particular how the Darwinian evolutionary paradigm does not apply in its primitive stages. The standard Darwinian paradigm is better at accounting for improvements than for inventions. At some point, the necessary mechanisms for evolution were able to emerge, by means that remain unclear.[37] Nevertheless, it is clear that a capacity to encode information is of decisive importance for evolution in general and evolvability in particular. And that, as we have seen, is critically dependent upon the organic chemistry of carbon, which permits the formation of long, stable chains.[38] No other element has this property; without it, RNA and DNA would be impossibilities, as would the replicative processes

36. For the argument, see Addy Pross, "On the Emergence of Biological Complexity: Life as a Kinetic State of Matter," *Origins of Life and Evolution of Biospheres* 35 (2005): 151–66, esp. 162–63.

37. For some possibilities, see Martin E. Feder, "Evolvability of Physiological and Biochemical Traits: Evolutionary Mechanisms Including and beyond Single-Nucleotide Mutation," *Journal of Experimental Biology* 210 (2007): 1653–60.

38. A feature of carbon chemistry which is familiar from graphite, and is of increasing importance in nanotechnology, following the discovery of molecules of carbon consisting of sixty or seventy or more linked carbon atoms: see Hugh Aldersey-Williams, *The Most Beautiful Molecule: The Discovery of the Buckyball* (New York: Wiley, 1995).

they control.[39] The capacity of evolution to fine-tune itelf is thus ultimately dependent on fundamental chemical properties which in themselves can thus be argued to represent a case of robust and fruitful fine-tuning.

In this chapter, we have considered the mechanism of evolution. Yet many now consider that the process of evolution itself has important insights to disclose concerning our theme. We shall explore these issues in the following chapter.

---

39. For recent speculation about how the genetic code works, see Brian Hayes, "The Invention of the Genetic Code," *American Scientist* 86 (1998): 8–14. For a substantial review of the current state of play, see Stephen J. Freeland, Tao Wu, and Nick Keulmann, "The Case for an Error Minimizing Standard Genetic Code," *Origins of Life and Evolution of Biospheres* 33 (2003): 457–77.

Chapter 14

The Outcomes of Evolution
The Directionality of Evolution

The Darwinian paradigm holds that evolution takes place by a process of descent with modification, through which a species adapts to an environment through iterations of replication under random variation followed by natural selection. Darwin's general theory was able to link together previously disparate phenomena, offering a powerful explanatory tool for an understanding of the biosphere. In particular, Darwin's theory of natural selection threw light on the perplexing question why some traits thrive at the expense of others. The neo-Darwinian paradigm, which accentuates the basic ideas of random variation followed by natural selection, has led to significant clarification of its underlying genetic mechanisms. Nevertheless, it is clear that the Darwinian paradigm is undergoing modification. In common with all scientific theories, it is subject to revision and modification in the light of growing evidence and theoretical development.

One of the most fundamental weaknesses with the neo-Darwinian evolutionary paradigm is that it contributes little to our understanding of developmental processes. Valuable though it is as an explanatory tool, neo-Darwinism seems to be unable to account for all, and perhaps even most, observable biological change.[1] As we noted earlier, until quite recently most biologists were more interested in explaining the outcomes of variation rather than its origins, perhaps assuming that the origin and maintenance of variability did not require discussion. During the 1990s, however, biologists began to explore this hitherto neglected aspect of neo-Darwinism, realizing that these issues required much closer attention.

It is now widely conceded that the underlying concept of natural selection offers little to explain how biological forms and phenotypes arise in the first place. We have already commented on the growing realization of the importance of evolvability, the capacity of an organism to generate heritable phenotypic variation, and the question of whether this trait is itself an object of natural selection. The notion of "fitness" has proved exceptionally difficult to define, not least because it is a property of neither organism nor environment, but emerges at the interface between them.[2] Furthermore, non-Darwinian processes—such as autopoiesis, epigenetic mechanisms, and symbiosis—are now realized to play a significant role in the evolutionary process, considered as a whole.[3] Nor can the process of generation of variation be considered to be completely random, since a series of convergent pressures must already have been in operation before any ensuing physical realization of organisms.[4]

THE TELEOLOGY OF EVOLUTION?

Perhaps the most important debate in contemporary philosophy of biology, for the purposes of the present volume, is whether evolution can be considered in any sense to be teleological.[5] The rejection of any form of teleology achieved the status of an axiomatic truth within neo-Darwinism from about 1970. Evolution was to be understood as an open-ended and indeterminate process, without any

1. See the alternative proposed by Robert G. B. Reid, *Biological Emergences: Evolution by Natural Experiment* (Cambridge, MA: MIT Press, 2007), 67–94.

2. See the important analysis in Costas B. Krimbas, "On Fitness," *Biology and Philosophy* 19 (2004): 185–204. Other important concerns are touched on in Elliott Sober, "The Two Faces of Fitness," in *Thinking about Evolution: Historical, Philosophical, and Political Perspectives*, ed. R. Singh et al. (Cambridge: Cambridge University Press, 2001), 309–21.

3. Note the points made in Gregory L. Challis and David A. Hopwood, "Synergy and Contingency as Driving Forces for the Evolution of Multiple Secondary Metabolite Production by *Streptomyces* Species," *Proceedings of the National Academy of Sciences* 100 (2003): 14555–61.

4. For example, mating is often assortative, in that mates appear to be chosen on the basis of traits they possess or lack, rather than at random: see Philip L. Munday, Lynne van Herwerden, and Christine L. Dudgeon, "Evidence for Sympatric Speciation by Host Shift in the Sea," *Current Biology* 14 (2004): 1498–1504; Anthony C. Little, D. Michael Burt, and David I. Perrett, "Assortative Mating for Perceived Facial Personality Traits," *Personality and Individual Differences* 40 (2006): 973–84; Alistair Blachford and Aneil F. Agrawal, "Assortative Mating for Fitness and the Evolution of Recombination," *Evolution: International Journal of Organic Evolution* 60 (2006): 1337–43.

5. For comment, see John Beatty, "Teleology and the Relationship of Biology to the Physical Sciences in the Nineteenth and Twentieth Centuries," in *Newton's Legacy: The Origins and Influence of Newtonian Science*, ed. Frank Durham and Robert D. Purrington (New York: Columbia University Press, 1990), 113–44.

predetermined goal. This view emerged at an early stage in the popular reception of Darwin's theory of natural selection. As is often pointed out, what seems to have impressed Thomas H. Huxley most forcibly on his first reading of the *Origin of Species* was the "conviction that teleology, as commonly understood, had received its deathblow at Mr. Darwin's hands."[6] Such a teleology was to be found in William Paley's *Natural Theology* (1802), which set out the view that nature was "contrived"—that is to say, designed and constructed with a specific purpose and intention in mind.[7]

Yet it has to be asked whether some Darwinists are indulging in precisely the same kind of metaphysical speculation, or allowing themselves to be trapped by the same (often unacknowledged) a priori metaphysical commitments that they identify in those affirming teleological approaches to biology. The increasing appeal to Darwinism by those wishing to invert Paley's approach and develop a natural *a*theology is of considerable significance, since it shows how a working assumption of evolutionary biology has been transposed into a dogma of fundamentalist atheism.[8] The term "teleonomy" was introduced into biological use in 1958 by the Princeton biologist C. S. Pittendrigh (1918–96) "in order to emphasize that recognition and description of end-directedness does not carry a commitment to Aristotelian teleology as an efficient causal principle."[9] This idea was developed further by Jacques Monod (1910–76),[10] who argued that *teleonomy* had displaced *teleology* in evolutionary biology. In using this term, Monod wished to highlight that evolutionary biology was concerned with identifying and clarifying the mechanisms underlying the evolutionary process. While the mechanisms which governed evolution were of interest, they had no goal. One thus could not speak meaningfully of "purpose" within evolution.

Monod's account, with its emphasis on "random" events, exemplifies a general trend within evolutionary biology which places an emphasis upon statistical approaches. This trend can be traced back to R. A. Fisher, Theodosius Dobzhansky,

6. Thomas H. Huxley, *Lay Sermons, Addresses, and Reviews* (London: Macmillan, 1870), 330. David Hull suggests that Darwin brought about the "final trivialization" of the notion: David L. Hull, *Darwin and His Critics: The Reception of Darwin's Theory of Evolution by the Scientific Community* (Cambridge, MA: Harvard University Press, 1973), 57.

7. Neal C. Gillespie, "Divine Design and the Industrial Revolution: William Paley's Abortive Reform of Natural Theology," *Isis* 81 (1990): 214–29. For comment, see Richard C. Francis, *Why Men Won't Ask for Directions: The Seductions of Sociobiology* (Princeton, NJ: Princeton University Press, 2004), 4–7.

8. See Abigail Lustig, "Natural Atheology," in *Darwinian Heresies*, ed. Abigail Lustig, Robert J. Richards, and Michael Ruse (Cambridge: Cambridge University Press, 2004), 69–83.

9. Colin S. Pittendrigh, "Adaptation, Natural Selection, and Behavior," in *Behavior and Evolution*, ed. Anne Roe and George Gaylord Simpson (New Haven, CT: Yale University Press, 1958), 390–416, esp. 394. Pittendrigh's allusion to Aristotelian teleology needs qualification, especially in the light of revisionist approaches to what Aristotle understood and intended by the notion: see, e.g., Monte Ransome Johnson, *Aristotle on Teleology* (Oxford: Clarendon Press, 2005), 40–63.

10. Jacques Monod, *Chance and Necessity: An Essay on the Natural Philosophy of Modern Biology* (New York: Alfred A. Knopf, 1971). Monod was particularly concerned to discredit his fellow Frenchmen Henri Bergson (1859–1941) and Pierre Teilhard de Chardin (1881–1955), both of whom had developed philosophies of life which were founded on the acceptance of biological evolution, yet interpreted this as having some kind of purpose.

and J. B. S. Haldane.[11] Yet, as Phillip Sloan has noted, the idealizing mathematical assumptions of these statistical reinterpretations of natural selection theory involved, at the theoretical level, the incorporation of assumptions of random and stochastic processes.[12] The emphasis on the "purposeless" character of natural selection, found within many popular neo-Darwinian accounts of the process, is thus little more than an "unwarranted rhetorical flourish," resting on "the reification of these foundational idealizations of population dynamics as realistic metaphysical claims about the world." Within a Reformed theological framework, for example, "random" can be translated as "nonpredictable" and thus contextualized within a generalized doctrine of divine providence.[13]

Furthermore, whether evolution exhibits design, intentions, or purposes or not, it unquestionably demonstrates a directionality.[14] Organisms have generally become larger, more complex, more taxonomically diverse, and more energetically intensive.[15] Does this imply a teleology? Answering this question demands careful reflection on what the term "teleology" actually means. There is widespread opinion that the use of the term is legitimate, at least in certain respects, within biology. The development of the notion of a "genetic program" by François Jacob and others in the 1970s can be seen as a partial validation of the notion. As Jacob remarked, teleology was rather like a "mistress"—someone that "biologists could not do without, but did not care to be seen with in public."[16]

Francisco Ayala argues that the notion of teleological explanation is fundamental to modern biology. It is required to account for the familiar functional roles played by parts of living organisms and to describe the goal of reproductive fitness which plays such a central role in accounts of natural selection.[17]

11. For an introduction, see John Beatty, "Dobzhansky and Drift: Facts, Values, and Chance in Evolutionary Biology," in *The Probabilistic Revolution*, ed. L. Krüger et al. (Cambridge, MA: MIT Press, 1987), 271–311.

12. Phillip R. Sloan, "Getting the Questions Right: Catholics and Evolutionary Theory," *Pax Romana* 64 (2003): 13–32. I am very grateful to Dr. Sloan for providing me with a copy of this important article, which is not widely available.

13. For an intriguing account of the apparent death and subsequent revival of notions of divine providence within a Darwinian context, see John Hedley Brooke, "Science and the Fortunes of Natural Theology: Some Historical Perspectives," *Zygon* 24 (1989): 3–22. The specific case of the American conservative Protestant theologian Benjamin B. Warfield (1851–1921) merits attention here: David N. Livingstone, "B. B. Warfield, the Theory of Evolution and Early Fundamentalism," *Evangelical Quarterly* 58 (1986): 69–83.

14. See the provocative discussion in William R. Stoeger, "The Immanent Directionality of the Evolutionary Process, and Its Relationship to Teleology," in *Evolutionary and Molecular Biology: Scientific Perspectives on Divine Action*, ed. Robert J. Russell, William R. Stoeger, and Francisco Ayala (Vatican City: Vatican Observatory Publications, 1999), 163–90.

15. For comment on these points, see John T. Bonner, *The Evolution of Complexity by Means of Natural Selection* (Princeton, NJ: Princeton University Press, 1988); John Maynard Smith and Eörs Szathmáry, *The Major Transitions in Evolution* (Oxford: W. H. Freeman / Spektrum, 1995).

16. For context, see Evelyn Fox Keller, *Making Sense of Life: Explaining Biological Development with Models, Metaphors, and Machines* (Cambridge, MA: Harvard University Press, 2002), 135–45. Jacob followed up this politically incorrect analogy by suggesting that the idea of a genetic program "made an honest woman of teleology."

17. Francisco J. Ayala, "Teleological Explanations in Evolutionary Biology," *Philosophy of Science* 37 (1970): 1–15, esp. 12.

A teleological explanation implies that the system under consideration is directively organized. For that reason, teleological explanations are appropriate in biology and in the domain of cybernetics but make no sense when used in the physical sciences to describe phenomena like the fall of a stone. Moreover, and most importantly, teleological explanations imply that the end result is the explanatory reason for the *existence* of the object or process which serves or leads to it. A teleological account of the gills of fish implies that gills came to existence precisely because they serve for respiration. If the above reasoning is correct, the use of teleological explanations in biology is not only acceptable but indeed indispensable.

Natural selection itself, the ultimate source of explanation in biology, is thus for Ayala a teleological process both because it is directed to the goal of increasing reproductive efficiency and because it produces the goal-directed organs and processes required for this. Teleological mechanisms in living organisms are thus biological adaptations, which have arisen as a result of the process of natural selection.

Ernst Mayr (1904–2005), widely credited with inventing the modern philosophy of biology, especially of evolutionary biology, sets out four traditional objections to the use of teleological language in biology:[18]

1. Teleological statements or explanations imply the endorsement of unverifiable theological or metaphysical doctrines in the sciences. Mayr has in mind Bergson's "élan vital" or the notion of "entelechy," formulated by Hans Driesch (1867–1941).[19]
2. A belief that acceptance of explanations for biological phenomena that are not equally applicable to inanimate nature constitutes rejection of a physicochemical explanation.
3. The assumption that future goals were the cause of current events seemed incompatible with accepted notions of causality.
4. Teleological language seemed to amount to an objectionable anthropomorphism. The use of terms such as "purposive" or "goal-directed" appears to represent that transfer of human qualities, such as purpose and planning, to organic structures.

As a result of these and other objections, Mayr points out, teleological explanations in biology were widely believed to be "a form of obscurantism." Yet paradoxically,

---

18. Ernst Mayr, *Toward a New Philosophy of Biology: Observations of an Evolutionist* (Cambridge, MA: Harvard University Press, 1988), 38–66, esp. 39–41. For comment on Mayr's appeal to history in this work, see John C. Greene, "From Aristotle to Darwin: Reflections on Ernst Mayr's Interpretation in *The Growth of Biological Thought*," *Journal of the History of Biology* 25 (1992): 257–84. For his more recent exploration of the same theme, published in time for his 100th birthday, see Ernst Mayr, *What Makes Biology Unique? Considerations on the Autonomy of a Scientific Discipline* (Cambridge: Cambridge University Press, 2004), 39–66, esp. 46–47.

19. On which see Horst H. Freyhofer, *The Vitalism of Hans Driesch: The Success and Decline of a Scientific Theory* (Frankfurt am Main: Peter Lang, 1982).

biologists continue to use teleological language, insisting that it is methodologically and heuristically appropriate and helpful.

There is no doubt that serious objections may be, and have been, raised about the notion of evolution as a conscious agent, actively planning its goals and outcomes, or drawn to a preordained goal by some mysterious force. Yet it must be pointed out that such anthropomorphic ways of speaking (and thinking) are evident in some sections of contemporary biology. An excellent example is provided by the "gene's-eye" view of evolution, popularized by Richard Dawkins, which entails envisaging the gene as an active agent.[20] While rightly cautioning that "we must not think of genes as conscious, purposeful agents," Dawkins goes on to argue that the process of natural selection "makes them behave rather as if they were purposeful."[21] This anthropomorphic way of speaking involves the attribution of both agency and intentionality to an entity which is ultimately a passive participant in the process of replication rather than its active director.[22] More seriously, in arguing that the gene is a replicator, Dawkins seems to confer upon it a degree of biological autonomy, which ignores its location within a *system*. Richard Lewontin's criticism of the "gene's-eye view" brings this point out with clarity and precision:[23]

> Nor are genes self-replicating. They cannot make themselves any more than they can make a protein. Genes are made by a complex machinery of proteins that uses the genes as models for more genes. When we refer to the genes as self-replicating, we endow them with a mysterious, autonomous power that seems to place them above the ordinary materials of the body. Yet if anything in the world can be said to be self-replicating, it is not the gene, but the entire organism as a complex system.

The emergence of this "gene's eye" approach must, of course, be contextualized and seen in the light of the rejection of higher-level forms of natural selection in George C. Williams's highly influential *Adaptation and Natural Selection* (1966).[24] Williams's sweeping critique of group selection theory marked the beginning of a new paradigm of genic selection, which held that natural selection is mostly, if not always, selection for and against single genes. Dawkins's *Selfish Gene* (1976) can, with the benefit of hindsight, be seen as marking the high tide of this approach and cementing its popular acceptance. Yet the tide has now

20. For a more refined version of this approach, see Michael J. Wade, "A Gene's Eye View of Epistasis, Selection and Speciation," *Journal of Evolutionary Biology* 15 (2002): 337–46.

21. Richard Dawkins, *The Selfish Gene*, 2nd ed. (Oxford: Oxford University Press, 1989), 196. For an early criticism of this viewpoint, see Stephen Jay Gould, "Caring Groups and Selfish Genes," in *The Panda's Thumb* (New York: W. W. Norton, 1980), 85–91.

22. For discussion of the wider issues, see Denis Noble, *The Music of Life: Biology beyond the Genome* (Oxford: Oxford University Press, 2006), 11–15.

23. Richard C. Lewontin, *Biology as Ideology: The Doctrine of DNA* (New York: HarperPerennial, 1992), 48. For a review of the issues here, see Peter Godfrey-Smith, "The Replicator in Retrospect," *Biology and Philosophy* 15 (2000): 403–23.

24. George C. Williams, *Adaptation and Natural Selection: A Critique of Some Current Evolutionary Thought* (Princeton, NJ: Princeton University Press, 1966), esp. 92–124.

turned, and multilevel or hierarchical approaches to natural selection appear to have regained the intellectual high ground.[25]

Yet as Mayr rightly points out, nature abounds in processes and activities that lead to an end or goal. However we choose to interpret them, examples of goal-directed behavior are widespread in the natural world; indeed, "the occurrence of goal-directed processes is perhaps the most characteristic feature of the world of living systems."[26] The evasion of teleological statements through their restatement in nonteleological forms invariably leads to "meaningless platitudes."[27] Although surrounding his conclusion with a thicket of qualifications, Mayr insists that it is appropriate to conclude that "the use of so-called 'teleological' language by biologists is legitimate; it neither implies a rejection of physico-chemical explanation nor does it imply noncausal explanation."[28]

EVOLUTION, CONTINGENCY, AND TELEOLOGY

So is there a directionality implicit within evolution, whether one chooses to interpret this teleologically or not? This particular phrasing makes it clear that we are posing a legitimate scientific question, not a speculative theological one. The view that evolution is open-ended, without predictabilities and indeterminate in terms of its outcomes, has achieved a dominant position in evolutionary biology.[29] Many writers who adopt the standard Darwinian paradigm argue for the essentially random and contingent nature of the evolutionary process. For example, Stephen Jay Gould (1941–2002) insisted that "almost every interesting event of life's history falls into the realm of contingency."[30] It is pointless to talk about purpose, historical inevitability, or direction. From its beginning to its end, the evolutionary process is governed by contingencies. "We are the accidental result of an unplanned process, . . . the fragile result of an enormous concatenation of improbabilities, not the predictable product of any definite process."[31] As Gould famously put this point, using the characteristically 1990s' analogy of a videotape, if we were to replay the tape of evolutionary history, we would not see the

---

25. See, e.g., David Sloan Wilson, "A Critique of R. D. Alexander's Views on Group Selection," *Biology and Philosophy* 14 (1999): 431–49; Michael J. Wade, "Community Genetics and Species Interactions," *Ecology* 84 (2003): 583–85; Peter J. Richerson and Robert Boyd, *Not by Genes Alone: How Culture Transformed Human Evolution* (Chicago: University of Chicago Press, 2005). For a useful review of developments, see Mark E. Borrello, "The Rise, Fall and Resurrection of Group Selection," *Endeavour* 29 (2005): 43–47. For a rounded statement of a multilevel selection theory, see David Sloan Wilson and Edward O. Wilson, "Rethinking the Theoretical Foundation of Sociobiology," *Quarterly Review of Biology* 82 (2007): 327–48.

26. Mayr, *Toward a New Philosophy of Biology*, 44–45.

27. Ibid., 55.

28. Ibid., 59.

29. Pier Luigi Luisi, "Contingency and Determinism," *Philosophical Transactions: Mathematical, Physical, and Engineering Sciences* 361 (2003): 1141–47.

30. Stephen Jay Gould, *Wonderful Life: The Burgess Shale and the Nature of History* (New York: W. W. Norton, 1989), 290.

31. Ibid., 101–2.

same thing happen each time. "Run the tape again and the first step from prokaryotic to eukaryotic cell may take 12 billion years instead of two." The influence of contingency is such that what happens is the product of happenstance. "Alter any early event, ever so slightly and without apparent importance at the time, and evolution cascades into a radically different channel."[32]

Gould argues that the role of contingency in biological evolution is so substantial that the tape will disclose different patterns on each individual replay.[33]

> I call this experiment "replaying life's tape." You press the rewind button and, making sure you thoroughly erase everything that actually happened, go back to any time and place in the past—say, to the seas of the Burgess Shale. Then let the tape run again and see if the repetition looks at all like the original. If each replay strongly resembles life's actual pathway, then we must conclude that what really happened pretty much had to happen. But suppose that the experimental versions all yield sensible results strikingly different from the actual history of life? What could we then say about the predictability of self-conscious intelligence? Or of mammals? Or of life on land? Or simply of multicellular persistence for 600 million difficult years?

It is, of course, an experiment that cannot be carried out, save in the rather restrictive laboratory of the human mind. But is it right? Is the process of intellectual development really so subject to the happenstance of history?[34]

To appreciate the issue in relation to intellectual development, consider the following question. If Darwin had never existed, would what we now term the "Darwinian theory of evolution" have emerged? The development of Darwin's theory is linked with certain specific events, observations, and personalities embedded within a historically contingent situation. So what would have happened if the *Beagle* had foundered off the coast of Patagonia, with the loss of all hands, including the ship's naturalist? From a scientific perspective, the answer is clear. The emergence of this way of thinking was not dependent upon the contingencies of Darwin's existence. It was something of an intellectual inevitability. If Darwin had not discovered this approach, someone else would have done so. Gould seems to agree.[35]

> I will grant one point to scientific colleagues and freely allow that if Charles Darwin had never been born, a well-prepared and waiting scientific world, abetted by a cultural context more than ready for such a reconstruction of nature, would still have promulgated and won general acceptance for evolution in the mid-19th century. At some point, the mechanism of natural selection would also have been formulated and eventually validated.

32. For an excellent critical study of the concepts of contingency implicit in Gould's analogy and its relevance to evolutionary theory, see John Beatty, "Replaying Life's Tape," *Journal of Philosophy* 103 (2006): 336–62.

33. Stephen Jay Gould, *The Structure of Evolutionary Theory* (Cambridge, MA: Belknap Press, 2002), 1019–20.

34. See here Kim Sterelny, "Understanding Life: Recent Work in the Philosophy of Biology," *British Journal for the Philosophy of Science* 46 (1995): 155–83, esp. 174–78.

35. Gould, *Structure of Evolutionary Theory*, 1342.

Yet Gould's emphasis on historical contingency is regarded with suspicion by many within the professional community of evolutionary biologists. This can be seen, for example, in Leigh van Valen's critique of Gould's use of the tape-of-life metaphor. What would happen, van Valen asked, if the tape of evolutionary history were to be replayed, as Gould suggested?[36] Van Valen immediately concedes, following Gould, that the first thing that an observer would be likely to notice was the differences between the two versions of the tape. The contingencies of history are such that the outcomes are different in each case. But on closer examination, the situation would prove to be more complex than Gould allowed. Despite the differences, similarities would emerge.

> Play the tape a few more times, though. We see similar melodic elements appearing in each, and the overall structure may be quite similar. . . . When we take a broader view, the role of contingency diminishes. Look at the tape as a whole. It resembles in some ways a symphony, although its orchestration is internal and caused largely by the interactions of many melodic strands.

Although the details will be different, van Valen argues that similarities and convergences are to be expected.

CONVERGENT EVOLUTION AND EVOLUTIONARY NAVIGATION

A similar approach is taken by the Cambridge paleobiologist Simon Conway Morris, whose pioneering work on the Burgess Shale was used by Gould, but in ways that Conway Morris clearly regarded as inadequate.[37] Although both Gould and Conway Morris recognize the role of contingency in the evolutionary process, they evaluate its importance in significantly different ways. For Gould, "the awesome improbability of human evolution" is a result of contingency in adaptive evolution. Conway Morris argues that if our planet were even slightly different from the way it actually is, then life might never have emerged. Although this seems similar to Gould's emphasis on historical contingency, it is important to note that Conway Morris emphasizes the way in which physical events create opportunities for life to emerge and adapt, where Gould instead emphasized the idiosyncratic nature of adaptation itself. Conway Morris thus characterizes his work as a refutation of "the notion of the 'dominance of contingency.'"[38]

36. Leigh M. van Valen, "How Far Does Contingency Rule?" *Evolutionary Theory* 10 (1991): 47–52.
37. For his correction of Gould at points of importance, see Simon Conway Morris, *The Crucible of Creation: The Burgess Shale and the Rise of Animals* (Oxford: Oxford University Press, 1998).
38. Simon Conway Morris, *Life's Solution: Inevitable Humans in a Lonely Universe* (Cambridge: Cambridge University Press, 2003), 297.

In *Life's Solution*, Conway Morris argues that the number of evolutionary end points is limited. "Rerun the tape of life as often as you like, and the end result will be much the same."[39] *Life's Solution* builds a forceful case for the predictability of evolutionary outcomes, not in terms of genetic details but rather their broad phenotypic manifestations. Convergent evolution is to be understood as "the recurrent tendency of biological organization to arrive at the same solution to a particular need."[40]

Conway Morris's case is based on a remarkable compilation of examples of convergent evolution, in which two or more lineages have independently evolved similar structures and functions. Conway Morris's examples range from the aerodynamics of hovering moths and hummingbirds to the use of silk by spiders and some insects to capture prey. "The details of convergence actually reveal many of the twists and turns of evolutionary change as different starting points are transformed towards common solutions via a variety of well-trodden paths."[41] And what is the significance of convergent evolution? Conway Morris is clear: it reveals the existence of stable regions in biological space. "Convergence occurs because of 'islands' of stability, analogous to 'attractors' in chaos theory."[42]

The force of Conway Morris's critique of Gould cannot be overlooked. While contingency is a factor in the overall evolutionary mechanism, it plays a significantly less decisive role than Gould allows. Evolution regularly appears to "converge" on a relatively small number of possible outcomes. Convergence is widespread, despite the infinitude of genetic possibilities, because "the evolutionary routes are many, but the destinations are limited."[43] Certain destinations are precluded by "the howling wildernesses of the maladaptive," where the vast majority of genotypes are nonviable, thus precluding further exploration by natural selection. Biological history shows a marked tendency to repeat itself, with life demonstrating an almost eerie ability to find its way to the correct solution, repeatedly. "Life has a peculiar propensity to 'navigate' to rather precise solutions in response to adaptive challenges."[44]

Examples of convergent evolution are legion. For those not familiar with the idea, two examples may be noted briefly:

1. *Photosynthesis*. In an earlier chapter, we noted the importance of photosynthesis. Three mechanisms are known to exist, usually referred to as Crassulacean acid metabolism (CAM), C-3, and C-4. The C-4 photosynthesis is known to have evolved independently at least 31 times in 18 different families of flowering plants during the past 8 million years, giving rise to a total of nearly

---

39. Ibid., 282.
40. Ibid., xii.
41. Ibid., 144; see the listing of such examples on 457–61.
42. Ibid., 127.
43. Ibid., 24: "Despite the almost crass simplicity of life's building blocks, perhaps we can discern inherent within this framework the inevitable and pre-ordained trajectories of evolution?"
44. Ibid., 225.

10,000 species of plants.[45] The CAM is also known to have evolved on multiple occasions.[46]

2. *The eye.* The evolution of the eye underwent dramatic development at the time of the Cambrian explosion.[47] This process combines remarkable morphological variability with genetic and developmental stasis across millions of years of evolution. Eyes have evolved on multiple independent occasions, taking at least nine distinct forms: pinhole eyes, two kinds of camera-lens eyes (found in vertebrates and octopuses),[48] curved reflector eyes, along with several kinds of compound, multilensed eyes. Compound eyes have evolved independently in crustaceans, annelid worms (sabellids), and bivalve molluscs. Camera-like eyes have evolved not only in vertebrates and octopuses, but also independently in jumping spiders, some snails, alciopid polychaete worms, cubozoan jellyfish, and the backward-looking eyes of coral reef shrimp.

The point Conway Morris hopes to make in assembling his matrix of convergence is that the number of evolutionary end points is limited. Time and time again, evolution "converges" on a relatively small set of possible solutions to the problems and opportunities that the environment offers to life.

This leads Conway Morris to make the point that even an essentially random search process will end up identifying stable outcomes in biological space. While the means of finding such islands of stability may seem erratic, its outcome is ultimately entirely intelligible. Gould suggested that directionality within evolution could be compared to a "drunkard's walk," in which organisms wander into greater complexity.[49] In effect, Conway Morris offers an alternative to the rigid dichotomy so often proposed between pure randomness (as seen in Gould's "drunkard's walk")[50] and tight directional progress toward a preestablished final goal. In making and defending this important point, Conway Morris offers an illuminating nonbiological analogy. He appeals to the discovery of Easter Island by the Polynesians, perhaps 1,200 years ago.[51] Easter Island is one of the most

45. See the excellent review of the research by Colin P. Osborne and David J. Beerling, "Nature's Green Revolution: The Remarkable Evolutionary Rise of C_4 Plants," *Philosophical Transactions of the Royal Society B* 361 (2006): 173–94.

46. Darren M. Crayn, Klaus Winter, and J. Andrew C. Smith, "Multiple Origins of Crassulacean Acid Metabolism and the Epiphytic Habit in the Neotropical Family *Bromeliaceae*," *Proceedings of the National Academy of Sciences* 101 (2004): 3703–8.

47. Andrew R. Parker, "Colour in Burgess Shale Animals and the Effect of Light on Evolution in the Cambrian," *Proceedings of the Royal Society of London: Biological Sciences* 265 (1998): 967–72.

48. Atsushi Ogura, Kazuho Ikeo, and Takashi Gojobori, "Comparative Analysis of Gene Expression for Convergent Evolution of Camera Eye between Octopus and Human," *Genome Research* 14 (2004): 1555–61.

49. For the image, see Stephen Jay Gould, *Full House: The Spread of Excellence from Plato to Darwin* (New York: Harmony Books, 1996), 149–51. For comment, see Peter A. Corning, *Nature's Magic: Synergy in Evolution and the Fate of Humankind* (New York: Cambridge University Press, 2003), 150–51.

50. Robert A. Martin, *Missing Links: Evolutionary Concepts and Transitions through Time* (Sudbury, MA: Jones & Bartlett, 2004), 59–61.

51. Conway Morris, *Life's Solution*, 19–21. The island was also "discovered" by Admiral Roggeveen on Easter Day 1722.

remote places on Earth, at least 3,000 kilometers from the nearest population centers, Tahiti and Chile. Yet though surrounded by the vast, empty wastes of the Pacific Ocean, it was nevertheless discovered by Polynesians. Is this, asks Conway Morris, to be put down to chance and happenstance? Possibly. But probably not. Conway Morris points to the "sophisticated search strategy of the Polynesians," which made its discovery inevitable. The same, he argues, happens in the evolutionary process: "Isolated 'islands' provide havens of biological possibility in an ocean of maladaptedness." It is these "islands of stability" which give rise to the phenomenon of convergent evolution.[52]

So can these "islands of stability" be *predicted*? Can one identify in advance, so to speak, points on which various evolutionary processes converge? Conway Morris is properly cautious at this point. After all, the scientific method is about a posteriori analysis, not a priori prediction. "Hindsight and foresight are strictly forbidden. . . . We can only retrodict and not predict."[53] Evolutionary theory may offer an account of what has been observed and is being observed, but it cannot predict future specifics. Yet the notion of islands of biological stability is perfectly valid and can be retrodicted on the basis of what is already known about parameters believed to be involved in the evolutionary process. Perhaps the identity of *individual* "islands of stability" can only be predicted with difficulty; yet the general phenomenon could be broadly predicted, and the identity of specific "islands" *retrodicted* on the basis of such an understanding of the forces of contingency, history, and adaptability entailed in the evolutionary process. The central point is that because organisms repeatedly arrive at the same biological solution—the camera-eyes of vertebrates and cephalopods being a case in point—this not only suggests that there is a degree of predictability to the evolutionary process, but also potentially points to a deeper structure to life, a "metaphorical landscape across which evolution must necessarily navigate."[54]

RETHINKING TELEOLOGY IN EVOLUTION

So where do these lines of thought take us? It is clear that Conway Morris's analysis points to some concept of teleology, yet one which cannot easily be accommodated within the spectrum of possibilities traditionally employed in such a discussion. Two fundamental points may be made, as follows.

First, most of the traditional objections to the appeal to the notion of teleology in biology noted by Mayr reflect a belief that an a priori metaphysical sys-

52. Ibid., 127.
53. Ibid., 11–12.
54. See Conway Morris's reflections in his 2005 Boyle Lecture: Simon Conway Morris, "Darwin's Compass: How Evolution Discovers the Song of Creation," *Science and Christian Belief* 18 (2006): 5–22.

tem, often theistic, is imposed upon the process of scientific observation and reflection, thus prejudicing its scientific character.[55] A close reading of Mayr suggests that he believes, not without good reason, that Kant's specific notion of teleology has exercised a generally adverse effect on the development of the philosophy of biology.[56] The origins and influence of Kant's concept of teleology have been the subject of intense scholarly investigation in recent years,[57] partly (though not entirely) validating Mayr's concerns about the intrusion of a priori metaphysical notions into the scientific endeavor.

From the standpoint of the scientific method, one may indeed protest against the imposition of a priori notions of goals and causes, such as those associated with many traditional approaches to teleology. The same intense suspicion of metaphysical notions lies behind the rise of "logical positivism" in the twentieth century.[58] Yet the ultimate failure of such radical empiricism rested in its a priori denial of the a posteriori possibility of metaphysical entities or principles.[59] The same point applies to teleological debates. The natural sciences rightly protest about the smuggling of preconceived teleological schemes into scientific analysis. But what if they arise from the process of reflection on observation? What if they are a posteriori inferences, rather than a priori assumptions? Conway Morris's evidence and analysis suggest that a form of teleology may indeed be inferred a posteriori as the "best explanation" of what is observed. This may not directly map onto a traditional Christian doctrine of providence; nevertheless, there is a significant degree of resonance with the notion which merits closer attention.

This is not necessarily, it should be noted, a matter of discerning "purpose"— a heavily metaphysically freighted notion—within the evolutionary sequence and inferring from this to a divine ordainer of purpose. Rather, we are reverting to the approach that is summarized in John Henry Newman's enlightening yet

---

55. Ayala clarifies the kind of teleology that is objectionable to Darwinians by making a distinction between an external "teleology," understood as a shaping action imposed by an external intelligence, and an immanent or internal teleology of a broadly Aristotelian kind that he finds unobjectionable and indeed indispensable in describing the living world: Ayala, "Teleological Explanations in Evolutionary Biology," 11.

56. For example, see the judicious comments in Mayr, *What Makes Biology Unique?* 90–91.

57. The best studies, which reward close reading, are Robert E. Butts, "Teleology and Scientific Method in Kant's Critique of Judgment," *Nous* 24 (1990): 1–16; Joan Steigerwald, "Kant's Concept of Natural Purpose and the Reflecting Power of Judgement," *Studies in History and Philosophy of Science C* 37 (2006): 712–34; John Zammito, "Teleology Then and Now: The Question of Kant's Relevance for Contemporary Controversies over Function in Biology," *Studies in History and Philosophy of Science* 37 (2006): 748–70. There is some useful introductory material in Michael Friedman, "Causal Laws and the Foundations of Natural Science," in *Cambridge Companion to Kant*, ed. Paul Guyer (Cambridge: Cambridge University Press, 1990), 161–99.

58. See, e.g., Rudolf Carnap, "The Elimination of Metaphysics through Logical Analysis," in *Logical Positivism*, ed. A. J. Ayer (New York: Free Press, 1959), 60–81, which rejects any notions that "transcend the realm of empirically founded, inductive science."

59. For a detailed analysis of the place of metaphysics in an a posteriori scientific theology, see Alister E. McGrath, *A Scientific Theology*, vol. 3, *Theory* (London: Continuum, 2003), 237–94.

curiously understudied remark: "I believe in design because I believe in God; not in God because I see design."[60] In line with the general approach adopted in this book, we are asking a rather more oblique question: might not the evolutionary process, despite its contingency, still be consonant with the achievement of purpose on the part of a creator God?[61]

Darwin's theory certainly indicates that it is no longer *necessary* to appeal to a creator God to account for the apparent design of living things, since this can be argued to come about through a complex and distinctive interaction between chance and necessity, between random and deterministic processes, in the process of natural selection. Yet while this demonstrates that a theistic account of biological design is not entailed, it does not entail the much stronger and rather more significant claim that either theism itself, or a theistic account of biological design, is *false*. As a result, theists are free to agree that natural processes are adequate to explain biological design, but they are also free to insist that theism provides another equally rational and plausible explanation which may ultimately prove to be the *best* explanation. Once more, the issue concerns the consonance or resonance of a Christian vision of reality with what is actually observed.

The teleonomic disclosures of evolutionary biology can be reconciled with a Christian vision of reality.[62] And as we have emphasized, the notion of "create" does not require to be interpreted as a single, once-for-all event but can equally—and many would now say rightly—be understood as a directed process. Charles Kingsley's words of 1871 bear further repetition here: "We knew of old that God was so wise that He could make all things: but behold, He is so much wiser than even that, that He can make all things make themselves."[63] The approach we have outlined in this work extends the scope of natural theology from the outcome of evolutionary processes to an appreciation of those processes themselves. Paley's essentially static view of nature inevitably focused attention on the present state

60. John Henry Newman, letter to William Robert Brownlow, April 13, 1870; in Charles Stephen Dessain et al., eds., *The Letters and Diaries of John Henry Newman*, 31 vols. (Oxford: Clarendon Press, 1963–2006), 25:97. See further Noel Keith Roberts, "Newman on the Argument from Design," *New Blackfriars* 88 (2007): 56–66.

61. A similar approach is taken in the excellent study of Ernan McMullin, "Cosmic Purpose and the Contingency of Human Evolution," *Theology Today* 55 (1998): 389–414. See also Francisco Ayala, "Intelligent Design: The Original Version," *Theology and Science* 1 (2003): 9–32; William E. Carroll, "At the Mercy of Chance? Evolution and the Catholic Tradition," *Revue des questions scientifiques* 177 (2006): 179–204.

62. For an excellent example, see Timothy Shanahan, "Darwinian Naturalism, Theism, and Biological Design," *Perspectives on Science and Christian Faith* 49 (1997): 170–78.

63. Charles Kingsley, "The Natural Theology of the Future," in *Westminster Sermons* (London: Macmillan, 1874), v–xxxiii. Note his further comment: "We might accept all that Mr. Darwin, all that Professor Huxley, has so learnedly and so acutely written on physical science, and yet preserve our natural theology on exactly the same basis as that on which Butler and Paley left it. That we should have to develop it, I do not deny. That we should have to relinquish it, I do [deny]." For comment, see Charles H. Muller, "Spiritual Evolution and Muscular Theology: Lessons from Kingsley's Natural Theology," *University of Cape Town Studies in English* 15 (1986): 24–34; James G. Paradis, "Satire and Science in Victorian Culture," in *Victorian Science in Context*, ed. Bernard Lightman (Chicago: University of Chicago Press, 1997), 143–75.

of things. Our approach, while not in any way diminishing the beauty and wonder of the natural world around us, extends that sense of wonder to the processes which brought it about. Process and outcome are alike the proper subject of a natural theology.

Yet there is a second point that must be made here. The rejection of any notion of "final causation" in biological accounts of natural selection ultimately rests upon how this idea is understood. For example, Charles S. Peirce's understanding of final causation and teleology causes some difficulties for even Mayr's cautious critique of teleology in biology.[64] Peirce argues that final causes are to be understood as general types that tend to realize themselves by determining processes of efficient causation. They are not future events, but general physical possibilities. For any given process, the indications of its final causation are that the end state of the process can be reached in different ways and that the process is irreversible.[65]

> We must understand by final causation that mode of bringing facts about according to which a general description of result is made to come about, quite irrespective of any compulsion for it to come about in this or that particular way; although the means may be adapted to the end. The general result may be brought about at one time in one way, and at another time in another way. Final causation does not determine in what particular way it is to be brought about, but only that the result shall have a general character.

Peirce, perhaps aware of the overtones of existing terminology, proposed an alternative to express what he regarded as the central point at issue here by apparently goal-directed activities: "If teleological is too strong a word to apply to them, we might invent the word *finious*, to express their tendency toward a final state."[66] It is fair to suggest that the inelegant term "finious" has yet to find wide acceptance; nevertheless, it clearly has potential as a means of illuminating the complex picture disclosed by contemporary evolutionary biology.[67] Yet quibbles about the gracefulness of the terminology apart, Peirce clearly recognized the need to find a metaphysically untainted word to describe the a posteriori phenomenon of biological processes tending toward certain end points.

Ernst Mayr and other philosophers are right to protest against any attempt to impose a predetermined teleology upon a scientific account of the evolutionary process. Yet Mayr's arguments really only have force when directed against a priori

64. See esp. Menno Hulswit, "Teleology: A Peircean Critique of Ernst Mayr's Theory," *Transactions of the Charles S. Peirce Society* 32 (1996): 182–214.

65. Charles S. Peirce, *Collected Papers of Charles Sanders Peirce*, ed. Charles Hartshorne and Paul Weiss, 8 vols. (Cambridge, MA: Harvard University Press, 1960), 1:211. For further discussion of this 1902 definition, see the magisterial analysis of T. L. Short, *Peirce's Theory of Signs* (Cambridge: Cambridge University Press, 2007), 91–174.

66. *Collected Papers of Charles Sanders Peirce*, 7:471. Mayr is aware of this notion: see Mayr, *What Makes Biology Unique?* 47.

67. See Short's early and somewhat neglected paper, clearly inspired by Peirce: T. L. Short, "Teleology in Nature," *American Philosophical Quarterly* 30 (1983): 311–20.

concepts of teleology, which are imported into biology from nonempirical metaphysical systems, whether theist or atheist. Throughout this section my argument is that some notion of teleology emerges from the study of the evolutionary process itself. Such a teleology is empirical, grounded in a posteriori discernment, not a priori imposition. It is abducted from the observation of the evolutionary process, not deduced from a nonempirical metaphysical system.[68] Peirce's notion of "finiousness," though clumsily framed, has the clear advantage of being an essentially empirical notion because it is derived from reflection on observation. The term "teleology" is more elastic than its critics appear to realize. It requires modification in the light of the empirical evidence, not abandonment in response to the dogmatic demands of those who maintain its inconceivability.

All of this points to the apparent ineradicability of teleological language and thinking in biology.[69] It is easy to portray this as an obsolete mode of speaking which will disappear with time and rigorous education in the scientific method. Yet this judgment is superficial and unhelpful. Teleological thinking persists in biology precisely because it appears to be a meaningful way of describing what is observed, which resonates with "natural" human ways of thinking. Just as one might speak of genes as "selfish," one might also speak of evolution as possessing "purpose." Both represent anthropomorphic ways of speaking, yet both may express valid insights. The observation that evolutionary biology must explain is the apparent navigation of the evolutionary search process to find stable regions of biological space.[70] It is very difficult to see how even a minimalist teleological language can be avoided. Conway Morris suggests, using the image of "Darwin's compass":[71]

> The view that evolution is open-ended, without predictabilities and indeterminate in terms of outcomes[,] is negated by the ubiquity of evolutionary convergence. The central point is that because organisms arrive repeatedly at the same biological solution, the camera-eyes of vertebrates and cephalopods perhaps being the most famous example, this provides not only a degree of predictability but more intriguingly points to a deeper structure to life, a metaphorical landscape across which evolution must necessarily navigate.

If it is correct to suggest that some notion of teleology emerges from reflection on the evolutionary process, the task which confronts Christian theology is to clarify the nature of this distinctive empirical notion of teleology and how it

68. There are obvious parallels here with the place of metaphysical notions in the natural sciences. While there is an overwhelming case to be made for excluding a priori notions of metaphysics from the sciences, there are no grounds for excluding metaphysical notions which emerge a posteriori from the observation of nature. See the detailed analysis in McGrath, *A Scientific Theology*, vol. 3, *Theory*, 237–94.

69. See the cri de coeur of David Hanke, "Teleology: The Explanation That Bedevils Biology," in *Explanations: Styles of Explanation in Science*, ed. John Cornwell (Oxford: Oxford University Press, 2004), 143–55.

70. For comment on the concept of "biological space," see Stuart L. Schreiber, Tarun M. Kapoor, and Günther Wess, eds., *Chemical Biology: From Small Molecules to Systems Biology and Drug Design* (Weinheim: Wiley-VCH Verlag, 2007), 828–32.

71. Simon Conway Morris, "Darwin's Compass: How Evolution Discovers the Song of Creation," *Science and Christian Belief* 18 (2006): 5–22.

relates to its alternatives. What relation does it bear to the concepts of teleology developed by Aristotle or Kant? Or rather more significantly for our purposes, how does it relate to a Christian notion of providence? Further exploration of this point lies beyond the present study.[72] Nevertheless, one may point out that a theological framework with which to explore this issue lies at hand in Augustine's notion of *rationes seminales*, to which we may now return.

EVOLUTION AND AUGUSTINIAN *RATIONES SEMINALES*

As we argued earlier, the classic Christian doctrine of creation enunciated by Augustine of Hippo during the period 401–15 offers an intellectual framework for reflecting on the evolution of the natural world, at both the cosmological and biological levels. As we noted earlier (see chap. 8), Augustine's basic approach consists of five elements, of which the fifth alone is shaped by the scientific assumptions of the late classical period:

1. God brought everything into being at one specific moment.
2. The action of creation included the embedding of causalities within the world, which would emerge or evolve at a later stage, as and when appropriate conditions pertained. These *rationes seminales* play a highly significant role in Augustine's concept of an emerging and developing creation.
3. This process of development is to be seen as directed by God's providence.
4. The image of a dormant seed is an appropriate but not exact analogy for these embedded causalities.
5. The generation of these dormant seeds leads to fixed and determinate biological forms.

Augustine's use of the metaphor of *ratio seminalis* is clearly open to evolutionary exploration, particularly when the fifth of his five elements of creation is seen as a historically situated notion, open to scientific revision and development. Augustine's views on the "eternity of kinds" (where we might say "fixity of species") have clearly been shaped, whether directly or indirectly, by Aristotle.[73] Augustine himself was painfully aware of the ease with which contemporary scientific theories could become incorporated into biblical interpretation and theological reflection, and he was adamant that the provisionality of such theories should be acknowledged. Otherwise, future biblical interpreters would be locked

---

72. I intend to explore this question myself in my 2009–10 Hulsean Lectures at the University of Cambridge, which will deal specifically with the relationship between Darwinism and natural theology.

73. For an account of Aristotle at this point, see Jiyuan Yu, *The Structure of Being in Aristotle's Metaphysics* (Dordrecht: Kluwer Academic Publishers, 2003), 193–94.

into hermeneutical approaches which were determined by the scientific views of previous generations. At this point, Augustine needs to be developed further, to correct Aristotle's views on the issue of biological fixity. It was not until the nineteenth century that this became possible.

The publication of Darwin's *Origin of Species* (1859) created new intellectual space for Augustine's approach, not least because Darwin himself explicitly allowed space for divine action through secondary causes in his account of natural selection.[74] Indeed, Darwin's notion of natural selection required him to postulate some means by which genetic characteristics might be "remembered" and hence transmitted to future generations without dilution. The genetic analogy he adopted was that of the "gemmule," a seedlike entity.[75] Although now known to be an incorrect hypothesis, the "gemmule" clearly represents a recognition of the potential heuristic value of seed-based analogues in Darwin's understanding of natural selection.

Darwin's theory of natural selection, then, might seem to have opened the doors for a major theological reevaluation, if not reappropriation, of Augustine's doctrine of creation. Yet it must be reported that virtually no writer of the later nineteenth century appears to have seen the potential of Augustine for the dialogue between Christian theology and Darwinian theory. An exception must be made in the case of the English Catholic biologist St. George Mivart (1827–1900). In his original discussion of how and to what extent biological evolution might be accommodated theologically, Mivart appealed to the arguments of Augustine, as set out in the major work we have been considering in the present chapter: "St. Augustine insists in a very remarkable manner on the merely derivative sense in which God's creation of organic forms is to be understood; that is, that God created them by conferring on the material world the power to evolve them under suitable conditions."[76]

74. Darwin's remarks toward the end of the *Origin of Species* merit close study: "Authors of the highest eminence seem to be fully satisfied with the view that each species has been independently created. To my mind it accords better with what we know of the laws impressed on matter by the Creator, that the production and extinction of the past and present inhabitants of the world should have been due to secondary causes." See Charles Darwin, *On the Origin of the Species by Means of Natural Selection*, 2nd ed. (London: John Murray, 1860), 489. On this point, see further Armand Maurer, "Darwin, Thomists, and Secondary Causality," *Review of Metaphysics* 57 (2004): 491–515, noting especially his comment (on 497) that Darwin's "argument for evolution by secondary causes" actually belongs to "natural theology, for it concerns God the creator and the laws he has implanted in matter." The parallels with Augustine are evident.

75. Darwin supposed that these hypothetical gemmules "circulate freely throughout the system, and when supplied with proper nutriment multiply by self-division, subsequently becoming developed into cells like those from which they were derived." For comment, see Gerald L. Geison, "Darwin and Heredity: The Evolution of His Hypothesis of Pangenesis," *Journal of the History of Medicine* 24 (1969): 375–411; P. Kyle Stanford, "Darwin's Pangenesis and the Problem of Unconceived Alternatives," *British Journal for Philosophy of Science* 57 (2006): 121–44.

76. St. George Mivart, *On the Genesis of Species* (New York: Appleton & Co., 1871), 281. Mivart appeals particularly to *De Genesi ad litteram* 5.5.14: "Terrestria animalia, tanquam ex ultimo elemento mundi ultima; nihilominus *potentialiter*, quorum numeros tempus postea visibiliter explicaret." He also correctly noted the theological potential of evolutionary convergence. Nevertheless, Mivart was regarded as unorthodox by many in the Catholic church of his day. For discussion, see Don O'Leary,

Augustine, we must again emphasize, neither accepted nor anticipated Darwinian evolutionary paradigms;[77] he shared the common human condition of being limited in his intellectual options on account of his historical location. Yet the potential of his approach to offer a theological framework for discussion of the evolutionary process in particular, and the historical development of the universe in general, cannot be overlooked; it clearly merits closer examination as part of a renewed natural theology.

Yet we must now move on to consider the implications of some of the points that we have explored in chapters 9–14 for an understanding of the notion of creation and its implications for a natural theology.

Roman Catholicism and Modern Science: A History (New York: Continuum, 2006), 78–93. Views similar to those of Mivart were expressed fifty years later by Henry de Dorlodot, *Le Darwinisme du point de vue de l'orthodoxie catholique* (Brussels: Vromant, 1921). For an excellent account of the significance of Augustine's doctrine of the *rationes seminales* in this context, see Michael J. McKeough, *The Meaning of the Rationes Seminales in St. Augustine* (Washington: Catholic University of America Press, 1926). McKeough is right to point out that Augustine shared his age's belief in the fixity of species, but he also observes that it is consistent with an evolutionary approach that affirms the gradual appearance of living beings through secondary causes and the operation of natural laws.

77. For a forcible statement of this point, see Henry Woods, *Augustine and Evolution: A Study in the Saint's "De Genesi ad litteram" and "De Trinitate"* (New York: Universal Knowledge Foundation, 1924).

Chapter 15

An Emergent Creation and Natural Theology

In chapter 8, we considered how Augustine of Hippo's doctrine of creation provides a theological framework which can act as the basis for approaching and interpreting contemporary scientific insights into the fabric of reality. Augustine wrote as a theologian, not as a scientist, and he must not be misunderstood as offering a prescientific account of the origins of reality. His concern is to articulate an intellectually defensible and explanatorily fecund approach to nature, an approach that is authentically Christian. The fundamental point is that God's creative activity is understood to involve both an act and process—the primordial origination of the cosmos, including the creation of the *rationes seminales*, and the subsequent emergence or evolution of things through God's providential agency:[1]

> These [*rationes seminales*] were made by God in the beginning, when he made the world, and simultaneously created all things, which were to be unfolded in the ages to come. They are perfected, in that in their proper

1. Augustine, *De Genesi ad litteram* 6.11.18. For reflections on models of divine agency which this might presuppose, see esp. William E. Carroll, "Divine Agency, Contemporary Physics, and the Autonomy of Nature," *Heythrop Journal* 49 (2008): 1–21.

natures, by which they achieve their role in time, they possess nothing that was not already present in them causally. They have, however, just begun, since in them are the seeds, as it were, of the future perfections that would arise from their hidden state, and which would be manifested at the appropriate time.

This aspect of Augustine's doctrine of creation has not been given due weight in recent discussions of the concept of emergence. Yet it is clear that the growing realization of the importance of emergent properties within nature, which is of growing importance to the dialogue between the natural sciences and Christian theology, can be accommodated within Augustine's theological framework. To understand the importance of this point for a right understanding of natural theology in particular, and the relation of the natural sciences to the Christian doctrine of creation in general, we may explore some aspects of the historical development of English natural theology since the seventeenth century.

THE CONCEPT OF CREATION IN CLASSIC NATURAL THEOLOGIES

In England during the late seventeenth and early eighteenth centuries, a great confluence of Christian theology and natural philosophy took place, giving rise to a form of natural theology that was intentionally apologetic and rooted in the best natural science of its day.[2] Substantially the same approach was set out in John Ray's *The Wisdom of God Manifested in the Works of Creation* (1691), the Boyle Lectures, and in William Paley's *Natural Theology* (1802).

A core assumption of the classical form of English natural theology from John Ray to William Paley is that the term "creation" designates an act by which the universe was brought into being several thousand years ago, more or less exactly as we now see it.[3] The fixity of the created order was held to be axiomatic,[4] although most Christian apologists suggested that there was evidence of a past catastrophe—often identified with Noah's flood—that had significantly impacted on both the physical and biological characteristics of Earth.[5] For Paley, only the Christian God

2. Alister E. McGrath, "Towards the Restatement and Renewal of a Natural Theology: A Dialogue with the Classic English Tradition," in *The Order of Things: Explorations in Scientific Theology* (Oxford: Blackwell Publishing, 2006), 63–96.

3. For a useful summary, see Robert Jurmain, *Essentials of Physical Anthropology*, 5th ed. (Belmont, CA: Thomson Wadsworth, 2004), 26–27. Some specific variations of this approach are of interest, such as the account of the origins of diurnal motion offered by Francis Lodwick (1619–94): William Poole, "Francis Lodwick's Creation: Theology and Natural Philosophy in the Early Royal Society," *Journal of the History of Ideas* 66 (2005): 245–63.

4. For an excellent study of this point, see John C. Greene, *The Death of Adam: Evolution and Its Impact on Western Thought* (Ames: Iowa State University Press, 1959).

5. A good example of this is found in the four volumes of Thomas Burnet's *Sacred Theory of the Earth* (1680–90). For comment, see Stephen J. Gould, *Ever since Darwin: Reflections in Natural History* (New York: W. W. Norton, 1977), 141–46.

could create such a complex natural world and also have the power to wipe out certain forms of life, as suggested by the fossil record.[6]

This view of creation was subjected to two major challenges in the nineteenth century. First, the geological record was increasingly recognized to point to Earth being much older than a literal reading of the biblical creation accounts suggests.[7] Calculations based on heat transfer carried out by W. T. Kelvin (1824–1907) pointed to Earth being at least 24 million years old, and probably much older.[8] Second, the publication of Charles Darwin's *Origin of Species* proposed an alternative account of biological origins, in which existing life-forms evolved over extended periods through a process of natural selection. The traditional doctrine of "special creation" was seen as clumsy and forced in the light of this more elegant explanation, even though some significant explanatory gaps remained in Darwin's original statement of his theory.[9]

These two developments raised some difficulties for some traditional Christian accounts of creation. The geological issues required a substantial expansion of the age of Earth, demanding that the Genesis creation accounts be interpreted in new ways—for example, by assuming significant interpolations of time within the narratives. The biological issues could be addressed by interpreting creation as an extended process, rather than as a primordial completed event. Both these processes of conceptual expansion and modification were well under way by the late nineteenth century, especially within Britain, and were generally not regarded as particularly problematic for academic theology,[10] even if they caused discomfort for populist approaches to biblical interpretation.

CREATION AND EMERGENCE

It is now clear that a third adaptation of the traditional conception of "creation" is required, already implicit within Augustine's account of creation: the view that

---

6. Keith A. Francis, *Charles Darwin and the Origin of Species* (Westport, CT: Greenwood Press, 2007), 45–47.

7. For major studies of this development, see Nicolaas A. Rupke, *The Great Chain of History: William Buckland and the English School of Geology (1814–1849)* (Oxford: Clarendon Press, 1983); Charles C. Gillispie, *Genesis and Geology: A Study in the Relations of Scientific Thought, Natural Theology and Social Opinion in Great Britain, 1790–1850* (Cambridge, MA: Harvard University Press, 1996).

8. F. D. Stacey, "Kelvin's Age of the Earth Paradox Revisited," *Journal of Geophysical Research* 105 (2000): 13155–58.

9. For an excellent account of these developments, see John Hedley Brooke, *Science and Religion: Some Historical Perspectives* (Cambridge: Cambridge University Press, 1991).

10. For some of these adaptive responses, see Frederick Gregory, "The Impact of Darwinian Evolution on Protestant Theology in the Nineteenth Century," in *God and Nature: Historical Essays on the Encounter between Christianity and Natural Science*, ed. D. C. Lindberg and R. L. Numbers (Berkeley: University of California Press, 1986), 369–90; Jon H. Roberts, *Darwinism and the Divine in America: Protestant Intellectuals and Organic Evolution, 1859–1900* (Madison: University of Wisconsin Press, 1988); Ronald L. Numbers, *Darwinism Comes to America* (Cambridge, MA: Harvard University Press, 1998).

creation entails the origination of a potentially multileveled reality, whose properties *emerge* under certain conditions which did not exist at the origins of the universe. Furthermore, these properties are not predictable by human observers a priori; they are discovered a posteriori. Since this notion may not be familiar to some theologians, we shall introduce the idea slowly in what follows.

The chemical sodium chloride (NaCl), better known as salt, is one of the major constituents of seawater and plays a major role in the chemistry of the human body. Chemically, the compound consists of an atom of sodium and an atom of chlorine. Yet the chemical and biological properties of sodium chloride could not be predicted from knowing that sodium is a soft, bright silvery metal, and chlorine is a greenish-yellow gas that acts a respiratory irritant. Its properties are emergent: they could not be predicted on the basis of our present knowledge of metallic sodium and gaseous chlorine.

Or consider gold. Its color and distinctive properties are well known, especially its malleability, which allows it to be beaten into gold leaf, typically four to five millionths of an inch thick. Yet these properties relate to metallic gold, consisting of large assemblies of gold atoms. They cannot be predicted from the behavior of individual gold atoms.[11] The collective, macroscopic properties of gold cannot be deduced from the quantum mechanical description of gold atoms. An understanding of the behavior of individual gold atoms does not allow us to predict the way in which large assemblies of such atoms will behave. The macroscopic properties of gold are to be considered as emergent. They are already inbuilt into the nature of gold; they exist as potentialities, however, and hence cannot be observed until certain conditions are achieved—in this case, when aggregates of gold emerge.

Or consider the behavior of chimpanzees and bonobos (two closely related groups of great apes, separated by the Zaire River, which were treated as a single group until the 1930s). Individual chimpanzees or bonobos behave in one way in isolation, and in quite another in groups. Their social behavior, in other words, is emergent: it cannot be predicted on the basis of a knowledge of individual apes. Although they are physically very similar, chimpanzees and bonobos show quite different patterns of social behavior, with females having a significantly higher status in bonobo than in chimpanzee communities.[12] Environmental differences may have played a significant role in causing these divergences to emerge.[13]

---

11. Stuart A. Kauffman, *Investigations* (New York: Oxford University Press, 2000), 127–28. In this work, a milestone in emergentist thinking, Kauffman argues that biological evolution is an inherently self-organizing process. Life arises spontaneously, and complexity evolves naturally in accordance with what he provisionally calls the "fourth law of thermodynamics": an innate tendency of life to explore the "adjacent possible" opportunities for building greater complexity.

12. Barbara Smuts, "Emergence in Social Evolution: A Great Ape Example," in *The Re-Emergence of Emergence: The Emergentist Hypothesis from Science to Religion*, ed. Philip Clayton and Paul Davies (Oxford: Oxford University Press, 2006), 166–86.

13. See the analysis in Richard W. Wrangham and Dale Peterson, *Demonic Males: Apes and the Origins of Human Violence* (Boston: Houghton Mifflin, 1996).

Or consider complex biological systems, such as cells or ecosystems. In each case, properties emerge which transcend those of their constituent parts.[14] Systems, by their very nature, are greater than the sum of their individual components. Ecosystems, for example, show emergent properties that stabilize over extended periods of time, resulting from a complex interaction between the environment and the individual biological components.[15] In the case of biological cells, complex signaling pathways emerge, demonstrating emergent properties such as integration of signals across multiple timescales, generation of distinct outputs depending on input strength and duration, and self-sustaining feedback loops.[16] Biochemical and biological systems persistently display properties that cannot be understood or predicted on the basis of purely reductive and analytical approaches—such as the biochemical phenomena or the emergence at a remarkably early stage of matching anticodons and amino acids by aminoacetyl-tRNA synthetase enzymes, the negative feedback in end-product inhibition first occurring in microbes, or the more biological phenomena of memory in animals and apical cells in plants.[17] Appreciating the sum of the parts that defines life will continue to elude us if we insist on constructing definitions that look no further than their physicochemical basis, treated in a fundamentally mechanistic manner.[18]

Each of these examples illustrates the phenomenon of *emergence:* the development of novel, unpredictable properties and behaviors at increasing levels of complexity.[19] Although there are some variations in definition of the concept of "emergence," the notion can be argued to have four general features:[20]

---

14. In connection with biological systems, this point is repeatedly made by William Bechtel and Robert C. Richardson, "Emergent Phenomena and Complex Systems," in *Emergence or Reduction?* ed. Ansgar Beckermann, Hans Flohr, and Jaegwon Kim (Berlin: de Gruyter, 1992), 257–88. The often-cited claim that the enzymatic efficiency of a protein is an emergent property should be noted here: Pier Luigi Luisi, "Emergence in Chemistry: Chemistry as the Embodiment of Emergence," *Foundations of Chemistry* 4 (2002): 183–200.

15. Eldor A. Paul, *Soil Microbiology, Ecology, and Biochemistry,* 3rd ed. (Burlington, MA: Academic Press, 2007), 224–25.

16. Upinder S. Bhalla and Ravi Iyengar, "Emergent Properties of Biological Signaling Pathways," *Science* 283 (1999): 381–87. For the emergence of cellular networks, particularly feedback mechanisms, see Uri Alon, *An Introduction to Systems Biology* (Boca Raton, FL: Chapman & Hall, 2007), 41–70.

17. See Robert W. Korn, "Biological Hierarchies, Their Birth, Death and Evolution by Natural Selection," *Biology and Philosophy* 17 (2002): 199–221; Jacques Ricard, "Reduction, Integration and Emergence in Biochemical Networks," *Biology of the Cell* 96 (2004): 719–25; Robert W. Korn, "The Emergence Principle in Biological Hierarchies," *Biology and Philosophy* 20 (2005): 137–51.

18. James Barham, "The Emergence of Biological Value," in *Debating Design: From Darwin to DNA,* ed. William A. Dembski and Michael Ruse (New York: Cambridge University Press, 2004), 210–26, esp. 218–22.

19. For an excellent introduction, see Michael Silberstein, "Reduction, Emergence, and Explanation," in *Blackwell Guide to the Philosophy of Science,* ed. Peter Machamer and Michael Silberstein (Oxford: Blackwell, 2002), 80–107.

20. See Philip Clayton, "Conceptual Foundations of Emergence Theory," in Clayton and Davies, *Re-Emergence of Emergence,* 1–31. Clayton has pioneered serious theological reflection on the notion: see esp. his essay "Toward a Constructive Christian Theology of Emergence," in *Evolution and Emergence: Systems, Organisms, Persons,* ed. Nancey C. Murphy and William R. Stoeger (Oxford: Oxford University Press, 2007), 315–43. For his important work on the emergence of mind, see Philip Clayton, *Mind and Emergence: From Quantum to Consciousness* (Oxford: Oxford University Press, 2004).

1. Everything that exists in the world of space and time is ultimately composed of the basic fundamental particles recognized by physics. However, physics proves inadequate to explain how this material comes to be structured.
2. When ensembles or aggregates of material particles attain an appropriate level of organizational complexity, genuinely novel properties begin to emerge.
3. These emergent properties cannot be reduced to, or predicted from, the lower-level phenomena from which they emerge.
4. Higher-level entities exercise a causal influence on their lower-level constituents.

The overall picture is that of the emergence of complexity from simpler previous physical structures, leading to the creation of higher levels with properties not possessed by lower levels. Inevitably, any account of this process of emergence will be hindered by contested definitions and concerns over potentially arbitrary demarcations.[21] An interesting taxonomy of emergence has been proposed by Harold Morowitz, who proposes twenty-eight stages of emergence within cosmic history.[22]

Morowitz's first seven steps lie in the domain of the physical sciences. Large-scale cosmic structuring leads to the formation of the stars, rich in hydrogen and helium, which in turn leads to nucleosynthesis and the creation of heavier elements. This in turn leads to the formation of solar systems and the evolution of planets with geospheres. The eighth proposed step is transitional, the emergence of a biosphere. This results in the formation of self-replicating protocells and hence competition for resources. As a result, Morowitz argues, the world becomes Darwinian.

Morowitz's next twelve steps are biological, leading through prokaryotes and eukaryotes to multicellular organisms, and hence to the evolution of mammals. The twenty-first step marks a transition, with the appearance of our primate ancestors. This is followed by a series of cultural developments, such as the emergence of societies of hominids and the evolution of language, philosophy, and spirituality.[23]

Morowitz's analysis is open to challenge. Yet our concern is not with the precise taxonomy that he proposes, but rather with the general principles that lie

21. Note the cautionary comments in John H. Holland, *Emergence: From Chaos to Order* (Oxford: Oxford University Press, 2000).

22. Harold J. Morowitz, *The Emergence of Everything: How the World Became Complex* (Oxford: Oxford University Press, 2002), 25–38.

23. The emergence of language, consciousness, and mind have attracted considerable attention in recent years. For representative contributions, see Terrence W. Deacon, *The Symbolic Species: The Co-Evolution of Language and the Human Brain* (New York: W. W. Norton, 1997); Jaegwon Kim, *Mind in a Physical World: An Essay on the Mind-Body Problem and Mental Causation* (Cambridge, MA: MIT Press, 1998); Nancey C. Murphy, *Bodies and Souls, or Spirited Bodies?* (Cambridge: Cambridge University Press, 2006).

behind it. Each stage of advancing complexity makes possible still further advances, which could not have taken place at earlier stages. The spontaneous self-organization of cosmological structures leads to the formation of planets; molecular and chemical evolution leads to living cells and life in general; and a Darwinian process of natural selection leads to the emergence of high-level functionality,[24] including the emergence of mind, with its capacity to reflect on the natural world.[25]

As I have emphasized, here I am not concerned to explore the phenomenon of emergence in greater detail, but rather with identifying its potential theological importance, in relation to natural theology in general, and more particularly in relation to the specific approach to natural theology set out in this work. I must also introduce a note of caution: the concept of "emergence" is in danger of being overexploited theologically, risking the charge of being discredited through conceptual inflation. The enthusiasm once demonstrated by theologians for quantum mechanical complementarity now seems to have been transferred to emergence. Although I believe that the notion of emergence is legitimate scientifically and valuable theologically, I feel I must express a degree of concern about its uncritical application in the science and religion dialogue.[26] In what follows, I shall adopt what I regard as a defensible and modest approach to the notion, avoiding the more extravagant claims that are increasingly being made about its theological potential.

EMERGENCE AND NATURAL THEOLOGY

The notion of emergence is significant for a Christian natural theology in three respects:

1. In speaking of "creation," the Christian tradition must come to understand that this notion implies potentialities which were not actualized in the first phase of the history of the universe, but which were enabled to emerge once suitable conditions arose.
2. The notion of "creation" thus designates a stratified entity, a series of layers or levels, rather than a single undifferentiated entity. This is consistent with forms of critical realism which acknowledge the stratification

24. George Ellis, "On the Nature of Emergent Reality," in Clayton and Davies, *Re-Emergence of Emergence*, 79–107.

25. The emergence of mind is one of the most significant and contentious issues to be discussed at present. See the useful review in Nancey C. Murphy, "Emergence and Mental Causation," in Clayton and Davies, *Re-Emergence of Emergence*, 227–43.

26. My concerns are clearly shared by Don Howard, the only critical voice in a recent collection of essays dealing with the significance of emergence: William R. Stoeger and Nancey C. Murphy, eds., *Evolution and Emergence: Systems, Organisms, Persons* (Oxford: Oxford University Press, 2007).

of reality, such as that developed within the social sciences by Roy Bhaskar,[27] and applied in a theological context in my *Scientific Theology*.[28]

3. Natural theology represents an engagement with "nature" in this full, extended, multilayered sense of the term.

Each of these points merits further comment.

It is clear that "creation" must be understood to designate an emerging reality. This is to be understood as a scientific amplification, not contradiction, of the classic Christian doctrine of creation. As noted earlier in this chapter, there have been those in the past who have argued that "creation" denotes a fixed state of affairs. This feature is typical of much popular natural theology of the eighteenth and early nineteenth centuries, and received its canonical statement in William Paley's *Natural Theology* (1802). Paley's version of natural theology was dealt a fatal blow through the publication and surprisingly rapid acceptance of Darwin's theory of natural selection within influential sections of the churches. Yet there were many who took the view that Paley's approach could be redeemed by developing an expanded account of the notion of creation. As Charles Kingsley put it in his 1871 lecture "The Natural Theology of the Future": "We knew of old that God was so wise that He could make all things: but behold, He is so much wiser than even that, that He can make all things make themselves."[29]

The basic idea that Kingsley develops is that of God endowing the creation with potentiality, so that its later developments are to be understood as continuous with the primordial creation. The original *donum* of creation is thus not limited to its specific *datum* at any given time. Kingsley argues that "the unknown *x* which lies below all phenomena, which is for ever at work on all phenomena," is none other than "The Breath of God; The Spirit who is The Lord and Giver of Life." However, he is careful to point out that this is a metaphorical way of speaking. The core idea is that of a creation which has been endowed with the capacity to develop, and whose developments as much as its original endowments are a testimony to its creator.[30]

Where Jean Baptiste Pierre Antoine de Monet, Chevalier de Lamarck (1744–1829), argued that all organic evolutionary change is governed by a primordial *sentiment intérieure* situated within an overarching teleology provided by

27. For an introduction, see Andrew Collier, *Critical Realism: An Introduction to Roy Bhaskar's Philosophy* (London: Verso, 1994).

28. See the detailed analysis in Alister E. McGrath, *A Scientific Theology*, vol. 2, *Reality* (London: Continuum, 2002). For comment on this approach from within the critical realist community, see Brad Shipway, "The Theological Application of Bhaskar's Stratified Reality: The Scientific Theology of A. E. McGrath," *Journal of Critical Realism* 3 (2004): 191–203.

29. Charles Kingsley, "The Natural Theology of the Future," in *Westminster Sermons* (London: Macmillan, 1874), v–xxxiii.

30. The idea is developed subsequently by other theologians, e.g., Jürgen Moltmann, *God in Creation: An Ecological Doctrine of Creation* (London: SCM Press, 1985), 9: "Through the energies and potentialities of the Spirit, the Creator himself is present in his creation."

an essentially Deistic universal power that orders the universe,[31] Kingsley restated this in terms of the transformative indwelling of the Spirit of God within creation. Deism, for Kingsley, offered only a "chilling dream of a dead universe ungoverned by an absent God"; Darwinism, when rightly interpreted, offered a vision of a living universe constantly improving under the wise direction of its benevolent creator.[32] "Of old it was said by Him without whom nothing is made: 'My Father worketh hitherto, and I work.' Shall we quarrel with Science if she should show how those words are true?"

Augustine of Hippo regularly cited John 5:17 (in which Jesus of Nazareth is reported as saying, "My Father is still working, and I also am working") in much the same way as Kingsley, affirming the continuing presence and activity of God within the natural order.[33] For Augustine, this points to the fundamental coordination of the ideas of creation and providence, in which the term "creation" has the extended meaning of an *original action* and a *continuing process*. This is developed in terms of the embedding or implanting of the primordial *rationes seminales*, followed by their actualization at appropriate moments. Though Augustine holds that the event and process are notionally distinct, the trajectory of divine agency is seen as continuous. Although Kingsley does not seem to explicitly invoke Augustine in developing his ideas,[34] there is clearly intellectual continuity between them.

While there is a healthy debate in progress concerning some of the religious implications of this kind of approach, it is clear that an emergent understanding of reality can be accommodated within a number of theological perspectives.[35] Although Charles Kingsley's 1871 account of the development of natural history is framed more in terms of "resultants" than "emergents,"[36] his framework for

31. For the background to Lamarck, see Phillip R. Sloan, "From Natural Law to Evolutionary Ethics in Enlightenment French Natural History," in *Biology and the Foundation of Ethics*, ed. Jane Maienschein and Michael Ruse (Cambridge: Cambridge University Press, 1999), 52–83.

32. To accept an emergentist account of things does not entail committing oneself to an understanding of God's engagement with the world or of the nature of the evolutionary process similar to that associated with Pierre Teilhard de Chardin. I am in sympathy with the account of de Chardin's evolutionary theory offered by David Grumett, especially his insistence that it rests upon Christian cosmological insights derived from patristic theology: David Grumett, "Teilhard de Chardin's Evolutionary Natural Theology," *Zygon* 42 (2007): 519–34. My concerns relate to the scientific basis of some of de Chardin's evolutionary beliefs, which seem highly speculative and divorced from empirical reflection.

33. See, e.g., Augustine, *De Genesi ad litteram* 4.11.21; 5.20.40.

34. Kingsley was generally hostile toward both Augustine and the Latin Christianity of his age, seeing it giving historical and theological support to a renewed Catholicism within England, which he regarded as a political and religious threat to the Church of England. See Leon B. Litvack, "*Callista*, Martyrdom, and the Early Christian Novel in the Victorian Age," *Nineteenth-Century Contexts* 17 (1993): 159–73.

35. See the brief overview of the literature provided in Niels Henrik Gregersen, "Emergence: What Is at Stake for Religious Reflection?" in Clayton and Davies, *Re-Emergence of Emergence*, 279–302.

36. For this distinction in G. H. Lewes's seminal 1877 discussion of the concept of emergence, see Achim Stephan, "Emergence—A Systematic View on Its Historical Facets," in Beckermann, Flohr, and Kim, *Emergence or Reduction?* 25–48, esp. 26–28.

discussing the concept of creation represents a significant move away from the static model of William Paley; Kingsley offers generous conceptual space for the articulation of more-recent, scientifically grounded notions of emergence.

To illustrate the importance of this point, we may reflect on the following question: did God create water? The standard theory of the origins of the universe holds that it began in an exceptionally hot, dense state some 15 billion years ago and transmuted into its present form through a process of expansion and cooling.[37] The formation of water, a chemically simple compound, requires the interaction of hydrogen and oxygen. The formation of atomic hydrogen was impossible in the first phases of the origin of the universe and only became possible during the "plasma era." The origins of oxygen (the third most abundant element in the universe) date from much later, when the formation of stars created the critical mass necessary for the synthesis of heavier elements in their cores.[38] Initially, water existed only in gaseous form; its condensation to form its bulk liquid phase, with its highly distinctive physical properties, came about at a much later stage.[39]

From even this quite brief account of the origins of water in the universe, it is clear that it is a relatively late arrival. Yet it was an inevitable arrival, given the physical processes and laws that determined the evolution of the cosmos. One can indeed speak of God "creating" water, provided this is not understood to mean its instantaneous origination, but the origination of orthogenetic processes that eventually led to its emergence.

EMERGENCE AND THE STRATIFICATION OF REALITY

From the analysis just presented, it can be seen that the related but not identical terms "creation" and "nature" should be understood to involve chronological and hierarchical development, in which more-complex levels of reality emerge over extended periods of time. Although all might be argued to be present, in some embryonic form, at the beginning of the universe, they must be recognized as coming into existence at later stages in its history.

Emergence is thus best understood as characterized by stratified, hierarchical structures, each with its own distinct level of order, descriptive language, and appropriate mode of analysis.[40] This idea is not new. For example, the German philosopher Nicolai Hartmann (1882–1950) argued that we need a critical

---

37. For standard accounts of this approach and its evidential foundations, see Martin J. Rees, *New Perspectives in Astrophysical Cosmology*, 2nd ed. (Cambridge: Cambridge University Press, 2000); V. F. Mukhanov, *Physical Foundations of Cosmology* (Cambridge: Cambridge University Press, 2005).

38. For an introduction to stellar nucleosynthesis of oxygen, see Donald D. Clayton, *Handbook of Isotopes in the Cosmos: Hydrogen to Gallium* (Cambridge: Cambridge University Press, 2003), 84–100.

39. For the details, see Philip Ball, *Life's Matrix: A Biography of Water* (New York: Farrar, Straus & Giroux, 2000).

40. Ellis, "On the Nature of Emergent Reality," 81.

ontology, sensitive to the complex, variegated nature of reality.[41] Hartmann offers a fourfold ascending stratification of reality,[42] as follows:

1. Inorganic being, including the categories of matter, substantiality, and causality.
2. Organic being, including the categories of metabolism, assimilation, and self-reproduction.
3. Mental being (*seeliges Sein*), including the categories of consciousness and pleasure.
4. Spiritual being, including the categories of thought, knowledge, and personality.

This marks a reaction against the prevailing logical positivism of the 1930s. Although Rudolf Carnap had also proposed a hierarchically organized approach to nature, he did not regard this as fundamentally ontological in nature, seeing it instead as an essentially heuristic process of categorization.[43] For Hartmann, reality itself—and not just the human perception of that reality—is multileveled, raising important questions about the appropriate method to be employed in the investigation of each level.

Today most natural scientists have managed to overcome the logical empiricist prejudice, occasionally degenerating into a dogma, which holds that there is one and only one right method for all scientific domains. While the provision of unified explanations of disparate phenomena is still widely prized as a worthy epistemic ideal, assertions of the methodological unity of science have gradually given way to a much more plausible emphasis upon the features which are distinctive of scientific practice in different domains. The idea of the "stratification" of reality thus presents no particular difficulties for the natural sciences and is entirely consonant with its methods and approaches. It is, however, open to a number of different interpretations. For example, in his 1936 essay "Physics and Reality," Albert Einstein wrote of the "stratification of the scientific system."[44] By this, he meant that the human attempt to make sense of the basic data of sense experience was multileveled; theoretical advance, however, could be expected to eliminate some of these layers as redundant.[45] This idea was taken up by Thomas F. Torrance (1914–2007), who regarded it as theologically significant.[46] Others

41. See, e.g., Nicolai Hartmann, *Zum Problem der Realitätsgegebenheit* (Berlin: Pan-Verlagsgesellschaft, 1931); idem, *Zur Grundlegung der Ontologie*, 3rd ed. (Meisenheim am Glan: Anton Hain, 1948).

42. Nicolai Hartmann, *Kleinere Schriften*, 3 vols. (Berlin: de Gruyter, 1955), 1:99–101.

43. Rudolf Carnap, *Der logische Aufbau der Welt* (Hamburg: Felix Meiner Verlag, 1998), 102–7.

44. Albert Einstein, "Physics and Reality," *Journal of the Franklin Institute* 221 (1936): 349–89, esp. 352–54.

45. Mara Beller, "Kant's Impact on Einstein's Thought," in *Einstein: The Formative Years, 1879–1909*, ed. Don Howard and John J. Stachel (Boston: Boston University, 2000), 83–107, esp. 94–96.

46. See the analysis in Tapio Luoma, *Incarnation and Physics: Natural Science in the Theology of Thomas F. Torrance* (Oxford: Oxford University Press, 2002), 117–19.

have held that "stratification" concerns the emergence of levels within reality itself, a notion that is especially important in the social sciences[47] yet also has clear implications for the natural sciences. It helps account, for example, for the quite different ways in which the same scientific object is represented and analyzed in different contexts, such as the quite different attitudes toward electrons in chemistry and physics, which offer their own "levels of explanation" of this entity.[48]

Roald Hoffmann, who won the Nobel Prize for Chemistry in 1981, makes this point in affirming the autonomy of chemistry over physics in certain respects:[49]

> There are concepts in chemistry which are not reducible to physics. Or if they are so reduced, they lose much that is interesting about them. . . . Think of ideas such as aromaticity, acidity and basicity, the concept of a functional group, or a substituent effect. Those constructs have a tendency to wilt at the edges as one tries to define them too closely. They cannot be mathematicized, they cannot be defined unambiguously, but they are of fantastic utility to our science.

This raises the question of whether chemistry and physics are to be understood as ontologically or epistemologically distinct, a debate that has caused interest and not a little confusion in recent years.[50] Yet much of this confusion can be eliminated if the relationship is approached through the notion of stratification, which plays a particularly important role in the form of critical realism developed by Bhaskar.

If it is conceded that ontology determines epistemology—a fundamental principle of Bhaskar's approach—it follows that the distinct characteristics of each emergent level demand its own characteristic mode of engagement and representation. As Bhaskar himself puts this:[51]

---

47. The emergence of "class" as a social construct is an excellent example: see Rosemary Crompton, *Class and Stratification: An Introduction to Current Debates*, 2nd ed. (Cambridge: Polity, 1998), 6–16.

48. Theodore Arabatzis and Kostas Gavroglu, "The Chemists' Electron," *European Journal of Physics* 18 (1997): 150–63. There is useful conceptual background material to such discussions in Mary Jo Nye, "Physics and Chemistry: Commensurate or Incommensurate Sciences?" in *The Invention of Physical Science: Intersections of Mathematics, Theology and Natural Philosophy since the Seventeenth Century*, ed. M. J. Nye, J. L. Richards, and R.H. Stuewer (Dordrecht: Kluwer Academic Publishers, 1992), 205–24.

49. Roald Hoffmann, *The Same and Not the Same* (New York: Columbia University Press, 1995), 20.

50. For a stronger statement of this position, see Olimpia Lombardi and Martín Labarca, "The Ontological Autonomy of the Chemical World: A Response to Needham," *Foundations of Chemistry* 8 (2006): 81–92. For a criticism, see Lee McIntyre, "Emergence and Reduction in Chemistry: Ontological or Epistemological Concepts?" *Synthese* 155 (2006): 337–43.

51. Roy Bhaskar, *The Possibility of Naturalism: A Philosophical Critique of the Contemporary Human Sciences*, 3rd ed. (London: Routledge, 1998), 3. This approach would, I think, bring greater clarity to the issues discussed, e.g., in Robin Le Poidevin, "Missing Elements and Missing Premises: A Combinatorial Argument for the Ontological Reduction of Chemistry," *British Journal for the Philosophy of Science* 56 (2005): 117–34.

> Naturalism holds that it is possible to give an account of science under which the proper and more or less specific methods of both the natural and social sciences can fall. But it does not deny that there are significant differences in these methods, grounded in real differences in their subject-matters and in the relationships in which these sciences stand to them. . . . It is the nature of the object that determines the form of its possible science.

Chemistry and physics can thus be seen as engaging distinct strata of reality, thus requiring distinct modes of engagement and means of representation.[52] Each is distinct; yet there are clearly connections between them. Bhaskar seems to identify at least four strata as follows:[53] psychological sciences, social sciences, biological sciences, molecular sciences. This can easily be expanded to suggest a stratification along the following lines: biology, chemistry, physics. Bhaskar argues that it does not follow that, because level A is rooted in and emergent from level B, it follows that level A is "nothing but" level B. Emergent strata possess features that are "irreducible," features that cannot be conceived solely in terms of lower levels. One cannot "reduce" chemistry to physics, precisely because the chemical stratum possesses characteristics which go beyond those in which it is rooted.

The stratification of reality allows us to affirm that we live in a world that is ontologically unitary, while conceding that our knowledge of it is methodologically diverse.[54] Ontological stratification leads to methodological pluralism. We must therefore recognize that there are multiple legitimate ways of investigating, describing, and explaining any natural process. Different sciences deal with different levels of organization and complexity, so that terms and concepts that may be applicable at one level are not necessarily appropriate at others.

A recognition that each level of reality must be engaged *kata physin*,[55] according to its own distinct identity, is a leading feature of the "scientific theologies" developed by Thomas F. Torrance and myself. This approach stresses that each stratum of reality must be engaged and represented according to its distinct nature.[56] Epistemology is determined by ontology. Each science develops a vocabulary and a working method which is appropriated or adapted to its object

---

52. A similar issue arises in biology, in which the ontological status of a series of entities which are primarily conceived in functional terms, such as the "gene," remains obscure. See Michael Snyder and Mark Gerstein, "Defining Genes in the Genomics Era," *Science* 300 (2003): 258–60. The term "ontology" is increasingly being used in biological circles to refer to specifications of biological entities, and their attributes and relationships in a domain of discourse—in other words, to how to organize a vast body of material in terms of perceived structures and relationships: Daniel L. Rubin, Nigam H. Shah, and Natalya F. Noy, "Biomedical Ontologies: A Functional Perspective," *Briefings in Bioinformatics* 9 (2008): 75–90.

53. As noted by Andrew Collier, *Critical Realism: An Introduction to Roy Bhaskar's Philosophy* (London: Verso, 1994), 45.

54. These points are emphasized in Steven P. R. Rose, *Lifelines: Biology, Freedom, Determinism* (Harmondsworth: Penguin, 1997). See also Steven P. R. Rose, "Précis of Lifelines: Biology, Freedom, Determinism," *Behavioral and Brain Sciences* 22 (1999): 871–921.

55. John Ruskin adopted the pen name "Kata Physin" for a series of articles in which he emphasized the need to respect, preserve, and appreciate things for what they are.

56. See esp. Thomas F. Torrance, *Theological Science* (London: Oxford University Press, 1969); McGrath, *A Scientific Theology*, vol. 2, *Reality*, 268–96.

and is to be determined a posteriori, not a priori. This issue arose during the controversy between Heinrich Scholz and Karl Barth during the early 1930s, with Scholz defending universal scientific criteria, and Barth insisting that each discipline—including theology—developed its own methodologies and criteria as an a posteriori response to its distinct subject matter.[57]

If natural theology represents an evaluation and appreciation of "nature," seen from a Christian perspective, as suggested throughout this work, it must therefore be noted that the character of these evaluations and appreciations will depend upon the level or stratum of nature being engaged. While natural scientists have proposed various strata within nature,[58] it can be seen that these multiple levels can and should, at least theoretically, be embraced by a comprehensive Christian natural theology. The focus of the present study is on a spectrum of approaches to nature, ranging from cosmology through chemistry to evolutionary biology. Yet it is important to point out that, on such a stratified approach to "nature," there is no reason why an engagement with the quest for beauty in human culture, or the human longing for something unattainable, should not also be seen as integral aspects of natural theology.[59] Natural theology is not limited to rational observation and reflection upon the biological or astronomical realms.

From what has been said in the present chapter, it can be seen that there is a case to be made for the concept of creation embracing both primordial actuality and emergent potentiality—an idea expressed, though in a nascent form, by Augustine of Hippo. There is clearly room for responsible theological development of this notion, which might be recommended to avoid some of the more-speculative approaches presently in circulation. This does not, it must be emphasized, involve the distortion or subversion of traditional Christian notions of creation, but is to be seen as their legitimate and necessary expansion.

---

57. See Alister E. McGrath, "Theologie als Mathesis Universalis? Heinrich Scholz, Karl Barth, und der wissenschaftliche Status der christlichen Theologie," *Theologische Zeitschrift* 62 (2007): 44–57.

58. See, e.g., Philip W. Anderson, "More Is Different," *Science* 177 (1972): 393–96; Ellis, "On the Nature of Emergent Reality," 80.

59. Each of these can easily be integrated into a Trinitarian natural theology: see, e.g., Alister E. McGrath, *The Open Secret: A New Vision for Natural Theology* (Oxford: Blackwell, 2008), 262–90. John Macquarrie's "new style" of natural theology can also be argued to point in this direction: see John Macquarrie, *Principles of Christian Theology*, 2nd ed. (London: SCM Press, 1977), 43–53.

Conclusion

This book, like so many others of its kind, has addressed some of the most fundamental questions of human existence: How do we make sense of the world around us? What is our place in the universe? What is the meaning of things? These questions have been debated since human beings began to think, and there is no reason to suppose that any form of closure is in sight or even possible. They remain frustratingly and tantalizingly open, a source of constant irritation to those who demand certainty in all things. The Enlightenment's grand quest for a single unified narrative of reality, which could be expressed in terms of the necessary and universal truths of reason, has faltered under the weight of evidence urged against it. Yet this has done nothing to discourage the quest for the most reliable account of the meaning of life and the place of humanity within the universe. The brash overconfidence of the Enlightenment may have eroded our confidence in the answers it gave to these questions; it has not, however, seen those questions lose their power or allure.

This book has set out an approach to natural theology, the age-old intellectual enterprise of exploring whether the natural world that we observe around us can disclose another realm, traditionally described by using the language of "the transcendent" or "the divine." William Paley advocated an approach to natural

217

theology based on intelligible and beautiful outcomes; the approach I adopted finds a new sense of wonder in the vast, complex processes which brought them about, adding to—not diminishing from—the sense of awe and amazement that arises from encountering and engaging nature. Paley and I both engage in dialogue with the sciences; yet we do so from different perspectives and with a different set of scientific spectacles through which to view the world. Richard Dawkins appears to believe that the case for a natural theology is weakened through recognizing the forces within nature that have led to the world as we know it. Far from it; we now have an additional source of wonder in those processes themselves, and in the "cosmic coincidences" that enabled them to operate in this manner. "We knew of old that God was so wise that He could make all things: but behold, He is so much wiser than even that, that He can make all things make themselves" (Charles Kingsley).[1] Paley's static vision of natural theology requires scientific revision, conceptual expansion, and theological elaboration, which this volume has attempted to provide.

Yet there is another point of difference between the approach adopted in this work and older forms of natural theology. Where some have argued that the existence and at least some of the characteristics of God can be deduced from the natural world, I argue for a more modest and realistic approach, based on the idea of resonance or "empirical fit" between the Christian worldview and what is actually observed. The Christian faith, grounded ultimately in divine self-revelation, illuminates and interprets the natural world; the "Book of Scripture" enables a closer and more fruitful reading of the "Book of Nature." Abduction, not deduction, is as characteristic of natural theology as it is of the natural sciences. The capacity of the Christian vision of reality to illuminate and explain what is observed is to be regarded as important in its own right, as well as constituting an indirect confirmation of its own veracity, in a manner analogous to "self-evidencing truths."[2]

To make this point is not to imply that Christianity is simply a way of understanding things. I have taken some care to point out that a fundamental theme of the Christian gospel is the transformation of humanity, traditionally and rightly articulated in terms of atonement and salvation. Yet part of that transformation is intellectual: the Christian faith gives rise to a renewal of the mind (Romans 12:1–2), which inevitably leads to seeing things in a new way. Augustine's view that salvation entails the "healing of the eyes of the heart" is an important statement of this point. To extend Augustine's imagery further, natural theology embraces both the healing of our spiritual vision and what we subsequently perceive in nature. It designates both the process of the believing engage-

1. Charles Kingsley, "The Natural Theology of the Future," in *Westminster Sermons* (London: Macmillan, 1874), v–xxxiii.
2. For this concept, see Carl G. Hempel, *Aspects of Scientific Explanation* (New York: Free Press, 1965), 370–74. This should not be confused with the superficially similar notion of "self-evident truths." This does not negate the importance of seeking external reasons for believing Christianity to be true, as pointed out by W. P. Paterson (1860–1939), in his 1905 Baird Lecture at Glasgow: W. P. Paterson, *The Rule of Faith*, 2nd ed. (London: Hodder & Stoughton, 1912), 7–9.

ment with nature and the understanding of nature which results. The approach here adopted thus represents rather more than a theology of nature: it enfolds both this process of assessment and engagement, and also its outcome.

Nor does this approach imply that natural theology is to be understood primarily as a sense-making activity. It is clearly far richer and deeper than this, extending to the aesthetic appreciation of the natural world and the moral inhabitation of its possibilities.[3] The central image of "seeing" embraces the notions of interpretation, appreciation, and principled action, since the way in which we "see" an object influences our attitudes toward it. Natural theology is about a theologically grounded quest for truth, beauty, and goodness within nature. It is my firm intention to explore the aesthetic and ethical aspects of nature in greater detail in further volumes. The present volume focuses on the sense-making aspects of natural theology, not in order to limit this enterprise to an appeal to reason, but in order to enable a more focused, detailed, and extended engagement with the sense-making dynamics of faith than would otherwise be possible.

Christian theology certainly makes possible a mapping of conceptual space, allowing the apparent ambiguities and riddles of experience to be accommodated within its overall vision of the nature of reality. Iris Murdoch (1919–99) knew of "the calming, whole-making tendencies of human thought," which, while respecting the singularities of experience and observation, is nonetheless able to transcend these particularities through generating a comprehensive vision of the world as a whole.[4] Similarly, the great American psychologist William James (1842–1910) spoke of the manner in which infants experience the world as being "one great blooming, buzzing confusion."[5] The intellectual, aesthetic, and moral ambiguity of the world often present a similar theological challenge, raising the question of how the noise of the world might be interpreted as a tune. The Christian faith, it is argued, offers a unitary and unifying vision of reality, which allows sense to be made of the bewildering complexity and apparent epistemic anarchy of the natural order. An authentically Christian theology provides us with a conceptual net to throw over our experience of the world, allowing us to make sense of its unity and live with its seeming contradictions.

Where others have argued that a natural theology offers a causal explanation of the natural order, I take the view that its distinct characteristics are better described in terms of "explanatory unification." Since the basic elements of this approach have been set out in my earlier book *The Open Secret* (2008) and the first part of the present book, I shall not repeat them in bringing this work to a close. The essential point is that natural theology is a way of "seeing" the natural world,

3. On which see Alister E. McGrath, *The Open Secret: A New Vision for Natural Theology* (Oxford: Blackwell, 2008), 221–31, 261–313.

4. Iris Murdoch, *Metaphysics as a Guide to Morals* (London: Penguin, 1992), 7. On the importance of respecting such singularities, see Alister E. McGrath, *A Scientific Theology*, vol. 3, *Theory* (London: Continuum, 2003), 34–43.

5. William James, *The Principles of Psychology* (Cambridge, MA: Harvard University Press, 1981), 462.

a seeing that arises from within the Christian tradition, deriving both its foundations and coherence from a Trinitarian ontology—and that this way of seeing things resonates strongly with our observation and experience of the world.

Yet recognition of an evangelical capacity to explain leads on to something much more significant: the capacity to confer meaning. And here we encounter one of the most distinctive and important aspects of the Christian faith: the throwing of a net of meaning over the raw data of experience. The gospel, we must remind ourselves, is not primarily an explanatory account of cosmic or human origins. Its essence lies in its conferral of *meaning*, expressed in such notions as purpose, value, significance, and agency.[6] The arguments set out in this book confirm the explanatory potential of faith, which needs to be converted into confidence in its related capacity to endow life with meaning. Christianity can never rest content with an Epicurean *dum vivimus vivamus* (let us live while we live = let us enjoy life); it speaks instead of transformation of that existence.

Yet our concern in this volume has been primarily with the explanatory potential of the Christian faith for an encounter with nature. The great English natural philosopher William Whewell (1794–1866) used a rich visual image to communicate the capacity of a good theory to make sense of, and weave together, observations. "The facts are known but they are insulated and unconnected. . . . The pearls are there but they will not hang together until some one provides the string."[7] The "pearls" are the observations, and the "string" is a grand vision of reality, a worldview, that *connects* and *unifies* the data. A grand theory, Whewell asserted, allows the "colligation of facts," establishing a new system of relations with each other, unifying what might have otherwise been considered to be disconnected and isolated observations.

Continuing with this imagery, this book can be said to be about identifying pearls and searching for the best string on which to thread them. The pearls are the anthropic phenomena that we have been exploring in the second part of the work; the string is the Trinitarian vision of reality that is characteristic of classical Christianity. Both the string and the pearls are of considerable interest in their own right; yet the manner of their "colligation" is perhaps even more interesting. It is hoped that the explorations set out in this book will stimulate further interest in the future of natural theology, the explanatory dimensions of Trinitarianism, and the significance of anthropic phenomena. I have sought to avoid the excesses of those theist enthusiasts who fix upon fine-tuning as certain evidence for the existence of God on the one hand, and their atheist counterparts on the other, who often seek refuge in the notion of a multiverse simply to avoid the theistic implications of the phenomena we have been surveying.[8]

6. Roy Baumeister, *Meanings of Life* (New York: Guilford Press, 1991), 29–57.
7. William Whewell, *Philosophy of the Inductive Sciences*, 2 vols. (London: John W. Parker, 1847), 2:36. Whewell's theory of induction is open to criticism: see, e.g., Laura J. Snyder, "The Mill-Whewell Debate: Much Ado about Induction," *Perspectives on Science* 5 (1997): 159–98.
8. See the comments of John Cornwell, *Darwin's Angel: A Seraphic Riposte to "The God Delusion"* (London: Profile Books, 2007), 53–58.

This book has focused on examples of fine-tuning in nature, using them as examples of "surprising facts" (Charles Peirce) which require explanation, or potential "clues to the meaning of the universe" (C. S. Lewis). These are the pearls that need to be strung together in such a way that they make the most sense. A Christian vision of reality offers us a way of seeing things in which these observations are no longer surprising; if anything, they are to be expected. In particular, I have noted how Augustine of Hippo's theology of creation offers an excellent theological platform from which to explore two of the most significant developments in the natural sciences in the last two hundred years: contemporary understandings of the origins of the universe, often referred to as the "big bang"; and our understanding of the development of life on Earth, particularly the process which is often still referred to as "Darwinian" evolution.

In this volume, I have made use of Charles Peirce's concept of abduction to illuminate the nature of both scientific and religious explanation. For Peirce, religion gives expression to a universal need to acknowledge and respond to an experienced sense of cosmic order and human "creatureliness." Peirce argued that musing on the beauty and order of the natural world was the basis of a "neglected argument" for the existence of God.[9] "In the Pure Play of Musement the idea of God's reality will be sooner or later to be found an attractive fancy," Peirce argued, since it supplied both an "ideal of life" and a "thoroughly satisfactory explanation" of the natural environment in which we find ourselves.[10] The extent to which the musings and reflections presented in this volume constitute an argument for God's existence, even in Peirce's subtle sense of the term, must be left to others to decide.

Yet there is little doubt that this discussion is set to continue, with the potential to illuminate and enrich both science and religion, and to further the human quest for meaning in this often puzzling and bewildering universe. A growing willingness on the part of empirical, nondogmatic scientists[11] to consider the metaphysical and religious implications of the scientific enterprise has created new and exciting conceptual possibilities. This is matched by an increasing awareness within the scientific community that the "scientific view of the world is hopelessly incomplete" and that there are "matters of value, meaning, and purpose that are outside science's scope."[12] Both Christian theology and the natural sciences have exaggerated their capacities in the past, doubtless with the best of intentions. The time is now right for both disciplines to acknowledge their

9. See John Haldane, "Philosophy, the Restless Heart, and the Meaning of Theism," *Ratio* 19 (2006): 421–40.

10. Charles Sanders Peirce, *Collected Papers of Charles Sanders Peirce*, ed. Charles Hartshorne and Paul Weiss, 8 vols. (Cambridge, MA: Harvard University Press, 1960), 6:465.

11. This position may be contrasted with the nonempirical and surprisingly dogmatic viewpoint often referred to as "scientism": see Mikael Stenmark, *Scientism: Science, Ethics and Religion* (Aldershot: Ashgate, 2001).

12. Francisco J. Ayala, "Intelligent Design: The Original Version," *Theology and Science* 1 (2003): 9–32, esp. 30. For similar reflections, see Peter B. Medawar, *The Limits of Science* (Oxford: Oxford University Press, 1985).

limitations and open the way to new possibilities of collaboration, dialogue, and sheer intellectual delight.

Natural theology, it seems, is back in fashion. This book offers a modest contribution to its further development. Yet there is much more that needs to be done to continue its rehabilitation and extend its horizons.

Bibliography

Abbott, Barbara. "Water = H_2O." *Mind* 108 (1999): 145–48.

Aczel, Amir D. *God's Equation: Einstein, Relativity and the Expanding Universe*. London: Piatkus, 2000.

Adam, Matthias. *Theoriebeladenheit und Objektivität: Zur Rolle von Beobachtungen in den Naturwissenschafte*. Frankfurt am Main: Ontos Verlag, 2002.

Aerts, Dirk. "Classical Theories and Nonclassical Theories as Special Cases of a More General Theory." *Journal of Mathematical Physics* 24 (1983): 2441–53.

Aguirre, Anthony. "Making Predictions in a Multiverse." In *Universe or Multiverse?* edited by Bernard Carr, 367–86. Cambridge: Cambridge University Press, 2007.

Albrecht, Michael von, and Gareth L. Schmeling. *A History of Roman Literature: From Livius Andronicus to Boethius; With Special Regard to Its Influence on World Literature*. 2 vols. New York: E. J. Brill, 1996.

Aldersey-Williams, Hugh. *The Most Beautiful Molecule: The Discovery of the Buckyball*. New York: Wiley, 1995.

Aliseda, Atocha. *Abductive Reasoning: Logical Investigations into Discovery and Explanation*. Dordrecht: Springer-Verlag, 2006.

———. "Logics in Scientific Discovery." *Foundations of Science* 9 (2004): 339–63.

Allori, Valia, Detlef Dürr, Shelly Goldstein, and Nino Zanghí. "Seven Steps towards the Classical World." *Journal of Optics B* 4 (2002): S482–88.

Alon, Uri. *An Introduction to Systems Biology: Design Principles of Biological Circuits*. Boca Raton, FL: Chapman & Hall / CRC, 2007.

Alston, William P. *Perceiving God: The Epistemology of Religious Experience*. Ithaca, NY: Cornell University Press, 1991.

Altmann, Alexander. "'Homo Imago Dei' in Jewish and Christian Theology." *Journal of Religion* 48 (1968): 235–59.

Alvarez, L. W., W. Alvarez, F. Asaro, and H. V. Michel. "Extraterrestrial cause for the Cretaceous-Tertiary Extinction." *Science* 208 (1980): 1095–1108.

Anatolios, Khaled E. *Athanasius*. London: Routledge, 2004.

Anders, Timothy. *The Evolution of Evil: An Inquiry into the Ultimate Origins of Human Suffering*. Chicago: Open Court, 1994.

Anderson, Bernhard W. *From Creation to New Creation: Old Testament Perspectives*. Minneapolis: Fortress, 1994.

Anderson, Douglas R. "An American Argument for Belief in the Reality of God." *Philosophy of Religion* 26 (1989): 109–18.
———. "The Esthetic Attitude of Abduction." *Semiotica* 153 (2005): 9–22.
———. "The Evolution of Peirce's Concept of Abduction." *Transactions of the Charles S. Peirce Society* 22 (1986): 145–64.
Andresen, Carl. *Logos und Nomos: Die Polemik des Kelsos wider des Christentums*. Berlin: de Gruyter, 1955.
Anstey, Peter R. "Boyle on Seminal Principles." *Studies in History and Philosophy of Science C* 33 (2002): 597–630.
Arabatzis, Theodore, and Kostas Gavroglu. "The Chemists' Electron." *European Journal of Physics* 18 (1997): 150–63.
Arbib, Michael A., and Mary B. Hesse. *The Construction of Reality*. Cambridge: Cambridge University Press, 1986.
Arnould, Marcel, Stephane Goriely, and Kohji Takahashi. "The R-Process of Stellar Nucleosynthesis: Astrophysics and Nuclear Physics Achievements and Mysteries." *Physics Reports* 450 (2007): 97–213.
Atran, Scott, and Ara Norenzayan. "Religion's Evolutionary Landscape: Counterintuition, Commitment, Compassion, Communion." *Behavioral and Brain Sciences* 27 (2004): 713–70.
Avery, Oswald, Colin MacLeod, and Maclyn McCarty. "Studies on the Chemical Nature of the Substance Inducing Transformation of Pneumococcal Types: Induction of Transformation by a Deoxyribonucleic Acid Fraction Isolated from *Pneumococcus* Type III." *Journal of Experimental Medicine* 79 (1944): 137–58.
Ayala, Francisco J. "Intelligent Design: The Original Version." *Theology and Science* 1 (2003): 9–32.
———. "Teleological Explanations in Evolutionary Biology." *Philosophy of Science* 37 (1970): 1–15.
Ayres, Lewis. *Nicaea and Its Legacy: An Approach to Fourth-Century Trinitarian Theology*. New York: Oxford University Press, 2004.
Babcock, William S. "A Changing of the Christian God: The Doctrine of the Trinity in the Seventeenth Century." *Interpretation* 45 (1991): 133–46.
Bachmann, Pascale Angelica, Pier Luigi Luisi, and Jacques Lang. "Autocatalytic Self-Replicating Micelles as Models for Prebiotic Structures." *Nature* 357 (1992): 57–59.
Baggini, Julian. *What's It All About? Philosophy and the Meaning of Life*. Oxford: Oxford University Press, 2005.
Bains, William. "Many Chemistries Could Be Used to Build Living Systems." *Astrobiology* 4 (2004): 137–67.
Ball, Philip. *Life's Matrix: A Biography of Water*. New York: Farrar, Straus, & Giroux, 2000.
Banavar, Jayanth R., Trinh Xuan Hoang, John H. Maddocks, Amos Maritan, Chiara Poletto, Andrzej Stasiak, and Antonio Trovato. "Structural Motifs of Biomolecules." *Proceedings of the National Academy of Sciences* 104 (2007): 17283–86.
Banner, Michael C. *The Justification of Science and the Rationality of Religious Belief*. Oxford and New York: Oxford University Press, 1990.
Baran, Enrique J. "Model Studies Related to Vanadium Biochemistry: Recent Advances and Perspectives." *Journal of the Brazilian Chemical Society* 14 (2003): 878–88.
Barham, James. "The Emergence of Biological Value." In *Debating Design: From Darwin to DNA*, edited by William A. Dembski and Michael Ruse, 210–26. New York: Cambridge University Press, 2004.
Barnes, Eric. "Explanatory Unification and the Problem of Asymmetry." *Philosophy of Science* 59 (1992): 558–71.
———. "Inference to the Loveliest Explanation." *Synthese* 103 (1995): 251–77.
Barnes, Michel René. "De Régnon Reconsidered." *Augustinian Studies* 26 (1995): 51–79.

———. "Rereading Augustine's Theology of the Trinity." In *The Trinity*, edited by Stephen T. Davis, Daniel Kendall, and Gerald O'Collins, 145–76. Oxford: Oxford University Press, 2001.

Barr, James. "The Image of God in the Book of Genesis: A Study of Terminology." *Bulletin of the John Rylands Library* 51 (1968): 11–26.

Barrett, Justin L. *Why Would Anyone Believe in God?* Lanham, MD: AltaMira Press, 2004.

Barrow, John D. *Between Inner Space and Outer Space: Essays on Science, Art, and Philosophy*. Oxford: Oxford University Press, 2000.

———. *The Constants of Nature: From Alpha to Omega*. London: Vintage, 2003.

———. *Theories of Everything: The Quest for Ultimate Explanation*. London: Vintage, 1992.

Barrow, John D., and Frank J. Tipler. *The Anthropic Cosmological Principle*. Oxford: Oxford University Press, 1986.

Bartelborth, Thomas. "Explanatory Unification." *Synthese* 130 (2002): 91–108.

———. "Verstehen und Kohärenz: Ein Beitrag zur Methodologie der Sozialwissenschaften." *Analyse and Kritik* 21 (1999): 97–116.

Barth, Karl. *Die christliche Theologie im Entwurf*. Munich: Kaiser Verlag, 1927.

———. *Der Römerbrief*. 2nd ed. Munich: Kaiser Verlag, 1922.

———. "Schicksal und Idee in Theologie." In *Theologische Frage und Antworten*, 54–92. Zurich: Evangelischer Verlag, 1957.

Bassham, James A. "Mapping the Carbon Reduction Cycle: A Personal Retrospective." *Photosynthesis Research* 76 (2003): 25–52.

Batterman, Robert W. *The Devil in the Details: Asymptotic Reasoning in Explanation, Reduction, and Emergence*. Oxford: Oxford University Press, 2002.

Battimelli, Giovanni. "Dreams of a Final Theory: The Failed Electromagnetic Unification and the Origins of Relativity." *European Journal of Physics* 26 (2005): S111–S116.

Baumeister, Roy. *Meanings of Life*. New York: Guilford Press, 1991.

Beatty, John. "Dobzhansky and Drift: Facts, Values, and Chance in Evolutionary Biology." In *The Probabilistic Revolution*, edited by L. Krüger, L. J. Daston, M. Heidelberger, G. Gigerenzer, and M. S. Morgan, 271–311. Cambridge, MA: MIT Press, 1987.

———. "Replaying Life's Tape." *Journal of Philosophy* 103 (2006): 336–62.

———. "Teleology and the Relationship of Biology to the Physical Sciences in the Nineteenth and Twentieth Centuries." In *Newton's Legacy: The Origins and Influence of Newtonian Science*, edited by Frank Durham and Robert D. Purrington, 113–44. New York: Columbia University Press, 1990.

Bechtel, William, and Robert C. Richardson. "Emergent Phenomena and Complex Systems." In *Emergence or Reduction?* edited by Ansgar Beckermann, Hans Flohr, and Jaegwon Kim, 257–88. Berlin: de Gruyter, 1992.

Behr, John. *Asceticism and Anthropology in Irenaeus and Clement*. Oxford: Oxford University Press, 2000.

Behrens, Georg. "Peirce's "Third Argument" for the Reality of God and Its Relation to Scientific Inquiry." *Journal of Religion* 75 (1995): 200–218.

Beiser, Frederick C. *The Sovereignty of Reason: The Defense of Rationality in the Early English Enlightenment*. Princeton, NJ: Princeton University Press, 1996.

Benner, Steven A., and Andrew D. Ellington. "Interpreting the Behavior of Enzymes: Purpose or Pedigree?" *Critical Reviews in Biochemistry and Molecular Biology* 23 (1988): 369–426.

Benner, Steven A., and Daniel Hutter. "Phosphates, DNA, and the Search for Nonterrean Life: A Second Generation Model for Genetic Molecules." *Bioinorganic Chemistry* 30 (2002): 62–80.

Benner, Steven A., Alonso Ricardo, and Matthew A. Carrigan. "Is There a Common Chemical Model for Life in the Universe?" *Current Opinion in Chemical Biology* 8 (2004): 672–89.

Benner, Steven A., Slim O. Sassi, and Eric A. Gaucher. "Molecular Paleoscience: Systems Biology from the Past." *Advances in Enzymology and Related Areas of Molecular Biology* 75 (2007): 1–132.

Benton, Michael J. *When Life Nearly Died: The Greatest Mass Extinction of All Time.* London: Thames & Hudson, 2003.

Bhalla, Upinder S., and Ravi Iyengar. "Emergent Properties of Biological Signaling Pathways." *Science* 283 (1999): 381–87.

Bhattacharji, S., N. Chatterjee, J. M. Wampler, P. N. Nayak, and S. S. Deshnukh. "Indian Intraplate and Continental Margin Rifting, Lithospheric Extension, and Mantle Upwelling in Deccan Flood Basalt Volcanism near the K/T Boundary: Evidence from Mafic Dike Swarms." *Journal of Petrology* 104 (1996): 379–98.

Bienert, Wolfgang A. "Zur Logos-Christologie des Athanasius von Alexandrien in *Contra gentes* und *De incarnatione*." In *Papers Presented to the Tenth International Conference on Patristic Studies*, vol. 2, edited by E. A. Livingstone, 402–19. Studia patristica 21. Leuven: Peeters, 1989.

Bird, Alexander. "Inference to the Only Explanation." *Philosophy and Phenomenological Research* 74 (2007): 424–32.

Blachford, Alistair, and Aneil F. Agrawal. "Assortative Mating for Fitness and the Evolution of Recombination." *Evolution: International Journal of Organic Evolution* 60 (2006): 1337–43.

Bloom, Jesse D., Sy T. Labthavikul, Christopher R. Otey, and Frances H. Arnold. "Protein Stability Promotes Evolvability." *Proceedings of the National Academy of Sciences* 103 (2006): 5869–74.

Boland, Vivian. *Ideas in God according to Saint Thomas Aquinas: Sources and Synthesis.* Leiden: Brill, 1996.

Bonanno, Alfio, and Martin Reuter. "Cosmology of the Planck Era from a Renormalization Group for Quantum Gravity." *Physics Review D* 65 (2002): 043508 (20 pages).

Bondi, Hermann. *Cosmology.* 2nd ed. London: Cambridge University Press, 1960.

Bonner, John T. *The Evolution of Complexity by Means of Natural Selection.* Princeton, NJ: Princeton University Press, 1988.

Borovik, A. J. "Characteristics of Metals in Biological Systems." In *Heavy Metal Tolerance in Plants: Evolutionary Aspects*, edited by A. Jonathan Shaw, 3–6. Boca Raton, FL: CRC Press, 1990.

Borrello, Mark E. "The Rise, Fall and Resurrection of Group Selection." *Endeavour* 29 (2005): 43–47.

Bostrom, Nick. *Anthropic Bias: Observation Selection Effects in Science and Philosophy.* New York: Routledge, 2002.

———. "Self-Locating Belief in Big Worlds: Cosmology's Missing Link to Observation." *Journal of Philosophy* 99 (2002): 607–23.

Bowler, Peter J. "Darwinism and the Argument from Design: Suggestions for a Reevaluation." *Journal of the History of Biology* 10 (1977): 29–43.

———. *The Mendelian Revolution: The Emergence of Hereditarian Concepts in Modern Science and Society.* London: Athlone Press, 1989.

Boyer, Pascal. *The Naturalness of Religious Ideas: A Cognitive Theory of Religion.* Berkeley: University of California Press, 1994.

Boyer, Pascal, and Charles Ramble. "Cognitive Templates for Religious Concepts: Cross-Cultural Evidence for Recall of Counter-Intuitive Representations." *Cognitive Science* 25 (2001): 535–64.

Braaten, Laurie J. "All Creation Groans: Romans 8:22 in Light of the Biblical Sources." *Horizons in Biblical Theology* 28 (2006): 131–59.

Brack, André E. "La chimie de l'origine de la vie." In *Les traces du vivant*, edited by M. Gargaud, D. Despois, J.-P. Parisot, and J. Reisse, 61–81. Pessac: Presses Universitaires de Bordeaux, 2003.

Breitenbach, Angela. "Mechanical Explanation of Nature and Its Limits in Kant's *Critique of Judgment*." *Studies in History and Philosophy of Science* 37 (2006): 694–711.

Brewster, David. *Life of Sir Isaac Newton*. London: Tegg, 1875.

Brockliss, L. W. B. "Aristotle, Descartes and the New Science: Natural Philosophy at the University of Paris, 1600–1740." *Annals of Science* 38 (1981): 33–69.

Brogaard, Berit. "Peirce on Abduction and Rational Control." *Transactions of the Charles S. Peirce Society* 35 (1999): 129–55.

Brooke, John Hedley. "Darwin and Victorian Christianity." In *The Cambridge Companion to Darwin*, edited by Jonathan Hodge and Gregory Radick, 192–213. Cambridge: Cambridge University Press, 2003.

————. "Like Minds: The God of Hugh Miller." In *Hugh Miller and the Controversies of Victorian Science*, edited by Michael Shortland, 171–86. Oxford: Clarendon Press, 1996.

————. *Science and Religion: Some Historical Perspectives*. Cambridge: Cambridge University Press, 1991.

————. "Science and the Fortunes of Natural Theology: Some Historical Perspectives." *Zygon* 24 (1989): 3–22.

Brooke, John Hedley, and Geoffrey Cantor. *Reconstructing Nature: The Engagement of Science and Religion*. New York: Oxford University Press, 2000.

Brooke, John Hedley, and Ian Maclean, eds. *Heterodoxy in Early Modern Science and Religion*. Oxford: Oxford University Press, 2005.

Brookfield, J. F. Y. "Evolution: The Evolvability Enigma." *Current Biology* 11 (2001): R106–R108.

Brunner, Emil. "Natur und Gnade: Zum Gespräch mit Karl Barth." In *Ein offenes Wort*, vol. 1, *Vorträge und Aufsätze 1917–1934*, edited by Rudolf Wehrli, 333–66. Zurich: Theologischer Verlag, 1981.

Burbidge, E. Margaret, Geoffrey R. Burbidge, William A. Fowler, and Fred Hoyle. "Synthesis of the Elements in Stars." *Review of Modern Physics* 29 (1957): 547–650.

Burchfield, Joe D. *Lord Kelvin and the Age of the Earth*. Chicago: University of Chicago Press, 1990.

Burns, Robert M. "Richard Swinburne on Simplicity in Natural Science." *Heythrop Journal* 40 (1999): 184–206.

Butts, Robert E. "Teleology and Scientific Method in Kant's Critique of Judgment." *Nous* 24 (1990): 1–16.

Byrne, Peter A. *Natural Religion and the Nature of Religion: The Legacy of Deism*. London: Routledge, 1989.

Byrne, Ruth M. J. *The Rational Imagination: How People Create Alternatives to Reality*. Cambridge, MA: MIT Press, 2007.

Caetano-Anollés, Gustavo, Hee Shin Kim, and Jay E. Mittenthal. "The Origin of Modern Metabolic Networks Inferred from Phylogenomic Analysis of Protein Architecture." *Proceedings of the National Academy of Sciences* 104 (2007): 9358–63.

Cairns-Smith, Graham. "Fine-Tuning in Living Systems: Early Evolution and the Unity of Biochemistry." *International Journal of Astrobiology* 2 (2003): 87–90.

————. *Genetic Takeover and the Mineral Origins of Life*. Cambridge: Cambridge University Press, 1982.

————. *Seven Clues to the Origin of Life*. Cambridge: Cambridge University Press, 1985.

Calhoun, Laurie. "The Underdetermination of Theory by Data, 'Inference to the Best Explanation,' and the Impotence of Argumentation." *Philosophical Forum* 27 (1996): 146–60.

Cameron, D. R., T. M. Lenton, A. J. Ridgwell, J. G. Shepherd, R. Marsh, and A. Yool. "A Factorial Analysis of the Marine Carbon Cycle Controls on Atmospheric CO_2." *Global Biogeochemical Cycles* 19 (2005): 1–12.

Campbell, Mary K., and Shawn O. Farrell. *Biochemistry*. 5th ed. Pacific Grove, CA: Brooks / Cole, 2006.

Carnap, Rudolf. *Der logische Aufbau der Welt*. Hamburg: Felix Meiner Verlag, 1998.
———. "The Elimination of Metaphysics through Logical Analysis." In *Logical Positivism*, edited by A. J. Ayer, 60–81. New York: Free Press, 1959.
Carr, Bernard. "Introduction and Overview." In *Universe or Multiverse?* edited by Bernard Carr, 3–28. Cambridge: Cambridge University Press, 2007.
———, ed. *Universe or Multiverse?* Cambridge: Cambridge University Press, 2007.
Carr, Bernard J., and Martin J. Rees. "Fine-Tuning in Living Systems." *International Journal of Astrobiology* 3 (2003): 79–86.
Carroll, William E. "At the Mercy of Chance? Evolution and the Catholic Tradition." *Revue des questions scientifiques* 177 (2006): 179–204.
———. "Creation, Evolution, and Thomas Aquinas." *Revue des questions scientifiques* 171 (2000): 319–47.
———. "Divine Agency, Contemporary Physics, and the Autonomy of Nature." *Heythrop Journal* 49 (2008): 1–21.
Carter, Brandon. "The Anthropic Principle and Its Implications for Biological Evolution." *Philosophical Transactions of the Royal Society* A 310 (1983): 347–63.
———. "Large Number Coincidences and the Anthropic Principle." In *Confrontation of Cosmological Theories with Observational Data*, edited by M. S. Longair, 291–98. Boston: Reidel, 1974.
Cascella, Michele, Alessandra Magistrato, Ivano Tavernelli, Paolo Carloni, and Ursula Rothlisberger. "Role of Protein Frame and Solvent for the Redox Properties of Azurin from Pseudomonas Aeruginosa." *Proceedings of the National Academy of Sciences* 103 (2006): 19641–46.
Catling, D. C., C. R. Glein, K. J. Zahnle, and C. P. McKay. "Why O_2 Is Required by Complex Life on Habitable Planets and the Concept of Planetary 'Oxygenation Time.'" *Astrobiology* 5 (2005): 415–38.
Cavalcanti, André R. O., and Laura F. Landweber. "Genetic Code: What Nature Missed." *Current Biology* 13 (2003): R884–R885.
Challis, Gregory L., and David A. Hopwood. "Synergy and Contingency as Driving Forces for the Evolution of Multiple Secondary Metabolite Production by *Streptomyces* Species." *Proceedings of the National Academy of Sciences* 100 (2003): 14555–61.
Chaplin, Martin F. "Water: Its Importance to Life." *Biochemistry and Molecular Biology Education* 29 (2001): 54–59.
Chauviré, Christiane. "Peirce, Popper, Abduction, and the Idea of Logic of Discovery." *Semiotica* 153 (2005): 209–21.
Chiti, Fabrizio, Niccolò Taddei, Elisa Giannoni, Nico A. J. van Nuland, Giampietro Ramponi, and Christopher M. Dobson. "Development of Enzymatic Activity during Protein Folding." *Journal of Biological Chemistry* 274 (1999): 20151–58.
Cirkovic, Milan M. "Ancient Origins of a Modern Anthropic Cosmological Argument." *Astronomical and Astrophysical Transactions* 22 (2003): 879–86.
Clark, Mary E. *In Search of Human Nature*. London: Routledge, 2002.
Clay, Jenny Strauss. *The Politics of Olympus: Form and Meaning in the Major Homeric Hymns*. Princeton, NJ: Princeton University Press, 1989.
Clayton, Donald D. *Handbook of Isotopes in the Cosmos: Hydrogen to Gallium*. Cambridge: Cambridge University Press, 2003.
———. *Principles of Stellar Evolution and Nucleosynthesis*. New York: McGraw-Hill, 1968.
Clayton, Philip. "Conceptual Foundations of Emergence Theory." In *The Re-Emergence of Emergence: The Emergentist Hypothesis from Science to Religion*, edited by Philip Clayton and Paul Davies, 1–31. Oxford: Oxford University Press, 2006.
———. *Explanation from Physics to Theology: An Essay in Rationality and Religion*. New Haven, CT: Yale University Press, 1989.
———. *Das Gottesproblem: Gott und Unendlichkeit in der neuzeitlichen Philosophie*. Paderborn: Schöningh Verlag, 1996.

———. "Inference to the Best Explanation." *Zygon* 32 (1997): 377–91.

———. *Mind and Emergence: From Quantum to Consciousness*. Oxford: Oxford University Press, 2004.

———. "Toward a Constructive Christian Theology of Emergence." In *Evolution and Emergence: Systems, Organisms, Persons*, edited by Nancey Murphy and William R. Stoeger, 315–43. Oxford: Oxford University Press, 2007.

Cleland, Carol E., and Christopher F. Chyba. "Defining 'Life.'" *Origins of Life and Evolution of the Biosphere* 32 (2002): 387–93.

Collier, Andrew. *Critical Realism: An Introduction to Roy Bhaskar's Philosophy*. London: Verso, 1994.

Collins, C. B., and Stephen Hawking. "Why Is the Universe Isotropic?" *Astrophysical Journal Letters* 180 (1973): 317–34.

Collins, Robin. "The Multiverse Hypothesis: A Theistic Perspective." In *Universe or Multiverse?* edited by Bernard Carr, 459–80. Cambridge: Cambridge University Press, 2007.

———. "A Scientific Argument for the Existence of God: The Fine-Tuning Design Argument." In *Reason for the Hope Within*, edited by Michael J. Murray, 47–75. Grand Rapids: Eerdmans, 1999.

Conover, S. "St. Bonaventure's Theory of the *Rationes Seminales*." *Round Table Franciscan Research* 12 (1947): 169–76.

Conway Morris, Simon. *The Crucible of Creation: The Burgess Shale and the Rise of Animals*. Oxford: Oxford University Press, 1998.

———. "Darwin's Compass: How Evolution Discovers the Song of Creation." *Science and Christian Belief* 18 (2006): 5–22.

———. *Life's Solution: Inevitable Humans in a Lonely Universe*. Cambridge: Cambridge University Press, 2003.

———. "A Palaeontological Perspective." *Current Opinion in Genetics and Development* 4 (1994): 802–9.

Corey, Michael A. *The God Hypothesis: Discovering Design in Our "Just Right" Goldilocks Universe*. Lanham, MD: Rowman & Littlefield, 2001.

Cornell, John F. "God's Magnificent Law: The Bad Influence of Theistic Metaphysics on Darwin's Estimation of Natural Selection." *Journal of the History of Biology* 20 (1987): 381–412.

Corning, Peter A. *Nature's Magic: Synergy in Evolution and the Fate of Humankind*. New York: Cambridge University Press, 2003.

Cornwell, John. *Darwin's Angel: A Seraphic Riposte to "The God Delusion."* London: Profile Books, 2007.

Costanzo, Giovanna, Raffaele Saladino, Claudia Crestini, Fabiana Ciciriello, and Ernesto Di Mauro. "Nucleoside Phosphorylation by Phosphate Minerals." *Journal of Biological Chemistry* 282 (2007): 16729–35.

Courtillot, Vincent. *Evolutionary Catastrophes: The Science of Mass Extinction*. Cambridge: Cambridge University Press, 1999.

Cracraft, Joel. "Avian Evolution, Gondwana Biogeography and the Cretaceous-Tertiary Mass Extinction Event." *Proceedings of the Royal Society B* 268 (2001): 459–69.

Craig, William Lane. "Barrow and Tipler on the Anthropic Principle versus Divine Design." *British Journal for Philosophy of Science* 38 (1988): 389–95.

———. *The Cosmological Argument from Plato to Leibniz*. London: Macmillan, 1980.

———. "The Existence of God and the Beginning of the Universe." *Truth: A Journal of Modern Thought* 3 (1991): 85–96.

———. "Timelessness and Creation." *Australasian Journal of Philosophy* 74 (1996): 646–56.

Craig, William Lane, and Quentin Smith. *Theism, Atheism, and Big Bang Cosmology*. Oxford: Clarendon Press, 1993.

Crayn, Darren M., Klaus Winter, and J. Andrew C. Smith. "Multiple Origins of Crassulacean Acid Metabolism and the Epiphytic Habit in the Neotropical Family *Bromeliaceae*." *Proceedings of the National Academy of Sciences* 101 (2004): 3703–8.

Crick, Francis H. C. *Life Itself: Its Origin and Nature*. London: Macdonald, 1982.

Crick, Francis H. C., and James D. Watson. "Molecular Structure of Nucleic Acids: A Structure for Deoxyribose Nucleic Acid." *Nature* 171 (1953): 737–38.

Crompton, Rosemary. *Class and Stratification: An Introduction to Current Debates*. 2nd ed. Cambridge: Polity, 1998.

Cronon, William. *Uncommon Ground: Toward Reinventing Nature*. New York: W. W. Norton, 1995.

Cross, Richard. "The Eternity of the World and the Distinction between Creation and Conservation." *Religious Studies* 42 (2006): 403–16.

Cunningham, David S. "Trinitarian Theology since 1990." *Reviews in Religion and Theology* 4 (1995): 8–16.

Dahm, Ralf. "Friedrich Miescher and the Discovery of DNA." *Developmental Biology* 278 (2005): 274–88.

Danneberg, Lutz. "Peirces Abduktionskonzeption als Entdeckungslogik: Eine philosophiehistorische und rezeptionskritische Untersuchung." *Archiv für Geschichte der Philosophie* 70 (1988): 305–26.

Darwin, Charles. *On the Origin of the Species by Means of Natural Selection*. 2nd ed. London: John Murray, 1860.

———. *On the Origin of the Species by Means of Natural Selection*. 6th ed. London: John Murray, 1872.

Darwin, Francis. "Reminiscences of My Father's Everyday Life." In *Charles Darwin: His Life Told in an Autobiographical Chapter*, edited by Francis Darwin, 66–103. London: John Murray, 1892.

Dau, Holger, Peter Liebisch, and Michael Haumann. "The Manganese Complex of Oxygenic Photosynthesis: Conversion of Five-Coordinated Mn(III) to Six-Coordinated Mn(IV) in the S2–S3 Transition Is Implied by XANES Simulations." *Physica Scripta* T115 (2005): 844–46.

Daugherty, Charles T. "Of Ruskin's Gardens." In *Myth and Symbol: Critical Approaches and Applications*, edited by Northrop Frye and Bernice Slote, 141–51. Lincoln, NE: University of Nebraska, 1963.

Davies, Paul. *The Goldilocks Enigma: Why Is the Universe Just Right for Life?* London: Allen Lane, 2006.

———. "Universes Galore: Where Will It All End?" In *Universe or Multiverse?* edited by Bernard Carr, 487–505. Cambridge: Cambridge University Press, 2007.

Davis, Bernard D. "On the Importance of Being Ionized." *Archives of Biochemistry and Biophysics* 78 (1958): 497–509.

Dawkins, Richard. *The Blind Watchmaker: Why the Evidence of Evolution Reveals a Universe without Design*. New York: W. W. Norton, 1986.

———. *The Selfish Gene*. 2nd ed. Oxford: Oxford University Press, 1989.

Day, John. *God's Conflict with the Dragon: Echoes of a Canaanite Myth in the Old Testament*. Cambridge: Cambridge University Press, 1985.

D'Costa, Gavin. "Revelation, Scripture and Tradition: Some Comments on John Webster's Conception of 'Holy Scripture.'" *International Journal of Systematic Theology* 6 (2004): 337–50.

De Dorlodot, Henry. *Le Darwinisme du point de vue de l'orthodoxie catholique*. Brussels: Vromant, 1921.

De Duve, Christian. *Singularities: Landmarks on the Pathways of Life*. Cambridge: Cambridge University Press, 2005.

De Vinck, José. "Two Aspects of the Theory of the *Rationes Seminales* in the Writings of Bonaventure." In *S. Bonaventura 1274–1974*, vol. 3, *Philosophia*, 307–16. Grottaferrata: Collegio S. Bonaventurae, 1973.

Deacon, Terrence William. *The Symbolic Species: The Co-Evolution of Language and the Human Brain*. New York: W. W. Norton, 1997.

Dear, Peter R. *The Intelligibility of Nature: How Science Makes Sense of the World*. Chicago: University of Chicago Press, 2006.

Decker, Heinz, and Nora Terwilliger. "Cops and Robbers: Putative Evolution of Copper Oxygen-Binding Proteins." *Journal of Experimental Biology* 203 (2000): 1777–82.

DeHart, Paul J. *Beyond the Necessary God: Trinitarian Faith and Philosophy in the Thought of Eberhard Jüngel*. Atlanta: Scholars Press, 1999.

Dell, Katharine J. *The Book of Proverbs in Social and Theological Context*. Cambridge: Cambridge University Press, 2006.

Delsemme, Armand H. "An Argument for the Cometary Origin of the Biosphere." *American Scientist* 89 (2001): 432–42.

Denton, Michael J. *Nature's Destiny: How the Laws of Biology Reveal Purpose in the Universe*. New York: Free Press, 1998.

Deuven, Igor, and Leon Horsten. "Earman on Underdetermination and Empirical Indistinguishability." *Erkenntnis* 49 (1998): 303–20.

Dicke, Robert H. "Dirac's Cosmology and Mach's Principle." *Nature* 192 (1961): 440–41.

Dihle, Albrecht. "Die Theologia tripertita bei Augustin." In *Geschichte—Tradition—Reflexion: Festschrift für Martin Hengel zum 70. Geburtstag*, edited by Hubert Cancik, 183–202. Tübingen: Mohr Siebeck, 1996.

Dirac, P. A. M. "The Cosmological Constants." *Nature* 139 (1937): 323–24.

Dixon, Thomas. "Scientific Atheism as a Faith Tradition." *Studies in History and Philosophy of Science C* 33 (2002): 337–59.

Dobson, Christopher M. "Chemical Space and Biology." *Nature* 432 (2004): 824–28.

Domning, Daryl P., and Monika Hellwig. *Original Selfishness: Original Sin and Evil in the Light of Evolution*. Aldershot: Ashgate, 2006.

Douglas, Michael R., and Shamit Kachru. "Flux Compactification." *Reviews of Modern Physics* 79 (2007): 733–96.

Douven, Igor. "Testing Inference to the Best Explanation." *Synthese* 130 (2002): 355–77.

Dowey, Edward A. *The Knowledge of God in Calvin's Theology*. New York: Columbia University Press, 1952.

Doyle, John P. "*Ipsum Esse* as God-Surrogate: The Point of Convergence of Faith and Reason for St. Thomas Aquinas." *Modern Schoolman* 50 (1973): 293–96.

Drake, Michael J., and Kevin Righter. "Determining the Composition of the Earth." *Nature* 416 (2002): 39–44.

Draper, David E. "A Guide to Ions and RNA Structure." *RNA* 10 (2004): 335–43.

Duhem, Pierre. *The Aim and Structure of Physical Theory*. Princeton, NJ: Princeton University Press, 1954.

Dupré, Louis K. *The Enlightenment and the Intellectual Foundations of Modern Culture*. New Haven, CT: Yale University Press, 2004.

Durrant, Marcus C. "An Atomic Level Model for the Interactions of Molybdenum Nitrogenase with Carbon Monoxide, Acetylene, and Ethylene." *Biochemistry* 43 (2004): 6030–42.

Dyson, Freeman J. *Disturbing the Universe*. New York: Harper & Row, 1979.

———. *Origins of life*. Rev. ed. Cambridge: Cambridge University Press, 1999.

Earl, David J., and Michael W. Deem. "Evolvability Is a Selectable Trait." *Proceedings of the National Academy of Sciences* 101 (2004): 11531–36.

Earman, John. "The SAP Also Rises: A Critical Examination of the Anthropic Principle." *American Philosophical Quarterly* 24 (1987): 307–17.

———. "Underdetermination, Realism, and Reason." *Midwest Studies in Philosophy* 18 (1994): 19–38.

Eco, Umberto. *Semiotics and the Philosophy of Language*. London: Macmillan, 1984.

Eder, Klaus. "The Rise of Counter-Cultural Movements against Modernity: Nature as a New Field of Class Struggle." *Theory, Culture and Society* 7 (1990): 21–47.

———. *Die Vergesellschaftung der Natur: Studien zur sozialen Evolution der praktischen Vernunft*. Frankfurt am Main: Suhrkamp, 1988.

Edwards, Mark J. "Justin's *Logos* and the Word of God." *Journal of Early Christian Studies* 3 (1995): 261–80.

Edwards, Rem B. *What Caused the Big Bang?* Amsterdam: Rodopi, 2001.

Ehrenfreund, P., W. Irvine, L. Becker, J. Blank, J. R. Brucato, L. Colangeli, S. Derenne, D. Despois, A. Dutrey, H. Fraaije, A. Lazcano, T. Owen, and F. Robert. "Astrophysical and Astrochemical Insights into the Origin of Life." *Reports on Progress in Physics* 65 (2002): 1427–87.

Eigen, Manfred. *Steps towards Life: A Perspective on Evolution*. Oxford: Oxford University Press, 1992.

Einstein, Albert. "Ist die Trägheit eines Körpers von seinem Energieinhalt abhängig?" *Annalen der Physik* 18 (1905): 639.

———. "Physics and Reality." *Journal of the Franklin Institute* 221 (1936): 349–89.

Eisenberg, David. "The Discovery of the α-Helix and β-Sheet, the Principal Structural Features of Proteins." *Proceedings of the National Academy of Sciences* 100 (2003): 11207–10.

Ellis, George. "Cosmology and Local Physics." *International Journal of Modern Physics* A17 (2002): 2667–72.

———. "On the Nature of Emergent Reality." In *The Re-Emergence of Emergence: The Emergentist Hypothesis from Science to Religion*, edited by Philip Clayton and Paul Davies, 79–107. Oxford: Oxford University Press, 2006.

Engel, Michael H., and Bartholomew Nagy. "Distribution and Enantiomeric Composition of Amino Acids in the Murchison Meteorite." *Nature* 296 (1982): 837–40.

England, Richard. "Natural Selection, Teleology, and the Logos: From Darwin to the Oxford Neo-Darwinists, 1859–1909." *Osiris* 16 (2001): 270–87.

Eschenmoser, Albert. "Chemical Etiology of Nucleic Acid Structure." *Science* 284 (1999): 2118–24.

Evans, Gillian R. *Augustine on Evil*. Cambridge: Cambridge University Press, 1990.

Feder, Martin E. "Evolvability of Physiological and Biochemical Traits: Evolutionary Mechanisms Including and beyond Single-Nucleotide Mutation." *Journal of Experimental Biology* 210 (2007): 1653–60.

Fedor, Martha J. "The Role of Metal Ions in RNA Catalysis." *Current Opinion in Structural Biology* 12 (2002): 289–95.

Feingold, Lawrence. *The Natural Desire to See God according to St. Thomas and His Interpreters*. Rome: Apollinare Studi, 2001.

Fenchel, T. M. *The Origin and Early Evolution of Life*. Oxford: Oxford University Press, 2002.

Festinger, Leon. *A Theory of Cognitive Dissonance*. Stanford, CA: Stanford University Press, 1957.

Fiddes, Paul S. "'Where Shall Wisdom Be Found?' Job 28 as a Riddle for Ancient and Modern Readers." In *After the Exile: Essays in Honor of Rex Mason*, edited by John Barton and David Reimer, 171–90. Macon, GA: Mercer University Press, 1996.

Filippenko, Alexei V. "Einstein's Biggest Blunder? High-Redshift Supernovae and the Accelerating Universe." *Publications of the Astronomical Society of the Pacific* 113 (2001): 1441–48.

Finney, John L. "Water? What's So Special about It?" *Philosophical Transactions of the Royal Society B* 359 (2004): 1145–65.

Fitzgerald, Allan D., ed. *Augustine through the Ages: An Encyclopedia.* Grand Rapids: Eerdmans, 1999.

Fölsing, Albrecht. *Albert Einstein: A Biography.* New York: Viking Books, 1997.

Ford, David. *Christian Wisdom: Desiring God and Learning in Love.* Cambridge: Cambridge University Press, 2007.

Forster, Malcolm R. "Unification, Explanation, and the Composition of Causes in Newtonian Mechanics." *Studies in History and Philosophy of Science* 19 (1988): 55–101.

Forster, Malcolm R., and Elliott Sober. "How to Tell When Simpler, More Unified, or Less Ad Hoc Theories Provide More Accurate Predictions." *British Journal for Philosophy of Science* 45 (1994): 1–35.

Forsyth, P. T. *Christian Aspects of Evolution.* London: Epworth Press, 1950.

Fortey, Richard. "Evolution: The Cambrian Explosion Exploded?" *Science* 293 (2001): 438–39.

Fortin, Ernest L. *Classical Christianity and the Political Order: Reflections on the Theologico-Political Problem.* Lanham, MD: Rowman & Littlefield, 1996.

Foster, Michael B. "The Christian Doctrine of Creation and the Rise of Modern Science." *Mind* 43 (1934): 446–68.

———. "Christian Theology and Modern Science of Nature (I)." *Mind* 44 (1935): 439–66.

———. "Christian Theology and Modern Science of Nature (II)." *Mind* 45 (1936): 1–27.

Fraassen, Bas C. van. *Laws and Symmetry.* Oxford: Clarendon Press, 1989.

———. *The Scientific Image.* Oxford: Oxford University Press, 1980.

Francis, Keith A. *Charles Darwin and "The Origin of Species."* Westport, CT: Greenwood Press, 2007.

Francis, Richard C. *Why Men Won't Ask for Directions: The Seductions of Sociobiology.* Princeton, NJ: Princeton University Press, 2004.

Frankel, Charles. *The End of the Dinosaurs: Chicxulub Crater and Mass Extinctions.* Cambridge: Cambridge University Press, 1999.

Franks, Felix. *Water: A Matrix of Life.* 2nd ed. Cambridge: Royal Society of Chemistry, 2000.

Fraser, Hilary. *Beauty and Belief: Aesthetics and Religion in Victorian Literature.* Cambridge: Cambridge University Press, 1986.

Freddoso, Alfred J. "Medieval Aristotelianism and the Case against Secondary Causation in Nature." In *Divine and Human Action: Essays in the Metaphysics of Theism,* edited by Thomas V. Morris, 74–118. Ithaca, NY: Cornell University Press, 1988.

Freeland, Stephen J., Tao Wu, and Nick Keulmann. "The Case for an Error[-]Minimizing Standard Genetic Code." *Origins of Life and Evolution of Biospheres* 33 (2003): 457–77.

French, Roger K. *Medicine before Science: The Rational and Learned Doctor from the Middle Ages to the Enlightenment.* Cambridge: Cambridge University Press, 2003.

Frenkel, Daan. "Introduction to Colloidal Systems." In *Soft Condensed Matter Physics in Molecular and Cell Biology,* edited by Wilson C. K. Poon and David Andelman, 21–47. New York: Taylor & Francis, 2006.

Fretheim, Terence E. *God and World in the Old Testament: A Relational Theology of Creation.* Nashville: Abingdon Press, 2005.

Freyhofer, Horst H. *The Vitalism of Hans Driesch: The Success and Decline of a Scientific Theory.* Frankfurt am Main: Peter Lang, 1982.

Friedman, Michael. "Causal Laws and the Foundations of Natural Science." In *Cambridge Companion to Kant,* edited by Paul Guyer, 161–99. Cambridge: Cambridge University Press, 1990.

————. "Explanation and Scientific Understanding." *Journal of Philosophy* 71 (1974): 5–19.

Friesen, Steven J. *Twice Neokoros: Ephesus, Asia, and the Cult of the Flavian Imperial Family*. Leiden: Brill, 1993.

Fry, Iris. "On the Biological Significance of the Properties of Matter: L. J. Henderson's Theory of the Fitness of the Environment." *Journal of the History of Biology* 29 (1996): 155–96.

Fulmer, Gilbert. "Faces in the Sky: The Anthropic Principle Design Argument." *Journal of American Culture* 26 (2003): 485–88.

Fyfe, Aileen. "The Reception of William Paley's *Natural Theology* in the University of Cambridge." *British Journal for the History of Science* 30 (1997): 321–35.

Gabora, Liane M. "Self-Other Organization: Why Early Life Did Not Evolve through Natural Selection." *Journal of Theoretical Biology* 241 (2006): 443–50.

Galhardo, Rodrigo S., P. J. Hastings, and Susan M. Rosenberg. "Mutation as a Stress Response and the Regulation of Evolvability." *Critical Reviews in Biochemistry and Molecular Biology* 42 (2007): 399–435.

Garber, Daniel. "How God Causes Motion: Descartes, Divine Sustenance, and Occasionalism." *Journal of Philosophy* 84 (1987): 567–80.

Gardiner, Brian G. "Linnaeus's Species Concept and His Views on Evolution." *The Linnean* [newsletter of The Linnean Society of London] 17 (2001): 24–36.

Gärtner, Bertil. *The Areopagus Speech and Natural Revelation*. Uppsala: Gleerup / Almqvist & Wiksells, 1955.

Gascoigne, John. "From Bentley to the Victorians: The Rise and Fall of British Newtonian Natural Theology." *Science in Context* 2 (1988): 219–56.

Gaukroger, Stephen. *Francis Bacon and the Transformation of Early-Modern Philosophy*. Cambridge: Cambridge University Press, 2001.

Geison, Gerald L. "Darwin and Heredity: The Evolution of His Hypothesis of Pangenesis." *Journal of the History of Medicine* 24 (1969): 375–411.

Gervino, G., A. Lavagno, and P. Quarati. "Modified CNO Nuclear Reaction Rates in Dense Stellar Plasma." *Nuclear Physics A* 688 (2001): 126–29.

Gest, Howard. "The Remarkable Vision of Robert Hooke (1635–1703): First Observer of the Microbial World." *Perspectives in Biology and Medicine* 48 (2005): 266–72.

Gestrich, Christof. *Neuzeitliches Denken und die Spaltung der dialektischen Theologie: Zur Frage der natürlichen Theologie*. Tübingen: Mohr, 1977.

Geyer, C. Ronald, Thomas R. Battersby, and Steven A. Benner. "Nucleobase Pairing in Expanded Watson-Crick-Like Genetic Information Systems: The Nucleobases." *Structure* 11 (2003): 1485–98.

Ghiretti-Magaldi, Anna, and E. Ghiretti. "The Pre-History of Hemocyanin: The Discovery of Copper in the Blood of Molluscs." *Experientia* 48 (1992): 971–72.

Giberson, Karl. "The Anthropic Principle: A Postmodern Creation Myth?" *Journal of Interdisciplinary Studies* 9 (1997): 63–90.

Gilbert, Walter. "The RNA World." *Nature* 319 (1986): 618.

Gillespie, John H. *The Causes of Molecular Evolution*. New York: Oxford University Press, 1991.

Gillespie, Neal C. "Divine Design and the Industrial Revolution: William Paley's Abortive Reform of Natural Theology." *Isis* 81 (1990): 214–29.

————. "Natural History, Natural Theology, and Social Order: John Ray and the 'Newtonian Ideology.'" *Journal of the History of Biology* 20 (1987): 1–49.

Gillispie, Charles C. *Genesis and Geology: A Study in the Relations of Scientific Thought, Natural Theology and Social Opinion in Great Britain, 1790–1850*. Cambridge, MA: Harvard University Press, 1996.

Gilmore, Richard. "Existence, Reality, and God in Peirce's Metaphysics: The Exquisite Aesthetics of the Real." *Journal of Speculative Philosophy* 20 (2006): 308–19.

Gilson, Étienne. "Pourquoi Saint Thomas a critiqué Saint Augustin." *Archives d'histoire doctrinale et littéraire du Moyen Age* 1 (1926–27): 5–127.

Ginsburg, R. N. "An Attempt to Resolve the Controversy over the End-Cretaceous Extinction of Planktic Foraminifera at El Kef, Tunisia Using a Blind Test; Introduction: Background and Procedures." *Marine Micropaleontology* 29 (1997): 67–68.

Glacken, Clarence J. *Traces on the Rhodian Shore: Nature and Culture in Western Thought from Ancient Times to the End of the Eighteenth Century.* Berkeley: University of California Press, 1973.

Glass, David H. "Coherence Measures and Inference to the Best Explanation." *Synthese* 157 (2007): 275–96.

Godfrey-Smith, Peter. "The Replicator in Retrospect." *Biology and Philosophy* 15 (2000): 403–23.

Goldblatt, Colin, Timothy M. Lenton, and Andrew J. Watson. "Bistability of Atmospheric Oxygen and the Great Oxidation." *Nature* 443 (2006): 683–86.

Goldsmith, Timothy H. "Optimization, Constraint, and History in the Evolution of Eyes." *Quarterly Review of Biology* 65 (1990): 281–322.

Gore, Charles. *The Permanent Creed and the Christian Idea of Sin.* London: John Murray, 1905.

Gould, Stephen Jay. "Caring Groups and Selfish Genes." In *The Panda's Thumb*, 85–91. New York: W. W. Norton, 1980.

———. *Ever since Darwin: Reflections in Natural History.* New York: W. W. Norton, 1977.

———. *Full House: The Spread of Excellence from Plato to Darwin.* New York: Harmony Books, 1996.

———. "Nonoverlapping Magisteria." *Natural History* 106 (1997): 16–22.

———. *Rocks of Ages: Science and Religion in the Fullness of Life.* London: Jonathan Cape, 2001.

———. *The Structure of Evolutionary Theory.* Cambridge, MA: Belknap Press, 2002.

———. *Wonderful Life: The Burgess Shale and the Nature of History.* New York: W. W. Norton, 1989.

Graesser, Michael L., Stephen D. H. Hsu, Alejandro Jenkins, and Mark B. Wise. "Anthropic Distribution for Cosmological Constant and Primordial Density Perturbations." *Physics Letters B* 600 (2004): 15–21.

Grant, Colin. "Why Should Theology Be Unnatural?" *Modern Theology* 23 (2007): 91–106.

Gray, John. *Enlightenment's Wake: Politics and Culture at the Close of the Modern Age.* London: Routledge, 1997.

Greene, John C. "From Aristotle to Darwin: Reflections on Ernst Mayr's Interpretation in *The Growth of Biological Thought.*" *Journal of the History of Biology* 25 (1992): 257–84.

———. *Science, Ideology, and World View: Essays in the History of Evolutionary Ideas.* Berkeley: University of California Press, 1981.

Gregersen, Niels Henrik. "Emergence: What Is at Stake for Religious Reflection?" In *The Re-Emergence of Emergence: The Emergentist Hypothesis from Science to Religion*, edited by Philip Clayton and Paul Davies, 279–302. Oxford: Oxford University Press, 2006.

Gregory, Frederick. "The Impact of Darwinian Evolution on Protestant Theology in the Nineteenth Century." In *God and Nature: Historical Essays on the Encounter between Christianity and Natural Science*, edited by D. C. Lindberg and R. L. Numbers, 369–90. Berkeley: University of California Press, 1986.

Grene, Marjorie, and David Depew. *The Philosophy of Biology: An Episodic History.* Cambridge: Cambridge University Press, 2004.

Gribbin, John R., and Martin J. Rees. *Cosmic Coincidences: Dark Matter, Mankind, and Anthropic Cosmology.* New York: Bantam Books, 1989.

———. *The Stuff of the Universe: Dark Matter, Mankind and Anthropic Cosmology.* London: Penguin, 1995.

Grosholz, Emily R. "Descartes' Unification of Algebra and Geometry." In *Descartes: Philosophy, Mathematics and Physics*, edited by Stephen Gaukroger, 156–68. Totowa, NJ: Barnes & Noble, 1980.

———. "Two Episodes in the Unification of Logic and Topology." *British Journal for the Philosophy of Science* 36 (1985): 147–57.

Gross, Charlotte. "Augustine's Ambivalence about Temporality: His Two Accounts of Time." *Medieval Philosophy and Theology* 8 (1999): 129–48.

Gross, Julius. *Geschichte des Erbsündendogmas: Ein Beitrag zur Geschichte des Problems vom Ursprung des Übels.* Munich: Reinhardt, 1960.

Grumett, David. "Teilhard de Chardin's Evolutionary Natural Theology." *Zygon* 42 (2007): 519–34.

Gunnlaugur, A. Jónsson, and S. Cheney Michael. *The Image of God: Genesis 1:26–28 in a Century of Old Testament Research.* Stockholm: Almqvist & Wiksell International, 1988.

Gunton, Colin E. *The Promise of Trinitarian Theology.* Edinburgh: T&T Clark, 1991.

———. *The Triune Creator: A Historical and Systematic Study.* Edinburgh: Edinburgh University Press, 1998.

Guth, Alan. "Inflationary Universe: A Possible Solution to the Horizon and Flatness Problems." *Physical Reviews* D23 (1981): 347–56.

———. *The Inflationary Universe: The Quest for a New Theory of Cosmic Origins.* Reading, MA: Addison-Wesley Publishing Co., 1997.

Haldane, John. "Philosophy, the Restless Heart, and the Meaning of Theism." *Ratio* 19 (2006): 421–40.

Halder, Georg, Patrick Callaerts, and Walter J. Gehring. "New Perspectives on Eye Evolution." *Current Opinion in Genetics and Development* 5 (1995): 602–9.

Hall, J. L., and Lorraine E. Williams. "Transition Metal Transporters in Plants." *Journal of Experimental Botany* 54 (2003): 2601–13.

Hall, Marie Boas. *Robert Boyle on Natural Philosophy: An Essay with Selections from His Writings.* Bloomington: Indiana University Press, 1965.

Halonen, Ilpo, and Jaakko Hintikka. "Unification—It's Magnificent but Is It Explanation?" *Synthese* 120 (1999): 27–47.

Hanke, David. "Teleology: The Explanation That Bedevils Biology." In *Explanations: Styles of Explanation in Science*, edited by John Cornwell, 143–55. Oxford: Oxford University Press, 2004.

Hankey, Wayne J. "Dionysian Hierarchy in Thomas Aquinas: Tradition and Transformation." In *Denys l'Aréopagite et sa postérité en Orient et en Occident: Actes du Colloque International Paris, 21–24 septembre 1994*, edited by Ysabel de Andia, 405–38. Paris: Institut d'Études Augustiniennes, 1997.

Hannerz, Ulf. *Cultural Complexity: Studies in the Social Organization of Meaning.* New York: Columbia University Press, 1992.

Hanson, N. R. "Is There a Logic of Scientific Discovery?" *Australasian Journal of Philosophy* 38 (1961): 91–106.

———. *Patterns of Discovery: An Inquiry into the Conceptual Foundations of Science.* Cambridge: Cambridge University Press, 1961.

Hardison, Ross C. "A Brief History of Hemoglobins: Plant, Animal, Protist, and Bacteria." *Proceedings of the National Academy of Sciences* 93 (1996): 5675–79.

Harker, David. "Accommodation and Prediction: The Case of the Persistent Head." *British Journal for Philosophy of Science* 57 (2006): 309–21.

Harman, Gilbert. "The Inference to the Best Explanation." *Philosophical Review* 74 (1965): 88–95.

Harriman, Anthony, and Jean-Pierre Sauvage. "A Strategy for Constructing Photosynthetic Models: Porphyrin-Containing Modules Assembled around Transition Metals." *Chemical Society Reviews* 25 (1996): 41–48.

Harrison, Edward Robert. *Cosmology: The Science of the Universe.* 2nd ed. Cambridge: Cambridge University Press, 2000.

———. *Darkness at Night.* Cambridge, MA: Harvard University Press, 1987.

Harrison, Peter. "'The Book of Nature' and Early Modern Science." In *The Book of Nature in Early Modern and Modern History*, edited by Klaas van Berkel and Arjo Vanderjagt, 1–26. Leuven: Peeters, 2006.

———. *The Fall of Man and the Foundations of Science.* Cambridge: Cambridge University Press, 2007.

———. "Natural Theology, Deism, and Early Modern Science." In *Science, Religion, and Society: An Encyclopedia of History, Culture and Controversy*, edited by Arri Eisen and Gary Laderman, 426–33. New York: Sharp, 2006.

———. "Physico-Theology and the Mixed Sciences: The Role of Theology in Early Modern Natural Philosophy." In *The Science of Nature in the Seventeenth Century*, edited by Peter Anstey and John Schuster, 165–83. Dordrecht: Springer-Verlag, 2005.

Hart, David Bentley. "The Mirror of the Infinite: Gregory of Nyssa on the *Vestigia Trinitatis.*" *Modern Theology* 18 (2002): 541–61.

Hart, Ray L. *Unfinished Man and the Imagination: Toward an Ontology and a Rhetoric of Revelation.* New York: Herder & Herder, 1968.

Hartmann, Nicolai. *Kleinere Schriften.* 3 vols. Berlin: de Gruyter, 1955.

———. *Neue Wege der Ontologie.* 4th ed. Stuttgart: W. Kohlhammer, 1964.

———. *Zum Problem der Realitätsgegebenheit.* Berlin: Pan-Verlagsgesellschaft, 1931.

———. *Zur Grundlegung der Ontologie.* 3rd ed. Meisenheim am Glan: Anton Hain, 1948.

Hauerwas, Stanley. *With the Grain of the Universe: The Church's Witness and Natural Theology.* Grand Rapids: Brazos Press, 2002.

Haught, John F. "Darwin and Contemporary Theology." *Worldviews* 11 (2007): 44–57.

Hawking, Stephen W., and Roger Penrose. *The Nature of Space and Time.* Princeton, NJ: Princeton University Press, 1996.

Hawthorn, Geoffrey. *Plausible Worlds: Possibility and Understanding in History and the Social Sciences.* Cambridge: Cambridge University Press, 1993.

Hayes, Brian. "The Invention of the Genetic Code." *American Scientist* 86 (1998): 8–14.

He, Wei-Zhong, and Richard Malkin. "Photosystems I and II." In *Photosynthesis: A Comprehensive Treatise*, edited by A. S. Raghavendra, 29–43. Cambridge: Cambridge University Press, 1998.

Hedley, Douglas. "Persons of Substance and the Cambridge Connection: Some Roots and Ramifications of the Trinitarian Controversy in Seventeenth-Century England." In *Socinianism and Arminianism: Antitrinitarians, Calvinists, and Cultural Exchange in Seventeenth-Century Europe*, edited by Martin Mulsow and Jan Rohls, 225–40. Leiden: Brill, 2005.

Helm, Paul. "John Calvin, the *Sensus Divinitatis* and the Noetic Effects of Sin." *International Journal of Philosophy of Religion* 43 (1998): 87–107.

Hempel, Carl G. *Aspects of Scientific Explanation.* New York: Free Press, 1965.

———. *Philosophy of Natural Science.* Englewood Cliffs, NJ: Prentice-Hall, 1966.

Henderson, Lawrence J. *The Fitness of the Environment: An Inquiry into the Biological Significance of the Properties of Matter.* New York: Macmillan, 1913; reprint, Boston: Beacon Press, 1958.

———. *The Order of Nature: An Essay.* Cambridge, MA: Harvard University Press, 1917.

Henke, Rainer. *Basilius und Ambrosius über das Sechstagewerk.* Basel: Schwabe, 2001.

Henry, John. "'Pray Do Not Ascribe That Notion to Me': God and Newton's Gravity." In *The Books of Nature and Scripture: Recent Essays on Natural Philosophy, Theology and Biblical Criticism in the Netherlands of Spinoza's Time and the British Isles of Newton's Time*, edited by James E. Force and Richard H. Popkin, 123–47. Dordrecht: Kluwer Academic Publishers, 1994.

Herschel, J. F. W. *Preliminary Discourse on the Study of Natural Philosophy*. London: Longman, Rees, Orme, Brown & Green, 1830.

Hesse, Mary B. *Models and Analogies in Science*. Notre Dame, IN: University of Notre Dame Press, 1966.

———. *Revolutions and Reconstructions in the Philosophy of Science*. Bloomington: Indiana University Press, 1980.

———. "What Is the Best Way to Assess Evidential Support for Scientific Theories?" In *Applications of Inductive Logic*, edited by L. Jonathan Cohen and Mary Hesse, 202–17. Oxford: Clarendon Press, 1980.

Hewison, Robert. *John Ruskin: The Argument of the Eye*. Princeton, NJ: Princeton University Press, 1976.

Heyd, Michael. "Un rôle nouveau pour la science: Jean Alphonse Turrettini et les débuts de la théologie naturelle à Genève." *Revue de théologie et philosophie* 112 (1982): 25–42.

Hick, John. *An Interpretation of Religion: Human Responses to the Transcendent*. London: Macmillan, 1989.

Hilton, Denis J., John I. McClure, and Ben R. Slugowski. "The Course of Events: Counterfactuals, Causal Sequences, and Explanation." In *The Psychology of Counterfactual Thinking*, edited by David R. Mandel, Denis J. Hilton, and Patrizia Catellani, 46–60. London: Routledge, 2005.

Himmelfarb, Gertrude. *The Roads to Modernity: The British, French, and American Enlightenments*. New York: Knopf, 2005.

Hirai, Hiro. *Le concept de semence dans les théories de la matière à la Renaissance: De Marsile Ficin à Pierre Gassendi*. Turnhout: Brepols, 2005.

Hitchcock, Christopher. "The Lovely and the Probable." *Philosophy and Phenomenological Research* 74 (2007): 433–40.

Hitchcock, Christopher, and Elliott Sober. "Prediction versus Accommodation and the Risk of Overfitting." *British Journal for Philosophy of Science* 55 (2004): 1–34.

Hochachka, Peter W., and George N. Somero. *Biochemical Adaptation: Mechanism and Process in Physiological Evolution*. Oxford: Oxford University Press, 2002.

Hoekstra, Hopi E., Kristen E. Drumm, and Michael W. Nachman. "Ecological Genetics of Adaptive Color Polymorphism in Pocket Mice: Geographic Variation in Selected and Neutral Genes." *Evolution: International Journal of Organic Evolution* 58 (2004): 1329–41.

Hoffmann, Michael. "Problems with Peirce's Concept of Abduction." *Foundations of Science* 4 (1999): 271–305.

Hoffmann, Roald. *The Same and Not the Same*. New York: Columbia University Press, 1995.

Hoffmann, Thomas Sören. *Philosophische Physiologie: Eine Systematik des Begriffs der Natur im Spiegel der Geschichte der Philosophie*. Stuttgart: Frommann-Holzboog, 2003.

Hogan, Craig J. "Why the Universe Is Just So." *Review of Modern Physics* 72 (2000): 1149–61.

Holder, Rodney D. *God, the Multiverse, and Everything: Modern Cosmology and the Argument from Design*. Aldershot: Ashgate, 2004.

Holladay, Carl R. *Theios Anēr in Hellenistic-Judaism: A Critique of the Use of This Category in New Testament Christology*. Missoula, MT: Scholars Press, 1977.

Holland, John H. *Emergence: From Chaos to Order*. Oxford: Oxford University Press, 2000.

Holm, Richard H., Pierre Kennepohl, and Edward I. Solomon. "Structural and Functional Aspects of Metal Sites in Biology." *Chemical Reviews* 96 (1996): 2239–2314.

Holte, Ragnar. "Logos Spermatikos: Christianity and Ancient Philosophy according to St. Justin's *Apologies.*" *Studia Theologica* 12 (1958): 109–68.

Hookway, Christopher. "Interrogatives and Uncontrollable Abductions." *Semiotica* 153 (2005): 101–15.

Horgan, John. *The End of Science: Facing the Limits of Knowledge in the Twilight of the Scientific Age.* Reading, MA: Addison-Wesley Publishing Co., 1996.

Horowitz, Maryanne Cline. "The Stoic Synthesis of the Idea of Natural Law in Man: Four Themes." *Journal of the History of Ideas* 35 (1974): 3–16.

Howell, Kenneth J. *God's Two Books: Copernican Cosmology and Biblical Interpretation in Early Modern Science.* Notre Dame, IN: University of Notre Dame Press, 2002.

Hoyle, Fred. "Hoyle on Evolution." *Nature* 294 (1981): 105.

———. "The Universe: Past and Present Reflections." *Annual Review of Astronomy and Astrophysics* 20 (1982): 1–35.

Hoyle, Fred, and N. C. Wickramasinghe. *Astronomical Origins of Life: Steps towards Panspermia.* Dordrecht: Kluwer Academic Publishers, 2000.

Huang, Ching-Hsien. "Studies on Phosphatidylcholine Vesicles: Formation and Physical Characteristics." *Biochemistry* 8 (1969): 344–52.

Hud, Nicholas V., and Frank A. L. Anet. "Intercalation-Mediated Synthesis and Replication: A New Approach to the Origin of Life." *Journal of Theoretical Biology* 205 (2000): 543–62.

Hull, David L. *Darwin and His Critics: The Reception of Darwin's Theory of Evolution by the Scientific Community.* Cambridge, MA: Harvard University Press, 1973.

Hulswit, Menno. "Teleology: A Peircean Critique of Ernst Mayr's Theory." *Transactions of the Charles S. Peirce Society* 32 (1996): 182–214.

Hummer, Gerard. "Water Pulls the Strings in Hydrophobic Polymer Collapse." *Proceedings of the National Academy of Sciences* 104 (2007): 14883–84.

Humphreys, Paul. *The Chances of Explanation: Causal Explanation in the Social, Medical, and Physical Sciences.* Princeton, NJ: Princeton University Press, 1989.

Huneman, Philippe. "Naturalising Purpose: From Comparative Anatomy to the 'Adventure of Reason.'" *Studies in History and Philosophy of Science* 37 (2006): 649–74.

Huniar, Uwe, Reinhart Ahlrichs, and Dimitri Coucouvanis. "Density Functional Theory Calculations and Exploration of a Possible Mechanism of N_2 Reduction by Nitrogenase." *Journal of the American Chemical Society* 126 (2004): 2588–2601.

Hunsinger, George. "The Mediator of Communion: Karl Barth's Doctrine of the Holy Spirit." In *Cambridge Companion to Karl Barth,* edited by John Webster, 177–94. Cambridge: Cambridge University Press, 2000.

Hunter, David G. *Marriage, Celibacy, and Heresy in Ancient Christianity: The Jovinianist Controversy.* Oxford Early Christian Studies. Oxford: Oxford University Press, 2007.

Hutchinson, G. Evelyn. *The Ecological Theater and the Evolutionary Play.* New Haven, CT: Yale University Press, 1965.

Hütter, Reinhard. "*Desiderium naturale visionis Dei—Est autem duplex hominis beatitudo sive felicitas*: Some Observations about Lawrence Feingold's and John Millbank's Recent Interventions in the Debate over the Natural Desire to see God." *Nova et vetera* 5 (2007): 81–132.

Hutton, Sarah. "Ralph Cudworth, God, Mind and Nature." In *Religion, Reason, and Nature in Early Modern Europe,* edited by Ralph Crocker, 61–76. Dordrecht: Kluwer Academic Publishers, 2001.

Huxley, Thomas H. *Lay Sermons, Addresses, and Reviews.* London: Macmillan, 1970.

Irlenborn, Bernd. "Abschied von der 'natürlichen Theologie'? Eine sprachphilosophische Standortbestimmung." *Theologie und Philosophie* 78 (2003): 545–57.
———. "Konsonanz von Theologie und Naturwissenschaft? Fundamentaltheologische Bemerkungen zum interdisziplinären Ansatz von John Polkinghorne." *Trierer theologische Zeitung* 113 (2004): 98–117.
Jablonski, David. "Geographic Variation in the Molluscan Recovery from the End-Cretaceous Extinction." *Science* 279 (1998): 1327–30.
James, William. *The Principles of Psychology.* Cambridge, MA: Harvard University Press, 1981.
———. *The Will to Believe.* New York: Dover Publications, 1956.
Janssen, Michel. "Of Pots and Holes: Einstein's Bumpy Road to General Relativity." *Annalen der Physik* 14, Supplement (2005): 58–85.
Jenson, Robert W. *The Triune Identity: God according to the Gospel.* Philadelphia: Fortress, 1982.
Jervell, Jacob. *Imago Dei: Gen 1, 26f. im Spätjudentum, in der Gnosis und in den paulinischen Briefen.* Göttingen: Vandenhoeck & Ruprecht, 1960.
Johnson, Jeff. "Inference to the Best Explanation and the Problem of Evil." *Journal of Religion* 64 (1984): 54–72.
Johnson, Monte Ransome. *Aristotle on Teleology.* Oxford: Clarendon Press, 2005.
Jones, Prudence. "The European Native Tradition." In *Nature Religion Today: Paganism in the Modern World,* edited by Joanne Pearson, Richard H. Roberts, and Geoffrey Samuel, 71–88. Edinburgh: Edinburgh University Press, 1998.
Jones, Todd. "Unification, Reduction, and Non-Ideal Explanations." *Synthese* 112 (1997): 75–96.
Joyce, Gerald F. "Foreword." In *Origins of Life: The Central Concepts,* edited by D. W. Deamer and G. R. Fleischaker, xi–xii. Boston, MA: Jones & Bartlett, 1994.
Jüngel, Eberhard. *God as the Mystery of the World.* Edinburgh: T&T Clark, 1983.
Jurmain, Robert. *Essentials of Physical Anthropology.* 5th ed. Belmont, CA: Thomson Wadsworth, 2004.
Kaiho, K., Y. Kajiwara, T. Nakano, Y. Miura, H. Kawahata, K. Tazaki, M. Ueshima, Z. Chen, and G. R. Shi. "End-Permian Catastrophe by a Bolide Impact: Evidence of a Gigantic Release of Sulfur from the Mantle." *Geology* 29 (2001): 815–18.
Kalbermann, German. "Ehrenfest Theorem, Galilean Invariance and Nonlinear Schrödinger Equations." *Journal of Physics A* 37 (2004): 2999–3002.
Kalckar, Herman M. "Origins of the Concept Oxidative Phosphorylation." *Molecular and Cellular Biochemistry* 5 (1974): 55–62.
Kärkkäinen, Veli-Matti. *Trinity and Religious Pluralism: The Doctrine of the Trinity in Christian Theology of Religions.* Aldershot: Ashgate, 2004.
Kasting, James F., and Janet L. Siefert. "Life and the Evolution of Earth's Atmosphere." *Science* 296 (2002): 1066–68.
Kauffman, Stuart A. *At Home in the Universe: The Search for Laws of Complexity.* Harmondsworth: Penguin, 1995.
———. *Investigations.* New York: Oxford University Press, 2000.
Keefe, Anthony D., and Stanley L. Miller. "Are Polyphosphates or Phosphate Esters Prebiotic Reagents?" *Journal of Molecular Evolution* 41 (1995): 693–702.
Keller, Evelyn Fox. *Making Sense of Life: Explaining Biological Development with Models, Metaphors, and Machines.* Cambridge, MA: Harvard University Press, 2002.
Kershaw, Steve. "Evolution of the Earth's Atmosphere and Its Geological Impact." *Geology Today* 6 (1990): 55–60.
Kim, Jaegwon. *Mind in a Physical World: An Essay on the Mind-Body Problem and Mental Causation.* Cambridge, MA: MIT Press, 1998.

Kim, Yoon Kyung. *Augustine's Changing Interpretations of Genesis 1–3: From "De Genesi contra Manichaeos" to "De Genesi ad litteram."* Lewiston, NY: Edwin Mellen Press, 2006.

King, Charles. "The Organization of Roman Religious Beliefs." *Classical Antiquity* 22 (2003): 275–312.

Kingsley, Charles. "The Natural Theology of the Future." In *Westminster Sermons*, v–xxxiii. London: Macmillan, 1874.

Kirschner, Marc W., and John Gerhart. "Evolvability." *Proceedings of the National Academy of Sciences* 95 (1998): 8420–27.

Kirschner, Marc W., and John C. Gerhart. *The Plausibility of Life: Resolving Darwin's Dilemma.* New Haven, CT: Yale University Press, 2005.

Kitcher, Paul. "Explanatory Unification and the Causal Structure of the World." In *Scientific Explanation*, edited by P. Kitcher and W. Salmon, 410–505. Minneapolis: University of Minnesota Press, 1989.

Klauber, Martin. "Jean-Alphonse Turrettini (1671–1737) on Natural Theology: The Triumph of Reason over Revelation at the Academy of Geneva." *Scottish Journal of Theology* 47 (1994): 301–25.

Klauck, Hans-Josef. "Nature, Art, and Thought: Dio Chrysostom and the *Theologia Tripertita.*" *Journal of Religion* 87 (2007): 333–54.

Kleiner, Scott A. "Explanatory Coherence and Empirical Adequacy: The Problem of Abduction, and the Justification of Evolutionary Models." *Biology and Philosophy* 18 (2003): 513–27.

———. "A New Look at Kepler and Abductive Argument." *Studies in History and Philosophy of Science* 14 (1983): 279–313.

———. "Problem Solving and Discovery in the Growth of Darwin's Theories of Evolution." *Synthese* 62 (1981): 119–62.

Klinck, Dennis R. "*Vestigia Trinitatis* in Man and His Works in the English Renaissance." *Journal of the History of Ideas* 42 (1981): 13–27.

Klinger, Eric. "The Search for Meaning in Evolutionary Perspective and Its Clinical Implications." In *The Human Quest for Meaning: A Handbook of Psychological Research and Clinical Applications*, edited by P. T. P. Wong and P. S. Fry, 27–50. Mahwah, NJ: Erlbaum, 1998.

Knuuttila, Simo. "Time and Creation in Augustine." In *The Cambridge Companion to Augustine*, edited by Eleonore Stump and Norman Kretzmann, 103–15. Cambridge: Cambridge University Press, 2001.

Kock, Christoph. *Natürliche Theologie: Ein evangelischer Streitbegriff.* Neukirchen-Vluyn: Neukirchener Verlag, 2001.

Kolakowski, Leszek. *Metaphysical Horror.* Chicago: University of Chicago Press, 2001.

Kolodner, Marc A., and Paul G. Steffes. "The Microwave Absorption and Abundance of Sulfuric Acid Vapor in the Venus Atmosphere Based on New Laboratory Measurements." *Icarus* 132 (1998): 151–69.

Korn, Robert W. "Biological Hierarchies, Their Birth, Death and Evolution by Natural Selection." *Biology and Philosophy* 17 (2002): 199–221.

———. "The Emergence Principle in Biological Hierarchies." *Biology and Philosophy* 20 (2005): 137–51.

Kragh, Helge. *Conceptions of Cosmos: From Myths to the Accelerating Universe; A History of Cosmology.* Oxford: Oxford University Press, 2007.

Krimbas, Costas B. "On Fitness." *Biology and Philosophy* 19 (2004): 185–204.

Krolzik, Udo. "Das physikotheologische Naturverständnis und sein Einfluss auf das naturwissenschaftliche Denken im 18. Jahrhundert." *Medizinhistorisches Journal* 15 (1980): 90–102.

Kuipers, Theo A. F. *From Instrumentalism to Constructive Realism: On Some Relations between Confirmation, Empirical Progress, and Truth Approximation.* Dordrecht: Kluwer Academic Publishers, 2000.

Kump, L. R., A. Pavlov, and M. A. Arthur. "Massive Release of Hydrogen Sulfide to the Surface Ocean and Atmosphere during Intervals of Oceanic Anoxia." *Geology* 33 (2005): 397–400.

Kurtz, Donald M. "Oxygen-Carrying Proteins: Three Solutions to a Common Problem." In *Essays in Biochemistry*, edited by David P. Ballou, 85–100. London: Portland Press, 1999.

Kvenvolden, Keith A., James Lawless, Katherine Pering, Etta Peterson, José Flores, Cyril Ponnamperuma, Isaac R. Kaplan, and Carleton Moore. "Evidence for Extraterrestrial Amino-Acids and Hydrocarbons in the Murchison Meteorite." *Nature* 228 (1970): 923–26.

Lambrecht, Jam. "The Groaning of Creation." *Louvain Studies* 15 (1990): 3–19.

Lane, Nick. *Oxygen: The Molecule That Made the World.* Oxford: Oxford University Press, 2002.

Lang, Helen S. *The Order of Nature in Aristotle's Physics: Place and the Elements.* Cambridge: Cambridge University Press, 1998.

Lange, Marc. "The Apparent Superiority of Prediction to Accommodation as a Side Effect." *British Journal for Philosophy of Science* 52 (2001): 575–88.

Lathe, Richard. "Fast Tidal Cycling and the Origin of Life." *Icarus* 168 (2004): 18–22.

Lazcano, Antonio, and Jeffrey L. Bada. "The 1953 Stanley L. Miller Experiment: Fifty Years of Prebiotic Organic Chemistry." *Origins of Life and Evolution of Biospheres* 33 (2004): 235–42.

Le Poidevin, Robin. "Missing Elements and Missing Premises: A Combinatorial Argument for the Ontological Reduction of Chemistry." *British Journal for the Philosophy of Science* 56 (2005): 117–34.

Lebedev, Y., N. Akopyants, T. Azhikinaa, Y. Shevchenkoa, V. Potapova, D. Stecenkoa, D. Bergb, and E. Sverdlov. "Oligonucleotides Containing 2-Aminoadenine and 5-Methylcytosine Are More Effective as Primers for PCR Amplification than Their Nonmodified Counterparts." *Genetic Analysis: Biomolecular Engineering* 13 (1996): 15–21.

Lee, Moon-Yeal, and Jonathan S. Dordick. "Enzyme Activation for Nonaqueous Media." *Current Opinions in Biotechnology* 13 (2002): 376–84.

Lehmann, Yves. *Varron théologien et philosophe romain.* Brussels: Latomus, 1997.

Lennox, James G. *Aristotle's Philosophy of Biology: Studies in the Origins of Life Science.* Cambridge: Cambridge University Press, 2001.

Leslie, John. *Universes.* London: Routledge, 1989.

Levene, Phoebus A. "The Structure of Yeast Nucleic Acid." *Journal of Biological Chemistry* 40 (1919): 415–24.

Levy, David M., and Sandra J. Peart. "Charles Kingsley and the Theological Interpretation of Natural Selection." *Journal of Bioeconomics* 8 (2006): 197–218.

Levy, Yaakov, and José N. Onuchic. "Water Mediation in Protein Folding and Molecular Recognition." *Annual Review of Biophysics and Biomolecular Structure* 35 (2006): 389–415.

Lewis, C. S. "Is Theology Poetry?" In *C. S. Lewis: Essay Collection*, 1–21. London: Collins, 2000.

Lewis, David. "Causal Explanation." In *Philosophical Papers,* vol. 2, 214–40. Oxford: Oxford University Press, 1987.

Lewontin, Richard C. "The Bases of Conflict in Biological Explanation." *Journal of the History of Biology* 2 (1969): 35–45.

———. *Biology as Ideology: The Doctrine of DNA.* New York: HarperPerennial, 1992.

Lichter, Werner. *Die Kategorialanalyse der Kausaldetermination: Eine kritische Untersuchung zur Ontologie Nicolai Hartmanns.* Bonn: Bouvier, 1964.

Lieberg, Godo. "Die Theologia tripartita als Formprinzip antiken Denkens." *Rheinisches Museum für Philologie* 125 (1982): 25–53.

———. "Die 'Theologia tripartita' in Forschung und Bezeugung." In *Aufstieg und Niedergang der römischen Welt*, vol. 1.4, edited by H. Temporini and W. Haase, 63–115. New York: de Gruyter, 1973.

Lienhard, Joseph T. "Reading the Bible and Learning to Read: The Influence of Education on St. Augustine's Exegesis." *Augustinian Studies* 27 (1996): 7–25.

Lindberg, David C., and Robert S. Westman, eds. *Reappraisals of the Scientific Revolution*. Cambridge: Cambridge University Press, 1990.

Linden, Stanton J. *Darke Hierogliphicks: Alchemy in English Literature from Chaucer to the Restoration*. Lexington: University Press of Kentucky, 1996.

Ling, Gilbert. "What Determines the Normal Water Content of a Living Cell?" *Physiological Chemistry and Physics and Medical NMR* 36 (2004): 1–19.

Lipmann, Fritz. "Metabolic Generation and Utilization of Phosphate Bond Energy." *Advances in Enzymology and Related Areas of Molecular Biology* 1 (1941): 99–162.

———. "Projecting Backward from the Present Stage of Evolution of Biosynthesis." In *The Origin of Prebiological Systems and of Their Molecular Matrices*, edited by S. W. Fox, 259–80. New York: Academic Press, 1965.

Lipton, Peter. *Inference to the Best Explanation*. 2nd ed. London: Routledge, 2004.

Little, Anthony C., D. Michael Burt, and David I. Perrett. "Assortative Mating for Perceived Facial Personality Traits." *Personality and Individual Differences* 40 (2006): 973–84.

Litvack, Leon B. "*Callista*, Martyrdom, and the Early Christian Novel in the Victorian Age." *Nineteenth-Century Contexts* 17 (1993): 159–73.

Liu, Maw-Shung, and K. Joe Kako. "Characteristics of Mitochondrial and Microsomal Monoacyl- and Diacyl-Glycerol 3-Phosphate Biosynthesis in Rabbit Heart." *Biochemical Journal* 138 (1974): 11–21.

Livingstone, David N. "B. B. Warfield, the Theory of Evolution and Early Fundamentalism." *Evangelical Quarterly* 58 (1986): 69–83.

———. *Darwin's Forgotten Defenders: The Encounter between Evangelical Theology and Evolutionary Thought*. Grand Rapids: Eerdmans, 1987.

Livingstone, David N., and Mark A. Noll. "B. B. Warfield (1851–1921): A Biblical Inerrantist as Evolutionist." *Isis* 91 (2000): 283–304.

Lockwood, Michael. *The Labyrinth of Time: Introducing the University*. Oxford: Oxford University Press, 2005.

Lombardi, Olimpia, and Martín Labarca. "The Ontological Autonomy of the Chemical World: A Response to Needham." *Foundations of Chemistry* 8 (2006): 81–92.

Luisi, Pier Luigi. "Contingency and Determinism." *Philosophical Transactions: Mathematical, Physical, and Engineering Sciences* 361 (2003): 1141–47.

———. "Emergence in Chemistry: Chemistry as the Embodiment of Emergence." *Foundations of Chemistry* 4 (2002): 183–200.

———. "Some Open Questions about the Origin of Life." In *Fundamentals of Life*, edited by Gyula Pályi, Claudia Zucchi, and Luciano Caglioti, 289–301. Paris: Elsevier, 2002.

Luoma, Tapio. *Incarnation and Physics: Natural Science in the Theology of Thomas F. Torrance*. Oxford: Oxford University Press, 2002.

Lustig, Abigail. "Natural Atheology." In *Darwinian Heresies*, edited by Abigail Lustig, Robert J. Richards, and Michael Ruse, 69–83. Cambridge: Cambridge University Press, 2004.

Lynden-Bell, Ruth M., and Pablo G. Debenedetti. "Computational Investigation of Order, Structure, and Dynamics in Modified Water Models." *Journal of Physical Chemistry B* 109 (2005): 6527–34.

Ma, Chung-Pei, and Edmund Bertschinger. "A Cosmological Kinetic Theory for the Evolution of Cold Dark Matter Halos with Substructure: Quasi-Linear Theory." *Astrophysical Journal Letters* 612 (2004): 28–49.

MacIntyre, Alasdair C. *Whose Justice? Which Rationality?* Notre Dame, IN: University of Notre Dame Press, 1988.

Macken, John. *The Autonomy Theme in the "Church Dogmatics" of Karl Barth and His Critics.* Cambridge: Cambridge University Press, 1990.

Mackie, J. L. *The Miracle of Theism: Arguments For and Against the Existence of God.* Oxford: Clarendon Press, 1982.

Macquarrie, John. "The Idea of a Theology of Nature." *Union Seminary Quarterly Review* 30 (1975): 69–75.

———. *Principles of Christian Theology.* 2nd ed. London: SCM Press, 1977.

Madsen, William G. *From Shadowy Types to Truth: Studies in Milton's Symbolism.* New Haven, CT: Yale University Press, 1968.

Magnani, Lorenzo. *Abduction, Reason, and Science: Processes of Discovery and Explanation.* New York: Plenum Publishers, 2001.

Majerus, Michael E. N. *Melanism: Evolution in Action.* Oxford: Oxford University Press, 1998.

Mandelbrote, Scott. "The Uses of Natural Theology in Seventeenth-Century England." *Science in Context* 20 (2007): 451–80.

Manson, Neil A. *God and Design: The Teleological Argument and Modern Science.* London: Routledge, 2003.

Marengo, Emilio, Maria Carla Gennaro, Elisa Robotti, Piero Rossanigo, Caterina Rinaudo, and Manuela Roz-Gastaldi. "Investigation of Anthropic Effects Connected with Metal Ions Concentration, Organic Matter and Grain Size in Bormida River Sediments." *Analytica Chimica Acta* 560 (2006): 172–83.

Markley, Robert. *Fallen Languages: Crises of Representation in Newtonian England, 1660–1740.* Ithaca, NY: Cornell University Press, 1993.

Marrone, Steven. "The Philosophy of Nature in the Early Thirteenth Century." In *Albertus Magnus and the Beginnings of the Medieval Reception of Aristotle in the Latin West,* edited by L. Honnefelder, R. Wood, M. Dreyer, and M. Aris, 115–57. Münster: Aschendorff, 2005.

Martin, Charles B., and John Heil. "The Ontological Turn." *Midwest Studies in Philosophy* 23 (1999): 34–60.

Martin, Michael F. *Atheism: A Philosophical Justification.* Philadelphia: Temple University Press, 1990.

Martin, Robert A. *Missing Links: Evolutionary Concepts and Transitions through Time.* Sudbury, MA: Jones & Bartlett, 2004.

Masel, Joanna. "Evolutionary Capacitance May Be Favored by Natural Selection." *Genetics* 170 (2005): 1359–71.

Matcheva, Katia I., Barney J. Conrath, Peter J. Gierasch, and F. Michael Flasar. "The Cloud Structure of the Jovian Atmosphere as Seen by the Cassini/CIRS Experiment." *Icarus* 179 (2005): 432–48.

Mather, Cotton. *The Christian Philosopher.* Edited by Winton U. Solberg. Urbana: University of Illinois Press, 1994.

Mathews, Gordon. *What Makes Life Worth Living? How Japanese and Americans Make Sense of Their Worlds.* Berkeley: University of California Press, 1996.

Maturana, Humberto, and Francisco Varela. *Autopoiesis and Cognition: The Realization of the Living.* Dordrecht: Reidel, 1973.

Maurer, Armand. "Darwin, Thomists, and Secondary Causality." *Review of Metaphysics* 57 (2004): 491–515.

May, Gerhard. *Creatio ex Nihilo: The Doctrine of "Creation out of Nothing" in Early Christian Thought.* Edinburgh: T&T Clark, 1995.

Maynard Smith, John, and Eörs Szathmáry. *The Major Transitions in Evolution.* Oxford: W. H. Freeman / Spektrum, 1995.

————. *The Origins of Life: From the Birth of Life to the Origin of Language.* Oxford: Oxford University Press, 1999.

Mayr, Ernst. *The Growth of Biological Thought.* Cambridge, MA: Belknap Press, 1982.

————. *This Is Biology: The Science of the Living World.* Cambridge, MA: Belknap Press, 1997.

————. *Toward a New Philosophy of Biology: Observations of an Evolutionist.* Cambridge, MA: Harvard University Press, 1988.

————. *What Makes Biology Unique? Considerations on the Autonomy of a Scientific Discipline.* Cambridge: Cambridge University Press, 2004.

Mazzarello, Paolo. "A Unifying Concept: The History of Cell Theory." *Nature Cell Biology* 1 (1999): E13–E15.

McCalla, Arthur. *The Creationist Debate: The Encounter between the Bible and the Historical Mind.* London: T&T Clark International, 2006.

McCarthy, Michael C. "'We Are Your Books': Augustine, the Bible, and the Practice of Authority." *Journal of the American Academy of Religion* 75 (2007): 324–52.

McCauley, Robert N. "The Naturalness of Religion and the Unnaturalness of Science." In *Explanation and Cognition,* edited by F. Keil and R. Wilson, 61–85. Cambridge, MA: MIT Press, 2000.

McClendon, James W., Jr., and James M. Smith. "Ian Ramsey's Model of Religious Language: A Qualified Appreciation." *Journal of the American Academy of Religion* 41 (1973): 413–24.

McGrath, Alister E. *Dawkins' God: Genes, Memes and the Meaning of Life.* Oxford: Blackwell Publishing, 2004.

————. *The Intellectual Origins of the European Reformation.* 2nd ed. Oxford: Blackwell, 2003.

————. "Karl Barth als Aufklärer? Der Zusammenhang seiner Lehre vom Werke Christi mit der Erwählungslehre." *Kerygma und Dogma* 81 (1984): 383–94.

————. *The Open Secret: A New Vision for Natural Theology.* Oxford: Blackwell, 2008.

————. *A Scientific Theology.* Vol. 1, *Nature.* London: Continuum, 2001.

————. *A Scientific Theology.* Vol. 2, *Reality.* London: Continuum, 2002.

————. *A Scientific Theology.* Vol. 3, *Theory.* London: Continuum, 2003.

————. "Theologie als Mathesis Universalis? Heinrich Scholz, Karl Barth, und der wissenschaftliche Status der christlichen Theologie." *Theologische Zeitschrift* 62 (2007): 44–57.

————. *Thomas F. Torrance: An Intellectual Biography.* Edinburgh: T&T Clark, 1999.

————. "Towards the Restatement and Renewal of a Natural Theology: A Dialogue with the Classic English Tradition." In *The Order of Things: Explorations in Scientific Theology,* edited by Alister E. McGrath, 63–96. Oxford: Blackwell Publishing, 2006.

————. "A Working Paper: Iterative Procedures and Closure in Systematic Theology." In *The Order of Things: Explorations in Scientific Theology,* edited by Alister E. McGrath, 194–203. Oxford: Blackwell Publishing, 2006.

McIntosh, Mark. "Faith, Reason, and the Mind of Christ." In *Reason and the Reasons of Faith,* edited by Paul J. Griffiths and Reinhart Hütter, 119–42. New York: T&T Clark, 2005.

McIntyre, Lee. "Emergence and Reduction in Chemistry: Ontological or Epistemological Concepts?" *Synthese* 155 (2006): 337–43.

McKeough, Michael J. *The Meaning of the Rationes Seminales in St. Augustine.* Washington: Catholic University of America Press, 1926.

McLaughlin, Peter. *Kant's Critique of Teleology in Biological Explanation: Antinomy and Teleology.* Lewiston, NY: Edwin Mellen Press, 1990.

McMullin, Ernan. "Cosmic Purpose and the Contingency of Human Evolution." *Theology Today* 55 (1998): 389–414.

———. "Fine-Tuning the Universe?" In *Science, Technology, and Religious Ideas*, edited by Mark H. Shale and George W. Shields, 97–125. Lanham, MD: University Press of America, 1994.

———. "Indifference Principle and Anthropic Principle in Cosmology." *Studies in the History and Philosophy of Science* 24 (1993): 359–89.

———. *The Inference That Makes Science*. Milwaukee: Marquette University Press, 1992.

———. "Introduction." In *Evolution and Creation*, edited by Ernan McMullin, 1–58. Notre Dame, IN: University of Notre Dame Press, 1985.

———. "Natural Science and Belief in a Creator." In *Physics, Philosophy, and Theology*, edited by Robert J. Russell, William R. Stoeger, and George V. Coyne, 49–79. Rome: Vatican Observatory, 1988.

———. "Plantinga's Defense of Special Creation." *Christian Scholar's Review* 21 (1991): 55–79.

Medawar, Peter B. *The Limits of Science*. Oxford: Oxford University Press, 1985.

Mendelsohn, Everett. "Locating 'Fitness' and L. J. Henderson." In *Fitness of the Cosmos for Life: Biochemistry and Fine-Tuning*, edited by John D. Barrow, Simon Conway Morris, Stephen J. Freeland, and Charles L. Harper, 3–19. Cambridge: Cambridge University Press, 2007.

Mettinger, Tryggve N. D. "Abbild oder Urbild? 'Imago Dei' in traditionsgeschichtlicher Sicht." *Zeitschrift für Alttestamentlicher Wissenschaft* 86 (1974): 403–24.

Mikkeli, Heikki. "The Foundation of an Autonomous Natural Philosophy: Zabarella on the Classification of Arts and Sciences." In *Method and Order in Renaissance Philosophy of Nature: The Aristotle Commentary Tradition*, edited by Daniel A. Di Liscia, Eckhard Kessler, and Charlotte Methuen, 211–28. Aldershot: Ashgate, 1997.

Miller, Fred D. *Nature, Justice and Rights in Aristotle's Politics*. Oxford: Clarendon Press, 1995.

Miller, Stanley L. "Production of Amino Acids under Possible Primitive Earth Conditions." *Science* 117 (1953): 528.

Mivart, St. George. *On the Genesis of Species*. New York: Appleton & Co., 1871.

Moltmann, Jürgen. *God in Creation: An Ecological Doctrine of Creation*. London: SCM Press, 1985.

Monod, Jacques. *Chance and Necessity: An Essay on the Natural Philosophy of Modern Biology*. New York: Alfred A. Knopf, 1971.

Moore, James F. "How Religious Tradition Survives in the World of Science: John Polkinghorne and Norbert Samuelson." *Zygon* 32 (1997): 115–24.

Moore, James R. *The Post-Darwinian Controversies: A Study of the Protestant Struggle to Come to Terms with Darwin in Great Britain and America, 1870–1900*. Cambridge: Cambridge University Press, 1979.

———. "Speaking of Science and Religion—Then and Now." *History of Science* 30 (1992): 311–23.

Morbidelli, Alessandro, John Chambers, Jonathan I. Lunine, Jean-Marc Petit, François Robert, Giovanni B. Valsecchi, and K. E. Cyr. "Source Regions and Timescales for the Delivery of Water to the Earth." *Meteoritics and Planetary Science* 35 (2000): 1309–20.

Morgan, David. *Visual Piety: A History and Theory of Popular Religious Images*. Berkeley: University of California Press, 1998.

Morgan, David T. "Benjamin Franklin: Champion of Generic Religion." *Historian* 62 (2000): 723–29.

Morley, Georgina. *John Macquarrie's Natural Theology: The Grace of Being*. Aldershot: Ashgate, 2003.

Morowitz, Harold J. *The Emergence of Everything: How the World Became Complex*. Oxford: Oxford University Press, 2002.

Morrison, Margaret. "A Study in Theory Unification: The Case of Maxwell's Electromagnetic Theory." *Studies in History and Philosophy of Science* 23 (1992): 103–45.

————. "Unification, Realism and Inference." *British Journal for Philosophy of Science* 41 (1990): 305–32.

————. *Unifying Scientific Theories: Physical Concepts and Mathematical Structures.* Cambridge: Cambridge University Press, 2000.

Mortensen, Beverly P. *The Priesthood in Targum Pseudo-Jonathan: Renewing the Profession.* Leiden: Brill, 2006.

Mukhanov, V. F. *Physical Foundations of Cosmology.* Cambridge: Cambridge University Press, 2005.

Müller, Achim. "Die inhärente Potentialität materieller (chemischer) Systeme." *Philosophia naturalis* 35 (1998): 333–58.

Muller, Charles H. "Spiritual Evolution and Muscular Theology: Lessons from Kingsley's Natural Theology." *University of Cape Town Studies in English* 15 (1986): 24–34.

Müller, Jörn, and Harald Lesch. "Woher kommt das Wasser der Erde?—Urgaswolke oder Meteoriten." *Chemie in unserer Zeit* 37 (2003): 242–46.

Muller, Richard A. "'Duplex cognitio Dei' in the Theology of Early Reformed Orthodoxy." *Sixteenth Century Journal* 10 (1979): 51–61.

Mullins, Phil. "Peirce's Abduction and Polanyi's Tacit Knowing." *Journal of Speculative Philosophy* 16 (2002): 198–224.

Munday, Philip L., Lynne van Herwerden, and Christine L. Dudgeon. "Evidence for Sympatric Speciation by Host Shift in the Sea." *Current Biology* 14 (2004): 1498–1504.

Munitz, Milton K. *The Mystery of Existence: An Essay in Philosophical Cosmology.* New York: Appleton-Century-Crofts, 1965.

Murdoch, Iris. *Metaphysics as a Guide to Morals.* London: Penguin, 1992.

Murdoch, John E. "The Analytic Character of Late Medieval Learning: Natural Philosophy without Nature." In *Approaches to Nature in the Middle Ages,* edited by Lawrence D. Roberts, 171–213. Binghamton, NY: Center for Medieval and Early Renaissance Studies, 1982.

Murphy, Nancey C. *Bodies and Souls, or Spirited Bodies?* Cambridge: Cambridge University Press, 2006.

————. "Emergence and Mental Causation." In *The Re-Emergence of Emergence: The Emergentist Hypothesis from Science to Religion,* edited by Philip Clayton and Paul Davies, 227–43. Oxford: Oxford University Press, 2006.

Musgrave, Alan. "Logical versus Historical Theories of Confirmation." *British Journal for Philosophy of Science* 25 (1974): 1–23.

Naddaf, Gerard. *The Greek Concept of Nature.* Albany: State University of New York Press, 2005.

Nadelman, Heather L. "Baconian Science in Post-Bellum America: Charles Peirce's 'Neglected Argument for the Reality of God.'" *Journal of the History of Ideas* 54 (1993): 79–96.

Nebelsick, Harold P. "Karl Barth's Understanding of Science." In *Theology beyond Christendom: Essays on the Centenary of the Birth of Karl Barth,* edited by John Thompson, 165–214. Allison Park, PA: Pickwick Publications, 1986.

Nelson, Paul A. "The Role of Theology in Current Evolutionary Reasoning." *Biology and Philosophy* 11 (1996): 493–517.

Newman, John Henry. *An Essay in Aid of a Grammar of Assent.* 2nd ed. London: Burns & Oates, 1870.

————. *The Idea of a University.* London: Longmans, Green & Co., 1907.

Newman, John Henry, Charles Stephen Dessain, and Thomas Gornall. *The Letters and Diaries of John Henry Newman.* 9 vols. Oxford: Clarendon Press, 1973.

Newman, William R. *Atoms and Alchemy: Chymistry and the Experimental Origins of the Scientific Revolution.* Chicago: University of Chicago Press, 2006.

Newton-Smith, W. H., and Steven Lukes. "The Underdetermination of Theory by Data." *Proceedings of the Aristotelian Society* 52 (1978): 71–91.

Nisbet, Barry. "The Rationalisation of the Holy Trinity from Lessing to Hegel." *Lessing Yearbook* 41 (1999): 65–89.

Noble, Denis. *The Music of Life: Biology beyond the Genome.* Oxford: Oxford University Press, 2006.

Noren, C. J., S. J. Anthony-Cahill, M. C. Griffith, and P. G. Schultz. "A General Method for Site-Specific Incorporation of Unnatural Amino Acids into Proteins." *Science* 244 (1989): 182–88.

Novak, David. *Natural Law in Judaism.* Cambridge: Cambridge University Press, 1998.

Numbers, Ronald L. *Darwinism Comes to America.* Cambridge, MA: Harvard University Press, 1998.

Nye, Mary Jo. "Physics and Chemistry: Commensurate or Incommensurate Sciences?" In *The Invention of Physical Science: Intersections of Mathematics, Theology and Natural Philosophy since the Seventeenth Century,* edited by M. J. Nye, J. L. Richards, and R.H. Stuewer, 205–24. Dordrecht: Kluwer Academic Publishers, 1992.

O'Collins, Gerald. *The Tripersonal God: Understanding and Interpreting the Trinity.* London: Continuum, 2004.

O'Connell, Robert J. *The Origin of the Soul in St. Augustine's Later Works.* New York: Fordham University Press, 1987.

Ogilvie, Brian W. "Natural History, Ethics, and Physico-Theology." In *Historia: Empiricism and Erudition in Early Modern Europe,* edited by Gianna Pomata and Nancy G. Siraisi, 75–103. Cambridge, MA: MIT Press, 2005.

Ogura, Atsushi, Kazuho Ikeo, and Takashi Gojobori. "Comparative Analysis of Gene Expression for Convergent Evolution of Camera Eye between Octopus and Human." *Genome Research* 14 (2004): 1555–61.

Okasha, Samir. "Van Fraasen's Critique of Inference to the Best Explanation." *Studies in History and Philosophy of Science* 31 (2000): 691–710.

Olafson, Frederick A. *Naturalism and the Human Condition: Against Scientism.* London: Routledge, 2001.

O'Leary, Don. *Roman Catholicism and Modern Science: A History.* New York: Continuum, 2006.

Oliver, Joan, and Randall S. Perry. "Definitely Life but Not Definitively." *Origins of Life and Evolution of Biospheres* 36 (2006): 515–21.

O'Loughlin, Taryn L., Wayne M. Patrick, and Ichiro Matsumura. "Natural History as a Predictor of Protein Evolvability." *Protein Engineering, Design and Selection* 19 (2006): 439–42.

Orgel, Leslie E. "Molecular Replication." *Nature* 358 (1992): 203–9.

Osborn, Eric F. *Irenaeus of Lyons.* Cambridge: Cambridge University Press, 2001.

Osborne, Colin P., and David J. Beerling. "Nature's Green Revolution: The Remarkable Evolutionary Rise of C4 Plants." *Philosophical Transactions of the Royal Society B* 361 (2006): 173–94.

Osler, Margaret, ed. *Rethinking the Scientific Revolution.* Cambridge: Cambridge University Press, 2000.

Ospovat, Dov. *The Development of Darwin's Theory: Natural History, Natural Theology, and Natural Selection, 1838–1859.* Cambridge: Cambridge University Press, 1995.

Outram, Dorinda. *The Enlightenment.* Cambridge: Cambridge University Press, 1995.

Paavola, Sami. "Abduction as a Logic of Discovery: The Importance of Strategies." *Foundations of Science* 9 (2005): 267–83.

———. "Hansonian and Harmanian Abduction as Models of Discovery." *International Studies in the Philosophy of Science* 20 (2006): 93–108.

———. "Peircean Abduction: Instinct or Inference?" *Semiotica* 153 (2005): 131–54.

Pace, Norman R. "The Universal Nature of Biochemistry." *Proceedings of the National Academy of Sciences* 98 (2001): 805–8.

Pais, Abraham. *Niels Bohr's Times, in Physics, Philosophy and Polity.* Oxford: Clarendon Press, 1991.

Paley William. *The Works of William Paley.* London: William Orr, 1844.

Pályi, Gyula, Claudia Zucchi, and Luciano Caglioti, eds. *Fundamentals of life.* Paris: Elsevier, 2002.

Pannenberg, Wolfhart. *Systematic Theology.* 3 vols. Grand Rapids: Eerdmans, 1991–98.

Paradis, James G. "Satire and Science in Victorian Culture." In *Victorian Science in Context,* edited by Bernard Lightman, 143–75. Chicago: University of Chicago Press, 1997.

Parascandola, John. "Organismic and Holistic Concepts in the Thought of L. J. Henderson." *Journal of the History of Biology* 4 (1971): 63–113.

Parker, Andrew R. "Colour in Burgess Shale Animals and the Effect of Light on Evolution in the Cambrian." *Proceedings of the Royal Society of London: Biological Sciences* 265 (1998): 967–72.

———. *In the Blink of an Eye: The Cause of the Most Dramatic Event in the History of Life.* London: Free Press, 2003.

Partridge, R. B. *3K: The Cosmic Microwave Background Radiation.* Cambridge: Cambridge University Press, 1995.

Pasorek, Günter. "Eine historische Notiz zur Scheidung von 'theologia civilis' und 'naturalis.'" In *Symmicta philologica Salisburgensia: Georgio Pfligersdorffer sexagenario oblata,* edited by Joachim Dalfen, Karl Forstner, Maximilian Fussl, and Wolfgang Speyer, 87–103. Rome: Edizioni dell'Ateneo, 1980.

Paterson, W. P. *The Rule of Faith.* 2nd ed. London: Hodder & Stoughton, 1912.

Paton, H. J. *The Modern Predicament: A Study in the Philosophy of Religion.* London: Allen & Unwin, 1955.

Pattison, Stephen. *Seeing Things: Deepening Relations with Visual Artefacts.* London: SCM Press, 2007.

Paul, Eldor A. *Soil Microbiology, Ecology, and Biochemistry.* 3rd ed. Burlington, MA: Academic Press, 2007.

Pauling, Linus, Robert B. Corey, and Herman R. Branson. "The Structure of Proteins: Two Hydrogen-Bonded Helical Configurations of the Polypeptide Chain." *Proceedings of the National Academy of Sciences* 37 (1951): 205–11.

Peebles, P. J. E. *Quantum Mechanics.* Princeton, NJ: Princeton University Press, 1992.

Peirce, Charles S. *Collected Papers of Charles Sanders Peirce.* Edited by Charles Hartshorne and Paul Weiss. 8 vols. Cambridge, MA: Harvard University Press, 1960.

Pelikan, Jaroslav. *Christianity and Classical Culture: The Metamorphosis of Natural Theology in the Christian Encounter with Hellenism.* New Haven, CT: Yale University Press, 1993.

Pelland, Gilles. *Cinq études d'Augustin sur les débuts de la Genèse.* Paris: Desclée, 1972.

Penrose, Roger. "Difficulties with Inflationary Cosmology." In *Proceedings of the 14th Texas Symposium on Relativistic Astrophysics,* edited by E. J. Fergus, 249–64. New York: New York Academy of Sciences, 1989.

———. *The Road to Reality: A Complete Guide to the Laws of the Universe.* London: Jonathan Cape, 2004.

Peperzak, Adriaan T. *The Quest for Meaning: Friends of Wisdom from Plato to Levinas.* New York: Fordham University Press, 2003.

Perl, Eric D. "St. Gregory Palamas and the Metaphysics of Creation." *Dionysius* 14 (1990): 105–30.

Peters, John W., and Robert K. Szilagyi. "Exploring New Frontiers of Nitrogenase Structure and Mechanism." *Current Opinion in Chemical Biology* 10 (2006): 101–8.

Peters, William A. M. *Gerard Manley Hopkins: A Critical Essay towards the Understanding of His Poetry.* London: Oxford University Press, 1948.

Philipp, Wolfgang. "Physicotheology in the Age of Enlightenment: Appearance and History." *Studies on Voltaire and the Eighteenth Century* 57 (1967): 1233–67.

Pittendrigh, Colin S. "Adaptation, Natural Selection, and Behavior." In *Behavior and Evolution*, edited by Anne Roe and George Gaylord Simpson, 390–416. New Haven, CT: Yale University Press, 1958.

Plantinga, Alvin. *God and Other Minds: A Study of the Rational Justification of Belief in God.* Cornell Paperbacks. Ithaca, NY: Cornell University Press, 1990.

———. "Reliabilism, Analyses and Defeaters." *Philosophy and Phenomenological Research* 55 (1995): 427–64.

———. "When Faith and Reason Clash: Evolution and the Bible." *Christian Scholar's Review* 21 (1991): 8–33.

Plutynski, Anya. "Explanatory Unification and the Early Synthesis." *British Journal for Philosophy of Science* 56 (2005): 595–609.

Polanyi, Michael. "Science and Reality." *British Journal for the Philosophy of Science* 18 (1967): 177–96.

———. *The Tacit Dimension.* Garden City, NY: Doubleday, 1967.

Polignac, François de. *Cults, Territory, and the Origins of the Greek City-state.* Chicago: University of Chicago Press, 1995.

Polkinghorne, John C. *Belief in God in an Age of Science.* New Haven, CT: Yale University Press, 1998.

———. "Physics and Metaphysics in a Trinitarian Perspective." *Theology and Science* 1 (2003): 33–49.

———. *Science and Creation: The Search for Understanding.* London: SPCK, 1988.

———. "Where Is Natural Theology Today?" *Science and Christian Belief* 18 (2006): 169–79.

Poole, William. "Francis Lodwick's Creation: Theology and Natural Philosophy in the Early Royal Society." *Journal of the History of Ideas* 66 (2005): 245–63.

Poon, Wilson C. K. "The Physics of a Model Colloid-Polymer Mixture." *Journal of Physics: Condensed Matter* 14 (2002): R859–R880.

Popa, Radu. *Between Necessity and Probability: Searching for the Definition and Origin of Life.* Berlin: Springer-Verlag, 2004.

Popper, Karl R. *The Logic of Scientific Discovery.* New York: Basic Books, 1959.

———. "Natural Selection and the Emergence of Mind." *Dialectica* 32 (1978): 339–55.

———. *Unended Quest: An Intellectual Autobiography.* Rev. ed. London: Fontana, 1976.

Posner, Michael I., and Steven E. Petersen. "The Attentional System of the Human Brain." *Annual Review of Neuroscience* 13 (1990): 25–42.

Potter, Vincent G. *Peirce's Philosophical Perspectives.* New York: Fordham University Press, 1996.

Powell, Samuel M. *Participating in God: Creation and Trinity.* Minneapolis: Fortress, 2003.

———. *The Trinity in German Thought.* Cambridge: Cambridge University Press, 2001.

Pozzi, Gianluca, Véronique Birault, Birgit Werner, Olivier Dannenmuller, Yoichi Nakatani, Guy Ourisson, and Susumu Terakawa. "Single-Chain Polyprenyl Phosphates Form 'Primitive' Membranes." *Angewandte Chemie International Edition* 35 (1996): 177–80.

Pratt, Andrew J. "The Curious Case of Phosphate Solubility." *Chemistry in New Zealand* 70 (2006): 78–80.

Prenter, Regin. "Das Problem der natürlichen Theologie bei Karl Barth." *Theologische Literaturzeitung* 77 (1952): 607–11.

Prescott, Lansing M., John P. Harley, and Donald A. Klein. *Microbiology.* 4th ed. Boston, MA: McGraw-Hill, 1999.

Prevost, Robert. *Probability and Theistic Explanation.* Oxford: Clarendon Press, 1990.

———. "Swinburne, Mackie, and Bayes' Theorem." *International Journal for the Philosophy of Religion* 17 (1985): 175–84.

Price, S. R. F. *Rituals and Power: The Roman Imperial Cult in Asia Minor*. Cambridge: Cambridge University Press, 1984.

Pross, Addy. "On the Emergence of Biological Complexity: Life as a Kinetic State of Matter." *Origins of Life and Evolution of Biospheres* 35 (2005): 151–66.

Psillos, Stathis. "The Fine Structure of Inference to the Best Explanation." *Philosophy and Phenomenological Research* 74 (2007): 441–48.

———. "Simply the Best: A Case for Abduction." In *Computational Logic: From Logic Programming into the Future*, edited by Fariba Sadri and Anthony Kakas, 605–25. Berlin: Springer-Verlag, 2002.

Rajendiran, T., M. Caudle, Martin L. Kirk, Ika Setyawati, Jeff W. Kampf, and Vincent L. Pecoraro. "Evaluating Hydrogen Bond Interactions in Enzymes Containing Mn(III)-Histidine Complexation Using Manganese-Imidazole Complexes." *Journal of Biological Inorganic Chemistry* 8 (2003): 283–93.

Ramsey, Ian T. *Models and Mystery*. Whidden Lectures. London: Oxford University Press, 1964.

Rariy, Roman V., and Alexander M. Klibanov. "Correct Protein Folding in Glycerol." *Proceedings of the National Academy of Sciences* 94 (1997): 13520–23.

Rasmussen, Steen, Liaohai Chen, Martin Nilsson, and Shigeaki Abe. "Bridging Nonliving and Living Matter." *Artificial Life* 9 (2003): 269–316.

Raymond, Jason, and Daniel Segré. "The Effect of Oxygen on Biochemical Networks and the Evolution of Complex Life." *Science* 311 (2006): 1764–67.

Rees, Martin J. *Just Six Numbers: The Deep Forces That Shape the Universe*. London: Phoenix, 2000.

———. *New Perspectives in Astrophysical Cosmology*. 2nd ed. Cambridge: Cambridge University Press, 2000.

Regier, Jerome C., and Jeffrey W. Schultz. "Molecular Phylogeny of Arthropods and the Significance of the 'Cambrian Explosion' for Molecular Systematics." *American Zoologist* 38 (1998): 918–28.

Reid, Duncan. *Energies of the Spirit: Trinitarian Models in Eastern Orthodox and Western Theology*. Atlanta: Scholars Press, 1997.

Reid, Robert G. B. *Biological Emergences: Evolution by Natural Experiment*. Cambridge, MA: MIT Press, 2007.

Renger, Gernot. "Oxidative Photosynthetic Water Splitting: Energetics, Kinetics and Mechanism." *Photosynthesis Research* 92 (2007): 407–25.

Rhee, Young Min, Eric J. Sorin, Guha Jayachandran, Erik Lindahl, and Vijay S. Pande. "Simulations of the Role of Water in the Protein-Folding Mechanism." *Proceedings of the National Academy of Sciences* 101 (2004): 6456–61.

Ricard, Jacques. "Reduction, Integration and Emergence in Biochemical Networks." *Biology of the Cell* 96 (2004): 719–25.

Richerson, Peter J., and Robert Boyd. *Not by Genes Alone: How Culture Transformed Human Evolution*. Chicago: University of Chicago Press, 2005.

Richmond, Alasdair. "Between Abduction and the Deep Blue Sea." *Philosophical Quarterly* 49 (1999): 86–91.

Ridderbos, Herman. *Paul: An Outline of His Theology*. Grand Rapids: Eerdmans, 1997.

Ridley, Mark. *Evolution*. 3rd ed. Malden, MA: Blackwell Science, 2004.

Rivers, Isabel. *Reason, Grace, and Sentiment: A Study of the Language of Religion and Ethics in England, 1660–1780*. 2 vols. Cambridge: Cambridge University Press, 1991.

Rizzotti, Martino, and André E. Brack, eds. *Defining Life: The Central Problems in Theoretical Biology*. Padua: University of Padua, 1996.

Roat-Malone, Rosette M. *Bioinorganic Chemistry: A Short Course*. 2nd ed. Hoboken, NJ: Wiley-Interscience, 2007.

Roberts, Jon H. *Darwinism and the Divine in America: Protestant Intellectuals and Organic Evolution, 1859–1900*. Madison: University of Wisconsin Press, 1988.

Roberts, Noel Keith. "Newman on the Argument from Design." *New Blackfriars* 88 (2007): 56–66.

Robinson, David. "Emerson's Natural Theology and the Paris Naturalists: Toward a Theory of Animated Nature." *Journal of the History of Ideas* 41 (1980): 69–88.

Robson, Jon M. "The Fiat and the Finger of God: The Bridgewater Treatises." In *Victorian Faith in Crisis: Essays on Continuity and Change in Nineteenth-Century Religious Belief*, edited by Richard J. Helmstadter and Bernard Lightman, 71–125. London: Macmillan, 1990.

Romano, Donatella, and Francesca Matteucci. "Contrasting Copper Evolution in Ω Centauri and the Milky Way." *Monthly Notices of the Royal Astronomical Society: Letters* 378 (2007): L59-L63.

Rose, Steven P. R. *Lifelines: Biology, Freedom, Determinism*. Harmondsworth: Penguin, 1997.

———. "Précis of Lifelines: Biology, Freedom, Determinism." *Behavioral and Brain Sciences* 22 (1999): 871–921.

Rosen, Frederick. *Classical Utilitarianism from Hume to Mill*. London: Routledge, 2003.

Rowley, H. H. "The Book of Job and Its Meaning." *Bulletin of the John Rylands Library* 41 (1958): 162–207.

Ruben, David-Hillel. *Explaining Explanation*. London: Routledge, 1990.

Rubin, Daniel L., Nigam H. Shah, and Natalya F. Noy. "Biomedical Ontologies: A Functional Perspective." *Briefings in Bioinformatics* 9 (2008): 75–90.

Rupke, Nicolaas A. *The Great Chain of History: William Buckland and the English School of Geology (1814–1849)*. Oxford: Clarendon Press, 1983.

Ruskin, John. *Works*. Edited by E. T. Cook and A. Wedderburn. 39 vols. London: Allen, 1903–12.

Rye, Robert, and Heinrich D. Holland. "Paleosols and the Evolution of Atmospheric Oxygen: A Critical Review." *American Journal of Science* 298 (1998): 621–72.

Salmon, Wesley C. *Scientific Explanation and the Causal Structure of the World*. Princeton, NJ: Princeton University Press, 1984.

———. "Scientific Explanation: Three Basic Conceptions." *Philosophy of Science Association* 2 (1984): 293–305.

Sanders, Fred. "Trinity Talk, Again." *Dialog: A Journal of Theology* 44 (2005): 264–72.

Sayers, Dorothy L. "Creative Mind." In *Letters of a Diminished Church*, 35–48. Nashville: W Publishing, 2004.

———. *The Mind of the Maker*. London: Methuen, 1941.

Schaffner, Kenneth F. *Discovery and Explanation in Biology and Medicine*. Chicago: University of Chicago Press, 1993.

Schickore, Jutta, and Friedrich Steinle, eds. *Revisiting Discovery and Justification: Historical and Philosophical Perspectives on the Context Distinction*. Dordrecht: Springer-Verlag, 2006.

Schlange-Schöningen, Heinrich. *Die römische Gesellschaft bei Galen: Biographie und Sozialgeschichte*. Berlin: de Gruyter, 2003.

Schmidt, James. "Civility, Enlightenment, and Society: Conceptual Confusions and Kantian Remedies." *American Political Science Review* 92 (1998): 419–27.

———. *What Is Enlightenment? Eighteenth-Century Answers and Twentieth-Century Questions*. Berkeley: University of California Press, 1996.

Schoedel, William R. "Christian 'Atheism' and the Peace of the Roman Empire." *Church History* 42 (1973): 309–19.

Schreiber, Stuart L., Tarun M. Kapoor, and Günther Wess, eds. *Chemical Biology: From Small Molecules to Systems Biology and Drug Design*. 3 vols. Weinheim: Wiley-VCH Verlag, 2007.

Schreiter, Robert J. *Constructing Local Theologies*. London: SCM, 1985.

Schulze-Makuch, Dirk, and Louis N. Irwin. *Life in the Universe: Expectations and Constraints*. Berlin: Springer-Verlag, 2006.

Schurz, Gerhard. "Scientific Explanation: A Critical Survey." *Foundations of Science* 1 (1995): 429–65.

Schweder, Rebecca. "A Defense of a Unificationist Theory of Explanation." *Foundations of Science* 10 (2005): 421–35.

Scott, Douglas. "The Standard Cosmological Model." *Canadian Journal of Physics* 84 (2006): 419–35.

Sebeok, Thomas A., and Jean Umiker-Sebeok. "'You Know My Method': A Juxtaposition of Charles S. Peirce and Sherlock Holmes." In *The Sign of Three: Dupin, Holmes, Peirce*, edited by Umberto Eco and Thomas A. Sebeok, 11–54. Bloomington: Indiana University Press, 1983.

Secord, James A. "Nature's Fancy: Charles Darwin and the Breeding of Pigeons." *Isis* 72 (1981): 163–86.

Shanahan, Timothy. "Darwinian Naturalism, Theism, and Biological Design." *Perspectives on Science and Christian Faith* 49 (1997): 170–78.

Shipway, Brad. "The Theological Application of Bhaskar's Stratified Reality: The Scientific Theology of A. E. McGrath." *Journal of Critical Realism* 3 (2004): 191–203.

Short, T. L. *Peirce's Theory of Signs*. Cambridge: Cambridge University Press, 2007.

———. "Teleology in Nature." *American Philosophical Quarterly* 30 (1983): 311–20.

Shults, F. Leron. "Constitutive Relationality in Anthropology and Trinity: Shaping and *Imago Dei* in Barth and Pannenberg." *Neue Zeitschrift für systematische Theologie und Religionsphilosophie* 39 (1997): 304–22.

Siegbahn, Per E. M., and Margareta R. A. Blomberg. "Transition-Metal Systems in Biochemistry Studied by High-Accuracy Quantum Chemical Methods." *Chemical Reviews* 100 (2000): 421–37.

Siegbahn, Per E. M., and Tomasz Borowski. "Modeling Enzymatic Reactions Involving Transition Metals." *Accounts of Chemical Research* 39 (2006): 729–38.

Silberstein, Michael. "Reduction, Emergence, and Explanation." In *Blackwell Guide to the Philosophy of Science*, edited by Peter Machamer and Michael Silberstein, 80–107. Oxford: Blackwell, 2002.

Silk, Joseph. *The Infinite Cosmos: Questions from the Frontiers of Cosmology*. Oxford: Oxford University Press, 2006.

Singer, S. J. "The Molecular Organization of Biological Membranes." In *Structure and Function of Biological Membranes*, edited by L. I. Rothfield, 145–222. New York: Academic Press, 1971.

Singer, S. J., and G. L. Nicolson. "The Fluid Mosaic Model of the Structure of Cell Membranes." *Science* 175 (1972): 720–31.

Skinner, H. Catherine W. "In Praise of Phosphates; or Why Vertebrates Chose Apatite to Mineralize Their Skeletal Elements." In *Frontiers in Geochemistry: Organic, Solution, and Ore Deposit Geochemistry*, edited by W. G. Ernst, 41–49. Columbia, MD: Geological Society of America, 2002.

Sloan, Phillip R. "From Natural Law to Evolutionary Ethics in Enlightenment French Natural History." In *Biology and the Foundation of Ethics*, edited by Jane Maienschein and Michael Ruse, 52–83. Cambridge: Cambridge University Press, 1999.

———. "Getting the Questions Right: Catholics and Evolutionary Theory." *Pax Romana* 64 (2003): 13–32.

———. "'The Sense of Sublimity': Darwin on Nature and Divinity." *Osiris* 16 (2001): 251–69.

Smith, Justin E. H., ed. *The Problem of Animal Generation in Early Modern Philosophy*. Cambridge: Cambridge University Press, 2006.

Smith, Mark S. *The Origins of Biblical Monotheism: Israel's Polytheistic Background and the Ugaritic Texts*. Oxford: Oxford University Press, 2001.

Smith, Michael D. *The Origin of Stars*. London: Imperial College Press, 2004.

Smith, Quentin. "Causation and the Logical Impossibility of a Divine Cause." *Philosophical Topics* 24 (1996): 169–91.

Smith, Robert W. *The Expanding Universe: Astronomy's "Great Debate," 1900–1931*. Cambridge: Cambridge University Press, 1982.

Smolin, Lee. *The Life of the Cosmos*. New York: Oxford University Press, 1997.

Smuts, Barbara. "Emergence in Social Evolution: A Great Ape Example." In *The Re-Emergence of Emergence: The Emergentist Hypothesis from Science to Religion*, edited by Philip Clayton and Paul Davies, 166–86. Oxford: Oxford University Press, 2006.

Snir, Yehuda, and Randall D. Kamien. "Entropically Driven Helix Formation." *Science* 307 (2005): 1067.

Snyder, Laura J. "Discoverers' Induction." *Philosophy of Science* 64 (1997): 580–604.

———. "The Mill-Whewell Debate: Much Ado about Induction." *Perspectives on Science* 5 (1997): 159–98.

Snyder, Michael, and Mark Gerstein. "Defining Genes in the Genomics Era." *Science* 300 (2003): 258–60.

Sober, Elliott. "The Two Faces of Fitness." In *Thinking about Evolution: Historical, Philosophical, and Political Perspectives*, edited by R. Singh, D. Paul, C. Krimbas, and J. Beatty, 309–21. Cambridge: Cambridge University Press, 2001.

Soderberg, Timothy. "Biosynthesis of Ribose-5-Phosphate and Erythrose-4-Phosphate in Archaea: A Phylogenetic Analysis of Archaeal Genomes." *Archaea* 1 (2005): 347–52.

Solberg, Winton U. "Science and Religion in Early America: Cotton Mather's 'Christian Philosopher.'" *Church History* 56 (1987): 73–92.

Spaemann, Robert. "Rationality and Faith in God." *Communio* 32 (2005): 618–36.

Sparkes, J. J. "Pattern Recognition and Scientific Progress." *Mind* 81 (1971): 29–41.

Spencer, Liam P., Bruce A. MacKay, Brian O. Patrick, and Michael D. Fryzuk. "Inner-Sphere Two-Electron Reduction Leads to Cleavage and Functionalization of Coordinated Dinitrogen." *Proceedings of the National Academy of Sciences* 103 (2006): 17094–98.

Stacey, F. D. "Kelvin's Age of the Earth Paradox Revisited." *Journal of Geophysical Research* 105 (2000): 13155–58.

Staehelin, L. Andrew. "Chloroplast Structure: From Chlorophyll Granules to Supra-Molecular Architecture of Thylakoid Membranes." *Photosynthesis Research* 76 (2003): 185–96.

Stamos, David N. "Popper, Falsifiability, and Evolutionary Biology." *Biology and Philosophy* 11 (1996): 161–91.

Stanford, P. Kyle. "Darwin's Pangenesis and the Problem of Unconceived Alternatives." *British Journal for Philosophy of Science* 57 (2006): 121–44.

Steigerwald, Joan. "Kant's Concept of Natural Purpose and the Reflecting Power of Judgement." *Studies in History and Philosophy of Science C* 37 (2006): 712–34.

Steinbeck, Christoph, and Clemens Robert. "The Role of Ionic Backbones in RNA Structure: An Unusually Stable Non-Watson-Crick Duplex of a Nonionic Analog in an Apolar Medium." *Journal of the American Chemical Society* 120 (1998): 11576–80.

Stenkamp, Ronald E. "Dioxygen and Hemerythrin." *Chemical Reviews* 94 (1994): 715–26.

Stenke, Johannes Maria. *John Polkinghorne: Konzonanz von Naturwissenschaft und Theologie*. Göttingen: Vandenhoeck & Ruprecht, 2006.

Stenmark, Mikael. *Scientism: Science, Ethics and Religion*. Aldershot: Ashgate, 2001.

Stephan, Achim. "Emergence—A Systematic View on Its Historical Facets." In *Emergence or Reduction? Essays on the Prospects of Nonreductive Physicalism*, edited by Ansgar Beckermann, Hans Flohr, and Jaegwon Kim, 25–48. Berlin: de Gruyter, 1992.

Sterelny, Kim. "Understanding Life: Recent Work in the Philosophy of Biology." *British Journal for the Philosophy of Science* 46 (1995): 155–83.

Sterelny, Kim, and Paul E. Griffiths. *Sex and Death: An Introduction to Philosophy of Biology*. Chicago: University of Chicago Press, 1999.

Stoeger, William R. "The Immanent Directionality of the Evolutionary Process, and Its Relationship to Teleology." In *Evolutionary and Molecular Biology: Scientific Perspectives on Divine Action*, edited by Robert J. Russell, William R. Stoeger, and Francisco Ayala, 163–90. Rome: Vatican Observatory, 1999.

Stoeger, William R., and Nancey C. Murphy, eds. *Evolution and Emergence: Systems, Organisms, Persons*. Oxford: Oxford University Press, 2007.

Sudduth, Michael Czapkay. "The Prospects for 'Mediate' Natural Theology in John Calvin." *Religious Studies* 31 (1996): 53–68.

Sullivan, John. *The Image of God: The Doctrine of St. Augustine and Its Influence*. Dubuque, IA: Priory Press, 1963.

Swift, Louis J. "Basil and Ambrose on the Six Days of Creation." *Augustinianum* 21 (1981): 317–28.

Swinburne, Richard. *The Existence of God*. 2nd ed. Oxford: Clarendon Press, 2004.

———. "Natural Theology, Its 'Dwindling Probabilities' and 'Lack of Rapport.'" *Faith and Philosophy* 21 (2004): 533–46.

Swoyer, Chris. "How Ontology Might Be Possible: Explanation and Inference in Metaphysics." *Midwest Studies in Philosophy* 23 (1999): 100–131.

Szekeres, Attila. "Karl Barth und die natürliche Theologie." *Evangelische Theologie* 24 (1966): 229–42.

Takano, Kazufumi, J. Martin Scholtz, James C. Sacchettini, and C. Nick Pace. "The Contribution of Polar Group Burial to Protein Stability Is Strongly Context-Dependent." *Journal of Biological Chemistry* 278 (2003): 31790–95.

Tang, Paul C. L. "On the Similarities between Scientific Discovery and Musical Creativity: A Philosophical Analysis." *Leonardo* 17 (1984): 261–68.

Tegmark, Max. "On the Dimensionality of Spacetime." *Classical and Quantum Gravity* 14 (1997): L69–L75.

Teixeira, José, Alenka Luzar, and Stéphane Longeville. "Dynamics of Hydrogen Bonds: How to Probe Their Role in the Unusual Properties of Liquid Water." *Journal of Physics: Condensed Matter* 18 (2006): S2353–62.

Teske, Roland J. "Augustine of Hippo on Seeing with the Eyes of the Mind." In *Ambiguity in Western Thought*, edited by Craig J. N. de Paulo, Patrick Messina, and Marc Stier, 72–87, 221–26. New York: Peter Lang, 2005.

———. "The Image and Likeness of God in St. Augustine's *De Genesi ad litteram liber imperfectus*." *Augustinianum* 30 (1990): 441–51.

———. "St. Augustine's View of the Human Condition in *De Genesi contra Manichaeos*." *Augustinian Studies* 22 (1991): 141–55.

Thagard, Paul. "The Best Explanation: Criteria for Theory Choice." *Journal of Philosophy* 75 (1978): 76–92.

———. *Computational Philosophy of Science*. Cambridge, MA: MIT Press, 1988.

Thomas, A. L. R. "The Breath of Life—Did Increased Oxygen Levels Trigger the Cambrian Explosion?" *Trends in Ecology and Evolution* 12 (1997): 44–45.

Tilley, Terrence W. "Ian Ramsey and Empirical Fit." *Journal of the American Academy of Religion* 45 (1977): 357 (Abstract), G:963–88 (in September Supplement).

Torchia, N. Joseph. *Creatio ex Nihilo and the Theology of St. Augustine*. New York: Peter Lang, 1999.

Torrance, Thomas F. "Divine and Contingent Order." In *The Sciences and Theology in the Twentieth Century*, edited by A. R. Peacocke, 81–97. Notre Dame, IN: University of Notre Dame Press, 1981.

———. "The Problem of Natural Theology in the Thought of Karl Barth." *Religious Studies* 6 (1970): 121–35.

———. *Theological Science.* London: Oxford University Press, 1969.

Tropp, Eduard A., Viktor Y. Frenkel, and Arthur D. Chernin. *Alexander A. Friedmann: The Man Who Made the Universe Expand.* Cambridge: Cambridge University Press, 1993.

Trost, Lou Ann. "Theology's Need for a New Interpretation of Nature: Correlate of the Doctrine of Grace." *Dialog: A Journal of Theology* 46 (2007): 246–54.

Tsumura, David T. *The Earth and the Waters in Genesis 1 and 2: A Linguistic Investigation.* Sheffield: Sheffield Academic Press, 1989.

Tuck, Richard. "The 'Christian Atheism' of Thomas Hobbes." In *Atheism from the Reformation to the Enlightenment*, edited by Michael Hunter and David Wootton, 102–20. Oxford: Clarendon Press, 1992.

Ulmschneider, Peter. *Intelligent Life in the Universe: From Common Origins to the Future of Humanity.* Berlin: Springer-Verlag, 2004.

Valentine, James W., David Jablonski, and Douglas H. Erwin. "Fossils, Molecules and Embryos: New Perspectives on the Cambrian Explosion." *Development* 126 (1999): 851–59.

Van Bavel, Tarsicius. "The Creator and the Integrity of Creation in the Fathers of the Church." *Augustinian Studies* 21 (1990): 1–33.

Van der Watt, J. G., ed. *Salvation in the New Testament: Perspectives on Soteriology.* Leiden: Brill, 2005.

Van Till, Howard J. "Basil, Augustine, and the Doctrine of Creation's Functional Integrity." *Science and Christian Belief* 8 (1996): 21–38.

Van Valen, Leigh M. "How Far Does Contingency Rule?" *Evolutionary Theory* 10 (1991): 47–52.

Vande Kemp, Hendrika. "The Gifford Lectures on Natural Theology: Historical Background to James's 'Varieties.'" *Streams of William James* 4 (2002): 2–8.

Veronese, Andrea, and Pier Luigi Luisi. "An Autocatalytic Reaction Leading to Spontaneously Assembled Phosphatidyl Nucleoside Giant Vesicles." *Journal of the American Chemical Society* 120 (1998): 2662–63.

Vetsigian, Kalin, Carl Woese, and Nigel Goldenfeld. "Collective Evolution and the Genetic Code." *Proceedings of the National Academy of Sciences* 103 (2006): 10696–701.

Vidal, Fernando, and Bernard Kleeberg. "Knowledge, Belief, and the Impulse to Natural Theology." *Science in Context* 20 (2007): 381–400.

Vijh, Uma P., Adolf N. Witt, and Karl D. Gordon. "Discovery of Blue Luminescence in the Red Rectangle: Possible Fluorescence from Neutral Polycyclic Aromatic Hydrocarbon Molecules?" *Astrophysical Journal Letters* 606 (2004): L65–L68.

Vilenkin, Alex. *Many Worlds in One: The Search for Other Universes.* New York: Hill & Wang, 2006.

Wade, Michael J. "Community Genetics and Species Interactions." *Ecology* 84 (2003): 583–85.

———. "A Gene's Eye View of Epistasis, Selection and Speciation." *Journal of Evolutionary Biology* 15 (2002): 337–46.

Wagner, Andreas. *Robustness and Evolvability in Living Systems.* Princeton, NJ: Princeton University Press, 2005.

Walker, Mark A., and Milan M. Cirkovic. "Astrophysical Fine Tuning, Naturalism, and the Contemporary Design Argument." *International Studies in the Philosophy of Science* 20 (2006): 285–307.

Walsh, Denis M. "Organisms as Natural Purposes: The Contemporary Evolutionary Perspective." *Studies in History and Philosophy of Science* 37 (2006): 771–91.

Ward, Keith. *Religion and Creation.* Oxford: Oxford University Press, 1996.

Ward, Peter D., and Donald Brownlee. *Rare Earth: Why Complex Life Is Uncommon in the Universe.* New York: Copernicus, 2003.

Ward, Peter D., and David W. Ehlert. *Out of Thin Air: Dinosaurs, Birds, and Earth's Ancient Atmosphere.* Washington, DC: Joseph Henry Press, 2006.

Webb, Mark O. "Natural Theology and the Concept of Perfection in Descartes, Spinoza and Leibniz." *Religious Studies* 25 (1989): 459–75.

Webster, John. *Barth.* 2nd ed. London: Continuum, 2004.

Werkmeister, W. H. *Nicolai Hartmann's New Ontology.* Tallahassee: Florida State University Press, 1990.

Wesson, Paul S. "Olbers's Paradox and the Spectral Intensity of the Extragalactic Background Light." *Astrophysical Journal* 367 (1991): 399–406.

Westheimer, Frank H. "Why Nature Chose Phosphates." *Science* 235 (1987): 1173–78.

Whewell, William. *Astronomy and General Physics Considered with Reference to Natural Theology.* 5th ed. London: William Pickering, 1836.

———. *Philosophy of the Inductive Sciences.* 2 vols. London: John W. Parker, 1847.

Wigner, Eugene. "The Unreasonable Effectiveness of Mathematics." *Communications on Pure and Applied Mathematics* 13 (1960): 1–14.

Wiles, Maurice. *Archetypal Heresy: Arianism through the Centuries.* Oxford: Clarendon Press, 1996.

Wilken, Robert L. *The Christians as the Romans Saw Them.* 2nd ed. New Haven, CT: Yale University Press, 2003.

Williams, George C. *Adaptation and Natural Selection: A Critique of Some Current Evolutionary Thought.* Princeton, NJ: Princeton University Press, 1966.

———. *Natural Selection: Domains, Levels, and Challenges.* New York: Oxford University Press, 1992.

Williams, Rowan. "Barth on the Triune God." In *Karl Barth: Studies of His Theological Method,* edited by S. W. Sykes, 147–93. Oxford: Clarendon Press, 1979.

———. "Sapientia and Trinity: Reflections on the *De Trinitate.*" In *Mélanges T. J. Van Bavel,* edited by Tarsicius J. van Bavel, Bernard Bruning, and Mathijs Lamberigts, 317–32. Leuven: Uitgeverij Peeters, 1990.

Williams, R. J. P. "The Inorganic Chemistry of Life." In *The New Chemistry,* edited by Nina Hall, 259–99. Cambridge: Cambridge University Press, 2000.

———. "Metal Ions in Biological Systems." *Biological Reviews* 28 (1953): 381–412.

Williams, R. J. P., and B. Abolmaali. *Bioinorganic Chemistry: Trace Element Evolution from Anaerobes to Aerobes.* Berlin: Springer-Verlag, 1998.

Williams, R. J. P., and J. J. R. Fraústo da Silva. *The Chemistry of Evolution: The Development of Our Ecosystem.* Boston: Elsevier, 2006.

———. "Evolution Was Chemically Constrained." *Journal of Theoretical Biology* 220 (2003): 323–43.

———. *The Natural Selection of the Chemical Elements: The Environment and Life's Chemistry.* Oxford: Clarendon Press, 1996.

Wilson, David Sloan. "A Critique of R. D. Alexander's Views on Group Selection." *Biology and Philosophy* 14 (1999): 431–49.

Wilson, David Sloan, and Edward O. Wilson. "Rethinking the Theoretical Foundation of Sociobiology." *Quarterly Review of Biology* 82 (2007): 327–48.

Wilson, James Q. *The Moral Sense.* New York: Free Press, 1995.

Witham, Larry. *The Measure of God: Our Century-Long Struggle to Reconcile Science and Religion.* San Francisco: HarperSanFrancisco, 2005.

Wolfson, Harry A. "Patristic Arguments against the Eternity of the World." *Harvard Theological Review* 59 (1966): 351–67.

Wolpert, Lewis. *The Unnatural Nature of Science.* Cambridge, MA: Harvard University Press, 1993.

Woods, Henry. *Augustine and Evolution: A Study in the Saint's "De Genesi ad litteram" and "De Trinitate."* New York: Universal Knowledge Foundation, 1924.

Woodson, Sarah A. "Metal Ions and RNA Folding: A Highly Charged Topic with a Dynamic Future." *Current Opinion in Chemical Biology* 9 (2005): 104–9.

Woodward, James. *Making Things Happen: A Theory of Causal Explanation.* Oxford: Oxford University Press, 2003.

Wrangham, Richard W., and Dale Peterson. *Demonic Males: Apes and the Origins of Human Violence.* Boston: Houghton Mifflin, 1996.

Wu, Rong, Prim B. Singh, and David M. Gilbert. "Uncoupling Global and Fine-Tuning Replication Timing Determinants for Mouse Pericentric Heterochromatin." *Journal of Cell Biology* 174 (2006): 185–94.

Wylen, Stephen M. *The Jews in the Time of Jesus: An Introduction.* New York: Paulist, 1996.

Yack, Bernard. *The Fetishism of Modernities: Epochal Self-Consciousness in Contemporary Social and Political Thought.* Notre Dame, IN: University of Notre Dame Press, 1997.

Yamagata, Yukio. "Prebiotic Formation of ADP and ATP from AMP, Calcium Phosphates and Cyanate in Aqueous Solution." *Origins of Life and Evolution of the Biosphere* 29 (1999): 511–20.

Yandulov, Dmitry V., and Richard R. Schrock. "Catalytic Reduction of Dinitrogen to Ammonia at a Single Molybdenum Center." *Science* 301 (2003): 76–78.

Ye, S., C. Kohrer, T. Huber, M. Kazmi, P. Sachdev, E. C. Y. Yan, A. Bhagat, U. L. RajBhandary, and T. P. Sakmar. "Site-Specific Incorporation of Keto Amino Acids into Functional G Protein-Coupled Receptors Using Unnatural Amino Acid Mutagenesis." *Journal of Biological Chemistry* 283 (2008): 1525–33.

Yeo, Richard R. "William Whewell, Natural Theology and the Philosophy of Science in Mid-Nineteenth Century Britain." *Annals of Science* 36 (1979): 493–516.

Yu, Jiyuan. *The Structure of Being in Aristotle's Metaphysics.* Dordrecht: Kluwer Academic Publishers, 2003.

Zachman, Randall. "Jesus Christ as the Image of God in Calvin's Theology." *Calvin Theological Journal* 25 (1990): 46–52.

Zahnle, Kevin, and Norman H. Sleep. "Impacts and the Early Evolution of Life." In *Comets and the Origin and Evolution of Life,* edited by P. J. Thomas, C. F. Chyba, and C. P. McKay, 175–208. New York: Springer-Verlag, 1997.

Zammito, John. "Teleology Then and Now: The Question of Kant's Relevance for Contemporary Controversies over Function in Biology." *Studies in History and Philosophy of Science C* 37 (2006): 748–70.

Zeitz, Lisa M. "Natural Theology, Rhetoric, and Revolution: John Ray's Wisdom of God, 1691–1704." *Eighteenth Century Life* 18 (1994): 120–33.

Zekiyan, Boghos Levon. *L'interioriso Agostiniano: La struttura onto-psicologica dell'interioriso Agostiniano e la "Memoria sui."* Genoa: Studio Editoriale di Cultura, 1981.

Zumft, Walter G. "Cell Biology and Molecular Basis of Denitrification." *Microbiology and Molecular Biology Reviews* 61 (1997): 533–616.

Index

abduction, 37, 45–49, 218
  in Charles Peirce, 43–45, 46–48, 83, 88
  as creative activity, 44, 46–47
accommodation versus prediction in scientific explanation, 59–60, 97
Alston, William P., 28
anthropic phenomena, xi–xii, 60, 86–93, 111–25, 120–25
  in cosmology, 111–25
  and counterfactual thinking, 86–93
  explanations of, 120–25
  and observation selection effects, 122–23
Antiphon the Sophist, 25
Aquinas, Thomas. See Thomas Aquinas
Areopagus address (Acts 17), 11–12, 64
arguments for God's existence, xi–xii, 16–19
  abductive, 37, 45–49, 218
  deductive, 37, 40–43
  from design, 16–17, 30, 68, 124, 128, 170, 184–91, 194–96
  from morality, 3n13
As You Like It, 4
Athanasius of Alexandria, 76
atheism, and nature, 18, 65, 78–79, 124, 185, 220

Augustine of Hippo, 25–26, 39, 76–77, 79, 98–108, 168–69, 199–201, 203–4, 211
Ayala, Francisco, 186–87, 195n55, 221n12

Bacon, Francis, 23
Balthasar, Hans Urs von, 39
Barrett, Justin, 67
Barrow, John D., 116–19, 142
Barth, Karl, 17, 18–20, 27, 71, 72, 80
Baumeister, Roy, 2
Bhaskar, Roy, 214–15
big bang, theory of origins of universe, 112–15, 132–33, 142
biocentric approaches to natural sciences, xiin14, 127–28, 145, 155
biology, and fine-tuning, 137–38, 164–65, 167–69
Bonaventure of Bagnoregio, 22
Bondi, Hermann, 88
books of nature and Scripture, 69–70, 71, 218
Bostrom, Nick, 122
Boyle Lectures, 16–17
Boyle, Robert, 23
Brunner, Emil, 74

Calvin cycle, 141
Calvin, John, 25–26, 63–65

Cambrian explosion, 161, 193
Carroll, William, 125
Carter, Brandon, xii, 116
chlorophyll, 158–59, 163
Clayton, Philip, 39n17, 40n21, 51n2,
    207n20
clues to the meaning of the universe, 1–2,
    3–4, 221
cognitive science of religion, 67
contingency in evolution, 189–94
convergence in evolution, 192–94
Conway Morris, Simon, 191–94, 198–99
counterfactual thinking, 86–93
Craig, William Lane, 40
creation, concept of
    emergent approaches to, 205–12
    ex nihilo, 72–74
    static approaches to, 204–5, 210
Cudworth, Ralph, 71

Darwin, Charles, 17–18, 30, 83–84, 107,
    171–72, 196, 200, 204–5
    and development of neo-Darwinian
        synthesis, 171–76
    and inference to the best explanation,
        48–49, 59–60
    views on teleology, 185
Dawkins, Richard, 17, 169, 188–89, 218
deductive-nomological reasoning, 37, 48
Deism, 62–64, 71–72, 78–79, 118
Derham, William, 22
Dennett, Daniel, 18
Descartes, René, 120–21
design, divine, 16–17, 30, 68, 124, 128,
    170, 184–91, 194–96
Dicke, Robert, 92–93, 122–23
Dirac, Paul, 92, 121–22
DNA, 136–38, 174–76
Duhem, Pierre, 56
Dyson, Freeman, 120

economy of salvation, 77–82
Eddington, Arthur, 92
Einstein, Albert, 45, 55, 77, 213
emergence, and doctrine of creation,
    203–16
Emerson, Ralph Waldo, 23
empirical fit, 57–58

evolution, biological, 167–200
evolutionary contingency, 189–94
evolutionary convergence, 192–94
evolvability, concept of, 178–80
explanation, and natural theology, 38–40,
    51–60, 95–96
    abductive explanation, 45–49, 218
    accommodation and explanation,
        59–60
    in biology, 176–77
    causal explanation, 37
    deductive explanation, 40–45
    inference to best explanation, 45–49,
        53–54
    logical-deductive explanation, 37,
        47–48
    prediction and explanation, 59–60, 89,
        97, 194
    self-evidencing explanations, 53–54, 218
    unificationist explanation, 54–56
eye, evolution of, 30, 167, 176, 193

faith and sense-making, 1–4, 37–40,
    53–60
fine-tuning, x–xii, 85–86, 92–93,
    137–38, 164–65, 167–69
finiousness, in Charles Peirce, 197–98
Foster, Michael Beresford, 73–74

Galen, Claudius, 99
gene, discovery of, 173–74
"gene's eye" view of evolution, 188–89
Genesis creation accounts, interpretation
    of, 70, 98–105
Gould, Stephen Jay, xiv, 189–90
Gunton, Colin, 70
Guth, Alan, 123

Hanson, Norwood R., 6, 16, 46
Harman, Gilbert, 44
Hartmann, Nicolai, 212–13
Hauerwas, Stanley, 62, 66, 80
Hawking, Stephen, 85, 116
hemoglobin, 158, 161, 163
Hempel, Carl, 37–38, 52
Henderson, Lawrence J., 127–29, 145,
    155
henotheism, 62

Hesse, Mary, 56
Hopkins, Gerard Manley, 4, 5, 74
Hoyle, Fred, 113, 131, 133–34
Hume, David, 53
Huxley, Thomas H., 168, 185
hydrogen bonding, and unusual properties of water, 147–48

imago Dei, 74–77
incarnation, doctrine of, 20, 65n20, 68, 70, 75–76, 81
inference to best explanation, 37–41, 45–49, 53–57, 59–60
    and abduction, 37, 45–49
inflation, cosmological, 115–16, 123–24
intelligibility of nature, 1–2
Irenaeus of Lyons, 68, 77–78
Islamic approaches to natural theology, 66–67

James, William, 1–2, 219
Jüngel, Eberhard, 65–66, 80

Kaufmann, Stuart, 136–37
Kingsley, Charles, 21, 168, 196, 210–12, 218
Kolakowski, Leszek, 144
K-T event, 45, 90–91

large number coincidences, 92–93, 121–22
Lewis, C. S., xiii, 3, 21, 221
life, definitions of, 129–32
life, origins of, 132–42
Lipton, Peter, 53–54, 97–98
Locke, John, 71
Long, Charles, 73
Luther, Martin, 80

MacIntyre, Alasdair, 15–16
Mackie, J. L., 40
Mather, Cotton, 12, 23
Mayr, Ernst, 89, 187–88, 194–95, 197
Mendel, Gregor, 172–73
Mill, John Stuart, 59
Miller, Hugh, 31
Miller, Stanley, 135
Mivart, St. George, 200–201

Moltmann, Jürgen, 70
Monod, Jacques, 185
multiverse hypothesis, 123–24, 220
Murchison meteorite, 134–35
Murdoch, Iris, 219
Murphy, Nancey, 208n23, 209n25

natural theology
    Barthian critique of, 17, 18–20, 27
    Deistic approaches to, 62–64, 71–72, 78–79, 118
    difficulty in defining, 15, 22, 26–27, 35
    and doctrine of creation *ex nihilo*, 72–74
    and economy of salvation, 77–82
    as empirical approach, 22–24
    Enlightenment approaches to, 5–6, 12–16, 25–27
    and *imago Dei*, 74–77
    in Islam, 66–67
    and meaning, 2–4
    as "proof" of God's existence, 56–57
    recent resurgence of, ix–x
    relation to revealed theology, 19–20
    as "seeing" nature in a specific way, 27–28, 31–33, 69–70, 218–19
    as sense-making activity, 29–31, 38–40, 51–60
    and *theologia tripartita*, 23–25
    as a theology of nature? 36
    Trinitarian approaches to, xiii–xiv, 35–37, 61–82
nature, concept of, 5–6, 27, 69–70
"neglected argument" for existence of God, 43–44
neo-Darwinian synthesis, 171–76
Newman, John Henry, 30–31, 53, 195–96
Newton, Isaac, 4, 52, 55
nitrogen fixation, 162–63
Noble, Denis, 169–70
nucleosynthesis, stellar, 132–34, 164–65

observation selection effects, 122–23
Olbers's Paradox, 87–89
oxygen transport mechanisms, 163–64

oxygenation of primitive atmosphere, 159–62

Paley, William, 16–17, 23, 30–31, 36–37, 48–49, 79, 83–84, 106, 118, 167–68, 185, 204–5, 217–18
Peirce, Charles S., xiii, 3n12, 42–45, 60, 83–84, 197, 221
  on abduction, 43–45, 46–48
  on "finiousness," 197–98
    "neglected argument" for existence of God, 43–44
  on "surprising facts" in theory development, 45–46, 60, 83–84, 88
Penrose, Roger, 85
Phillips, D. Z., 42
Philo of Alexandria, 75
phospholipids, 150–51
photosynthesis, 158–59, 192–93
Plantinga, Alvin, 18n29, 38, 102n40, 124n43
Polanyi, Michael, 2, 3
Popper, Karl, 89
prediction versus accommodation in scientific explanation, 59–60, 97
purpose within nature? 124, 128, 170, 184–91, 194–96

Ramsey, Ian T., 57
rationes seminales, 101–6, 125, 142–43, 168–69, 199–201, 203–4
Ray, John, 22, 204
Raymond of Sebonde, 26
Rees, Martin, 85, 119–20
RNA world, 136–37
Ruskin, John, 5, 29, 30–31, 79, 81–82

self-evidencing explanations, 53–54, 218
Shakespeare, William, 4
Smolin, Lee, xi

standard cosmological model, 114–15
steady state theory of cosmos, 113
stratification of reality, 212–16
"surprising facts" in theory development, 45–46, 60, 83–84, 88
Swinburne, Richard, 18, 37, 41–43

teleological explanations in biology, 124, 128, 170, 184–91, 194–96
teleonomy, concept of, 185, 196
Temple, Frederick, 168
theologia tripartita, 23–25
Thomas Aquinas, 12n4, 63–65, 68–69, 97n6, 106n54
Tipler, Frank J., 116–18
Torrance, Thomas F., 20, 213–14, 215–16
transition metals, biological roles of, 156–65
Trinity, doctrine of, x, xii–xiv, 27, 33, 35–36, 54, 58–59, 61–82, 95–97, 101, 105, 120
"two books" tradition, 69–70, 71, 218

Urey, Harold, 35

Varro, Marcus Terentius, 24

watchmaker, God as, 16–17, 30, 68
water, 143–53
  biological functions of, 147–51
  hydrogen bonding, and unusual properties of, 147–48
  origins of, 151–53
  properties of, 145–47
  as solvent, 147–49
Westheimer, Frank, 140–41
Weyl, Hermann, 92
Whewell, William, 59, 145, 220–21
Williams, R. J. P., 157
Wittgenstein, Ludwig, 38